Before Leonard

The Early Suitors of Virginia Woolf

Before Leonard

The Early Suitors of Virginia Woolf

Sarah M. Hall

PETER OWEN

LONDON AND CHESTER SPRINGS

PETER OWEN PUBLISHERS

73 Kenway Road
London SW5 0RE

Peter Owen books are distributed
in the USA by
Dufour Editions Inc.,
Chester Springs,
PA 19425-0007

First published in Great Britain
by Peter Owen Publishers 2006

ISBN 0 7206 1222 5

A catalogue record for this book is
available from the British Library

Printed and bound by Cambrian Printers Ltd

To the people who, more than anyone, made this book possible – Bryan, Beryl and Amanda

Acknowledgements

THE FAMILIES OF my subjects were extremely generous and helpful during my research into their relatives. Grateful thanks are due to the following. John and Charlotte Waterlow, who talked to me at length about their father and gave permission to quote extensively from their father's unpublished writings. John was kind enough to lend me his father's correspondence and the pictures of him that appear in this book. Charlotte allowed me to read her memoirs (unpublished at time of writing), 'From Bloomsbury to Balham and Beyond', and quote from a paper about her father. Wayland and Elizabeth Young, Lord and Lady Kennet, for talking to me about Hilton Young and for permission to reproduce extracts and photographs from the Kennet Papers in Cambridge University Library. Louisa Young for help with pictures of Hilton Young. Alison Bagenal for sharing her memories of Saxon Sydney-Turner, allowing me access to Saxon's letters to Barbara Bagenal and lending some of the photographs of Saxon which appear in this book; other photographs were scanned for me by Barbara's granddaughter, Vanessa Pawsey. Henrietta Phipps and Mary Lamb, who very kindly told me what they knew about Walter and Rose Lamb. Henrietta Phipps and Norman Lamb, MP, for granting permission to reproduce extracts from Walter Lamb's letters. Moira Lamb, for a rare photograph of Walter Lamb and family. Thomas Pakenham for permission to reproduce Henry Lamb's sketch of Lytton Strachey. Hugh Cecil for permission to publish extracts from Desmond MacCarthy's memoir of Sydney Waterlow. Stephen Headlam, for information about Walter Headlam's ancestors. Sir George Young, MP, Helen Winnifrith and Mary Keynes for information about the Young family. George Skipton, whom I was not able to trace, for notes on Hilton Young's maternal family tree.

Others who were very helpful were Paul Levy, P.N. Furbank and Charlotte Chesney for trying to help me trace H.O. Meredith's descendants (although I was in the end unsuccessful), and Beatrice Newton and Lady Campbell of Croy, for information about Walter and Rose Lamb. Professor Geoff Burrows of the

University of Melbourne kindly allowed me to read chapters from his unpublished biography of Hilton Young and corrected inaccuracies in my own chapter.

Many librarians and archivists aided my researches: Dr Rosalind Moad, Elizabeth Pridmore and Dr Patricia McGuire of the Modern Archive Centre, King's College Library, Cambridge; Joy Eldridge and Fiona Courage of the Special Collections Department of the University of Sussex; Jonathan Smith and the staff of the Trinity College Library, Cambridge; Andrew Potter of the Royal Academy of Arts Library; Godfrey Waller, Superintendent of the Manuscripts Reading Room at Cambridge University Library; Helen R.M. Smith, David Colquhoun and Sean McMahon of the Alexander Turnbull Library, Wellington, New Zealand; the staff of the Humanities and Manuscripts departments of the British Library; Dominic Persad and Laura Whitton at the Tate Gallery; Helen Trompeteler, Matthew Bailey and Antonia Leak at the National Portrait Gallery. Thanks also to Jeremy Crow at the Society of Authors and Catherine Trippett at Random House for their patience and good humour in dealing with my many enquiries.

Personal thanks are due to several people. Above all to my partner Bryan Greene, my most loyal friend and sponsor, who asked me awkward questions about the first draft and thereafter made my way as easy as possible. This book would quite literally not exist without him. My sister, Amanda Matravers, my most astute reader, who consistently pinpointed the perfect phrase and suggested much-needed structural improvements, as well as providing bed, board and entertainment during research trips to Cambridge. My mother, Beryl Hall, for constant encouragement and unfailing kindness. Vanessa Curtis for valuable support, advice on publishers and illustrations, lending books and looking up seemingly endless page numbers. Pascale Rose and Geoff Licence for their unshakeable belief that this book would be published and Geoff again for his imagination and energy. Stephen Barkway for sending items of interest and for repeated book loans. Sheila M. Wilkinson for permission to reproduce two of her photographs. Stuart N. Clarke for his encyclopaedic knowledge and for donating a useful book. David Sutherland of Crayon Design and Ruth Webb for help with an important picture. Members of the Reading Group of the Virginia Woolf Society of Great Britain for their enthusiasm and inspiration. Antonia Owen, Daniel McCabe and Nick Pearson at Peter Owen Publishers for help and support throughout the publishing process. Helen Parry for the assiduous proofreading.

And last but definitely not least, Virginia Woolf, for providing such a fertile area of research for her readers.

Contents

Illustrations

Saxon Sydney-Turner with Barbara Bagenal's daughter Judith in about 1920
Used with the kind permission of the Bagenal family

Saxon Sydney-Turner in old age with Barbara Bagenal, outside his Hendon lodgings in the late 1950s
Used with the kind permission of the Bagenal family

Sketch of Lytton Strachey by Henry Lamb, 1910
Private collection

Lytton Strachey with Virginia Woolf at Garsington, 1923
National Portrait Gallery

The Mill House, Tidmarsh, near Pangbourne in Berkshire, the home of Lytton Strachey and Carrington from 1917 to 1924
Used with the kind permission of Sheila M. Wilkinson

51 Gordon Square, the Strachey family's London home from 1919 to 1963

Hilton Young at Cambridge in 1901, when he was President of the Union, with members of the Magpie and Stump, the most long-lived of the university's debating societies
Cambridge University Library; used with the kind permission of Lord Kennet

Hilton Young at the time of the East Worcestershire election in 1910, when he stood as a Liberal candidate against the Conservative Austen Chamberlain
Cambridge University Library; used with the kind permission of Lord Kennet

The Lacket, Lockeridge, Wiltshire, purchased by Hilton Young in 1908 and still owned by the family. Lytton Strachey lived here from October 1913 to September 1915
Used with the kind permission of Lord Kennet

Hilton Young in naval uniform in the 1920s, after losing an arm at Zeebrugge in April 1918
Used with the kind permission of Lord Kennet

Walter Lamb, probably taken between 1907 and 1913 when he was a Trinity fellow
Trinity College, Cambridge

Walter Lamb and family, *c*. 1903–5
Used with the kind permission of Moira Lamb

Nineteen-year-old Rupert Brooke in summer 1906, before he went up to Cambridge
King's College, Cambridge; used with the kind permission of the Brooke Trustees

Rupert Brooke in the garden at the Old Vicarage, Grantchester, summer 1911
King's College, Cambridge; used with the kind permission of the Brooke Trustees

Rupert Brooke in Ottawa, July 1913, during the year he spent travelling
King's College, Cambridge; used with the kind permission of the Brooke Trustees

The last photograph of Rupert Brooke, suffering from sunstroke in Egypt, 2 April 1915
King's College, Cambridge; used with the kind permission of the Brooke Trustees

Sir Sydney Waterlow in Greece, where he was British Minister 1933–9
Used with the kind permission of John and Charlotte Waterlow

Sydney Waterlow in the garden at Parsonage House
Used with the kind permission of John and Charlotte Waterlow

Parsonage House, Oare, Wiltshire, taken in the 1920s. The house was leased by Sydney Waterlow in 1918
Used with the kind permission of John and Charlotte Waterlow

Chronology

This is not a complete chronology, for which the reader is referred to Virginia Woolf's letters and diaries, but lists dates related to Virginia Woolf and her early suitors. Dates of publication for her major works are taken from *The Letters of Virginia Woolf*, edited by Nigel Nicolson and Joanne Trautmann. Where a particular date is not known, the event is listed first for that year.

1866
15 February   Walter Headlam born

1878
22 October   Sydney Waterlow born

1879
20 March   Hilton Young born
30 May   Vanessa Stephen born

1880
1 March   Lytton Strachey born
8 September   Thoby Stephen born
28 October   Saxon Sydney-Turner born
25 November   Leonard Woolf born

1881
16 September   Clive Bell born

1882
5 January   Walter Lamb born
25 January   Virginia Stephen born

1883
27 October   Adrian Stephen born

1885
21 January   Duncan Grant born

1887

3 August — Rupert Brooke born

1893

Summer — The Stephen and Brooke families meet at St Ives (probable date; possibly 1892)

1895

5 May — Death of Julia Stephen, aged forty-nine

1896

October — Sydney Waterlow goes up to Trinity College, Cambridge, to study classics

1897

19 July — Death of Stella Duckworth, aged twenty-eight

1899

October — Thoby Stephen goes up to Trinity College, Cambridge, where he meets Leonard Woolf, Lytton Strachey, Clive Bell, Saxon Sydney-Turner, Hilton Young and (in 1901) Walter Lamb

1900

Mid June — Virginia meets Clive Bell at the Trinity College ball; she may also have met Thoby's other friends at the same occasion; Sydney Waterlow goes down from Trinity College

1901

Sydney Waterlow is appointed attaché in Washington

Summer — The Stephen and Strachey families stay at Lyndhurst, Hampshire

October — Walter Lamb goes up to Trinity College, Cambridge, to study classics

1902

Virginia sends Walter Headlam a critique of his work

April — Leslie Stephen diagnosed with cancer; Sydney Waterlow becomes engaged to Alice Pollock

10 November — Sydney Waterlow marries Alice Pollock

1904

22 February — Death of Leslie Stephen, aged seventy-one

March–May — Stephens go to Manorbier (Wales), Italy and Paris; Virginia has an idea for her first novel

Summer — Virginia has a mental breakdown and makes her first suicide attempt; Vanessa arranges the move to 46 Gordon Square for the four siblings, but Virginia is too unwell to move in until November

19 November — Leonard Woolf leaves for Ceylon (arrives 16 December)

6 December	Virginia lunches with Adrian Stephen and Walter Headlam in Cambridge: Vanessa and Violet Dickinson discourage Virginia from a close relationship with him

1905

16 March	First of Thoby Stephen's 'Thursday evenings' at 46 Gordon Square: Saxon Sydney-Turner is the only guest who is not a relative
20 March	Virginia and Thoby attend an evening party at the Youngs'
Mid June	Virginia and Vanessa attend the Trinity College ball and have tea with Walter Headlam in Cambridge
End June– beginning July	The Stephen and Strachey families stay with friends at Forest Row, Sussex
Early August	Clive Bell proposes to Vanessa and is rejected
Summer	Lytton Strachey falls in love with his cousin Duncan Grant
September	Saxon Sydney-Turner stays with the Stephens in Carbis Bay, Cornwall

1906

31 July	Clive Bell proposes to Vanessa and is again rejected
8 September	Virginia, Vanessa and Violet Dickinson travel to Greece to meet Thoby and Adrian, who had left England on 3 August
14 October	Thoby Stephen leaves Greece and returns home
Mid October	Rupert Brooke goes up to King's College, Cambridge
1 November	Virginia, Vanessa and Adrian return home to find Thoby ill; Vanessa and Violet are also ill
20 November	Thoby Stephen dies of typhoid fever
22 November	Vanessa agrees to marry Clive Bell; Virginia is at first happy for her sister, but her opinion of Clive quickly degenerates
c. 10 December	Walter Headlam becomes Virginia's mentor and offers to dedicate his translation of *Agamemnon* to her

1907

7 February	Vanessa marries Clive Bell
Mid March	Virginia's flirtation with Walter Headlam develops; he urges her to get married
25 March	Virginia and Adrian move to 29 Fitzroy Square, leaving 46 Gordon Square to Vanessa and Clive
c. 29 March– 12 April	Walter Headlam writes Virginia three letters while she is in Paris
May	Virginia has a lovers' tiff with Walter Headlam in Cambridge; later he sends her a poem
September	Saxon Sydney-Turner and Walter Lamb stay with Virginia and Adrian in Playden, Sussex

September/ October	Virginia begins writing 'Melymbrosia' (*The Voyage Out*)
Autumn	Walter Lamb is elected a Trinity fellow; for the next two years he combines lecturing at Newnham with teaching at Clifton College, Bristol
27 December	First meeting of Clive's Play Reading Society, which continued until 15 January 1909

1908

4 February	Birth of Julian Bell
Mid April	Rupert Brooke's first Apostles meeting, a reading party near Salisbury Plain with Lytton Strachey, Maynard Keynes, Desmond MacCarthy, E.M. Forster and G.E. Moore
22 April	Virginia starts a substantial correspondence with Lytton Strachey
End April	Virginia's flirtation with Clive begins while she is staying with the Bells in St Ives
10 May	Rupert Brooke meets Noel Olivier at a Fabian party: he is twenty; she is fifteen
20 June	Walter Headlam dies suddenly, aged forty-two: Virginia is dismissive of him and his work, but Rupert Brooke is devastated by his death
Mid July	Lytton Strachey discovers that Duncan Grant is having an affair with Maynard Keynes
1–17 August	Virginia goes to Wells, Somerset, where she expects a visit and a proposal from Hilton Young, neither of which materializes
Autumn	Hilton Young buys The Lacket
October	Virginia gives Clive drafts of 'Melymbrosia' to assess: despite minor misgivings, he is convinced of its merit
Mid November	Lytton Strachey stays with Virginia and Adrian at the Lizard, Cornwall
December	Virginia is asked by Cecil Headlam to contribute to Walter Headlam's memoir and declines
25 December	Lytton Strachey begins to encourage Leonard Woolf to marry Virginia

1909

	Hilton Young becomes assistant editor of *The Economist*
January– February	Letter-writing game between Virginia, Vanessa and Clive Bell, Lytton Strachey, Saxon Sydney-Turner and Walter Lamb
17 February	Lytton Strachey proposes and Virginia accepts: they both agree to retract immediately
28 February	Virginia and Adrian Stephen meet Rupert Brooke for tea
1 March	Virginia goes with Rupert Brooke and Harry Norton to visit James Strachey in his Cambridge lodgings
15–17 May	Virginia spends the weekend in Cambridge; Hilton Young proposes to her and is rejected
June	Rupert Brooke moves to the Orchard, Grantchester

6 to end August	Virginia, Adrian and Saxon Sydney-Turner go to Bayreuth and Dresden, where Virginia observes Saxon's eccentricities; Leonard Woolf and Lytton Strachey correspond about whom Virginia might marry
November–December	James Strachey gossips to Lytton about a possible affair between Virginia and Marjorie Strachey, and a match between Virginia and Duncan Grant

1910

	Hilton Young becomes financial editor of the *Morning Post*
1 January	Virginia offers to address envelopes for the cause of women's suffrage
10 February	Virginia, with Adrian Stephen, Duncan Grant and three others, takes part in the Dreadnought Hoax, to the disapproval of Clive Bell
c. 25 March–15 April	Virginia stays with Vanessa and Clive at Studland to recover her health
May	Olive Ilbert (wrongly) suspects a reconciliation between Virginia and Hilton Young
7 to *c.* 27 June	Virginia stays with Vanessa and Clive in Blean, near Canterbury
End June	Virginia enters Jean Thomas's nursing home in Twickenham
Late July	Rupert Brooke and Noel Olivier become secretly engaged
Mid Aug–early September	Virginia stays in Cornwall with Jean Thomas
4 September	Virginia assures Clive Bell that she does not mean to marry Lytton Strachey or Hilton Young, but Clive remains jealous and later this year banishes Lytton from Gordon Square
Mid September–mid October	Vanessa and Clive Bell stay at Studland: Virginia is there when Sydney Waterlow and Walter Lamb are guests
29 September	Sydney dines with Virginia at The Cottage, Studland
8 November	'Manet and the Post-Impressionists' opens (closes 15 January 1911)
8 December	Sydney Waterlow dines with the Bells and Virginia in London and begins to be interested in Virginia
c. 20 December	Rupert Brooke moves to the Old Vicarage, Grantchester
27 December	Virginia is taken by Saxon Sydney-Turner to meet his parents in Hove

1911

January	Virginia leases Little Talland House in Firle, East Sussex
February	Rupert Brooke meets Elisabeth van Rysselberghe in Munich and begins an affair with her
Spring	Clive Bell suspects that Oliver Strachey will propose to Virginia
27 May	Virginia attends the wedding of Gwen Darwin and Jacques Raverat and soon afterwards is depressed about her single state
29 May	Virginia lunches with Walter Lamb at Trinity College
Early June	Leonard Woolf arrives in England, having sailed from Ceylon on 16 May
c. 13 June	Sydney Waterlow separates from his first wife Alice

15 June	Sydney meets Norah Finberg and begins an affair with her
17 June	Rupert Brooke meets Leonard Woolf
3 July	Virginia, Walter Lamb and Duncan Grant visit 46 Gordon Square, where Leonard Woolf is dining with the Bells
8 July	Virginia invites Leonard Woolf to Firle, but he does not visit until September
20 July	Walter Lamb makes a near-proposal to Virginia in Richmond Park
23 July	Walter Lamb writes a passionate love letter to Virginia
24 July	Walter tells Sydney Waterlow of his proposal to Virginia
14–19 August	Virginia stays with Rupert Brooke in Grantchester; one evening they bathe nude in the moonlight
15 August	Sydney Waterlow has tea with Virginia and Rupert at Grantchester
16 August	Virginia and Rupert dine with Sydney at the Cambridge Union
19 August	Rupert returns with Virginia to Little Talland House; between now and the end of the year he visits her several times in Firle and meets her in London
27 August	Rupert Brooke arrives at the Neo-Pagan camp at Clifford Bridge: Lytton Strachey, Leonard Woolf, Gerald Shove and G.E. Moore are staying near by at Becky Falls
30 August	Rupert writes 'Dining-Room Tea'; Virginia and Ka Cox join the camp at Clifford Bridge
16 September	Leonard Woolf stays with Virginia at Firle; Marjorie Strachey is also staying
Mid October– beginning November	Rupert Brooke temporarily takes Duncan Grant and Maynard Keynes's rooms at 21 Fitzroy Square; Virginia is at no. 29
Late October	Virginia leases Asheham House with Vanessa
3 November	Sydney Waterlow lunches with Virginia and Adrian and talks to Virginia all afternoon
4 November	Sydney dines with Virginia and the Cornfords in Grantchester
5 November	Virginia and Ka Cox have tea with Sydney in Cambridge
17 November	Virginia moves from 29 Fitzroy Square to 38 Brunswick Square (spends her first night there on the 20th)
25–7 November	Sydney Waterlow spends the weekend with Virginia at Little Talland House
27 November	Decree nisi granted for Sydney's divorce from Alice
29 November	Sydney proposes to Virginia in London and is rejected
4 December	Leonard Woolf moves into 38 Brunswick Square; Rupert Brooke's *Poems* published
28 December	Rupert Brooke arrives in Lulworth, Dorset for a Bloomsbury/Neo-Pagan reading party; others attending are Lytton, James and Marjorie Strachey, Maynard Keynes, Duncan Grant, Ka Cox, Henry Lamb, Justin Brooke, Ferenc Békássy and, later, Gerald Shove and Harry Norton
31 December	Ka Cox confesses to Rupert her love for Henry Lamb; Rupert leaves Lulworth the next day but returns to see Ka

1912

Early January	Rupert Brooke has a mental breakdown which lasts about two months
11 January	Leonard Woolf proposes to Virginia, but they are interrupted by Walter Lamb
13 January	Virginia writes to Leonard asking if they can remain as friends for the present
16 February	Virginia enters Jean Thomas's nursing home for a fortnight
March	Sydney Waterlow reopens a correspondence with Virginia and asks if they can be friends
Spring	Clive Bell begins an affair with Molly MacCarthy that lasts until the beginning of 1915
April	Rupert Brooke and Bryn Olivier come to tea with Virginia at Asheham; a long walk with Walter Lamb leaves Virginia bored and frustrated
29 May	Virginia agrees to marry Leonard Woolf
10 August	Marriage of Virginia Stephen and Leonard Woolf in St Pancras Registry Office; they spend their honeymoon in Somerset, France, Spain and Italy
Mid August	Rupert Brooke quarrels with James Strachey about James's Bloomsbury friends
3 October	Virginia and Leonard return from honeymoon
5 October	Second Post-Impressionist exhibition opens (closes 31 January 1913): Leonard Woolf acts as secretary until December; Henry Lamb's portrait of Lytton Strachey is one of the exhibits
Late October	The Woolfs move from 38 Brunswick Square to 13 Clifford's Inn
Early November	Rupert visits Virginia at Clifford's Inn and thinks her changed by her marriage

1913

January	Virginia begins to suffer from ill health; Sydney Waterlow takes over from Leonard Woolf as secretary for the Second Post-Impressionist exhibition
8 March	Rupert Brooke hears that he has been elected a King's fellow
April/May	Sydney's first marriage is legally ended
22 May	Rupert Brooke sails for America and the South Seas
Summer	Sydney marries Margery Eckhard
July–August	Virginia becomes very ill and enters Jean Thomas's nursing home, but her condition deteriorates on her return
9 September	Virginia takes an overdose of veronal – her second suicide attempt; her life is saved by Maynard Keynes's brother, Geoffrey, a doctor
October	Lytton Strachey rents The Lacket from Hilton Young until September 1915; he writes half of *Eminent Victorians* here
15 October	Rupert Brooke lands in Honolulu, and goes from there to Samoa, Fiji and Tahiti

5 December	Walter Lamb appointed Secretary of the Royal Academy
December	The Woolfs' belongings are moved from 13 Clifford's Inn to Asheham; during Virginia's lengthy illness she has been living chiefly at Dalingridge Place in Sussex (George Duckworth's house)

1914

5 April	Rupert Brooke leaves Tahiti for San Francisco
5 June	Rupert arrives back in England
28 June	Assassination of Archduke Ferdinand
4 August	Outbreak of First World War
16 October	The Woolfs move to 17 The Green, Richmond; Walter Lamb lives near by at Kew
October	Sydney and Margery Waterlow rent Asheham and complain about the dirt but stay until July 1915
5–8 December	The Woolfs borrow The Lacket from Lytton Strachey

1915

February	Clive Bell begins an affair with Mary Hutchinson that lasts until 1927
March	The Woolfs move to Hogarth House, Richmond, their London house until 1924
25 March	Virginia enters a nursing home and remains ill for nearly six months
26 March	*The Voyage Out* published by Duckworth and Co.
4 April	Dean Inge reads Rupert Brooke's sonnet 'The Soldier' during the Easter Sunday service in St Paul's Cathedral
23 April	Death of Rupert Brooke, aged twenty-seven
May	Alfred Brooke killed in action
May	Hilton Young elected Liberal MP for Norwich; he retains his seat until 1929 with only a year's break from 1923 to 1924
Winter	Lytton Strachey meets Carrington at Asheham

1916

	Saxon Sydney-Turner meets and falls in love with Barbara Hiles
14 May	Virginia tries to persuade Vanessa to lease Charleston Farmhouse
16 October	Vanessa moves into Charleston with Duncan Grant and Bunny Garnett; her two sons follow later
25 October	Carrington visits Virginia to clear up a misunderstanding (possibly their first meeting)
29 November	Virginia invites Barbara Hiles to dinner in order to meet her

1917

January–February	Saxon Sydney-Turner stays at Asheham with Barbara Hiles and Carrington
24 April	The Woolfs' first printing press is delivered

July	The first publication of the Hogarth Press is *Two Stories*, comprising Leonard's 'Three Jews' and Virginia's 'The Mark on the Wall'
December	Lytton Strachey moves to Tidmarsh with Carrington, who moved in on 22 November

1918

1 February	Barbara Hiles marries Nicholas Bagenal
19 March	Virginia encounters Hilton Young at Ka Cox's house
23 April	Hilton Young is wounded at Zeebrugge and later has his right arm amputated
9 May	Lytton Strachey's *Eminent Victorians* published
Summer	Sydney Waterlow leases Parsonage House, in Oare, Wiltshire
11 November	Armistice Day: the First World War ends
27 December	Virginia appeals in the *Times Literary Supplement* for more balanced reporting of the death of Rupert Brooke

1919

January	Paris Peace Conference begins; Sydney Waterlow attends on behalf of the Foreign Office and is later decorated with a CBE and the Legion of Honour
28 April	League of Nations founded
28 June	Treaty of Versailles is signed
1 July	The Woolfs buy Monk's House at an auction
20 October	*Night and Day* published by Duckworth and Co.

1921

	Hilton Young appointed Financial Secretary to the Treasury
16 January	Sydney Waterlow writes to Virginia about his depression
March	*Monday or Tuesday* published by the Hogarth Press, as are all of Virginia's subsequent books
April	Lytton Strachey's *Queen Victoria* published, bearing a dedication to Virginia
21 May	Carrington marries Ralph Partridge

1922

February	Saxon Sydney-Turner's father dies
3 March	Hilton Young marries Kathleen Scott (née Bruce), the widow of Captain R.F. Scott
27 October	*Jacob's Room* published

1924

13 March	Virginia and Leonard move to 52 Tavistock Square; Saxon Sydney-Turner and his mother move into Hogarth House
15 July	Carrington and Ralph Partridge leave Tidmarsh to move into Ham Spray; Lytton moves in a few weeks later

1925

22 March	Virginia expresses regret for her flirtation with Clive in a letter to Gwen Raverat
23 April	First *Common Reader* published
14 May	*Mrs Dalloway* published

1926

c. March	Sydney Waterlow appointed British Minister in Bangkok
May	Hilton Young joins the Conservative Party
September	Walter Lamb meets Rose Brooks in France

1927

15 January	Walter Lamb marries Rose Brooks
Early February	Clive parts permanently from Mary Hutchinson
5 May	*To the Lighthouse* published
Summer	Hilton Young awarded GBE

1928

	Sydney Waterlow appointed British Minister in Addis Ababa
11 October	*Orlando* published
December	Lytton Strachey's *Elizabeth and Essex* published

1929

	Sydney Waterlow appointed British Minister in Sofia
30 May	Hilton Young is elected Conservative MP for Sevenoaks and retains his seat until 1935
24 October	*A Room of One's Own* published

1931

3 February	Virginia is keen for the Hogarth Press to publish Rupert Brooke's letters, but the plan comes to nothing
8 October	*The Waves* published
Early November	Hilton Young is appointed Minister of Health
November	Lytton Strachey falls ill; Virginia knows nothing of it until mid December

1932

22 January	Death of Lytton Strachey
11 March	Death of Carrington
13 October	Second *Common Reader* published

1933

	Sydney Waterlow appointed British Minister in Athens
5 October	*Flush* published
30 July	Virginia refers in her diary to writing memoirs about Walter Headlam and Hilton Young (these have never been found)

1935

July Hilton Young leaves the Cabinet and becomes 1st Baron Kennet of the Dene

1937

15 March *The Years* published

12 May Coronation of George VI; Hilton Young, as Lord Kennet, attends

1938

Clive Bell and Walter Lamb express opposing points of view in *Art in England*

2 June *Three Guineas* published

1939

Early June Sydney Waterlow reluctantly retires from his post as British Minister in Athens

Mid August The Woolfs move from 52 Tavistock Square to 37 Mecklenburgh Square, but do not spend much time at their new house

3 September Britain declares war on Germany

1940

25 July *Roger Fry* published

18 September 37 Mecklenburgh Square suffers severe bomb damage, but Virginia's diaries are saved; the Hogarth Press is moved to Rodmell and then Letchworth

16 October 52 Tavistock Square is destroyed by a bomb

1941

28 March Death of Virginia Woolf, aged fifty-nine

17 July *Between the Acts* published

1944

4 December Death of Sydney Waterlow, aged sixty-six

1945

8 May Victory in Europe, marking the end of the Second World War

1947

25 July Death of Hilton Young's wife Kathleen

1951

31 December Walter Lamb retires from the Royal Academy

1955

Autumn Saxon Sydney-Turner moves into a house for the elderly, leaving his Percy Street flat to Vanessa and Duncan

1960

11 July   Death of Hilton Young, aged eighty-one

1961

27 March   Death of Walter Lamb, aged seventy-nine

7 April   Death of Vanessa Bell, aged eighty-one

1962

4 November   Death of Saxon Sydney-Turner, aged eighty-two

1964

18 September   Death of Clive Bell, aged eighty-three

1969

14 August   Death of Leonard Woolf, aged eighty-eight

1978

9 May   Death of Duncan Grant, aged ninety-three

2004

5 February   Death of Frances Partridge, the last of 'Bloomsbury', aged one hundred and three

Introduction

‘I WISH EVERYONE DIDN'T tell me to marry. Is it crude human nature breaking out? I call it disgusting,' wrote Virginia Stephen to her friend Violet Dickinson on New Year's Eve 1906.[1] It was the first of a series of irritated outbursts on the issue of marriage. If the subject was not immediately dropped, Virginia threatened, she would ban the marriage-brokers from her house and compose for them a salacious essay on desires of the flesh.[2] Virginia Stephen was a few weeks away from her twenty-fifth birthday. Two days after the death of her older brother Thoby from typhoid, her sister Vanessa had become engaged to his close friend, leaving Virginia bereft of two siblings at one stroke.

Now that the elder sister was disposed of, convention demanded that the younger find a husband, and Virginia was being plagued by queries from family and friends about her single state. To one friend she complained of all the interfering women, old and young, who gave her the same unsolicited advice – that she should marry (and presumably rid herself of her virginity) as soon as possible.[3] Soon even her male acquaintances were adding their voices to the chorus: her parents' friend Walter Headlam expressed concern that she might be pining away without a husband.[4] But her irritation with the meddlers was only partly genuine. Despite her protests she concurred with Oscar Wilde's dictum that it was better to be talked about than not to be talked about. It was she who kept the pot of gossip simmering, confiding in her sister and other close friends every time a man approached her with romantic intentions. Where he had none, she would often invent them for the amusement of her correspondents, describing an innocent encounter as though it were an amorous adventure. Little wonder then that there was such interest in her romances.

Until Quentin Bell's biography was published in 1972 Virginia Woolf's readers knew none of this. Very few details of her private life reached the public during the thirty years following her death. Her biographical standing has changed significantly since the early 1970s, when Joan Russell Noble, the compiler of *Recollections of Virginia Woolf*, found twenty-four books and 167 articles of literary criticism on her works but little in the way of biography and only scraps of information about Virginia's character.[5] Thirty years on Virginia Woolf is an international literary star and her image an iconic one: the much-reproduced 1902 Beresford picture of the twenty-year-old writer-in-embryo is a National Portrait Gallery bestseller. The number of criticisms and biographies has increased exponentially. Woolf's own writings, having been translated into French and German soon after their publication in English, are now sold in many foreign-language editions, including Arabic, Bulgarian, Greek, Hebrew, Icelandic, Punjabi and Serbo-Croat. There are biographies spotlighting almost every aspect of her life: her family and background; her relationship with her sister; her alleged abuse by her half-brothers; her place in the Bloomsbury group; her affiliation with the city of her birth; her close friendships with other women; her marriage to Leonard Woolf; her affair with Vita Sackville-West; her mental illness. With access to her letters and diaries, and personal memoirs from friends and fellow writers, we feel justified in believing we know more about Virginia Woolf than we do about our own friends and families.

There is, however, a glaring gap in the otherwise comprehensive coverage: Woolf's male admirers. Her friendships with women have been well documented, but who were the important men in her life, those who had an interest in her during her formative years, before she married Leonard Woolf; when she was Miss Stephen, daughter of the late Sir Leslie and sister of the handsome Thoby, rather than Virginia Woolf the Writer? An intelligent, independent and beautiful woman, she was surely much admired and even adored by men in her youth, but by whom?[6] The names of several men are mentioned in biographies, but about those less central to Bloomsbury there is precious little to go on. Virginia wrote about some of them in her journals and correspondence, but her responses are very personal and do not give the complete picture. Did they have an influence, these men, on her thought and her writing? Did they feature as characters in her novels? Where did they come from; what were they like; and what was the nature of their relationships with Virginia? How many of them wanted to marry her?[7] Did she seriously consider their proposals and why, in the end, did she reject them?

It is a challenge to pin down those of Virginia Woolf's early admirers who got close enough to her to be considered as suitors. It was easy enough to define as suitors those who proposed, but other men maintained relationships with her that are also deserving of the name of 'affair' – so long as we bear in mind that a sexual affair is not at all what we are talking about. Virginia was a virgin on her wedding day, and – famously – near celibate for the years after it. The word 'affair' is used throughout this book to indicate a love affair of a more amorphous kind than it usually denotes today. Some of the affairs were serious, some were not. Some involved serious courtship and aimed at marriage; others were precarious and incomplete. Most were relatively short-lived, although they all sprang out of existing friendships. During each affair there were 'dates' – often walks and visits; an exchange of letters – perhaps flirtatious; generally an acknowledgement by Virginia that someone was paying court to her and an amused interest in how things would progress; and a peak of intimacy (sometimes a proposal of marriage) followed by a descent – into friendship, ridicule or absence.

Gathering evidence from letters, diaries, memoirs and biographies of Virginia and her friends it gradually became clear who her admirers were. I felt justified in referring to these men as 'suitors' because in their relations with her they all exhibited 'courting' behaviour; although this does not necessarily mean that her admirer was in love with her or that he was contemplating marriage. Those I consider her suitors are listed below, in roughly chronological order of their period of intimacy with her.[8]

Walter Headlam (1866–1908), classical scholar and fellow of King's College; a friend of the Stephen family, with whom Virginia maintained a flirtation during 1907

Clive Bell (1881–1964), art critic, bon viveur and brother-in-law of Virginia, who became intimate with him from April 1908

Saxon Sydney-Turner (1880–1962), brilliant classical scholar who spent his entire working career in the Treasury; a close friend of Virginia's from around 1908

Lytton Strachey (1880–1932), ground-breaking historical biographer, a confirmed homosexual who nevertheless proposed to Virginia in February 1909 but agreed with her to retract the same day

Hilton Young (1879–1960), financial journalist, later a Member of Parliament; another family friend, who courted Virginia throughout 1908 and proposed in May 1909

Walter Lamb (1882–1961), brother of the painter Henry; fellow of Trinity College and later Secretary of the Royal Academy, who came very close to a proposal in July 1911

Rupert Brooke (1887–1915), 'Neo-Pagan' and poet, a childhood friend, with whom Virginia was very friendly in the summer of 1911

Sydney Waterlow (1878–1944), diplomat, ambassador and writer, who proposed to Virginia in November 1911

Some of these men (Clive Bell, Lytton Strachey, Rupert Brooke) are famous for their own writings, as well as in connection with Virginia Woolf, and their intimacy with Virginia has attracted the attention of biographers. Clive Bell's flirtation has been covered by Virginia's and Vanessa's biographers, mainly for the effect it had on the relationship between the two sisters. Lytton has his own chunky biography by Michael Holroyd, who observes the mutual attraction and notes how close the two came to marriage. In books about Rupert Brooke his friendship with Virginia is mentioned in passing, but she appears as a very minor character in his tortuous love life with its assorted muses. The lesser-known suitors occasionally come to the surface in memoirs, although they do not loom large in studies of Virginia Woolf. Cecil Headlam wrote a memoir of his brother Walter after his death, in which he neglects to mention the friendship with Virginia, although he was well aware of it, having asked her to contribute to the book. Louisa Young covers briefly Hilton Young's proposal to Virginia in her biography of her grandmother, Kathleen Scott, the woman Hilton eventually married. In her 1933 diary Virginia refers to a memoir she is writing about Walter Headlam and Hilton Young, but this was either lost or destroyed – at any rate it has never yet come to light.[9] This is the one and only time Walter Headlam is mentioned in Virginia's journals. For him, and for Walter Lamb, Saxon Sydney-Turner, Hilton Young and Sydney Waterlow, information relating to their relationships with Virginia is hard to come by; and no one, it seems, has drawn all these threads together in a thorough examination of her romances and friendships before Leonard.

Why the neglect? Are there simply too many other interesting aspects of Virginia Woolf's work and life to concentrate on? Or perhaps the gap has been caused by an assumption that on the whole her early suitors were not very important and had little effect on her writing and ideas. I don't think this is true at all. Autobiography – the interpretation of memory – has a way of insinuating itself into fiction. Virginia's own love affairs, for instance, and observation of the affairs of her family and friends often worked their way into her books. Her first two novels, *The Voyage Out*, with male protagonists based on Clive Bell and Lytton Strachey, and *Night and Day*, with a Leonard-like hero, are largely concerned with the possibilities and dangers inherent in love and marriage for an Edwardian woman of Virginia's class and upbringing. At that time a woman's choice of a husband meant a serious and considered decision about what kind of a life she wanted to lead. The success and failure of marriages and partnerships interested Virginia profoundly: *Mrs Dalloway* explores Clarissa's choice of the reliable although inexpressive Richard over the intuitive but emotional Peter; *To the Lighthouse* is a study of the successful, although ultimately tragic, union of her parents; part of *Between the Acts* concerns the ailing marriage of the romantic Isa and the boorish Giles. Among the short stories, 'Lappin and Lapinova' shows how a marriage inhabiting a fantasy world requires the full participation of both spouses and is unlikely to thrive if fantasy is its only basis. Occasionally Virginia's friends suspected that she was 'collecting' interesting experiences and people in order to turn them into fiction. It is easy to believe that she sometimes toyed with her suitors with the intention of observing the characteristics of love affairs for the sake of her writing.

It is generally accepted that Leonard Woolf, Virginia's eventual spouse, helped to provide the physical and psychological environment in which it was possible for Virginia to write her novels. It is highly significant that although she had been writing stories and essays since childhood, and began a novel in 1907, she gained the confidence to complete and publish her first book only after her marriage. Leonard's iron self-mastery was well matched to Virginia's innate self-discipline, resulting in a dual affirmation to dedicate time and energy to their writing. Leonard's regimented programme during Virginia's periods of illness, while frustrating, gave her valuable breathing spaces in which to think and resolve novelistic problems of character, plot and – most of all – style.

But if Leonard helped Virginia achieve mental and physical well-being, the men who preceded him provided context, ideas and subject matter and, in Clive Bell's case, encouragement and valuable criticism in addition. Their lives

enriched hers; some of their beliefs and principles – in the areas of art, literature, politics, personal values and philosophy of life – she aligned herself with;
others she rejected. Ideas current among one's friends and peers often provoke
a reaction in one's own beliefs or may set off ripples with distant consequences.

Virginia's friendship with the classicist Walter Headlam was closely associated
with her early obsession with classical literature and Ancient Greece. No doubt
he fed her longing to see Greece with descriptions of 'that lovely land of
amethystine haze and twilight coffee' and the view from the Acropolis, 'one of
the finest things in the world'.[10] If Walter Headlam contributed to her interest
in classics, Walter Lamb and Clive Bell helped to bring to her attention theories
of art (Clive having been influenced in his turn by Roger Fry). Walter and Clive
stood on either side of the divide about art's traditions and its future. While she
was not a direct participant in these debates, Virginia was well aware of their
preoccupations and showed a remarkable empathy with the painter's artistic
endeavours – familiar to her from those of her sister Vanessa, Duncan Grant
and Roger Fry – in the character of Lily Briscoe in *To the Lighthouse*. Clive was
Virginia's first real critic and the first among her Bloomsbury friends (who
were not, as a rule, given to praising each other's work) to recognize her literary
skill. Perhaps partly in gratitude for this she created a sympathetic portrait of
him as Terence Hewet in *The Voyage Out*.

Sadly, the erudite Saxon Sydney-Turner accomplished nothing of lasting
worth, but his procrastinations and the waste of his polymathic talents in the
Treasury made Virginia all the more determined not to fritter away her own life
and gifts. Lytton Strachey's revolution in historical biography was the counterpart to Virginia's youthful reading of the classic authors of the English canon
and to Leslie's work on the *Dictionary of National Biography*. Strachey is also
immediately detectable as the model for St John Hirst in Woolf's début novel,
The Voyage Out.

Hilton Young, on the surface a model Edwardian gentleman of the type that
Bloomsbury rebelled against, was the kind of man the youthful Virginia had in
mind when she contemplated marriage: smart, respectable and with a promising future. He did not share Virginia's personal beliefs but may have been the
inspiration for Richard in *Mrs Dalloway*. That there was more to him than met
the critical eye of Bloomsbury was borne out by his eventual choice of a wife –
the courageous and adventurous sculptor Kathleen Scott, the widow of

Captain Robert Scott. Rupert Brooke, a fellow writer, shared Virginia's love for words and literary craftsmanship. His sensitivity was on a par with hers; and his deep depressions had features in common with her mental illnesses. Sydney Waterlow was an international diplomat, and his concerns were more closely aligned with those of Leonard than of Virginia. But his 'extra-curricular' interests in philosophy and the French concept of '*unanimisme*' had an impact on Virginia's thought and writing and especially on what is generally accepted as her most original achievement, *The Waves*. He and Walter Lamb, being in her eyes 'establishment' figures, most frequently of all the suitors suffered her ridicule and acid wit.

Clive Bell, Saxon Sydney-Turner and Lytton Strachey were what might be called 'inner' Bloomsbury and remained close friends of Virginia throughout her life. Intimacies of a kind existed with all three men during 1908–9. While Vanessa was preoccupied with her first baby, Julian, Clive and Virginia carried on a flirtation which Virginia later regretted and for which they have often been censured in print. Saxon and Virginia wrote flirtatious letters and admired one another's intellect in a fairly sexless manner. Lytton, highly strung and sensitive, moulded from similar clay to Virginia, became so anxious that someone outside their circle might carry off Thoby's beautiful and witty sister that he proposed to her himself.

Further proposals of marriage came from Hilton Young and Sydney Waterlow. Hilton was the most outwardly conventional of Virginia's suitors both in his courting and his person. Over the period of a couple of years he visited, wrote letters in her absence and delivered a romantic proposal on a Cambridge punt. Sydney was the most unconventional; his proposal came while he was married to someone else. The cautious Walter Lamb gave Virginia reasons why he could not propose and asked her to wait while he plucked up the courage (he never did, and she did not wait). Walter Headlam flirted with Virginia by letter, as he had with other women, and their friendship came to a sudden and mysterious end just before his premature death. Rupert Brooke was not drawn romantically to Virginia, but their friendship was for a time intimate, and he felt personally slighted when she married someone else, as he did whenever he lost a friend to marriage.

Virginia's suitors had one key characteristic in common – they came from the limited pool of 'Cambridge men' who had been to Trinity or King's in the early 1900s. Upper-middle-class England at the turn of the twentieth century was a very small world. Many of the male members of this exclusive club had been to one of a dozen public schools and one of two universities: most were destined to be 'movers and shakers' in law, politics or some other niche of the ruling class. At first glance, therefore, they all seem to be privileged intellectuals. But a closer look at their backgrounds and families reveals more variety.

Walter Headlam, from a family of reverends and lawyers, became a classical scholar, as his family had expected since he was a child, and Hilton Young took up the navy and politics, of which his ancestors would doubtless have approved. Lytton Strachey's upbringing with a highly literate and rather offbeat family prepared him for a career writing innovative warts-and-all biographies of those generally accepted as heroes of the Victorian era. Walter Lamb, the son of a social-climbing professor of mathematics, led the respectable life of the well-fed upper middle class, associating with artists and royalty. Sydney Waterlow, the Lord Mayor's grandson, continued the mayoral tradition of entertaining foreign royals, while nursing leanings towards the more artistic accomplishments of his mother's family, the Beauchamps. This family included Kathleen, who became the writer Katherine Mansfield.

Some of the suitors broke with family traditions. Clive Bell, whose *nouveau riche* forebears made their money from the coal industry, fled the life of a country squire to become an art critic. Saxon Sydney-Turner's unpromising and obscure beginnings (poor and shabby, in Virginia's eyes) did not impede his career in the Treasury – although they may have hampered his ambitions. Rupert Brooke, from a family of Anglican ministers, decided early on that he would not be guided by God and turned himself into a kind of pagan demi-god, an Adonis, to his admirers.

My main purpose in this book is to examine the nature of Virginia's relationship with each of her early suitors and the significance of their friendship to Virginia's life and her work. I try to provide a solid biographical base and 'read between the lives', often remarkable in their own right, in order to reveal the backgrounds, characters and accomplishments of these men of Bloomsbury and Bloomsbury's fringes. What emerges is a part of the social history of Cambridge-educated young Englishmen during the first half of the twentieth century

You will probably notice as you read – if you do not already know – how interrelated are all the performers on the Bloomsbury stage. Apart from her brother-in-law Clive Bell, Virginia was distantly related to at least two more of her suitors, Lytton Strachey and Hilton Young. The links within Bloomsbury and its fringes are seductive and surprising and encourage belief in a localized variant of the 'six degrees of separation' theory. Here are two examples that lead from one of her suitors back to Virginia: Hilton Young proposed to Virginia in 1909 and later married Kathleen Scott, who in her youth was a great friend of the dancer Isadora Duncan, who had an affair with Edward Gordon Craig, the son of Ellen Terry. At this point we can retreat further into the past and note that Ellen was photographed by Virginia's great-aunt Julia Margaret Cameron and was married at sixteen to Julia's friend G.F. Watts or, alternatively, that Craig's sister Edith (Edy) was a companion of Virginia's friend Vita Sackville-West. Another interesting line also runs via the well-connected Kathleen Scott, who knew Aleister Crowley, who married Rose, the sister of Clive Bell's friend Gerald Kelly, who was President of the Royal Academy when another of Virginia's suitors, Walter Lamb, was Secretary there. Aleister Crowley also appeared as a minor character in Sydney Waterlow's story, when he tried to recruit the lover of Sydney's friend J.W.N. Sullivan into his Sicilian harem. Waterlow and Lamb were connected via Sydney's friend Sir Eric Phipps, whose son, long after Sydney's death, married Henrietta, Walter's niece. Rupert Brooke and Lytton Strachey were connected through Brooke's lover Elisabeth van Rysselberghe, who after his death had an affair with André Gide, beloved of Lytton's sister Dorothy Bussy. Chains like these run throughout the lives of the people featured in this book, and connect figures as disparate as Winston Churchill, Oscar Wilde, Captain Robert Falcon Scott, Augustus John, Henry James, T.E. Lawrence, Max Beerbohm, J.M. Barrie, Elizabeth Jane Howard and several British monarchs. The scene of the action spreads from Bloomsbury to wartime France and Belgium and as far as the Antarctic, New Zealand and the South Seas.

The first decades of the twentieth century, the period during which our protagonists matured and grew old, saw a number of major political and social changes. It is not surprising, therefore, that history impinges upon the narrative in many places, for example, the First World War (or the Great War, as it was called until renamed after the onset of another) and its aftermath, leading to the formation of the League of Nations, politics between the wars, the turbulent years of the rise of the Labour Party and the attendant decline of the Liberals. Even the tragic consequences of Scott's second (and last) expedition to the South Pole has its place in this story. Looked at another way, the personal history of each suitor overlaps with other, larger histories. As a result, the perspective of the narrative often broadens to look at the general impact of the suitors' lives. I describe the social and professional background of each of these very different individuals, scrutinize him in relation to Virginia, then replace him in his historical niche. I examine the suitors at work and at leisure; what they did when they were following their professions as well as when they were courting Virginia. The contextual framework enriches the story of course, but my main theme and my overwhelming interest are centred on Virginia Stephen/Woolf, without whom the lives of the suitors and of her readers and admirers would have been a good deal poorer.

The Highly Eligible Miss Stephen

URING THE TWO years between the move from her childhood home and the death of her brother, Virginia Stephen learned the true meaning of freedom. She had grown up at 22 Hyde Park Gate in Kensington, a house inhabited by seventeen or eighteen people (including servants), with three water closets, one bathroom and little privacy. Relatives and friends who came topour out their woes to the lady of the house, the sympathetic Julia Stephen, were often overheard by others in the adjoining room, and Virginia regularly saw a neighbour washing in the bedroom opposite.[1] Both Leslie and Julia Stephen had been married before, and relics from their former lives came tumbling out of the over-packed cupboards.[2]

Laura, Leslie's daughter by his first wife, was mentally disturbed and disruptive but lived in the family home until she was twenty. Julia's two sons, George and Gerald Duckworth, handsome and thoroughly Victorian in outlook, were superficially respectable but took an unhealthy interest in the young Virginia. The alarming behaviour of these half-siblings had a damaging effect on Virginia's developing psychology. Laura's uncontrollable behaviour and the family attitude towards her bred in Virginia a lifelong fear of mental instability, and the attentions of her half-brothers were highly detrimental to her view of sexuality. But there were more immediate tragedies.

In 1895 Virginia's beloved mother died, followed two years later by her recently married half-sister Stella Duckworth. Leslie was plunged into deep grief and gloom after the first of these losses and insisted that the rest of the family followed suit. Always a demanding man, he became increasingly more so, frequently bewailing the loss of his wife, the burden of his work editing the monumental *Dictionary of National Biography* and the lack of emotional and practical support from his unsympathetic offspring. Virginia, loving her father but enraged by his behaviour, felt smothered by the confusion of passion and sentiment that engulfed their lives. In 1904 Leslie, too, died, and the young Stephens, all in their twenties, left the Hyde Park Gate life behind.[3]

At the new Bloomsbury house, 46 Gordon Square, the Stephen siblings – Virginia, Vanessa, Thoby and Adrian – made a new beginning. The rooms were light and airy, Victorian clutter was banished and time-worn habits abolished. Virginia had a room to decorate as she wished. She could be as private or as sociable as she wanted; and her father's legacy had provided her with the means to develop her writing career at her own pace. Her life during 1905 and 1906 was filled with meeting new people, making friends of both sexes, reading at a prodigious rate and laying the foundations of her career as a writer. All the young Stephens were more than content with the new domestic arrangements they had made after the death of their father. These signalled emancipation from the Victorian conventions under which they had grown up – from the dark furnishings and the claustrophobic, over-populated house in respectable Kensington. They were freed from dressing for dinner and calling with cards; from constant discussions about servant problems, engagements and weddings, illness and death; from the intimidating and tiresome etiquette of parties and social chit-chat. As well as family visitors curious to observe their fall from grace (which is how many relatives viewed their relocation from Kensington to Bloomsbury), the Stephens, thanks to Thoby's gift for friendship at Cambridge, had guests who were interested not in their domestic surroundings but in the discussion of ideas.

Thoby Stephen was the pivot for what became the Gordon Square 'at home' evenings, when his Cambridge friends continued their practice of debating such abstract concepts as 'beauty', 'good' and 'reality'. Although they did not speak of their affection until after his death, his friends adored him; as did his family – 'noble boy', his aunt, the romantic novelist Anny Thackeray, could not forbear from sighing. They admired him for his good looks – a classical head on broad shoulders – and for his charm and charisma, much more than for his intellect. He was clever, although not outstandingly so; he had had an indifferent school record, failing an entrance examination for Eton and being sent to Bristol's Clifton College instead. He was good at drawing birds and animals and was an enthusiastic butterfly and moth hunter, but he was not so proficient in Latin and Greek, and his handwriting was boyishly untidy.[4] He was reserved and unsentimental, feeling awkward and embarrassed by his father's outburst of grief after his mother's death.[5] But there was in him, as in all his siblings and his parents, a sensitive and melancholy side, a vulnerability. When he was delirious during a bout of influenza at school in 1894 he tried to throw himself out of a window.[6] Thoby's suicidal urge foreshadowed Virginia's attempted suicide ten years later, when, during a period of mental illness, she, too, tried to throw herself from a window.[7] Thoby's friends, however, failed to pick up this darker side and unanimously saw a Greek god in his face and figure. After his death Lytton Strachey wrote of Thoby's grandeur; even the normally level-headed Leonard Woolf was moved to described the monolithic qualities that had suggested his nickname, 'the Goth'.[8] For his sisters he was a brother whose attention was to be competed for and for his younger brother a role model who, sadly, could never be matched.

At the Gordon Square 'Thursday evenings' the Stephen women were required only to use their brains – dress and manners went unnoticed, but opinions and arguments were taken apart and criticized regardless of who had spoken them. There was no allowance made for their gender. And there was no talk of love and marriage. It was almost as far from the Hyde Park Gate era as it was possible to be. To Virginia, it seemed out of the question that any of these young men should fall in love with them or they with the young men. Because marriage was never discussed, Virginia assumed they considered it a subject not worth their notice, and she shared their opinion.[9] She had no romantic interest in men or any idea of getting married in the foreseeable future – all that had been left behind with the red plush and black paint at Hyde Park Gate. She accepted Thoby's university friends – intellectual and witty but mostly socially inept and shabbily dressed – as extensions of him rather than as prospective suitors. It was only after Thoby's death and Vanessa's marriage that she came to think of them as such. Much later she confessed in a memoir, 'Old Bloomsbury', that her ideas about a suitable husband – unlike her other ideas – had at that time not yet left the Victorian age. On the rare occasions she was forced to consider marriageable partners she still thought about 'young men who had been in the Eton Eleven and dressed for dinner'.[10] And Thoby's friends, she recognized at once, fell very far short of this. They were equipped for philosophical argument rather than for polite social intercourse. When George Duckworth proudly introduced his bride Lady Margaret Herbert to Saxon Sydney-Turner, that unworthy gentleman did not pause in the delicate and exacting task of lighting his pipe; he merely half rose from his chair and nodded in her direction. But how refreshing that kind of behaviour must have been for the sisters, whose socially ambitious half-brother had forced them into 'society', dragging them out to parties and subjecting their clothes and behaviour to the closest scrutiny. She and Vanessa no longer had to undergo the post-mortem George Duckworth had put them through when they accompanied him to social events – had they dressed properly, had they talked of suitable subjects, had they made a conquest of an acceptable young man? Suddenly none of these things mattered.

The Stephens must have known that the harmonious period at 46 Gordon Square could not last long. All of them were, after all, extremely eligible. They were physically very attractive, intelligent, had a measure of financial independence and the additional advantage of illustrious relatives. (Not that they wished to exploit their connections, but the connections were there nevertheless.) Women, and some men, found Thoby irresistible. As early as March 1905 Vanessa wrote to her cousin-in-law Madge Vaughan of her fears that their idyllic life would suddenly come to an end when Thoby fell in love.[11] A few months later, having been courted assiduously by Clive Bell, she recognized that it might not be her brother who would be the first to break the charmed circle. She faced the fact that sooner or later they would all walk down the aisle and began to feel quite comfortable with the idea. Virginia, three years younger, was less sanguine about marriage and felt the possibility looming like a great shadow over their future happiness.[12] During that summer Clive proposed to Vanessa and was prevaricatingly refused, and the fragile unity of the foursome remained intact for another year or so. But ultimately it was not to be marriage that separated them. The division, when it came, was final and irrevocable.

In 1906 all four Stephens made an ambitious trip to Greece and Turkey, following in the footsteps of Desmond MacCarthy, who had been there four years earlier. In August Adrian and Thoby started out on horseback from Trieste and travelled through Montenegro and Albania to Greece, where Virginia, Vanessa and their friend Violet Dickinson joined them, having sailed from Italy.[13] Greece had caught the imagination of Thoby and Adrian and many of their Cambridge contemporaries. In Ancient Greek literature and art they thought they detected a model civilization – but they found that modern twentieth-century Greece did not always live up to their high ideals. Of course the Stephens were not naïve enough to think they would find undisturbed the Greece of Plato, Theocritus and Sophocles, but they had hoped and expected to find in the modern Greeks traces of their noble ancestry.

Virginia ridicules their (and her own) expectations in her satirical early story 'A Dialogue upon Mount Pentelicus', written shortly after her return. Here she describes in fiction a real journey the Stephens made up the mountainside. Although modern Greek citizens, the guides appointed by the English tourists in the story are not at all representative of that ancient race who strike noble poses in Greek sculpture, friezes and pottery: they are as animated and voluble as children. Where is the dignity, the gravity, the distinction of their forefathers? The true heirs of Ancient Greece are not these barbarians, the young Englishmen conclude, but those who have learned their Greek at Harrow.[14]

Virginia tackled the same feelings of bathos in *Jacob's Room* where the narrator states that the idealization of Greece is an 'illusion'. Modern Greece is 'ramshackle'; but at least it has efficient trams. The waiter in Jacob's hotel has the classically allusive name of Aristotle but is grubby and far from dignified.[15] During their own trip to Greece the Stephens' friends the Noels, whom (like Desmond in 1902) they visited at Euboea and who had lived in Greece for generations, told them bluntly that all Greeks were dirty, dishonest and ignorant.[16] Moreover, Virginia observed, even the language had been tainted and had branched out into three varieties: the demotic of everyday speech, an 'impure dialect' which no one could write; the formal language of the newspapers, which even the Noels could not read; and the classical, which no one could read and which the locals did not understand (Virginia tried her best).[17]

Nevertheless the country was exotic and colourful, and the Stephens found enough poetry in the rural peasants and ruined Greek architecture to feed their aesthetic appetites. Virginia remembered the words of Homer among the ruins of Mycenae, and she imagined an ancient city in the desert and the purple and gold of a royal procession. She kept a highly descriptive travel diary to exercise her literary muscles, emphasizing the earthiness and sensuality of Greece. From the vantage point of the early twenty-first century her experiences seem enviably authentic: ancient statues seen *in situ* rather than in glass cases; trotting up Mount Pentelicus on muleback; eating freshly plucked grapes in a vineyard; watching dolphins leaping in the sea; a visit to the huts of nomad shepherds. But, for the most part, Ancient Greece was dead, and modern Greece was no substitute.[18]

But the idea of 'Greekness' explored in 'A Dialogue upon Mount Pentelicus' reaches a different conclusion from the diary. During a discussion, one of the young Englishmen points out to another that his ideas of Ancient Greek civilization are deluded – his net is spread so wide that it catches up all that is beautiful or true, whatever its provenance, and calls it 'Greek'. Then a monk emerges from nearby bushes and for a moment all six of the young men are entranced, seeing a vision of the continuity of the ages embodied in this timeless figure and sensing Plato and Sophocles close by. When the monk greets him the young man who is guilty of attributing all good things to Ancient Greece takes this as a sign that he has been chosen as a worthy heir.[19]

Unfortunately Vanessa fell ill as soon as they reached Greece and was intermittently unwell throughout the trip, nursed by the kindly Violet. Thoby returned to London in October as planned, while the others continued on to Turkey. When they returned to England on 1 November they found that Thoby had contracted a fever, initially misdiagnosed as malaria. Vanessa and Violet had also become ill enough to take to their beds, but they would ultimately recover. Only Thoby did not, and on 20 November, after three weeks of medical bungling, he died from typhoid, for which there was no cure at that time. His death at the age of twenty-six cemented his almost mythical standing in the minds of his family and friends. Virginia soon realized how little she actually knew of her brother's inner life and how he had spent his time away from home, but it was to be another sixteen years before she explored them in fiction, in *Jacob's Room*.

Jacob's Room (1922) is full of snatches of Thoby's physical appearance and bearing and conjectures about his personality and private life. At nineteen Jacob Flanders seems powerfully built, shy and rather clumsy to a fellow passenger on the Cambridge train. In King's College Chapel he has misogynistic and patriarchal thoughts on the plain wives of learned men. With university friends he discusses right and wrong, sometimes answering the earnest and steadfast opinions only with laughter.[20]

On a boating holiday a trivial quarrel with a friend casts a gloom over Jacob; he is careless, breaking the Primus stove and leaving a book where it gets swept overboard. At a dinner party he is silent and awkward but distinguished. In his desire for truth he composes a letter to the papers complaining about an edition of Wycherley that has had all the indecencies removed.[21] Clara Durrant, one of his many admirers, thinks him unworldly and without pretensions, but his mother is merely irritated by his clumsiness. Drunken friends think him great and heroic. Strangers think he is beautiful or mistake him for a military man.[22] He speaks with an authoritative air about Greek plays but has only a rudimentary knowledge of the language. He sees in the face of his lover, the beautiful but stupid Florinda, a noblewoman of Ancient Greece. He has a beautiful voice, thinks another female admirer, but is awkward, aloof and slightly overbearing.[23]

With artist friends in France Jacob reverts to the robust schoolboy jargon of Thoby's letters from Evelyns and Clifton: 'juggins', 'jolly well have to', 'hang it all'.[24] He exchanges Greek for politics and becomes abstracted and stern-looking. He is still plagued by glooms: only his friend Bonamy, who bears him an unspoken love, understands that he must be left alone with his melancholy.[25] Jacob meets a married woman who talks about Greek, French and Russian literature and who exposes his youth and callowness. Bonamy's prediction comes true: Jacob has fallen in love with a woman with a Greek profile – a caryatid at Athens reminds him of her. Her views of him are contradictory: he is sometimes a 'mere bumpkin'; at other times Alceste from Molière's *Misanthrope*.[26] A girl pining for Jacob sees his image in the Greek heads of the British Museum. A clergyman friend of the family sees him, tall and statuesque, in the street. And then suddenly he is dead, like the real Thoby, leaving nothing but a collection of hints.[27]

Virginia speculated years after Thoby's death that, had he lived, his passion for G.E. Moore's dictum of intellectual honesty, as well as the Stephen lawgiving gene, would have resulted in his career as a lawmaker, Mr Justice Stephen. She imagined him having written and illustrated a book on birds, published by the Hogarth Press, as well as works on law, art, literature and public affairs.[28] But his real accomplishment, given the fact of his early death, was in bringing together a number of disparate young men and introducing them to his brother and sisters. The quartet of Stephens was an irresistible combination that attracted at first a trickle, then a flood, of visitors. With Vanessa Thoby shared statuesque good looks, a rock-like eternal quality and reserve; with Virginia a thirst for knowledge and debate and a rare talent for attracting loyal and adoring friends. Now the other three would have to manage without him, but his friends – now their friends – remained.

However, one of these young men wanted to be much more than a friend. Vanessa had refused Clive Bell's proposals of marriage on two earlier occasions and on 7 November had written to Clive to suggest that they should part for a year.[29] But now, barely two weeks later, the family circle had been broken completely and she seemed to abandon her earlier self-sufficiency. She had no further reason to procrastinate. Snatching a chance of happiness from the emptiness of their shared loss, she accepted an awkwardly timed third proposal two days after her beloved brother's death.

Thus within the space of three months, from November 1906 to February 1907, the young Virginia Stephen's life was irrevocably changed. Thoby's death and Vanessa's marriage – one might almost say on the rebound from the tragedy – reduced the Stephen household to two unhappy and rather incompatible siblings, Virginia and Adrian. For Adrian the series of shocks had also been great. Since leaving the cocoon of Cambridge in the summer of 1905 Adrian had found it difficult to settle. Virginia considered that he had not taken his education very seriously and looked upon it as entertainment.[30] This lack of application was reflected in the third-class degree he was eventually awarded. He worked for his Bar examinations but had not found his niche – and would not do so for many years.

The newly married Bells now needed the house at 46 Gordon Square to themselves, so while they were on their honeymoon Virginia found an alternative dwelling place near by at 29 Fitzroy Square, formerly inhabited by George Bernard Shaw, to share with her younger brother. In 1907 the houses of Fitzroy Square were mainly offices, workshops and flats, retaining little of their original grandeur. Duncan Grant recalled that the Stephens were the only people in the square to have an entire house.[31] Virginia's rooms were on the second floor and Adrian had a study at the front of the ground floor, where visitors would congregate. In the evenings he would play the pianola for hours at a stretch in the large first-floor drawing-room, where Watts's portrait of Leslie had followed them from Gordon Square, probably at Virginia's instigation (Adrian had few fond memories of his father). Duncan Grant remembered Virginia during the Fitzroy years as shy, fierce and aloof, especially when introduced unexpectedly to a stranger. Determined not to be insincere merely out of politeness, she would greet a newcomer with an abrupt phrase or two, then subside into silence.[32] There was no small talk – the 'say nothing that is not true' tenet of the Cambridge philosopher G.E. Moore had put a stop to this in Bloomsbury.

Adrian was the only one of the four to reject Moore's philosophy outright. He had always been the odd one out. The less favoured brother in terms of looks and charisma, he had been his mother's pet as a child, which had caused some friction with the others. Finding himself often excluded from their games (many years later his analyst hinted that it was because Virginia had not paired with him but made a trio with the older two), he made isolation a deliberate policy. In the nursery he set up newssheets to rival the *Hyde Park Gate News*, the family newspaper created by Virginia and Thoby, and refused to join in with butterfly-hunting; and at Cambridge he set himself apart by repudiating the philosopher who was so highly regarded by Thoby's friends. Owing partly to Adrian's own efforts, Virginia always saw him as different from herself and the others. He seemed to her much younger than he was and in need of looking after – her perception of him as the 'baby brother' never really altered over the years.[33]

Although united by a deep if unspoken fraternal love (and Virginia wrote words of great affection for him as well as criticism), as housemates the pair were not a great success. Virginia's highly strung nature and Adrian's bouts of lethargy and sullenness were not compatible. Adrian had been as a child nervous and stubborn by turns, and in adulthood his aimlessness plunged her into despair. Sometimes he sat all day in an armchair reading and needed to be forced into any kind of physical activity. Virginia was often impatient with her brother, and Adrian knew just how to tease his sister for maximum effect. Occasionally their domestic conflicts brought a return to nursery ways, throwing pats of butter across the room at each other which adhered to the walls in silent but greasy reproach.[34]

After the loss of Vanessa to Clive, both Virginia and Adrian immediately felt the lack of her stabilizing and protective influence. Although Virginia's intentions were good, she was not capable of taking a maternal role in relation to her brother, as Vanessa had done with Thoby from his babyhood. She talked, in a wifely way, of making a home for Adrian, but this worked better in theory than practice.[35] On the break-up of the Gordon Square household, Sophie Farrell, the Stephen family cook, explained that her decision to go to Fitzroy Square with the younger two was taken largely because Virginia was so scatterbrained that she would not be able to manage.[36] (Radical as they intended to be, the burden of supervising household matters was apparently still to fall to the sister rather than the brother.)

Thrown into relief by all the paeans sung by his friends in praise of Thoby is the absence of anything approaching the same hero-worship of Adrian. But the latter had his own admirers nevertheless. Duncan Grant's immediate attraction to him, at their first meeting in Paris in 1907, had matured into love by 1909. Adrian, although flattered and encouraged by Duncan's attention, was confused about his own inclinations. A sexual relationship developed with Duncan, but Adrian also visited female prostitutes and fell in love with women. Rupert Brooke's muse Noel Olivier rejected Adrian's proposal of marriage and resented his ardent pursuit but was nevertheless struck by his 'radiant beauty' at Asheham in late 1913 when he came down to dinner in his pyjamas.[37] Adrian's second cousin, Fredegond Shove, also saw the Stephen beauty shining through him when she wrote to Vanessa in 1916 of his resplendent figure in light-brown velvet, and she thought him 'almost the best person in the world'.[38] Lytton Strachey, spending Easter 1908 on Salisbury Plain with Cambridge friends, wished that Adrian would appear in his purple stockings.[39] (The light-brown velvet suit and purple stockings suggest that Adrian could be something of a dandy.) Adrian's only biographer to date, Jean MacGibbon, herself had an affair with him in the 1940s. From their first meeting, she says, she thought of him as a special person, larger than life in spirit as well as in body.[40]

In her more loyal moods Virginia claimed distinction and charm for Adrian, but she did not idolize him as she had Thoby, and his spirit did not haunt her fiction as Thoby's does *Jacob's Room* or *The Waves*. A sympathetic portrait of his childhood and adolescence is painted in *To the Lighthouse*, where he features as the youngest son James, alternately indulged by Mrs Ramsay and subjected to the harsh but inescapable truths of Mr Ramsay. But Virginia invested her younger brother with no mysteries. Dying young and handsome, Thoby's memory was subject (as Rupert Brooke's later was) to the accretion of adulation and the tragedy of unfulfilled promise, while Adrian had to get by in the real world.

After Vanessa's marriage Virginia was frequently (or so it felt to her) encouraged to leave her maiden state behind. There was no corresponding urgency to pair Adrian off, but the mores of Jane Austen's Britain had not completely been eradicated even by the early twentieth century, and to the more conventional members of her family Virginia must have seemed conspicuously eligible. Given this pressure to marry, it is unsurprising that she began to observe the men around her with a new eye and that male friends and acquaintances sensed this and responded. Eligible, intelligent and lovely as she was, Virginia did not lack for attention. The unsettled interval of 1907–11 saw her with a sequence of overlapping love affairs, flirtations and proposals. Quentin Bell states that before Vanessa's marriage in February 1907 'All Virginia's passions, her jealousies and tenderness [were] kept for her own sex.'[41] This is why, understandably, many biographers focus on her female intimates. But there is another story to be told.

While Virginia's intimate friendships and sexually explicit letters during this period were mainly reserved for Vanessa and for her close friend Violet Dickinson, she was not immune to the effect her beauty, intelligence and wit had on the young (and the not-so-young) men of her acquaintance. She had seen the mysterious effect of love on her shy and passive half-sister Stella Duckworth and Stella's fiancé Jack Hills, which for her transposed them from the mundane world into figures of high romance.[42] But Vanessa's courtship and marriage was the first time Virginia was able properly to witness how love affairs worked themselves out. She began to be intrigued by the power she could exert over her admirers and tried out these powers even where her heart was very little engaged. No suitable candidate for marriage was to be found among these men, although Virginia was flattered by their attentions and did little to discourage them. While she would often profess love – and sometimes passion – to her female correspondents (and continued to do so for the rest of her life), she does not appear to have been truly 'in love' with any of those males who put themselves forward for consideration before Leonard Woolf.

None of Virginia's male suitors broke suddenly upon the scene. She did not go to house parties searching for love at first sight among the new faces. Stella had married an Eton friend of her brother George, and, unexpectedly following in her half-sister's footsteps, Vanessa, rather conventionally, married a Cambridge friend of Thoby's. Virginia selected her intimates mainly from the readily available set of men that paid social calls to Fitzroy or Gordon Square. These, with the exception of Walter Headlam (sixteen years older than Virginia) and Rupert Brooke (five years younger), were all student contemporaries of her late brother Thoby and had become acquainted with her chiefly through him. The suitors knew one another and were familiar with others in the inner or outer circle of Bloomsbury. That Virginia, like Thoby, had a gift for friendship is borne out by the fact that in most cases the suitors stayed in touch with her after the period of intimacy was over, even when they had suffered a rejection at her hands – with the exception, perhaps, of Lytton Strachey.

While all the candidates for Virginia's affections came with the commendation of friendship with her brother or parents, the first was almost a member of the family. He was Walter Headlam, an old friend of the Stephen clan, who had been familiar to Virginia since childhood.

A Fine Romance: Walter Headlam

VIRGINIA'S RELATIONSHIP WITH Walter Headlam was her first direct experience of heterosexual romance, albeit one which was not accompanied by the usual accoutrements of courtship. It was no coincidence that for her first 'romance' she chose, or was chosen by, an older man who shared some of her father's qualities. But as well as the familiarity and safety represented by a male family friend whom she could look upon as a father or older brother, there was also the element of risk which denoted a rebellion against her family. After all, this man had flirted with her stepsister and her mother, and there were rumours of a fetish for little girls. Whether Virginia knew about these things or not, she sensed the family reservations about him and knew she was playing a slightly dangerous game. But she needed to demonstrate to herself and others that men found her attractive and that she was single because of her own selective nature, not because of a lack of offers. This compulsion to prove her allure would be a recurring theme in Virginia's relationships with men. It did not seem to matter that her heart was disengaged. Of course, everyone of her acquaintance was potential raw material for her writing, and it was very interesting to get to know people on intimate terms. In her relationship with Walter a few of the key elements of a love affair were present: the common external interest, the gentle early wooing, the lovers' tiff and even a brief fit of jealousy, exhibited by Walter when he thought he was being neglected. But in reality it was only the shadow of a romance.

Virginia's mother, although far from sentimental, had considered marriage the duty of a woman. Julia had been a keen observer of budding amours and a compulsive matchmaker, and Virginia had witnessed several marriages-in-the-making. The romances she attended to most closely were those of her parents, her stepsister Stella and her sister Vanessa. The first two examples were not encouraging. Her parents' marriage ended with the death at forty-nine of her mother, owing to rheumatic fever, contracted during a period of illness brought on by incessant ministering to the needs of others. Julia was a tireless letter-writer on behalf of the unemployed and a frequent visitor to the poor and bereaved, providing practical help and sympathy to an apparently ever-increasing number of unfortunates. But by far the greatest demands on her were made by her husband Leslie, who had a constant need for sympathy and reassurance from his wife. Effectively, this suggested to Virginia that caring for others, and especially for her husband, had killed her.

The second romance ended prematurely and tragically when Stella died three months after her wedding from peritonitis, complicated by the fact that she was in the early stages of pregnancy. One of her nurses told Stella's friend Violet Dickinson that she had died after a gynaecological defect had been aggravated by sexual intercourse. Again, there is the inference that her death was a direct result of marriage and in Stella's case the obligatory sexual relationship that went with it.[1]

Vanessa, more robust and less submissive respectively than her mother and her stepsister, survived pregnancy and other hazards of marriage. Her example alone was sufficiently joyous and life-affirming to fire Virginia with enthusiasm for the state of marriage and for the possibility of a romantic relationship for herself. But where was she to find a wooer? At the time of Vanessa's marriage in early 1907 most of Virginia's male acquaintances appeared to be more interested in abstract discussion than in feminine charms. Virginia was never fooled into thinking Walter Headlam a perfect match, but he was a man who was attracted to her, with whom she could talk about her interests and her intellectual pursuits.

Born at 24 Norfolk Square, near London's Hyde Park, on 15 February 1866, Walter George Headlam was the second son of Edward and Mary. His father was one of twelve children born to the Venerable John Headlam, Archdeacon of Richmond in Yorkshire, and his wife Maria. Maria was descended from the notorious Master of Trinity, Richard Bentley (1662–1742), the brilliant but quarrelsome classical scholar celebrated in the two-volume *Life of Dr Bentley* by the Bishop of Gloucester, J.H. Monk, in 1830. Virginia wrote about this work, commenting on its subject's domineering character and his scholarly feuds, in an essay, 'Outlines: Dr Bentley', first published in the *Common Reader* in 1925, no doubt aware of the connection with Headlam. Indeed, she could have been thinking of him when she wrote in the article of those gowned scholars, glimpsed scurrying through a college courtyard at dusk, who read Pindar as most people read the newspaper and seem to live in the company of the Greeks rather than of their contemporaries.[2]

The charming and diligent Edward won a scholarship to Cambridge and was a fellow of St John's College, *en route* to becoming a barrister and director of examinations in the Civil Service Commission. His five surviving brothers also distinguished themselves academically, and his sister was skilled in languages. Walter's mother, Mary – lively, pretty and matching her husband in personal charm – had aesthetic leanings and passed these on to her second son. He received a literary grounding of sorts from his aunts, who had married the brothers John and Thomas Storey Spedding, relations of the literary scholar James Spedding. Now largely forgotten, James Spedding was a friend of Leslie Stephen's father and had written a dauntingly comprehensive multi-volume study of Francis Bacon. Leslie kept the work in his library and lent it to Virginia. Spedding's 'salon' was comparable to that of Virginia's Prinsep relatives. Frequent visitors were historians J.A. Froude and Thomas Carlyle (also an acquaintance of Leslie's), poet and translator Edward Fitzgerald and poet laureate Alfred Tennyson. Walter never met these illustrious guests, but conversations and anecdotes reflecting their characters echoed in the houses of his Spedding relatives just as they echoed through those of Virginia's family.[3]

Walter's extensive family was based along the borders of North Yorkshire and Durham and is traceable today across ten generations. Branches of it sprouted a half-a-dozen offspring; consequently Walter had a dizzying number of uncles, aunts and cousins. Prodigious numbers of children were also born into the family in Walter's generation. His father's brother Morley, a justice of the peace, had eleven children.[4] Edward himself had six children, and another brother, Francis, produced eight offspring. Maurice married the daughter of an earl, Cuthbert was a baronet, Thomas was a lieutenant-colonel and Hugh was a brigadier-general. Another of Walter's uncles, the Reverend Arthur William Headlam, married Agnes Sarah Favell, who could trace her descent from Oliver Cromwell. Walter's cousins, Arthur and James, became respectively Bishop of Gloucester and Professor of Greek and Ancient History at Queen's College, London. Thus Walter's family abounded in members of the ruling class: churchmen and lawgivers, professors and military men, aristocrats and landowners. Walter had a considerable amount to live up to and, in some respects, he did so – although not in the important task of continuing the dynasty.[5]

Walter was brought up in London but went to school at Elstree, Hertford-shire (the school was later moved to Berkshire), and then to Harrow. At the age of sixteen he suffered three tragic losses in quick succession: in July 1882 his eleven-year-old brother Arthur died and, not long afterwards, both parents. Despite these family tragedies Walter won a scholarship to King's College, Cambridge, going up in 1884. A string of academic qualifications and accolades followed. By 1903 he had been awarded three Sir William Browne gold medals, the Porson prize, a first-class degree in Classics, a King's fellowship, Master of Arts and Doctor of Literature. Academic success was built into the Headlam family genes and in the field of classics above all. In his brother Cecil's opinion, Walter 'came of a stock which was likely to produce a classical scholar of genius'.[6] When he was made a King's fellow in 1890, he took the corner room on the ground floor of the Gibbs Building. His cousin James (later the Greek professor of Queen's College, London) and Goldswor-thy Lowes Dickinson (later a friend of Leonard Woolf and E.M. Forster) lived along the corridor.

Walter spent the rest of his short life teaching and researching with Cambridge as his base. He taught students in his rooms, walking around declaiming poetry, surveyed by portraits of Leslie and Julia Stephen and surrounded by precarious towers of books and papers. In 1891 these towers grew taller still. The *Mimes* of Herodas were discovered, and Headlam was selected to work on the manuscripts and to produce a complete edition for the Cambridge University Press. Close scrutiny of an obscure text was his great passion, and he delighted in explaining how he had deciphered the many-layered nuances of a certain Greek word. His work with the manuscripts secured his status as a recognized authority on Herodas while he was still in his twenties. A scholarly figure resembling Walter appears as a minor character in *Jacob's Room*. Professor Huxtable of Trinity writes his letters in Greek, as Walter was fond of doing, and he is extremely learned – into his brain would fit the intellects of a dozen ordinary men. Huxtable is compared intellectually with Dr Bentley, Master of Trinity, whom Virginia probably knew was an ancestor of Walter's. When deep in scholarly thought he is ennobled, but in the sordid world of painful corns and bill-paying he is a grumbling miser.[7] Walter did not have miserly tendencies as far as we know, but he certainly had problems coping with everyday affairs; or, rather, he merely forgot them, being engrossed in his work. E.F. Benson related a tale of one item of research leading to another until shaving water boiled dry, lunch brought to Headlam's room was neglected until dinner time, and his pipe, although lit many times, was not actually smoked. This scholarly eccentricity was of course not a particular drawback for one whose life was spent in an institution such as King's and was generally viewed as endearing. Headlam's sudden boyish and rather impractical enthusiasms – for composing music after hearing a Schubert symphony, although he could not read music or play the piano; for horse-riding, after spending an afternoon at the Newmarket races – were received the same way.[8]

It was during the 1880s that Walter came into the Stephen family circle. He was a friend of Virginia's half-brother Gerald Duckworth (Julia Stephen's younger son from her first marriage), writing him lines in Greek for his eighteenth birthday in 1888 and accompanying him on a trip to St Moritz a decade later. He became a protégé of both Leslie and Julia. Leslie, in the *Mausoleum Book*, names Headlam as one of the two young men who were Julia's favourites.[9] No doubt the fact that he was parentless added poignancy to his situation. Walter looked on Leslie as a role model, but Julia was a friend and confidante to whom he wrote about some of his deeper feelings. He told her of the conflicting drives within him: one to work diligently, and one, when he was feeling trapped by the narrow, monastic life he had chosen as a King's fellow, to give it all up. In 1893 he wrote of his desire to start living fully, after deferring it for so long. He was then twenty-seven. Half of him wanted to 'go to the devil' and half to be Julia's friend, he said, well aware that these impulses were mutually exclusive.[10] Sexual frustration perhaps played a part in his discontent. King's College was not the best of places to meet young women, although he did teach some of the Newnham students, several of whom found him charming.

Walter's friendship with the Stephen family meant that he visited them at Hyde Park Gate and St Ives while Virginia was a girl. She resented the constant presence of the promising young scholars taken under Leslie's wing. They were commemorated in *To the Lighthouse* in the character of pharmacist's son Charles Tansley. The young men came to pay their tribute to Leslie, to talk to him about their work and listen to him talk about his own. He had a scholarly integrity and scrupulous honesty that they emulated: it is worth noting that in *To the Lighthouse* Charles Tansley, as well as Mr Ramsay, feels compelled to predict disappointment for James, whose heart is set on a boat trip. Tansley's walk into St Ives with Mrs Ramsay may have been inspired by Virginia's vivid memory of Walter accompanying her mother to a St Ives public house to purchase rum for the children's moth-hunting.[11] But the charming summers at Talland House were only one side of the picture; Walter's friendship with the family brought him into much murkier waters. In November 1891 he had what must have been a very alarming experience with his friend and Virginia's cousin, J.K. (Jem or Jim) Stephen.

Jem was the son of Leslie's older brother, James Fitzjames Stephen, and was Leslie's favourite nephew. Virginia remembered him as a deep-voiced and powerfully built young man with very blue eyes who reminded her of Homer's Achilles.[12] He was a King's fellow, well known and widely admired as a public speaker and the author of a volume of parodies and other verse, *Lapsus Calami* (literally, 'slip of the pen'). He had founded the TAF (Twice A Fortnight) Club, whose members included Walter, Gerald Duckworth, M.R. James, later Provost of King's and today known for his ghost stories, and E.F. Benson, author of the Mapp and Lucia stories. The TAF met every Sunday night for talk and supper in a member's rooms. A photograph of the group shows Gerald in the accoutrements of a gentleman student: straw boater, monocle, cravat, waistcoat, jacket with protruding handkerchief, watch chain. The bulky Jem lounges at the back of the group in a light-coloured striped blazer, smoking a pipe. Walter himself looks something of a dandy: diminutive, smart, in cream flannels with a bow tie, glasses, a buttonhole in his jacket, and neat, dark, slicked-back hair. His brother Cecil described Walter at this time as 'striking and original', with blue eyes, a 'mobile lip', a vivacious wit and intelligence and 'a resonant, clear voice' with an occasional stammer.[13]

In the years preceding 1891 Jem had been suffering mental disturbances. At the age of twenty-seven he had received a blow to the head from a windmill sail while horse-riding in Felixstowe, and his conduct became increasingly irrational.[14] This was not entirely due to brain damage from the accident, but it appears that the blow triggered the manic depression which was a characteristic of the Stephen family. Although their symptoms manifested themselves differently, Thomas Caramagno (in *The Flight of the Mind*) puts Jem and Virginia into the same psychiatric grouping of 'bipolar manic-depressive illness' in his chart of the family's mental disorders.[15] Jem's disturbing behaviour was witnessed by the Stephens, whom he visited frequently while he was ill. He would drive about in a hansom cab all day and leave Leslie to pay the fare. He laboured under the delusion that he was a great artist and painted a portrait of Virginia on a piece of wood. He became obsessed with Virginia's half-sister Stella Duckworth and wrote her passionate but confused love letters. He pursued her aggressively, paying unannounced visits to the house in the hope of seeing her – unluckily he lived only a couple of streets away from Hyde Park Gate. Virginia and her siblings were instructed that if they met him they were to say she was not at home. On one occasion, recalled by Virginia in 'A Sketch of the Past' (*Moments of Being*), Jem rushed into the nursery at 22 Hyde Park Gate and attacked the bread with his swordstick. On another he interrupted the Stephens' breakfast and laughingly told them that Dr Savage's considered medical opinion was that he would either die or go insane.[16] While Leslie and Julia were sympathetic and recognized the significance of his symptoms, Jem's father could not face the awful truth and hid his fears, with the consequence that Jem did not receive the appropriate medical attention.

In November Walter was called urgently to Jem's Cambridge lodgings. He arrived with a family doctor having been alerted by the distressed landlady to Jem's strange behaviour. Gerald, then a student at Clare College, probably got his information straight from his friend Walter. He wrote to tell Julia Stephen of the crisis, describing how Walter had discovered her favourite nephew in a manic state, standing naked in front of his bedroom window, singing and hurling his possessions into the street. Walter and the doctor managed to calm Jem down and called for his brothers Harry and Herbert Stephen. Jem was confined in St Andrew's, a psychiatric hospital in Northampton, where he died on 3 February 1892 of mania and exhaustion, having refused all food and rest.[17] He was three weeks short of his thirty-third birthday.

His friend's death greatly distressed Walter. Two days later he wrote a sonnet for the *Cambridge Review* entitled 'In Memoriam J.K.S.' He quotes lines from Jem's poem 'In a Garden', which describes a twilight walk by three friends (Jem, Walter and E.F. Benson). In Walter's poem, only two grieving friends remain, and the 'flowers' of the garden, symbolizing Jem's potential, have been destroyed while still in bud:

> Now, when scarce afresh we see
> Flowers upon the earth,
> Two are mourners of the three;
> Blasted ere their birth
> Are the flowers that were to be.[18]

As a friend of Jem's and Gerald's and an admirer of her parents Walter must have appeared to the young Virginia as a member of their extended family, but there is no evidence to suppose a mutual attraction until much later. He was sixteen years older than her, and she probably regarded him initially as a friend of her parents. In the view of Virginia's nephew Quentin Bell, Walter's later claim upon Virginia's attention was his high scholarly reputation among classicists.[19] Virginia took her own classical education very seriously. It began when Thoby, on a visit home from Evelyns, told her about the Greeks and Trojans while they marched up and down the stairs to cover his embarrassment about talking shop.[20] She had already read some Greek at home when she began a ladies-only class in Greek in November 1897 with Dr George Warr at King's College, Kensington. She progressed to private lessons with Clara Pater, sister of the writer Walter Pater. Warr was a translator of classical authors and Clara Pater classics tutor at Somerville College, Oxford. Virginia thus had the benefit of professional teaching although she did not attend a prep school or university like her brothers. Greek was her 'daily bread', she told her cousin Emma Vaughan. She wanted company in her studies and told Emma to encourage her sister Marny to reacquaint herself with her Greek books. Leslie's friend Charles Eliot Norton talked to Virginia about Greek and advised her to read Edward Fitzgerald's translation of Sophocles.[21] By 1902 she was taking lessons with Janet Case, admiring her teacher's thoroughness, precision and lack of sentimentality and spending a part of each morning making translations from Greek. She kept Thoby up to date on her progress.[22] For Virginia the Greek language and the culture and art of Greece were always a link to Thoby and his belief – shared with many of his Cambridge friends – in the civilizing influence of the Ancient Greeks. It is not surprising that Virginia should strike up a friendship with a classical scholar, especially one who had strong connections to her family.

The nature of the Walter–Virginia friendship is somewhat mysterious. It grew slowly over a matter of years, came to a head and declined rapidly thereafter. Virginia first developed a one-to-one relationship with Walter at some point in 1902, in the wake of her father's diagnosis with cancer. The sixteen-year age gap between Walter and Virginia invites speculation that she was searching for a father surrogate; not exactly a filial replacement but an older male with whom she could talk about books and continue the literary exchanges and intellectual flirtatiousness that had characterized her relationship with Leslie. For Walter the friendship was part of his love affair with all the women of the family. Walter Lamb remembered of late 1906:

> [I] walked & talked a good deal with Walter Headlam of King's, who had once loved Leslie Stephen's wife, Mrs Duckworth, & had since her death been very fond of her younger daughter, Virginia Stephen. He also greatly admired Vanessa . . .[23]

Virginia's friendship with Walter was at this time mainly scholarly. She sent him three pages of criticism of the manuscript of his translation of Aeschylus' *Agamemnon*, a sign that their relationship was already one of equals, rather than the father–daughter or uncle–niece acquaintance that might be expected between a family friend and a daughter of the family.[24] She had been studying Greek for several years, although still only twenty, while Walter must have studied the subject for at least fifteen years. There are two likely explanations why he chose to submit himself to the criticism of such a young and comparatively inexperienced woman. One is that his admiration of Virginia's intellect surmounted the barriers of age and her lack of a university education. The other is that he had conceived a romantic fancy for the daughter of his old friend and chose to woo her in the only way he knew, through classical literature. Perhaps it was a combination of the two.

A balancing friendship grew up at the same time with Violet Dickinson, formerly a friend of Stella's. In these relationships with old family friends Virginia did not seek substitutes for her parents but a more informal echo of them. In Walter she found someone with whom she could develop her own literary ideas, perhaps preparing herself for the inevitable break from Leslie. In Violet she found a sympathetic and maternal figure who offered help and encouragement. She leaned on both her friends in the aftermath of Leslie's death in 1904, finding especial comfort in Walter's esteem for her father.

Virginia's family losses were suffered at a less immediate level by Walter – he had also known and loved Jem, Julia, Stella and Leslie, but, save in Jem's case, his grief cannot have been so deep as Virginia's. While she suffered a suicidal breakdown at the Welwyn home of Violet, Walter's behaviour after Leslie's death was uncharacteristically pleasure-seeking. During the summer of 1904, whether looking anew at his life or finally 'going to the devil' as he could not in Leslie's and Julia's lifetimes, Walter relaxed his customarily strict regime and freed himself from certain restraints in his behaviour. In London he visited public art galleries but also indulged in the less intellectual pleasures of drinking beer, gin and cocktails. He wrote to his sister Ida that he felt happier the more 'rules' he broke.[25] His behaviour suggests that mourning was mixed with a sense of relief and prefigures the new freedoms enjoyed by the Stephen siblings at Gordon Square.

Meanwhile Virginia's own mixed feelings had brought on serious mental illness. She agreed to the lengthy convalescent regime prescribed by Dr Savage (who had sent her cousin J.K. Stephen to an asylum), but his prohibition on reading and writing made her life miserable. She always submitted to the treatment, however reluctantly, mindful perhaps of her cousin, who had not obeyed his doctors.

In December Virginia suffered a further bout of illness and was sent to recover at her aunt Caroline Emelia's house in Cambridge. She wrote to tell Violet that she had recently met Walter ('whom I always like') while lunching with Adrian, then in his final year at Trinity.[26] Virginia, although fond of Walter, was aware that Violet and Vanessa considered him a flirt. She tried to plead his cause by claiming that her attraction was due to the fact that he was an 'artist'. She reminded Violet of Walter's admiration for Leslie and Julia, whose portraits he kept in his rooms. This fact meant much to Virginia, who missed her father dreadfully. Virginia takes great pains to justify her own attraction to Walter, classing him as a 'simple and sincere' artist, like Vanessa.[27] The latter perhaps read the letter or received one with similar sentiments – her own, written the following day, is almost a reply to it. She points out that, even if Walter is an artist, it isn't a prerequisite of an artist to be flirtatious. Oddly judgemental, Vanessa calls his behaviour 'degrading'. She hastens to add that she does not suspect her younger sister of such underhand dealings, although a couple of years later, suffering from Virginia's continued intimacy with Clive, she would have cause.[28]

Virginia was not the only young woman with whom Walter practised his flirtations, however harmless his intentions. His brother Cecil relates an incident, probably pre-dating his friendship with Virginia, which serves to illustrate this. Three Newnham students of Walter's acquaintance, one a pupil, found him an amusing companion and were in the habit of walking with him. During one such walk Walter broke his hunting-crop opening a gate for them. Since it had been damaged in their service the students bought him a new one.

He expressed his thanks by means of a poem, written partly in Greek, in which he imagined the crop a magic wand with which he could conjure them up, in place of his tedious books.

> To-day when the weather is wettish
> I stay disappointed at home;
> Yet bring me my mystical fetish!
> No need for diversion to roam:
> For the strange power of my whip is,
> This wonder of wonderful sticks,
> It will show to my fancy Philippis
> And Niko and Psix
> [...]
> Were I but a wizard enchanter!
> O Wand, could I wave you, and bring
> To my door in a musical canter
> The real satisfactory thing!
> The books that oppress and bore me
> Should remain on their several shelves,
> And there should be gracious before me
> The ladies themselves ...[29]

Cecil Headlam evidently intended this anecdote to illustrate his brother's charm, and the poem, although unambiguously flirtatious, is remarkably naïve – contemporary commentators would have a field-day with the whip/ wand imagery, for instance, which was almost certainly not intended to have sexual connotations.[30]

Flirting was not Walter's only foible. Like Adrian Stephen he was an inveterate luggage-loser but never let this deter him from travelling, resigning himself to disasters en route. In 1906 he appealed to his friend Mrs George Wherry to find him a 'lady fair' – not as an *amour* but to help with his holiday packing, of which he professed himself incapable.[31] Another of Walter's weaknesses was a tendency to hypochondria. He was especially prey to anxieties connected with his work, fearing that he would go blind or die before completing his studies. He would pore over medical dictionaries checking his latest symptoms – the usual discomforts of a scholar, such as headache, lack of appetite and fatigue – and more often than not diagnosing himself at death's door.[32] Sadly his fears were to prove justified, although not in any way he could have predicted or prevented.

Walter's reputation was sufficiently high during his lifetime that, when Regius Professor of Greek R.C. Jebb died suddenly in 1905, Walter was considered among those worthy of replacing him. He made a formal application for the post in December 1905 and in January 1906 delivered a public lecture, or praelection, on the subject of Aeschylus' *Agamemnon* to the university senate council. This impressed not only the council but also one of his rivals for the post, who afterwards wrote to declare his admiration. In his speech Walter gallantly gave precedence for selection to his colleague Henry Jackson, twenty-five years his senior, but expressed an interest in a future vacancy. Jackson was duly selected, and it was widely predicted that Walter would follow him into the professorship after Jackson's retirement or death.[33]

Walter's high standing cannot have escaped Virginia's notice, and she enjoyed telling Vanessa and Violet about his attentions to her. She revealed to Violet in December 1906 that Walter was to act as her literary critic as she had done for him in 1902. And she is, she announces, to be the new dedicatee of Headlam's *Agamemnon* translation, with Swinburne (the original dedicatee) passed over for her sake – flattery indeed.[34] Despite the flippant tone she adopted to amuse her gravely ill correspondent, Virginia's letter reveals her elation about being taken seriously as a woman and a writer. Walter is teasingly portrayed as the only person who will tell her the hard truth about herself, the intimation being that Violet and everyone else are feeding her mere flattery.[35] However, in terms of her work the opposite was true. Violet was not averse to giving negative comments, while Walter appears to have provided encouragement rather than incisive criticism.[36] If he made any unenthusiastic remarks, Virginia did not record them.

Virginia's friendship with Walter blossomed through the first half of 1907. She visited him at King's, probably while staying with her aunt Caroline Emelia, and Walter came to tea with her in London. They exchanged books, and she gave him her manuscripts to read. They had at least one serious talk about marriage. With ambiguous motives, Walter told Virginia that he was sad that she had not married, because he did not like to see her despondent and alone. He may have been testing the ground for himself, but Virginia saw this as another comment on her failure to secure a husband and assumed the role of martyred spinster.[37]

There was no passionate declaration on either side, neither is any serious falling-out recorded. Their friendship was not undisturbed by conflict, but their arguments were often drummed up by Virginia for amusement. In a letter to Clive in March 1907 Virginia gratuitously introduces a diversionary paragraph about Walter's opinion of Vanessa. Walter, she reports, claimed rashly that he could see no beauty in Vanessa and charged her with an indifference to people; Virginia came to her beloved sister's defence with all guns blazing and demolished his argument.[38] Given Vanessa's already unfavourable opinion of Walter, it was more than usually tactless of Virginia to pass word of this comment on to Clive and therefore to Vanessa herself (since they generally read one another's letters), even if her intention was to prove her own loyalty. It certainly cannot have endeared Walter to Vanessa but served rather to fuel her dislike.

Violet, to whom many of the confidences about Walter were addressed, also had her doubts. During a short trip to Paris in April 1907 Walter made sure Virginia did not forget him by sending three letters across the Channel. When she told Violet of his pursuit it was not without a foreknowledge of Violet's 'cynical' reaction. Virginia disclosed that Walter signed one of the letters with a pledge of fraternal love.[39] It is difficult not to read her attitude as provocative. In another letter to Violet Virginia is playful and flirtatious, thanking her friend for some 'polite' remarks about her writing and comparing them with those she received from Walter. As usual she provides only tantalizing hints: 'Headlam thinks – many things too subtle to be said here – about my style.'[40] This is mock modesty – after all, she has already stated her belief in Walter's veracity and trustworthiness. Her vanity was flattered by his appreciation of her intellectual powers. She wanted others to know of his approbation, lest they should think that only the voluptuous and sensual Vanessa was worthy of male attention. But she also teased her correspondents. Virginia had a great desire to be loved and used evidence of affection and admiration from others to arouse jealousy in those she loved best to coax them into expressing their own affection for her.

Sadly, no letters from Virginia to Walter have been found and only one from him to her, but it is evident from the letters to Violet and Vanessa that, in her friendship with him, Virginia was signalling her independence from the opinions of friends and family.[41] Walter was a useful foil against those who urged her to marry simply because she was of an age so to do. But why did Virginia's beloved sister and her closest friend disapprove of Walter? Probably their objections stemmed from his rather dubious reputation among the Stephen family. Walter had courted Stella for a time and, like many of her hopeful lovers, was rewarded by a friendship with her mother, who took pity on him. In her 1893 St Ives diary Stella, ever-mindful of her mother's travails, noted irritably that her mother had home tired and upset after a long walk with Walter, and she wondered what had happened. Margaret Lushington, a guest at Talland House, also noted the upset in her diary: 'Poor poor little man but she is too tired & full of things to be bother'd ... too dreadful I realised it all.'[42] Anthony Curtis speculates that Headlam, mistaking his own gratitude for ardour, made an approach to Julia during the walk. The following day Walter left and Stella recorded in her diary: 'I cannot think of him without a shudder & yet he is much to be pitied – it is awful.'[43] The attitude of compassion mixed with repulsion found in Stella's and Margaret's diaries was probably a mirroring of Julia's own attitude. But Curtis also suggests that Stella was upset on her own behalf as well as her mother's that Walter's attentions were straying.[44]

Quentin Bell believed that both Vanessa and Violet distrusted Walter not just because of his flirtatiousness but also because of a rumour that he had a predilection for little girls.[45] There may even have been some improper behaviour to which certain members of the Stephen family were privy. Whether Virginia knew of Stella's attitude towards Walter is not certain, but it is probable that Violet – who had been close to Stella – was aware of it.

What is certain is that Walter was attracted to children and to little girls especially. His brother notes that 'he loved children, and had something of the Lewis Carroll cult for girl-children'.[46] This may have been harmless admiration for their perceived purity and innocence, a common enough attitude in Victorian times. There was something of the child in Walter's own nature, and his friends tell of his naïve simplicity and unworldliness. He hosted children's tea parties, and in a poem entitled 'After All' listed little girls as one of the things that made life worth while. He wrote to a female friend that little girls were perhaps the only 'naturally graceful things' that human beings produced.[47] In some cases his affection was certainly returned. He was visited regularly by Bee, the young daughter of his friend Mrs George Wherry, who would call for him at his Gibbs Building rooms to come and play, waiting, patient and barefoot, until he pitched himself over the windowsill to join her. Fortunately his rooms were located on the ground floor. In another poem, 'Seven Years Old', addressed to a young cousin, we may be disturbed by lines such as 'Your sweet lips half asunder' that read like a love poem. But we should also consider that its author, who was twenty-one at the time and probably shared the romantic outlook of other late Victorian writers, also expresses a wish in the same poem that his young cousin be free from 'danger or distress'.[48] Ultimately, seeking confirmation of Walter's rumoured misdemeanours within his poetry is as speculative as finding in J.K. Stephen's misogynistic verses evidence that he was Jack the Ripper.[49]

By May 1907 Virginia's friendship with Walter had developed into what could be termed a courtship. But Walter may have been reading into it more than was there; Virginia clearly had the upper hand. When a letter of hers went missing in the post he behaved like a jealous lover, accusing her of caprice and neglect. Virginia wrote to Violet of Walter's consternation and dropped loaded clues about how she compensated him for his disappointment: 'he ... thought me fickle and cold and treacherous. But we made it up – a subtle phrase secret and ambiguous. How d'you think we made it up?'[50] Much of this may be taken with a pinch of salt – both Virginia and Walter had flirtatious tendencies and Virginia, at least, was going through the motions of courtship without serious intentions or great depth of feeling. The 'affair' proceeded ambiguously, with frequent reports to Violet. Virginia was still seeking attention and affection from her beloved friend, and she was careful to protest no love for Walter. She hoped to tease Violet into an interest in her real feelings for her 'beau assumptive', but on the whole her own attitude towards him was mocking. In another letter to Violet she lays her cards on the table, confessing that she craves attention, and throws down a challenge in the shape of a poem from Walter. The poem arrived in her hour of need, she hints, exhibiting his attentions as a model for Violet to follow.[51] Many of Walter's published poems are undated, but one, entitled 'Seville', is dated 1907, and this may be the poem he sent to Virginia. The poet stands ruminating in a Spanish street and in his mind's eye sees sunlight streaming from the house of his beloved, although she lives in a street of tall buildings where little light penetrates:

> Gazing I stood; the passers-by
> Turned, wondering what I mused apart:
> They guessed, maybe, the painter's eye,
> But ah, guessed not the lover's heart![52]

Then suddenly, having perhaps outlived his usefulness, Walter all but disappears from Virginia's life. The flirtation dwindled into nothing, and there is no more teasing of Vanessa or Violet. The sudden silence about Walter is curious – there is no reference in Virginia's letters or diaries of a serious quarrel; no mention that she has dropped her friend or is tired of him. She occupied herself with lunching with aristocratic friends, writing articles and holidaying in Playden, Sussex, where she had tea with her father's old friend Henry James. She lectured to the working men of Morley College on Keats, was drawn by artist Francis Dodd, visited her cousin H.A.L. (Herbert) Fisher in Oxford and displayed her acting talents in Clive Bell's Play Reading Society. She was coming to terms with the fact of Vanessa's marriage, becoming fonder of Clive, and seeing more of her sister as the couple emerged from their bower of bliss and began to accept social invitations. Perhaps she was simply too busy and too little inclined to spare the time to maintain the friendship, which had few connections with the rest of her life and friends. Another possibility, if we give credence to the family rumours about Walter, is that Violet or Vanessa felt that the friendship had strayed on to dangerous ground and told Virginia about their suspicions.

In the autumn Walter's *Book of Greek Verse* was published, and was well received in the press and by colleagues. He was proclaimed a true Greek poet who had picked up and reproduced exactly the rhythms of Sophocles, Theocritus, Aeschylus and Sappho. Success was at last within his grasp, and he looked forward to putting his long years of research into practice. But he had left it too late. On 15 June 1908 he attended a King's College ball in Cambridge, revelling until 6 a.m., another party in the Fellows' Gardens on 17 June and a cricket match at Lord's two days later. On 20 June he died suddenly in London, aged forty-two. He had reportedly fallen ill and died within the space of twenty-four hours, perhaps of a recurring illness from which he was believed to have recovered. One medical opinion was that he died from strangulation of the bowels; his brother reported 'an accidental twist of an intestine' (sometimes the result of an untreated hernia). In death his large family welcomed him back into the fold. He was buried with many other members of the Headlam family at the church of Wycliffe, Yorkshire, where his grandfather John Headlam had been rector. Walter's cousin, the Reverend Morley Headlam, conducted the burial service.[53]

Virginia received the news dispassionately, being rather more objective and less distressed than might be expected on hearing of the death of a formerly close friend. Summing up Walter's character for Madge Vaughan, the daughter of his old friend J.A. Symonds, Virginia described Walter as 'charming' but 'difficult', a disappointed man who was quarrelsome with his contemporaries.[54] Just like his ancestor Dr Bentley, in fact. And, like Leslie, Walter liked to elicit compassion from women and complained to Virginia about his lack of recognition and his arguments with Cambridge colleagues. This need for sympathy she might have found attractive at first – as a reminder of her recently dead father – but later tired of. So that at Walter's death, his life's work – work for which she had some admiration – is dismissed as 'some edition of Aeschylus'.[55] Walter's arguments with colleagues no doubt originated with his criticism of commentators whose work added little to the sum of knowledge. One of his books, *On Editing Aeschylus*, is a lengthy critique of the editorial methods of his colleague Dr A.W. Verrall. Walter's readiness to draw attention to sub-standard work did not endear him to many of his colleagues, but some revered him for the integrity of his search for knowledge. One obituary noted his wide knowledge and insight but also his scholarly detachment.

Other classics scholars admired his work. Professor Gilbert Murray, Regius Professor of Greek at Oxford, praised Walter for his studies and translations of Greek lyrics, saying he had an 'exquisite ear for that remote and marvellous music'.[56] Professor Ulrich von Wilamovitz-Moellendorf, editor of a later complete edition of Aeschylus, wrote elegiac verses in *The Spectator*. Walter's friend and protégé Rupert Brooke, who considered Walter his valued guide to English literature and a genius, a better man by far than the celebrated R.C. Jebb, wrote to his mother: 'It was a terrible shock. It made me feel quite ill and miserable for days ... the whole thing makes one so rebellious; to think what the world has lost.' And what the world had lost, in his opinion, was 'about the best writer of Greek there has been since the Greeks'.[57]

Even today Walter is recognized as an authority in classical studies, and his name occasionally appears in academic papers as a learned translator and interpreter of Greek poetry. He was among the first to take the holistic approach, laying stress upon the social and historical context in which the Greek poets wrote, exploring their allusions to an earlier tradition and detecting in their works the seeds of a later one. Cecil Headlam claimed that his brother's intention was to 'invade every province of knowledge' for the illuminations each gave him about classical literature.[58] He read widely, for instance, in anthropology and the history of ideas, and all his studies prepared the ground for his scholarly approach to Greek literature. His bibliographer, Lawrence Haward, noted that his reading for studies of Aeschylus and Herodas covered the whole of Greek literature to the twelfth century AD.[59]

Several months after his death Walter's brother Cecil asked Virginia to contribute a memoir to a collection of her friend's letters and poems (published as *Walter Headlam: His Letters and Poems* by Duckworth and Co. in 1910). The problem with this, she told Lytton Strachey, is that the memoir would have to contain 'lies'.[60] Her reaction is puzzling, even if she is empathizing with the sardonic wit of her correspondent. In the event Cecil had to do without her memoir, and her friendship with Walter is not even mentioned in the book.

In Virginia's imagination, Walter joined George Duckworth in the legions of the disreputable, becoming a butt of her jokes. When in 1918 Roger Fry claimed to have an interesting story to tell about Leslie and Julia and involving a 'mistake', Virginia's mind ran riot on the possibilities, creating strange fantasies. She speculated that Vanessa might be the illegitimate daughter of George – suggesting a very precocious incestuous relationship between her mother and her stepbrother, given that George was eleven when Vanessa was born – or Adrian the bastard son of Walter Headlam.[61] These jokes are unexpected and rare slurs on her beloved and venerated mother, unless we assume that Virginia's fantasy presupposes the molestation of Julia in each case. The association of Walter with George is also surprising, given George's overly affectionate and perhaps abusive treatment of his half-sister. This linking of their names may indicate that Virginia had heard the rumours about Walter's alleged preferences; or it may simply suggest that she viewed both men as inappropriately demonstrative to her mother.

Virginia told the Cambridge classicist J.T. (Jack) Sheppard, later Provost of King's College, that Walter appeared in the character of William Rodney, the Elizabethan scholar who is engaged to Katharine Hilbery in *Night and Day*.[62] Rodney, like Walter, takes care over his appearance, stammers occasionally and has a keen intelligence and wit. But Rodney's over-developed sense of propriety – he is scandalized when Katharine leaves the house without gloves – and his hypocrisy – he is willing enough to sacrifice his morals as long as no one else knows of it – and his eagerness to express his feelings, all these are inspired by George Duckworth, teaming him up with Walter once more. (See pp. 132–3 for William Rodney and Lytton Strachey.)

Quentin Bell believed that the character of William Bankes in *To the Lighthouse* may have been based on Walter.[63] If true, this suggests a considerable mellowing of Virginia's attitude towards him in the 1920s, since Bankes is one of the more sympathetic characters in the novel. Lily Briscoe, whose insights we most trust, thinks during a walk along the seashore that he may be the finest person she knows. She respects him for his lack of vanity, his detachment and his integrity. But Lily acknowledges that Bankes is no superman: he has small but very human vices such as his tendency to complain about dogs sitting on furniture and salt in the vegetables.[64] But it does not seem to me that Woolf would use Headlam as a model for Bankes, since the real man was a flirtatious classical scholar – an 'artist', as Virginia insisted – and the fictional character a rational, if fastidious, scientist.

Only once did Virginia seek to explain her change of heart about Walter in writing, and it is not a very convincing explanation. In a 1919 letter to Vanessa she asserts that neither of the sisters indulges in a dog-like loyalty to their ex-admirers. She compares their earliest romances: Jack Hills, who courted Vanessa after Stella died, means nothing to her now; likewise Virginia feels nothing for Walter except a vague feeling of gratitude that he provided useful copy for her fiction.[65] This is interesting because of the assumed parallel of Walter with Jack Hills, with whom Vanessa had a fairly serious relationship, one that George Duckworth feared would result in an illicit marriage abroad (it would have been illegal in England, since Vanessa was the half-sister of Jack's dead wife).[66] In comparing her feelings for Walter with Vanessa's feelings for Jack, Virginia must have been aware of the disparity.

But her eagerness to claim a romance for herself may be the key to her flirtation, indeed to many of her relationships with men before her marriage. As a writer she was eager to undergo everything that life threw at her. Unpleasant as well as pleasant incidents fed her imagination and helped her writing. Death, she told Vita Sackville-West, would be the only experience she would never describe.[67] She acknowledged that even her periods of depression and illness were put to use as intervals of calm in which to think and plan her novels. Seeing Vanessa blossom after her engagement and marriage to Clive, Virginia must have been curious and longing for the transformation herself; thus, she tried to extract the most out of her flirtation in order to approximate a love affair, but her reservations about her suitors must have rendered it a shadowy and insubstantial business. Her next flirtation would not only be more passionate, but more forbidden, and its impact sent reverberations through the rest of her life.

Turning the Knife: Clive Bell

ALTER HEADLAM WAS treated as a member of the family; Clive Bell was one. Married to her well-loved sister, Clive inspired in Virginia mixed feelings that were never completely resolved. She felt Vanessa's marriage as an abandonment, and although her sister had married comparatively late (at twenty-seven) Virginia was all too ready to criticize the man who had finally parted them. She could not deny that Vanessa appeared to be extremely happy, but she viewed Clive as a rival. She had another when the Bells' first child arrived a year later, absorbing all of his mother's time and attention. But this time Clive, too, was neglected in favour of the new arrival, and he and Virginia began their ill-judged flirtation. Virginia was later to regret her actions; however, in his son Quentin's opinion, Clive only regretted that he had not achieved his goal of a full-blown affair.

Arthur Clive Heward Bell was born on 16 September 1881 in East Shefford, Berkshire. His family's wealth, unlike that of the Stephens and the Stracheys, was fairly new. Four generations earlier Clive's mother's family, the Corys, had been farmers, until his great-grandfather William Cory (1783–1862) set up in business as a coal merchant and moved to London. Cory's son, also William, inherited a thriving company. It was his daughter, Hannah Taylor Cory, who married into the Bell family. Her husband, another William, was drawn into the Cory coal dynasty; not unwillingly perhaps, as this was the golden age of the industry. By the 1870s William Heward Bell, civil engineer, had become an English country gentleman on the proceeds of this black gold.

With his new wealth he purchased a country seat, Cleeve House at Seend in Wiltshire, in 1883. Since 1865 Seend had been a source of high-quality iron ore, and blast furnaces for smelting had been built there. If William moved to Seend because of the iron works he was disappointed: they closed six years later. Neither did Cleeve House entirely satisfy him. It had been built in 1857, and by 1894 William thought it was due for a major overhaul. He had it extensively rebuilt and extended in mock-Jacobean style. But it was still far from ideal. The water supply was unreliable; there were no flush toilets and even twenty years later guests were discouraged from bathing. Inside, much of the space was occupied by a medieval-style great hall, complete with minstrels' gallery and laid out as if in tribute to warfare and taxidermy, with displays of weapons and stuffed creatures in glass cases or mounted on the walls.[1]

There were four children: two sons, William Cory Heward and Arthur Clive Heward (both used their middle names, although Clive's mother wrote to him as Arthur until the 1930s), and two daughters, Elsie Lorna, also known by her middle name, and Dorothy. Cory, Clive's senior by six years, attained the post of Lieutenant-Colonel in the British Army and fought in the First World War, where he was awarded a DSO and a Croix de Guerre. After the war he became a Conservative MP. Clive's son Quentin remembered him as a man with a resounding voice and a jolly sense of humour. Lorna married during the First World War and had two children; she reminded Quentin of Aunt Norris in Jane Austen's *Mansfield Park*. Dorothy married a man of intelligence and technical aptitude, but he astounded his wife by revealing homosexual tendencies.[2]

Apart from the inconveniences of Cleeve House, all the appurtenances of an upper-middle-class life were enjoyed by the Bell family, including a high standard of education for their sons. Clive was sent to school at Marlborough (where he had a miserable time) and in 1899 went up to Trinity College, Cambridge, as an exhibitioner, to study history. Also starting that year at Trinity were Thoby Stephen, Leonard Woolf, Saxon Sydney-Turner and Lytton Strachey. As a family, the Bells had a limited interest in culture, literature, music or painting and must have been somewhat puzzled as to how Clive emerged from their numbers. While most of the Bells, Virginia maintained in one of her kinder moments, were 'good country people' who were 'without culture or pretension', Clive read and quoted Shelley, Keats and Shakespeare, wrote poetry and, along with his Mooreist friends, pondered the nature of good and beauty.[3]

Thoby Stephen was proud of his Cambridge friends and as willing to talk about them to Virginia as she was to listen. Home for the holidays, Thoby described Clive as an unlikely mix of Shelley and a country squire.[4] He had the curls of the poet (albeit red) and a taste for verse. On the country squire side, he was self-assured and genial, favouring manly pursuits such as riding to hounds, shooting birds and animals and having mistresses. These attributes (save the last) were doubtless the reason why he was the only friend of Thoby's in whom his half-brother George Duckworth, stickler for propriety and the conventions, had any confidence. The others were shabby, unorthodox and lacked – or ignored – social etiquette. Clive had an urbane charm that set him apart from Leonard, Lytton and Saxon. It was his odd mixture of characteristics that appealed to Thoby, as well as their shared enthusiasm for hunting. Clive kept horses at Cambridge to indulge his passion, and Leonard Woolf remarked that his first sight of Clive was in full hunting regalia, striding across the college grounds.[5]

Virginia first met Clive at the Trinity College ball in June 1900. It was her first ball, and she spent most of it gossiping with friends and relations because Thoby did not know many young men who cared to dance. Clive was the only one of Thoby's friends who was not overawed by beautiful young women; on the contrary, he relished their company and went out of his way to encounter them. He called on Thoby's sisters in the absence of his friend as early as January 1903, and, since Virginia reported that it was a long visit, he cannot have lacked conversation. The following year Clive played host to the three Stephens in Paris.

Clive had gone to Paris with a purpose very different from its outcome. Awarded an Earl of Derby scholarship despite obtaining only a second-class history degree, he had determined upon an investigation of the British government's standpoint at the 1822 Congress of Verona. His research in the Paris archives altered the course of his life. He began to spend a great deal of time in the Louvre and took up with Gerald Kelly, another Cambridge graduate who was now studying painting and living the life of an artist in Montparnasse. Clive gradually abandoned his political research and joined his friend and other British and American artists in the cafés and studios of Paris, talking of art and observing its practitioners. The Stephens stopped at Paris during their trip to continental Europe after Leslie's death in 1904. By the time they arrived Clive was sufficiently at ease in the artists' milieu to act as their representative, and Virginia and her siblings were initiated into bohemian life. Virginia recalled, as if it were the dawning of a new era, staying up till 11.30 one evening, arguing in a café about art and music, and smoking cigarettes – then a rather *risqué* activity for women. The next day Clive and Gerald Kelly ('He is only 24 and has 5 pictures in the Salon,' Vanessa told her friend Margery Snowden, impressed) took them to see Rodin's studio.[6] Vanessa was in her element, but Virginia's enjoyment of the trip appears to have been chiefly retrospective. She was approaching a bout of mental illness, most probably as a delayed reaction to her father's death. She was, she admitted, very irritable and temperamental in Paris and found it difficult to write.[7]

Years later memories of Paris filtered through to her third novel, *Jacob's Room*. Jacob Flanders, visiting the artist Edward Cruttendon and his girlfriend Jinny Carslake in the French capital, thinks them very remarkable people and revels in their unconventionality. With the benefit of hindsight, the author takes a different view. The conversation is exuberant but schoolboyish, with little to justify Jacob's high regard for his friends. The author condemns Cruttendon to a future painting Kentish orchards. However, Gerald Kelly, on whom Cruttendon is partly based, did not disappear into obscurity. From a bohemian artist he transformed himself into a member of the art establishment and was President of the Royal Academy from 1949 to 1954. A bon viveur and a natural entertainer, Kelly was the first President to appeal to a wide audience using television broadcasts, during which he shocked the more prim viewers by using colourful language. He was, partly because of this, the first television art celebrity. He met many famous and infamous artists but observed frankly that the conversation of these great men (and they were all men) had made no lasting impression on him.[8]

Vanessa had been favourably impressed by Clive and his artist friends. A few months after their Paris trip he was invited to stay with the Stephens in Teversal, Nottinghamshire. Vanessa's friend Margery Snowden was also a guest. Virginia, convalescing from the breakdown that had started on her return from Paris, found Clive very easy-going in comparison with the more silent, intellectual contingent of Thoby's friends and much easier to converse with. Vanessa, for her part, found him a sympathetic companion, one of the few people outside her art-school friends who shared her interests. His friendship with Vanessa and Virginia made Clive the envy of Thoby's other friends, who admired the Stephen sisters from a distance but found them unapproachable and aloof. By the summer of 1905 Clive was passionately in love with Vanessa and proposed, prepared even to give up his beloved hunting for her sake.[9] Vanessa refused but left him room for manoeuvre. To Margery Snowden, however, she represented her rejection as unconditional: 'I could no more marry him than I could fly – so there's an end of it.'[10] Thoby, who knew of the attraction, was told of the proposal. He had foreseen the result of introducing his sisters to his friends but wrote sympathetically to Clive.[11]

If Thoby was not surprised, however, Vanessa appeared to be. Clive's proposal had come, it seemed to her, out of a clear blue sky. Vanessa protested that she had been led to believe that Clive had a very low opinion of her brain-power – even that he disliked her and talked to her merely out of politeness. The proposal was a blow to Virginia's self-esteem and to her supposition – engendered by her father and bolstered, as she thought, by her brother's friends – that the mind was more important than the body. Did Vanessa have a *femme fatale* attraction that she was exerting without effort, without even being conscious of it? Perhaps Saxon Sydney-Turner and Ralph Hawtrey, bookish and reticent friends of Thoby's, were silently and secretly in love with Vanessa as well, she observed sardonically. How could one tell? Virginia worshipped Vanessa as a mysterious and enigmatic being, but in any competition for male attention she was accustomed to success. Her lively wit and curious mind made her a very attractive companion. She had been her father's favourite and Thoby's confidante; she had even been eager to please George Duckworth by accompanying him to parties in place of the silent Vanessa. She might have felt justified in assuming that her cleverness would outshine Vanessa's reserve outside the family circle, too. But now Vanessa's beauty and 'womanly' qualities had netted a proposal. Virginia, in a pose of self-pity that was only half in jest, pointed out to Violet that no one had asked for *her* hand in marriage. Not that she was prepared, either emotionally or intellectually, for marriage, and she certainly did not want Clive for herself; but a proposal was, after all, a tribute. Within a few years she would exact from Clive a tribute of another kind.

Although she would later place her trust in Clive's literary opinions, Virginia's initial estimation of his tastes was prompted by *Euphrosyne*, a collection of graduate verse which included his own poems as well as those by Lytton Strachey, Leonard Woolf, Walter Lamb and Saxon Sydney-Turner. Published in 1905, but not to a wide audience, it was reviewed favourably (unsurprisingly) by Thoby Stephen in the *Cambridge Review*, presided over at that time by Walter Lamb. To attract more buyers and so cover the publishing costs Walter himself wrote an 'attack' (bad publicity was better than good publicity, even in those days), and Clive Bell answered with a 'priggish' letter.[12] Virginia ridiculed *Euphrosyne* for its slightness and inconsequentiality.[13] She did not know it, but the forthright Leonard Woolf agreed with her low opinion of the book. Receiving a copy from Lytton Strachey in Ceylon, Leonard felt revulsion on reading it: 'It is a queer medley. There are only 3 things in it wh. I ever want to read again.' Most of the poems, he said uncompromisingly, 'made me very nearly as sick as when I read my own'.[14]

Virginia's first letter to Clive in November 1906, just before Thoby's death, gives no flavour of their future correspondence. It is simply a note to change the time of an appointment with Vanessa, who was recovering from suspected appendicitis. Clive is addressed as 'Mr Bell'; in letters to Violet he is 'Bell', then 'dear Peter Bell' (his nickname was from Wordsworth's 1819 poem). Clive stayed with Vanessa for lengthy periods during her convalescence, spending more time with her than did Virginia, who began to sense the inevitability of their marriage. She played up the tragedy for Violet, angling for sympathy: 'One day I shall look him in the eye and say your [sic] not good enough – and then he will kiss me, and Nessa will wipe a great tear, and say we shall always have a room for you.'[15] She told Clive quite bluntly – or at least reported so to Violet: 'You are all sensitive appreciations, Mr Bell; you have no character. You want bottom.'[16] Part of Virginia's objection to the match was that in her eyes no one would have been good enough for Vanessa. Nevertheless she behaved well towards Clive, and once, when he was looking particularly miserable, even invited him to become part of the family. Perhaps on this occasion she felt more sorry for him than she did for herself and could afford to be magnanimous.

With encouragement from both sisters Clive understandably felt confident enough to propose to Vanessa for a third time, two days after the death of Thoby Stephen, and was at last accepted. Virginia, who was still concealing the fact of Thoby's death from Violet, was entrusted with the task of announcing the engagement to her. Painfully aware of what she was soon to lose, Virginia remarked to friends how happy Vanessa was and how radiantly beautiful she looked, sitting by the fire in her pink Turkish cloak with a rose behind her ear. 'Peter is an angel,' she told Violet.[17] But she was not blind to the fact that the 'angel' was taking up a lot of Vanessa's time and attention. Virginia hovered around the lovers, hoping some of the magic would rub off on her. She was absorbed by their love affair. During Clive's frequent visits she would hear incessant talk and laughter coming from Vanessa's room. Like a neglected child she once asked them what they had been talking about: 'Art,' they replied simply, underscoring Virginia's exclusion.[18] Even in Clive's absence, Vanessa seemed preoccupied with thinking about him. When she went to Newbury with Margery Snowden to convalesce, Virginia speculated that they would find Clive a more rewarding subject for conversation than art.[19]

By mid December, Vanessa had recovered sufficiently to be taken to meet her future in-laws. On New Year's Eve 1906 Virginia and Adrian went to see her and the Bells at Cleeve House. A hunting, shooting and fishing mentality reigned. Virginia noted with amusement that the inkwell in her room was made from a horse's hoof – to her, this was a symbol of their philistinism.[20] Vanessa, resenting the waste of her time (to her, time that was not spent painting was wasted), wrote to Virginia in later years about the dullness of the conversation and the bad taste of her in-laws: 'I look at these surroundings and feel thankful that he [the baby, Julian] is too young to know the difference between ugliness and beauty.'[21] Playing the dutiful daughter-in-law at Seend was not appealing to Vanessa, who avoided her own relatives and had no desire to spend time with the Bells. She tolerated it only for Clive's sake – her in-laws did not appeal to her exacting tastes. Mrs Bell had the nervous, slightly startled appearance of a rabbit, and Mr Bell was uncultured – he fell asleep while reading a review written by Virginia in the *Cornhill* – and prone to bellowing at his offspring. Clive's sisters, Lorna and Dorothy, were archetypal daughters of the provinces: hunting, tennis or hockey in the daytime, blue satin dresses and hair ribbons in the evening.

Virginia used an exaggerated version of life at Seend as a model for her short story 'Lappin and Lapinova', where the shy bride is faced with bumptious and brutish in-laws and can endure the ordeal only by creating a fantasy world of rabbits and hares. Clive's mother, described by Virginia as 'rabbit faced', may have provided inspiration for the rabbit fantasy.[22] The sporting atmosphere that reigned at Cleeve House resonates in another Woolf story, 'The Shooting Party'. Here a degenerate and crumbling aristocracy hunts animal quarry, a practice equated with a love of violence and a relish of gore. Quentin Bell recounts a memory of a dinner at Cleeve that would fit neatly into this setting:

> [Uncle] Cory, always a clumsy fellow, managed to break the stopper of a decanter. 'You hog,' roared my grandfather. 'That's what you are, a hog, a hog!' Lieutenant-Colonel Cory Bell (retired), MP DSO, Croix de Guerre [and aged fifty], sat mute and shamefaced while his father shouted at him.[23]

While Virginia's feelings for the Bell family were clear, her feelings for Clive were ambivalent. She wished to think well of him and must have been aware that failing to get on with him could lead to a disastrous rift with her sister. Vanessa had already proved where her loyalties lay. Virginia felt, as her father had about his stepdaughter Stella's marriage, that she should be glad for the bride's sake, if not for her own.[24] She managed to maintain the illusion of happiness for several weeks while Vanessa was still within reach, but when Vanessa left to stay with the Bells the first signs of resentment emerged. Virginia sketched Clive's character for Madge Vaughan, hinting at shortcomings as well as virtues: 'He is very honest, and unselfish and scrupulous; he is clever, and cultivated – more taste, I think, than genius; but he has a gift for making other people shine, and he is very affectionate.'[25] She told Clive that she and Vanessa's friends thought that no man could deserve her. She proposed that he should provide a description of himself, his life and prospects, in order to plead his case.[26]

Only a few weeks after the engagement, Virginia's view of Clive had degenerated. She described a beautiful snowy Christmas Day to Violet, noting that Clive would call it 'obvious'. She referred to him as 'pompous and polished'.[27] Irritably she takes exception to Clive's complaints about his family: 'Nobody is ever too good for their own flesh and blood' – a statement very obviously at odds with her opinions of many of her own relations.[28] Her irritability turned to physical disgust. She began to question Vanessa's choice and to make malicious comments about Clive's appearance. She compared him to her father with his noble and austere profile, to Thoby with his Grecian build – and found Clive wanting. She wondered 'what odd freak there is in Nessa's eyesight' that she should find her diminutive red-haired husband so adorable.[29] This was unkind of Virginia, but she was not the only one to question Vanessa's choice. Two of Thoby's closest friends, Leonard Woolf and Lytton Strachey, had their own doubts.

The Stephen sisters were a source of fascination to Thoby's friends. Even Leonard, as a colonial administrator in Ceylon, was kept up to date on their movements. He and Lytton had begun corresponding about Clive's passion for Vanessa at the time of his first proposal in 1905. Neither expected her to accept. Lytton, treating the episode as a comic interlude, presented a lurid picture of Clive as a lovesick hero from a Victorian melodrama: 'He's haunted, desperately haunted, by visions of Vanessa; his frightened pathetic face shows it; and his small lascivious body oozes with disappointed lust.'[30] Leonard replied with some surprise that he had long believed Clive to be in love with Virginia. He speculated that Clive's love for Thoby Stephen sprung from the fact he was the male version of the beloved Vanessa. (Leonard then startled Lytton by confessing his own admiration for Vanessa and suggesting that it was founded on his love for 'the Goth'. Ergo, the reverse of Clive's case.)[31]

Both Lytton and Leonard were despondent at hearing news of Vanessa's engagement to a man they deemed their intellectual inferior. It came hard upon the heels of Thoby's death, which they were still mourning. It seemed to them in particularly bad taste to propose so soon afterwards. 'I am too weary to mind the mockery of it all,' Leonard wrote resignedly.[32] But mixed with the shock was a grudging admiration. They wondered how Clive had accomplished the coup. While they had worshipped the sisters from afar, their more worldly and impulsive friend had leapt in recklessly and carried off the prize. Leonard allowed a fortnight to pass before writing the briefest of congratulatory notes to Clive, couching it in conventional words and appending a note describing his devastation on hearing of Thoby's death. When two years later Clive went to Italy with both Stephen sisters Lytton was again amazed at his luck: 'Don't you think it's the wildest romance? That that little canary-coloured creature we knew in New Court should have achieved that? – The two most beautiful and wittiest women in England!'[33] The Bells' marriage forced Lytton and Leonard to acknowledge that he who dares sometimes wins.

Henry James, an old friend of Leslie Stephen, was no great fan of Clive. He lamented that he had ever let Leslie's daughters stray so far as to keep such company. He disliked their friends and could not reconcile himself to the choice Vanessa had made (although three decades earlier he had been surprised at Julia Duckworth's willingness to take on Leslie Stephen). Like Virginia, he compared Clive to Thoby and found him lacking. Clive was stooping where Thoby had been tall and straight; Clive was third-rate where Thoby had had a superior intellect – it was like comparing a poodle to a mastiff, he exclaimed.[34] There was a certain amount of class snobbery inherent in these criticisms, Clive's family, unlike those of Thoby's other friends, having attained their fortune and country seat through what Oscar Wilde would have called 'the purple of commerce' rather than by accident of birth. For similar reasons, Lytton's brother James and his friend Rupert Brooke found Clive boisterous and unsubtle and agreed between themselves that he was 'no gentleman'.[35]

The cause of Virginia's resentment was different. Vanessa's marriage would mean the end of their 'very close conspiracy'.[36] The parting of the Stephen sisters was especially hard for Virginia, who was still emotionally dependent on her elder sibling, although in her mid twenties. From nursery days the sisters had been on intimate terms. Years later Virginia remembered the first sign of mutual interest in a discussion of whether black cats had tails.[37] From her late teens Virginia had invested Vanessa with goddess-like characteristics. The picture we now have of the granitic, passionate, reserved and enigmatic Vanessa is due chiefly to Virginia's descriptions and letters. In their relationship it was chiefly Virginia who did the courting, Vanessa who graciously received her sister's compliments and admiration. The division of roles continued when they were in company: Virginia sparkled and Vanessa was all but silent. All at once, on Vanessa's marriage, the partnership – with which Virginia must have been content since it worked so much in her favour – was broken up. The two 'wise virgins' had become one happily married wife and one lonely and restless spinster.

The Bells' marriage was initially very successful. Even Virginia had to acknowledge her sister's obvious happiness: 'It is clear to the most prejudiced eye that God made her for marriage; and she basks there like an old seal on a rock.'[38] Together Vanessa and Clive discovered the joys of marriage (although Clive had already learned some of these joys as a bachelor). Initiated into sex, Vanessa was reborn, extolling the virtues of copulation and revelling in them. After years of being a dependable daughter and sister she now had someone to spoil her, and she made the most of it. Her sensuality was in the ascendant. Regally, she and Clive received guests from their bed, an almost unheard-of bohemianism for that era. Their 'at home' evenings for their friends at Gordon Square were mirrored by those of Virginia and Adrian at Fitzroy Square, setting up an element of competition between the two salons. The Bloomsbury universe now had two suns, but Virginia felt keenly her paler light.

Clive's *joie de vivre* and his skills as a host were his chief personal charms. Conversation and the art of bringing people together were his forte. When he founded the Play Reading Society in late 1907 he provided Virginia with an opportunity to shine. Half-a-dozen 'inner circle' Bloomsberries, including Clive and Vanessa Bell, Virginia and Adrian Stephen, Saxon Sydney-Turner and Lytton Strachey, met every few weeks at Gordon or Fitzroy Square between 27 December 1907 and 15 January 1909.[39] Whether by design or not, the Play Reading Society offered the friends an exceptionally good way of becoming more intimate. The *risqué* language and subject matter of their readings helped to break down social barriers. Virginia's story of Lytton's releasing Bloomsbury from its reticence about sex by pointing at a stain on Vanessa's dress and querying 'Semen?' is well known.[40] She does not date this watershed, but presumably it had not taken place before an incident in 1908 when she blushed at having to pass Clive to reach a train lavatory. Lytton's audacity may have been a direct result of the freer dialogue the Bloomsberries were allowed under the guise of their Play Reading Society roles, and the newly married Bells must take some of the credit for the liberties that had already been taken with Edwardian sexual mores. The first reading was of John Vanbrugh's partner-swapping play *The Relapse*. Virginia played two deceitful women, one of whom married the character played by Clive. Later she took the part of another treacherous woman, Dalila, in Milton's *Samson Agonistes*.

It is clear from the society's high-spirited minute-book, written by Saxon Sydney-Turner and later by Clive, that all the participants enjoyed performing. Even during her pregnancy and subsequent convalescence Vanessa missed only one meeting, acting as the audience on two occasions when she was not well enough to take part. There are hints that the readings sometimes dissolved into hilarity: Clive's note for the 16 December meeting suggests that 'What this society needs most is more self-control.'[41] Clive occasionally used his position as minute-taker to tease Virginia or to flirt with her. Of her performance in Swinburne's *Atalanta in Calydon* he remarked: 'Virginia, as Alathaea, read her seven hundred lines with freedom and beauty, and gave the impression of understanding all that she read', then he wrote in pencil and deleted, perhaps after her protests or thinking better of it: 'an achievement, as some conjecture, well nigh miraculous'.[42] He reserves his highest praise for her final performance, reading Spenser's *Epithalamion*: 'I can only say that to me it revealed beauties at which I could never have come unaided. The poem possesses, henceforth, a new loveliness and an added associations [*sic*].'[43] With such undercurrents it is hardly surprising that Vanessa was reluctant to miss a meeting.

Gradually Virginia began to sense that there might be a niche for her within the Bell marriage. A gap opened up with the birth of their first son, Julian. For Vanessa motherhood was an all-consuming occupation – her time and energies were almost wholly taken up with the infant's needs. Even when the baby was not in the room she would hold up her hand to halt conversation if she thought she heard a cry. Clive became a stimulating companion for his sons when they reached an age for rational conversation, but for babies he had no particular affection. The fragility of their bodies made him nervous, their crying made him tense and their bodily emissions made him nauseous. For her part, Virginia felt slighted by the constant interruptions the baby caused, and she and Clive began to leave the house for walks together, leaving Vanessa to cope alone.

Thus, a prolonged mutual flirtation between them began in rebellion against Vanessa's neglect. For the first time they spent long periods of time alone together. In turning his attentions to the younger sister Clive found an intelligent, witty and sympathetic companion, unfettered by the demands of motherhood. Spending time with Clive Virginia rediscovered her brother-in-law's merits – he was sensitive, affable and a good conversationalist; interested in people, literature, art and ideas. Clive told Virginia she was mysterious and disconcerting and that the dream-like state into which she sometimes fell fascinated him (there are hints here of *Night and Day*'s Katharine Hilbery). He did not have a high opinion of women generally: observe her fellow creatures if she would, he told her, but she must admit that on the whole women were inferior to men. However, he was careful to demonstrate that he considered her far above the average woman – she was more beautiful, more intelligent and her conversation unparalleled. After a trip to St Ives Clive reminded her of their 'talk about intimacy and the really exciting moments in life . . . Did we ever achieve the heights?'[44] He yearned for a more physical intimacy and brought Marvell-like sophistry to his aid:

> I wished for nothing in the world but to kiss you . . . it's of very little consequence if we say or do those things that we ought not to have said and done. What does matter is that we should not leave unsaid & undone those things which, by some divine emotion, we know that we ought to say and do.[45]

Virginia, susceptible to flattery, told Clive she had been disposed to kiss him once but that he had missed the opportunity. She warned him that his high opinion would turn her head. But she was careful both to preserve and to display her loyalty to Vanessa. With mock modesty she compared the faintness of her own light to the radiance of her sister: 'Nature has done so much more for her than for me.'[46] She emphasized her affection for them both. It was vital to remain on good terms with Vanessa, since it was her love Virginia valued above all. There were two essential threads to her strategy, if her idiosyncratic efforts at diplomacy can be given such a name. One was to continue to woo her sister with the 'goddess' illusions she had created for her in childhood. She recalled their youthful bond in a biographical sketch of Vanessa's early life (later published as 'Reminiscences' in *Moments of Being*) and in her letters to Clive expressed almost a lover's passion for Vanessa, anticipating that the letters would be read aloud. Virginia's second concern was to make sure Vanessa understood that she was not in love with Clive, despite their lengthy and romantic conversations, and that she had no intention of stealing her sister's husband.

Even at the height of their flirtation, Vanessa was left in no doubt as to Virginia's opinion of Clive. Virginia wrote to her about a friend who wanted to know whether Clive was a 'genius' – not a word Virginia used without due consideration. She went on to describe him:

> An exquisite, fastidious little Chipmonk, with the liveliest affections, and the most tender instincts – a man of parts, and sensibilities – a man of character and judgment – a man with a style, who writes some of the best letters in the English tongue, and meditates a phrase as other men meditate an action – But a man of genius?[47]

Was this meant to reassure Vanessa that her flirtation with Clive was not to be taken seriously? Perhaps. Several weeks later Virginia accompanied the Bells on a trip to Italy, so reassurance may have been required. Vanessa may also have been comforted by the advent of a more serious suitor, Hilton Young, that summer.

Clive played a dual role in Virginia's life. Aside from helping to convince her of her physical and intellectual attractions, he also acted as a literary adviser. At this stage in her career Virginia had considerable potential but little to show for her writing ambitions. She needed a mentor, someone to reassure her that she was a 'proper' writer. The second, less perilous phase of their flirtation began when Clive assumed this role. Virginia was flattered by Clive's interest in her writing (her respect of his opinions was tempered a little by the discovery that he had compared Lytton's poems to those of Catullus). Clive, for his part, was gratified by her respect for his literary opinions. She gave him early drafts of *The Voyage Out* (then called 'Melymbrosia'), recognizing that his critical faculty was free from malice and envy.[48] She was grateful for his criticisms, even though they could be fairly harsh: 'some places [are] jagged like saws', he complained.[49] He noted examples of what he melodramatically called the 'smaller excrescences, which fill me with horror and some fear'.[50] But his overall judgement was that 'the wonderful thing that I looked for is there unmistakeably'.[51] This 'wonderful thing' he later identified as genius. Of all the clever people he had known in his life, he wrote in his seventies, only Virginia and Pablo Picasso had had the quality of genius: a quality that marked them out as 'a species distinct from the common; their mental processes were different from ours; they arrived at conclusions by ways to us unknown'.[52]

Clive's views were important to Virginia as she embarked on her novelistic career, but as she became more confident of her own powers she began to outgrow him. Many of his comments about 'Melymbrosia' chimed with her own opinions and suspicions about her work, and she began increasingly to rely on her own judgement, writing and rewriting draft after draft until she was satisfied. Later she would show no one the manuscripts of novels in progress. Even Leonard would only read them on completion. Virginia wrote to Clive in later years that he had been the first person to take her seriously as a writer. This statement was not strictly true – after all, Violet Dickinson and Walter Headlam had preceded him – but was one which Clive valued and made much of. With these friends Virginia used her work to reach a level of intellectual intimacy. We do not know what Walter made of her writing or whether he saw early drafts of 'Melymbrosia', but Violet stated her opinions frankly – sometimes a little too frankly for Virginia's liking. Clive, although critical, never failed in faith. He constantly reassured her that she was a good writer and might be a great one. It was no doubt this that made his negative comments more palatable.[53]

The intimacy between Virginia and Clive altered the sisters' relationship permanently. Vanessa was perfectly well aware of what was going on but never confronted Virginia. It was a Bloomsbury conviction that friendship was one of the greatest goods of society (à la Moore); besides, Vanessa's temperament did not incline her to the melodramatic. She did, however, refer, sometimes wistfully, to the friendship of her husband and her sister in her letters to them. It is painfully evident that the earlier exclusion of Virginia from Clive's and Vanessa's idyll had effectively been reversed, with Vanessa now debarred. News of Virginia came to her sister mainly through reports from Clive, with whom Virginia spent much time. Meanwhile the shift of loyalties had become apparent to others. During early 1909 a few Bloomsbury friends indulged in a letter-writing game in which they each took on an *alter ego*. These disguises allowed them to correspond about thorny topics that their unconventional Bloomsbury mores would, paradoxically, have prohibited. Lytton wrote pseudonymously to Virginia about Clive's attentions and Vanessa's unhappiness. Virginia acknowledged that Clive was a little in love with her but would admit no responsibility for the situation.[54] Later she would see more clearly. The trust between the sisters, although not the affection, was destroyed. Vanessa was guarded about her later affairs with Roger Fry and Duncan Grant, fearing perhaps another *ménage à trois* in which she would come to play second fiddle. Many years afterwards Virginia recognized the damage she had done, telling Gwen Raverat that the flirtation had 'turned more of a knife in me than anything else has ever done'.[55]

Eventually the flirtation ran its course and was overtaken by the advent of other suitors for Virginia. Walter Headlam had died in June 1908; but by then Hilton Young was on the scene. Clive was forced to take a back seat, but his tack was to denigrate Hilton's intellect, aware that this would produce doubts in Virginia: 'You will not have to bear a literary rival in your future tyrant. A Cato he will be, but never, I think a Cicero, still less a Tacitus.'[56] Clive also made it plain that his frankness would have to be curbed on her marriage. 'I am writing on the hypothesis that you are still a disengaged young woman, if I mistake, stop here and return the unread letter,' he wrote disingenuously.[57] Walter Lamb, too, was exhibiting a romantic interest in Virginia. He wrote of her in flattering terms in letters to Clive, presumably unaware of his correspondent's confidence in the futility of his suit. 'I must leave him to fight his own battles, only too happy to escape his fate,' Clive wrote teasingly to Virginia.[58]

During 1909 Virginia received two proposals and ruminated on marriage. Her intimacy with Clive had passed its zenith, but he disliked her references to other men: 'To speculate on what exactly it is you want to say to the man you will love is not a congenial occupation: that way ill-temper and irritation lies, if not madness.'[59] Even Lytton's elder brother Oliver, who paid some attention to Virginia in the spring of 1911, was briefly under suspicion:

> Whether or not Oliver will have proposed to you before this letter arrives I can't tell. The one thing for certain is that he will, unless you freeze him off ...
> I think him splendid [but] I implore you not to forget me ... You went off with him tonight, so I can't help writing.[60]

But Virginia considered Oliver's interest just a passing phase of susceptibility to women. Ray Costelloe confided to Virginia that she was falling in love with Oliver, and they married later that year.[61]

By late 1910 Clive was finding Lytton's close friendship with Vanessa and Virginia too much to bear. There was a quarrel, and Lytton was asked to stay away from Gordon Square. Virginia rather relished the outbreak of hostilities, gleefully telling Ottoline Morrell that she planned a fancy-dress ball at which Clive and Lytton, each costumed as the other's ideal, would fall for one another.[62] She reassured Clive that she would be more 'appreciative' of him in future and that she was not considering marrying Lytton or Hilton Young.[63] But Clive could also be jealous of her female friends. On one occasion, for example, Virginia had to explain to her aggrieved brother-in-law why she had allowed Mary Sheepshanks to interrupt their tête-à-tête.[64] In subsequent years Virginia became less considerate of Clive's feelings, possibly as a result of his continuous teasing, which she hated, and a suspicion that he was more irritated than heartbroken at losing her affections.

On Virginia's engagement to Leonard in 1912 Clive was forced to give up his claim to a primary place in her affections. He did so grudgingly, feeling that she belonged to him despite the fact they were both attached to other people: 'You know, whatever happens, I shall always cheat myself into believing that I appreciate and love you better than your husband does.'[65] In his jealousy Clive was, to say the least, a little hypocritical. He had never been a believer in lifelong devotion. He was a serial seducer of women and even in old age was despondent if his life lacked a love interest. In his later years Clive still exhibited signs of jealousy and occasionally became peevish with Virginia, who was not very discreet and often disparaging about his romances. For her part she believed that most of them were undertaken out of vanity rather than passion.[66]

But Clive's string of lovers testifies if nothing else to his sexual charisma. Before his marriage there had been a liaison with a married woman, Annie Raven-Hill, the wife of a *Punch* illustrator. A neighbour of his parents in Seend, Annie provided the initial stages of Clive's sexual education. The affair continued on and off until he married Vanessa, but he also sought solace from his ex-lover during 1909–14. Vanessa, who met Annie at Seend in April 1908, was refreshed and amused by her 'wildly improper' topics of conversation, which included sex and contraception. She was even keen to ask Annie's advice on family planning, probably unaware at this time that Annie had been

Clive's lover.[67] Vanessa was certainly told later, however, and in 1921 Clive read a paper to the Memoir Club describing the liaison. Virginia, also attending, was surprised to hear about the recommencement of the affair, relating its timing to her intimacy with Clive: 'She coincided with his attachment to me then.'[68]

During his marriage Clive was almost always romantically involved with at least one other woman. As his flirtation with Virginia had shown, Clive had no qualms about playing close to home – one of his conquests included his friend Desmond MacCarthy's wife Molly. Clive got on well with both of the MacCarthys, who were an important element of Bloomsbury. While Desmond's good humour and conversation were well known in London circles, Molly was considered an accomplished letter-writer, but the more *risqué* members of Bloomsbury occasionally felt that her slightly prudish presence inhibited their conversation. She had an original mind, and Virginia considered her a good writer (she published a novel, *A Pier and a Band*, and a book of reminiscences, *A Nineteenth Century Childhood*), but she never wholeheartedly embraced the tenets of Bloomsbury. In spring 1912, with Vanessa's attention firmly fixed on her lover Roger Fry, Virginia's on her soon-to-be fiancé Leonard and Desmond's on his new friend Violet Asquith, Clive began to write flirtatious letters to Molly. Molly at first resisted intimacy, keeping her letters to everyday matters and gossip about friends, but Clive wore down her resistance and Molly eventually allowed the affair to become physical. But her lack of interest in sex soon led him to seek other companions, and by the beginning of 1915 the affair had run its course. Clive took Molly's decision to end the affair badly, venting his feelings on both the MacCarthys.[69] However, he had already identified Molly's successor, Mary Hutchinson, with whom he conducted his longest extra-marital relationship.

Mary Hutchinson (née Barnes), related to the Stracheys, was a well-dressed and highly literate woman. She was married to barrister St John (Jack) Hutchinson and numbered among her friends T.S. Eliot and Aldous Huxley.[70] Vanessa, with some acerbity, pronounced her more suitable for fashionable salons than Bloomsbury drawing-rooms: Mary was too taken up with the superficialities of dress and parties and too little concerned with work for Vanessa's taste.[71]

By February 1915 Mary was conducting an affair with Clive. Vanessa was preoccupied with Duncan Grant and was therefore prepared to tolerate Mary as the price of her own freedom. Mary was soon an *habituée* of Bloomsbury, attending parties and accepted publicly as Clive's mistress, often accompanying him to friends' country houses. (After they spent a weekend with Lytton and Carrington in 1920, Carrington's verdict was that they were both too elegant and pseudo-French.[72]) Mary even sat to Vanessa for a portrait; perhaps understandably in the circumstances, the result was unflattering.[73] Several times Clive tried to end the affair with Mary, but they found their lives too empty without each other and soon drifted together again. He prevaricated, unable to leave one woman until he had found another. In 1921, still with Mary, he had an amorous interlude with a Spanish woman, Juana de Gandarillas, which he made a great deal of, irritating his friends. According to Virginia Juana was beautiful and wildly extravagant, which helped one to forget that her intelligence was under par.[74] Vanessa referred to her uncharitably as 'the Guano'.[75] Juana's letters, discreet and charming, make it clear that Clive was smitten and sought reassurance of her affection. She teases him gently about his lady friends and expresses her pleasure at meeting Vanessa and Duncan in Paris.[76] Within a year it was all over and Clive was considering moving from Gordon Square to set up a permanent home with Mary in Chelsea. In the end, though, Vanessa was the only woman with whom he lived on a domestic basis. The others had always to accept a few days or weeks of him at a time. In 1927, after numerous separations and reconciliations, Clive and Mary finally parted for good.

Virginia believed that Clive was becoming dissipated and pursuing his place in 'society' to the detriment of his health and intellect. She maintained that his brain was softening through too many cocktails and friendships with pretty women, and that his Don Juan persona was undignified. Indeed she wrote to his younger son Quentin to tell him so.[77] (Quentin had some sympathy with her point of view.) By 1929 she was trying to persuade a mutual friend to tell Clive that his stories of affairs with girls half his age bored everyone and to suggest that he should take up some real work, such as writing a book.[78] Vanessa's constant fear (she was long past jealousy) was that he would try to introduce his new friends into Bloomsbury, as he had done with Mary.

One of the paramours of Clive's middle age was Benita Jaeger, whom he continued to see for six years during the 1930s. Benita had been brought up in Germany and now lived at 26 Brunswick Square, near to where Virginia and Leonard had lived before their marriage. Like Mary, Benita was a great socialite. She and Clive went to parties and fashionable restaurants and travelled widely together, a trip to Cannes one year and a West Indies cruise another. She began a novel, upon which Virginia pronounced the sentence of death, and also tried her hand at painting and acting before becoming a sculptor of heads. She eventually married an artist, John Armstrong. Vanessa knew her a little and, perhaps surprisingly, liked her. The fact that Benita did not try to infiltrate Vanessa's circle may have rendered her more agreeable.[79]

Also among Clive's lovers was Beatrice Meinertzhagen (nicknamed 'Bobo'), a niece of leading Fabian Beatrice Webb. The Meinertzhagens had been friends of the young Stephens, but in Virginia's view Bobo was 'a sentimental Jewess'.[80] Like many of Virginia's harsher judgements this came with qualifications: she was attracted to Bobo's seductive and sinuous charm. It was Bobo who in February 1927 was permitted to take the drastic step of cutting Virginia's hair off, so freeing her from the tyranny of hairpins.

Romance was one of Clive's chief *raisons d'être*. But it would be wrong to condemn him as merely a Don Juan or a sybarite. He held strong and controversial (if changeable) views on art and politics. His interest in art had started in the early 1900s when, as a young man in Paris, he was the companion of artists and art critics. His marriage to Vanessa and friendship with Roger Fry helped to cement his position in the art world. He was Roger's aide on both Post-Impressionist exhibitions, supporting Roger's aims and travelling to Paris with Desmond MacCarthy to collect exhibits.[81] While Roger was the driving force behind introducing the new French painters to Britain, Clive was the spokesperson for the concept of 'significant form'. When in 1913 Roger Fry was asked by Chatto and Windus to write a book for them on Post-Impressionism he was too busy with the impending opening of the Omega Workshops to take up the offer. Instead he handed the project over to Clive.[82] The result, *Art* (1914), was a manifesto of the beliefs that Clive shared with Roger on the subject of modern art, as well as a few of his own that Roger rejected.

When war broke out in 1914 Clive was one of the first in Bloomsbury to appreciate the seriousness of the situation and its possible repercussions. Civilization would never be the same again; more wars would soon follow. When conscription was introduced he became a conscientious objector, and his pamphlet *Peace at Once* (1915), which called for negotiation rather than armed conflict, was burned by order of the Lord Mayor. History and Maynard Keynes (in *The Economic Consequences of the Peace*) have proved

Clive right in the main, but Georgian England was in no mood to listen and the force of patriotic sentiment overwhelmed rational argument.

By his mid forties Clive's socialism had all but evaporated. His 1928 *Civilization: An Essay* was a refutation of the socialist ideal. Although Virginia liked the book when she read it in manuscript (so she told Clive, at least), she later observed that his idea of civilization was a good lunch with his Bloomsbury friends. There was more than a grain of truth in this. Clive propounded the theory that culture and enlightened thinking were the most important aims of a civilized society; the masses, unable to appreciate the finer things of life, should serve the needs of their intellectual masters. This belief is diametrically opposed to democracy: there is no means to sustain this kind of society except by an autocracy. This time he was on the 'wrong' side. The dictatorship which was emerging in 1930s Germany not only proved itself unappreciative of European culture but was distinctly hostile to any other sort. Not just Clive's but Bloomsbury's pacifism practically disappeared in the face of the Nazi threat, and Clive even joined the Home Guard.

In his old age Clive took up with Saxon's old flame Barbara Bagenal, separated from her husband Nick. In the 1940s Barbara began to chauffeur Clive about, deal with the practicalities of his life and keep him amused and entertained. In their social appetites and taste for gossip they were two of a kind. Vanessa could only feel relieved that the whole burden of Clive was not falling to her, but although she was grateful to Barbara she could not bring herself to like her unreservedly. At Charleston Barbara was referred to as 'Little Ba' and was 'something of a family joke, but not an unkind joke'.[83] Virginia had been very fond of Barbara (then Hiles) in the Hogarth Press days, finding her sensible, amusing and an authority on plants, but Vanessa was often impatient with her chirpiness and boundless energy and avoided her company. Age did not render her immune to the irritant. From Venice in 1957 Vanessa wrote to her daughter Angelica complaining of Barbara's chattering presence. Staying at La Souco three years later Vanessa made an early departure – regular visits from the lively Barbara were hindering her enjoyment.[84]

Women thought Clive charming; only on rare occasions did his bonhomie backfire. Irene Cooper-Willis, a friend of Desmond MacCarthy (himself a bit of a charmer), said that Clive's company was a little too rich for her digestion: he made her feel as if a meringue had been set before her at breakfast.[85] Ottoline Morrell was not much more enamoured, finding him lightweight and lacking in depth; this did not prevent her, however, from inviting him frequently to stay at Garsington.[86] His closest friends found him irritating and refreshing in equal measure. Virginia borrowed some of his characteristics for Mrs Manresa in her final, posthumously published novel *Between the Acts*. Mrs Manresa, who has Mary Hutchinson's painted nails and jewellery, is married to a rich Jew who has made his money through commerce. She breezes in to the middle of the Olivers' sedate lunch with champagne, a picnic basket, snippets of London gossip and a young man in tow. She flirts with butler and patriarch alike, but her companions are grateful for her vulgarity, which enables them to 'take advantage of the breach of decorum, of the fresh air that blew in, to follow like leaping dolphins in the wake of an ice-breaking vessel'.[87] Together with Roger Fry Clive acted as a vital force in Bloomsbury, bringing life and pleasure into the intellectualized and rather severe coterie.

Clive died in London on 18 September 1964, two days after his eighty-third birthday. Vanessa had died in 1961 and a memorial exhibition of her paintings was held that year at the Art Council's Galleries in London's St James's Square. Critics praised the honesty, sincerity and vitality of her work. But posterity decreed that Clive would be remembered more for his friend-ships than for his work. Although his art criticism was accomplished, it is now widely recognized that the most well known of his theories, that of 'significant form', was originated by his friend Roger Fry. But his enthusiasm and forward-thinking had helped introduce the Post-Impressionists into Britain, and among young artists he was very influential for a time. His reputation faded following his death, however, and *The Times* suggested that the memory of his bonhomie would outlive his critical influence. Perhaps he had been a little inflexible in his tastes and dogmatic about expressing them, a shade too fond of courting controversy. Nevertheless, his criticism was witty and learned and always provoked interest and discussion.[88] To Virginia Woolf's readers he would be remembered as both villain and hero: as the partner-in-crime with whom she irreparably damaged her beloved sister's trust; but also as Virginia's first real critic and literary guide, who assured her that, despite the flaws of her first novel, she was a fledgeling genius.

The Strangest Mind:
Saxon Sydney-Turner

AFTER HER PROLONGED but unconsummated affair with Clive, Virginia's attentions began to stray beyond the family circle. The flurry of passion expressed by Clive and jealousy suppressed by Vanessa had taken its toll on all three of them. Even as she was extricating herself from Clive during 1909–10, Virginia was developing cooler, more intellectual friendships with Saxon Sydney-Turner and Lytton Strachey. Like Clive, both seemed ineligible for marriage: Saxon because of his apparent asexuality (although he later fell in love with Barbara Hiles) and Lytton because of his well-known preference for beautiful young men. Virginia's friendship with Saxon was free from physical attraction on both sides, but it enriched her existence. He was a puzzling man, intellectually brilliant and with a remarkably retentive memory in certain areas of knowledge, but unusually passive, sometimes remote and absorbed in his own thoughts, often entirely silent for hours on end. Despite his widely acknowledged intellect, in a group of high achievers he was the exception, but his engaging eccentricity secured him a place at the heart of Bloomsbury.

But what, you may ask, is Saxon Sydney-Turner doing in a book about Virginia's 'suitors'? Did he ever propose? Were there romantic inclinations on either side? What evidence is there even of a mutual attraction? Although we can only guess what was going on in the mind of the enigmatic Saxon – even his most intimate friends did not know for certain – there was unquestionably an intimate friendship between him and Virginia. She was occasionally frustrated by his silent self-absorption and his terminal indecisiveness but for the most part loved him for his quirkiness. There was never a full-blown 'affair' or even a courtship, but the two of them were drawn to one another from the time of Thoby's death in 1906. Before her marriage Virginia often invited Saxon to dinner and tea, spent time with him alone and in company, made a trip to the Bayreuth opera with him and her brother Adrian, was taken to meet Saxon's family and made flirtatious remarks – both to him and to her friends about him. After she married Leonard she signalled that the friendship would continue unabated by writing to Saxon from her honeymoon hotel in Pisa.

Unlike most of his peers Saxon Arnoll Sydney-Turner did not possess a clutch of illustrious ancestors. A friend who knew him in old age said: 'I never thought of him as a person with forebears – just Saxon, a curious, slightly strange, one-off human being.'[1] His great-grandfather, the lawyer and historian Sharon Turner (1768–1847), was his best-known ancestor. Sharon Turner was an authority on Icelandic and Anglo-Saxon culture and language (hence, probably, his great-grandson's name). He was a friend and correspondent of the poet laureate Robert Southey and a business associate of John Murray, who consulted him about legal matters, including the repercussions of publishing Byron's infamous *Don Juan*. Much of Sharon Turner's life was devoted to the study and interpretation of ancient documents in the British Museum, in pursuance of his ambition to write a complete history of England to the present day. Between 1799 and 1829 he wrote the twelve historical volumes that made him famous. These were distinguished by their lengthy titles, beginning with the *History of England from the Earliest Period to the Norman Conquest* and continuing his historical survey to the end of the Elizabethan age. But it was on his earlier historical work that his reputation rested, and for this he numbered among his admirers Tennyson, Hallam, Macaulay and Scott, who gave him an honourable mention in the dedication of *Ivanhoe*.[2]

Even with his dual career as businessman and historian, Sharon Turner found time to keep a record of his work and of everyday incidents in a diary, which survived into the next century and was passed down to Saxon. In 1926, hearing of the diary, Virginia asked to borrow it and for a while considered publishing it through the Hogarth Press. She derived great enjoyment from reading about Turner's idiosyncrasies, musing that Saxon's ancestor resembled him not only in his erudition, diligence and sincerity but also – unfortunately – in his tendency to bore others. Sharon Turner was by Virginia's time almost a forgotten figure, but he was not destined to be rescued from obscurity by the Woolfs. Virginia returned the diary to Saxon in 1930, fully perused but with no plans for publication. But Sharon Turner's habit of keeping detailed diaries permeated succeeding generations. Frances Marshall (later Partridge) remembered seeing those of Saxon's father and two grandparents in 1928.

His father had kept a diary for thirty years in one enormous book with long pages, so that it was possible to compare what happened on April 3rd for thirty successive years at a glance. This absolutely delighted Saxon, and I strongly suspect he keeps one himself on the same plan.[3]

Saxon's father was Alfred Moxon Sydney-Turner, a doctor who treated mentally disturbed patients at his home at 42 Ventnor Villas in Hove, East Sussex, aided by his wife. Dr Turner, as he was known in Bloomsbury Circles, a Member of the Royal College of Surgeons, LSA (Licentiate of the Society of Apothecaries) and a Justice of the Peace – a man of some standing although not of wide reputation. Virginia first met Saxon's parents in 1910, and by 1916 she and Leonard were on sufficiently friendly terms with them to think of calling in from nearby Brighton.[4] Dr Turner was also Duncan Grant's first port of call when there were anxieties about Vanessa's breast milk shortly after Angelica's birth.[5] (On this occasion, understandably, Dr Turner could not help. He was the 'wrong' sort of doctor.) Virginia maintained that Saxon and his family were very poor, but this was probably only when compared with the inherited wealth of the Stephens, the Stracheys and the Bells – at his death in 1922 Dr Turner left £1,118 (a modest fortune, the equivalent of over £40,000 today) and two houses.[6]

Saxon, born on 28 October 1880, grew into a well-behaved child with a quick brain but a poor appetite. His mother told Virginia proudly that he had conquered the alphabet even before he could talk.[7] He was educated at Westminster School and won a university scholarship to Trinity College. Part of the scholarship examination was a translation of a Greek passage containing a riddle. Most candidates managed the translation, but Saxon was the only one who was able to solve the riddle. This was a skill which never left him, and he was later a great cruciverbalist (crossword-puzzle solver) and loved all sorts of word games. At Trinity he was the first person to befriend Leonard Woolf. Meeting in front of a noticeboard, they became engaged in a conversation which was absorbing enough to continue in Leonard's rooms in New Court. They acquired other friends, with whom they would form the core of 'Old Bloomsbury': Lytton Strachey, Thoby Stephen and Clive Bell. According to Lytton, freshman Saxon was quite a different animal to the later incarnation. During his first term Saxon was a spirited young man with a wide literary knowledge, who discussed, read and wrote poetry well into the night and declaimed it in the college courtyard. But by the second term Saxon's ebullience had mysteriously disappeared, and he began to spend more and more time on the private (and often obscure) obsessions that would occupy the rest of his life.[8]

Although he was taciturn, Saxon's brilliance must have commanded the respect of his peers, for, like Leonard and Lytton, he was invited to the extremely select Thursday evening gatherings of the philosopher J.E. McTaggart.[9] In October 1902 he was elected to the Apostles, the colloquial title for the supposedly secret Cambridge Conversazione Society, founded by twelve under-graduates in 1820 as an exclusive debating club for Cambridge's *crème de la crème*. Early members had included Tennyson and Hallam (Tennyson resigned after only four months).[10] Despite his many extra-curricular pursuits Saxon did not neglect his studies, and in 1903 he outshone all his friends with a double first in classics. He and Leonard stayed on at Cambridge an extra year to study for the Civil Service examinations. Saxon was the only candidate to keep his coat on during the examinations in the sweltering August heat of 1904. But the tempera-ture did not impair his performance, and he did well enough to be offered a position in the Civil Service. Leonard did badly and left for Ceylon as a colonial administrator. Saxon, never a profuse or captivating letter-writer, intermittently wrote him dull letters, but their friendship was effectively put on hold until Leonard's return to England in 1911.

Leonard, like most other people who knew him, found Saxon a mystery: 'Saxon was a very strange character with one of the strangest minds I have met with.'[11] An inconspicuous-looking man, short and thin with light brown hair and moustache, a bird-like appetite (he later acquired a taste for good food prepared by others) and nocturnal habits, Saxon moved about silently, ghost-like, seeming hardly to disturb the surrounding air. At Cambridge Leonard would often look up from his studies to find Saxon sitting next to him when he had thought himself alone. Leonard and Lytton considered him, with all his subtlety and complexity, a creature straight out of a novel by their early hero Henry James. However, they were disappointed when at last the writer and their friend met – Henry James was not at all impressed by the silent and rather shabby Saxon and wholly missed the purported similarity to his fictional characters.[12]

Saxon alternately intrigued and irritated his friends. Leonard and Lytton were more baffled by Saxon the better they knew him. They attempted to illu-minate his hidden depths by means of amateur psychology, but the harder they tried, the more he retreated, enveloping himself in a cocoon of obsessions:

He seemed, even at the age of twenty, to have deliberately withdrawn himself from life . . . He was thus in the process of successfully stifling his creativeness, his sensitive and subtle intelligence, his affections . . . Beneath the façade and the veils one felt that there might be an atrophied Shelley.[13]

Clive Bell remembered Saxon as the most erudite and the best reader of the Midnight Society of which they were both members at Cambridge.[14] (It was perhaps for this reason that he asked him to join his Play Reading Society in 1907.) Maynard Keynes called him 'a quietist' – strictly speaking, an adherent to a religion requiring submission of the will. And indeed he was a peculiarly passive character. On the first of Thoby Stephen's Thursday 'at home' evenings at Gordon Square (16 March 1905) Saxon was the only guest who was not a family member. He did not make much conversation. Thoby, asked by an intrigued Virginia why he considered his friend such a genius, replied that Saxon was not witty and entertaining but that his rarely vocalized sentences were always pronouncements of utter truth.[15] That autumn, when Saxon stayed with the Stephen siblings at Carbis Bay in Cornwall, bringing with him a bag full of books, she was no more impressed by his brilliant silences than she had been at Thoby's Thursday evenings. There was no sign yet that he would become a valued friend.

At this time, before she had got to know them well, Virginia was disappointed with Thoby's intellectual friends, whose self-conscious iconoclasm inhibited them in social situations. Throughout Thoby's school and university years she had envied him the social aspect of his education, knowing that lectures and seminars were only one side of the story. She yearned for the kind of conversations her brother had at Cambridge with those heroic-sounding figures whose sayings and doings Thoby had repeated for her entertainment.

In reality, Virginia found, they were far from heroic. To add insult to injury she was excluded from their male elite. In the company of women most of Thoby's friends (with the marked exception of Clive Bell) were guarded in their behaviour and speech, ill-equipped by their expensive education to respond to the conversational gambits of attractive young females. At Cambridge, as at school, theirs had been a thoroughly male camaraderie, and many had no idea how women lived or how their minds worked. Virginia fictionalized this lack of understanding in her first two novels. In *The Voyage Out* Terence Hewet is curious about Rachel Vinrace's seemingly uneventful existence with her elderly aunts; in *Night and Day* Ralph Denham wonders what lady of leisure Katharine Hilbery does with her time. Virginia, frustrated by the young men's reluctance to attempt communication, complained bitterly that their company had become 'a great trial. They sit silent, absolutely silent, all the time; occasionally they escape to a corner and chuckle over a Latin joke . . . The worst of it is they have not the energy to go.'[16] In the world of the Edwardian drawing-room these intellectuals were like fish out of water.

But after Thoby's death his friends' responses proved that their manners and sympathies had not completely deserted them. Saxon was among those of Thoby's friends who came immediately to pay their respects and offer help, and Virginia never forgot his kindness. He spent quite some time at Gordon Square, giving up two weeks of his precious six weeks' holiday allowance, as Virginia gratefully noted.[17] She dated her intimacy with Saxon from this period and a decade later wrote to him: '[Thoby's] death meant almost more to you and me than to anyone, and I think we shared together some of the worst things.'[18]

Most of the time, however, Saxon had his nose stuck into some abstruse piece of learning. Even as late as September 1907, when he visited Adrian and Virginia at Playden with Walter Lamb, Saxon seemed unconscious of the fact Virginia was female. He was constantly busy on some intellectual problem, contemplating his next chess move or composing an opera at the piano.[19] Virginia was ambivalent about being accepted by Thoby's Cambridge set: she wanted to be on equal terms intellectually, with no exceptions made for her gender, but still she longed for her femaleness to be acknowledged and appreciated. After Vanessa's marriage her fear of her own personal unattractiveness became more acute. While Vanessa and Clive wallowed in connubial bliss, she despaired of Thoby's other friends, who seemed remote, untouched – and untouchable – by female hand.

An accomplished solver of riddles, puzzles and acrostics, Saxon was bookish but not a writer, an opera buff but not a musician, more able to appreciate the creations of other people than create anything himself. He set riddles and word puzzles for friends and was supposed by them to compose poetry, sonatas and snatches of opera, but only a few verses ever saw the light of day.[20] He tweaked and polished and hinted to his friends that great things were approaching; but an essential spark was missing. His friends waited in vain for his great work to appear – he never managed to find a satisfactory outlet. Recently a half-finished play written by Saxon has come to light. Competent rather than original, it is an untitled and undated Shakespearian light drama or comedy with shades of *As You Like It* and *Twelfth Night*. It comes to a halt during the first scene of Act III, just as the hero begins an intrigue with a mystery woman and things start hotting up. As it stands, it includes a skilful dialogue about women's deceitfulness, a developing sub-plot and a lover's tryst, but it does not make for gripping drama and has not enough jokes for a comedy. It is cleverly wrought but passionless, like an accomplished student exercise.[21]

Virginia's friendship with Saxon received a helping hand when Clive's Play Reading Society, the successor of his Midnight Society at Trinity, was established in late 1907. The society encouraged wallflowers such as Saxon to take the floor. Reading plays forced him into speech (albeit someone else's words) instead of allowing him to lapse into his customary silence. Reluctantly he agreed to be the minute-taker, and the minute book testifies to his humour and his love of rarefied language. For the reading of Ben Jonson's *Every Man Out of His Humour* Saxon gave special mention to 'the nice Latinity of Cordatus [Virginia] and the proper submissiveness of Mitis [Vanessa]'. He even allowed a measure of praise for 'a really admirable performance by myself as the Third Rustic'.[22] He was not always so easy to please. Following a reading of Ibsen's *Rosmersholm*, Virginia was castigated for her lack of intensity: 'Virginia did not always give me the feeling of concentrated nervous force that I desiderate in Rebecca.'[23] Saxon himself played the eponymous hero and was modest about his performance: 'My own Rosmer was I suppose dull; but it appears to have been so far right that it suggested imminent dissolution.'[24]

For *Aureng-Zebe*, Dryden's 'heroic' play of 1675, Saxon observed ambiguously that Virginia and Lytton were 'comparatively untroubled' by the difficult rhyming couplets.[25] (Is there a hint that their sang-froid is misplaced?) He confessed he found the rendition tame: 'On the whole I should have liked a little more rant.'[26] He took another opportunity to remind his readers that he had done more than his fair share of note-taking: '[I] am quite willing to surrender the office of critic and recorder to any one whom a spirit of emulation or a sense of justice may move to desire its reversion.'[27] Eventually Clive put Saxon out of his misery and began to take the notes himself.

Literature was one of Saxon's principal interests; music was another. He was a devoted opera fan and collector of opera data. In the summer of 1908, he and Adrian Stephen went to Bayreuth to hear Wagner's Ring cycle. The letters Virginia wrote to him there from Wells were similar in tone to her letters to

Violet Dickinson or Clive, suggesting that Saxon was by now regarded as a close friend. Some of Saxon's peculiarities reminded Virginia of her father; others mirrored her own. She tells him sympathetically of her own experiences of 'difference': how the people of Wells laugh at her dishevelled appearance after she has been walking in the rain; how they stare in surprise when she applauds a band of outdoor musicians; how she has managed to offend a theology student at her boarding house.[28] Like Saxon, she had the sort of oddness that attracted amused glances from strangers. Leonard described how, despite her beauty and distinction, Virginia always appeared slightly ridiculous to others: 'To the crowd in the street there was something in her appearance which struck them as strange and laughable.'[29] Perambulating the streets thinking out her novels and speaking the words aloud, she seemed distracted and preoccupied, separated by her musings from the rest of humanity. Saxon's tendency to retire into a world of his own struck a chord, allowing her to revel not only in her own unorthodox behaviour but also in the 'Bloomsbury' disregard for convention. One of Virginia's letters to Saxon from this period touches on topics that her parents' generation would have considered highly inappropriate for a spinster to pen to a bachelor – dogs in heat; the mistress of Louis XIV; the marriage service; and deserted spouses.[30]

In 1909 Virginia herself was one of the Bayreuth party. She found Saxon endearingly odd, diverting herself by observing his gentle but ineffectual habits – like an old cat trying to lick itself clean. At one boarding-house breakfast he managed to spill some ink. Virginia was amused to see that he used a handkerchief dipped in milk to clean it off a chair and a piece of bread to wipe a pair of inky scissors. She also noted that he was unable to decide what to eat, admired the 'sensible' Germans, spent the day 'dormant' in the world of his own private thoughts and was rather cross when interrupted.[31] Saxon's idiosyncrasies fascinated her and she reported them gleefully to Vanessa: 'He hops along, before or behind, swinging his ugly stick, and humming, like a stridulous grasshopper.'[32] He spent one evening absorbed in making up a song in German addressed to a goose called Nicholas.[33] He was prone to bursts of garrulousness late at night, when he might throw into the ring for discussion some innocent remark made weeks before by Adrian or Virginia, asking for clarification. (Leonard, too, had noticed this quirk at Cambridge.) On one occasion, when Saxon asked Virginia the meaning of an observation she had made three years earlier, she was compelled to improvise. He was pleased with her answer and told her she was very clever – the greatest compliment she had yet received from him.[34]

Saxon's eccentricities, taciturnity and love of routine, remarked on by many friends, were possibly due to a psychological condition. They have much in common with the symptoms of Asperger's syndrome – that is, a milder form of the better-known condition of autism.[35] Unknown during most of Saxon's lifetime, Asperger's could account for Saxon's restricted but obsessive interests and his social awkwardness. People with 'high functioning' Asperger's tend to be socially naïve but are often of above average intelligence. Many have an unusual gait and are physically clumsy – characteristics that Virginia noticed in Saxon while they were in Bayreuth. Also associated with the condition is an in-depth knowledge of particular subjects and an unusually retentive memory for facts. Saxon's encyclopaedic mind contained details of all the opera performances he had ever seen, where he had seen them, who had sung the parts, and so on; similarly for cricketing data. Friends receiving letters about Saxon's long walks in Sussex or Wiltshire soon learned to expect a list of signposts passed or meals eaten rather than descriptions of the beauty of the countryside. When Saxon met a refugee from post-Revolutionary Russia, what he found fascinating was not the political situation but the speed of the postal system and the cost of bootlaces.[36] Virginia was moved to wonder why Saxon did not put his considerable mental powers to a more sociable use, such as making interesting conversation. Listening to him was 'like reading a dictionary' – informative, certainly, but not enthralling.[37] Upon his favourite subjects Saxon loved to soliloquize, unconcerned by the boredom of his listeners – he could hold forth until the early hours of the morning without noticing that his friends had long been ready for bed. (Insomnia is typical of those with Asperger's.) In 1917 Virginia remonstrated with Saxon for keeping late hours – his letters were written at 2 a.m. – and asked Barbara Hiles to keep an eye on his bedtime.[38]

While Leonard was in Ceylon he gathered from Lytton's letters that a friendship had developed between Virginia and Saxon and suggested jokingly that she might marry him. It was true that Virginia greatly admired Saxon's intellectual powers and that his unsophisticated innocence appealed to her ('There is certainly something very attractive – not physically – about Saxon. His purity of mind is such,' she wrote to Vanessa), but Lytton dismissed his right to be considered Virginia's suitor: '[Saxon] certainly is *not* upon the tapis,' he told Leonard unequivocally.[39] When Virginia went to Bayreuth with

Saxon and it looked as though there might be a romance between them, Lytton assured Leonard: 'you're safe so far as *he's* concerned'.[40] Lytton was clearly right about Saxon's unfitness for marriage to Virginia. His apparently asexual nature would have suited her (Lytton thought of him almost as a eunuch), but his characteristic taciturnity would not have been satisfactory in a husband, although she came to accept it in a friend.

The combination of Virginia's unmarried status and her flirtatious nature made it difficult for her to be among admiring friends without giving the impression that she favoured one of them. All her bachelor acquaintances were fair game for her teasing remarks, and the more unlikely the candidate, the better the joke. She told Vanessa that she had intended to close a letter to Saxon with the word 'affectionately' but was saved from this passionless conclusion by a lack of space.[41] She also fantasized about using Saxon as an excuse not to see her half-brother George Duckworth. Suffering from a bout of illness, she was about to enter a nursing home; she would notify George only that she would be 'confined' for the next few weeks and leave him to work out the full story. Naturally he would suspect the worst, assume Saxon was implicated and pull strings to have him promoted. Then, as nominal head of the family, he would motor down to the south coast to extract a promise of funds from Saxon's father.[42]

Virginia was also writing flirtatious letters to the inscrutable Saxon, who was in the habit of employing his learning to write to his friends in Latin. Unfamiliar with the language and its syntax Virginia pleaded: 'Write to me, in one of the living languages, preferably Romance.'[43] Saxon replied in the most romantic of the romance languages – French. Virginia responded appreciatively with remarks about Saxon's eighteenth-century wit and wisdom. He is again compared to a cat – this time an elegant black cat with white paws.[44] She even introduces an amorous note while on a convalescent trip to Cornwall. Describing the nuisance of stumbling across fervent lovers on the cliffs, Virginia tells him that if *she* is ever in a similar position she will endeavour to appear friendly and approachable to avoid embarrassing hapless passers-by.[45]

Virginia appreciated Saxon's erudition and his quiet charms, but she also found cause to pity him. On 27 December 1910 Saxon took her on an unscheduled visit to his family home in Hove. Staying at the Pelham Arms in Lewes for Christmas, Virginia went for a day trip to Brighton and met Saxon at the Pavilion, assuming they would lunch near by. But Saxon escorted her to

Hove to meet his parents. In her customary report to Vanessa, she paints a shabby, depressing picture: the street has an atmosphere of poverty, the house is chilly and sparsely furnished. Vanessa's portrait of Saxon, hanging on the dining-room wall, looks strange in its dull surroundings. Some details are reminiscent of Katharine Hilbery's visit to the Highgate home of the Denhams in *Night and Day*, but the Denhams are cheerful and vital. The inhabitants of the house at Hove, as portrayed by Virginia, are Dickensian. Saxon's parents were old and thin and surrounded by shadowy minor characters – a bald and starved-looking old lady, a man with numerous unnamed afflictions and a Mr Palmer upstairs in bed – described as 'patients' of Dr Turner.[46] Offal was served for lunch – small portions because the patients had to be fed from the same meagre pot.

Saxon maintained his habitual silence during lunch, then discreetly left the room leaving his mother and Virginia to talk. Mrs Turner took advantage of her son's absence to tell Virginia proudly of his precociousness as a child, entering into vivid detail about his ailments. Assuming an *affaire de coeur* between her son and her lovely visitor, she asked Virginia to keep an eye on Saxon's health and confided her wish that he should marry a good woman. All the ingredients for a typical Virginia comic interlude are present, but while she drew a melodramatic picture of the paucity and dankness in which Saxon's family lived Virginia laid stress upon his integrity:

> I feel that one ought to think very kindly of Saxon. It is such a poverty-stricken middle class family, and if I were as distinguished and nice as Saxon, I should be much more arrogant . . . he is completely placid and sincere, and always remembers his mother's hard lot.[47]

Virginia had a bleak afternoon in the suburbs, reminding her of unpleasant days spent with her Fisher relatives. She was faced with mentally disturbed individuals and had to eat a revolting lunch in their company. She was left alone to make desultory conversation with Mrs Turner. All the worst things, in fact, to which Saxon could have subjected her and which, under other circumstances, could have left her bored, irritated, alarmed and upset. Virginia's affection for Saxon was such that she did not allow this disagreeable visit to tarnish her image of him. Instead of derision and mockery there is sympathy and a gentle humour in her description.

Is it possible that this surprise meeting with his parents was a mild attempt at courtship by Saxon? Evidently Virginia did not think so, even if Saxon's mother did. A few years later he confessed to Virginia that there were two reasons why he had never been in love with her: because Thoby's death had made them intimate enough; and because he had always known that she would marry Leonard.[48] These reasons seemed good enough in hindsight, but in truth perhaps Saxon knew that Virginia was spiky and critical where he was placid and tolerant and that their approaches to life were not compatible. She certainly found him tame and hesitant compared to the intrepid and decisive Leonard.[49]

Saxon did fall in love, for the first and only time in his life, in 1916. Barbara Hiles was a former student of Chelsea's Slade School of Art and one of the group of friends that Virginia called the 'Bloomsbury bunnies' or 'cropheads', because of their penchant for trousers and short haircuts. They included (Dora) Carrington, Dorothy Brett, Faith Henderson and Alix Sargant-Florence.[50] These young women were the younger generation, born ten or fifteen years after the older Bloomsberries whose hard-won freedoms they seemed to take for granted. Barbara was dark-haired and pretty, with an air of common sense mixed with merriment – Ottoline Morrell compared her to a respectable barmaid, cheerful and level-headed.[51] Barbara lived and painted at a studio in Hampstead and frequently threw parties there – it was at one of these that Saxon first met and fell in love with 'the one completely satisfactory person that I ever hope to meet, that somehow found out that somewhere inside me there was still something that could wake up and play'.[52] But Barbara was already being courted by another man, and Saxon soon found himself involved in a *ménage à trois*. His rival was Nicholas Bagenal, the brother of Barbara's friend Faith Henderson, and he was stationed with the Irish Guards in France. Faith naturally enough thought her brother more worthy of Barbara but suspected that 'Bloomsbury' had an unfavourable opinion of his intellect and supported Saxon's suit.

Virginia invited Barbara to dine at Richmond on 29 November 1916. She was keen to meet Saxon's first love and wanted to check that Barbara had a proper appreciation of his charms. 'I do want someone to explore all the exquisiteness of your nature,' she wrote to him affectionately.[53] She admitted to a flutter of jealousy, such as she felt when Lytton took up with Carrington, but was glad he had finally found someone to love, even though the presence of Nick Bagenal complicated the situation.

In an attempt to further Saxon's romance Virginia suggested that he should go to Asheham with Carrington and Barbara at the end of January 1917, while she and Leonard stayed at Hogarth House. Saxon, whose health was suffering under the strain of unrequited love, had been advised to take a rest cure by his doctor. His activities on arriving at Asheham were hardly conducive to his rest. In a gallant attempt to make his fellow guests comfortable he spent much of the weekend with his arms in freezing cold water, clearing ice out of the cistern and pipes. Carrington was amused to see that instead of changing his shirt he kept on the wet one and flapped his arms about in front of the fire in an attempt to dry it. 'Saxon is as I suspected a lunatic,' she wrote to Lytton.[54] For once Saxon excelled as a host. He read Swinburne aloud to a party of guests from Charleston and chivalrously organized a day of versifying in honour of the absent Nick Bagenal – Saxon's poem, inevitably, had classical allusions. They went tobogganing on the snow-covered downs and icy ponds using a tea-tray or Maynard Keynes's dispatch case. In a singularly energetic mood Saxon even suggested they play badminton instead of writing letters.[55]

By the autumn Virginia had become Saxon's confidante and they had frequent conversations about his romance. She encouraged him to be tenacious in love – better to have loved and lost than to have spent all one's days in an office and on tube trains, she advised him. Saxon assured Virginia that he thought her marriage the best advertisement for matrimony he had come across.[56] But his strong sense of fair play made him anxious about the ethics of his situation. Was it morally right for him to take advantage of his rival's absence? And surely he himself was too old for Barbara, being eleven years her senior? Wasn't he too dull and middle-aged (he was thirty-seven) for such a lively young lady? Having caught sight of Nick bathing, Saxon thought his rival would make a better husband. Virginia pondered the sort of husband Saxon would make – not an appropriate one for her, she decided – too prevaricating.[57]

For a brief period that winter Saxon appeared to be in Barbara's good favour. A couple of weeks later, however, everything had changed. Believing that 'it would kill Nick' if she married Saxon, and inspired by Bloomsbury precedents such as the Clive–Vanessa–Duncan triangle, Barbara announced a bold plan of marrying Nick while keeping Saxon as a lover.[58] Vanessa, whose situation was the result of accident rather than planning, was critical of an arrangement deliberately calculated along the same lines: 'half the year with one, half with the other, a child by each, etc., and no one to have any jealousy or cause for complaint'; it was doomed to failure, she pronounced.[59] Virginia, too, was dubious, wondering whether Barbara was in love or just marrying Nick because he wanted it so much.[60]

Nevertheless, they married on 1 February 1918. Saxon stepped aside self-effacingly, convincing himself (and perhaps Barbara) that it would make no difference if she married Nick: 'You're a wonderful creature, that can make me happier just by existing.'[61] Although he tried to maintain, in G.E. Moore's phrase, a 'good state of mind', he found that he was more often than not the gooseberry of the threesome. He felt wretched and excused himself from visiting the Woolfs because he could not bear to see any happily married couple at close quarters.[62] These feelings he considered unworthy and tried to suppress – and succeeded to the extent that Virginia, seeing him pick up the threads of his old life and happily contemplate the next opera season, wondered whether he had really been in love at all.[63] When Barbara gave birth to Nick's baby in November Saxon seemed resolved to treat the little girl as if she were his own daughter and even chose her name, Judith. He managed the larger issues well, but his anxieties were channelled into the smaller ones. When attacked by headache and rheumatism two weeks later he told Virginia and Leonard he had lost the will to live. (When the headache went, his will to live returned.)[64]

The brave new world that he, Barbara and Nick had tried to create had not come to pass. Convention reigned – Barbara was with her husband and child, and Saxon was alone. He began to sense that he had lost his only opportunity for marriage and felt so rootless that he considered emigrating.[65] On the last day of what was probably the worst year of his life, he wrote to Barbara suggesting that they should stop seeing one another. But he was still deeply in love with her:

> You were right in thinking that it [Barbara's marriage to Nick] wouldn't kill me: you were wrong in thinking that it could go on making no difference . . . But in case what I have written seems cold and unmindful of all you have given me I want to say that I thank you and that I always shall thank you for having taught me what love means and having given me the greatest happiness that I have ever known. There is no shadow of reproach in my thoughts of you and even if I never see you again you will always remain for me the most perfect human being that I have ever met or can hope to meet.[66]

Barbara, realizing how much she had hurt her unassertive but devoted lover, suggested that the three of them live together. But Saxon, although he concurred with their wish to remain friends, knew that he cared too much for Barbara to live with her while sharing her with another man. It was not sexual jealousy of Nick, he explained with scrupulous honesty, but something more fundamental:

> I have never thought – except perhaps one night when we were all at Asheham – of your copulating with Nick as a thing to mind about. Even then I think it was more a feeling of being shut out than anything else. I suppose that when one cares very much about somebody one would always like to feel that one came first with them. If that's being jealous perhaps I have been but it has been so impersonal that it seems absurd to call it being jealous of him.[67]

Virginia was sorry that her old friend's altruism and idealism had disadvantaged him. Her sensitivity on his behalf was poignant. One evening, after they had had tea together, she asked him to dine 'remembering old lonely evenings of my own, when the married couple seemed so secure & lamplit'.[68] Saxon never did find the comfort and security of those lamplit evenings but remained devoted to Barbara, writing to her regularly and often for the rest of his life, in a friendship which outlasted her marriage.

In February 1922 Saxon's father died, among his bequests to his son the Hove house where Virginia had lunched in 1910. Mrs Turner was unable to cope alone, so Saxon took charge of the funeral arrangements and replied to the messages of condolence from his father's former colleagues. Virginia portrayed him to Vanessa as a man who had found his calling, happy to have something useful to do.[69] He planned to live with his mother in Richmond – perhaps with two old ladies who had been patients of his father – and asked Virginia (who was living there) to help him find a house. Virginia repeated for Clive Bell a dialogue with Saxon about his future home and prospects, giving a strong flavour of the rambling style of his conversation:

V. But what about the lunatics?

S. Um-m. They might of course come too – at least the two old ladies might – but the eldest of them, who is 90 next May, is certified. I am not sure that we should be allowed to keep her. Besides ...

V. Is she quite mad?

S. Um-m. She can't talk so that you understand. Sometimes she shouts. She did at Christmas. Lady Young, who is getting old herself, and has some complaint, I don't know exactly what it is – she lives at Eastbourne now – Lady Young forgot to send her anything. This upset her a good deal. She would have had no presents if I hadn't bought her a box of chocolates . . .

V. But, Saxon, how much money have you got? – I mean by your father's will? –

S. I have a mortgage on a house at Portslade . . . Um – I may foreclose. I'd better ask Niemeyer about that . . . Peonies.

V. Peonies?

S. Niemeyer has purple peonies in his garden. They come from Copenhagen.

V. Shall you like living with your mother?

S. Um-m-m. I don't think Thersites is a good character altogether, do you?

V. Shakespeare?

S. Well, I believe there is a play by the Elder Nashe; but I meant Shakespeare.[70]

Virginia, on the other hand, found Richmond too far from Bloomsbury and began looking for a London house. One plan (which fell through) was to take a house in Woburn Square and let a floor to Saxon.[71] Eventually, in spring 1924, the Woolfs moved to 52 Tavistock Square, letting Hogarth House to Saxon and his mother (plus four 'lunatics', according to Virginia) for the next two years. Within a few months there had been a number of farcical misfortunes at Hogarth: bits of the bedroom ceiling detached themselves; there was a plague of beetles; and a lark made its home in the boiler, flying out to alarm the cook every morning.[72] These stories delighted Virginia as much as hearing that Saxon had been reading obscure Latin works in a café in Vichy, seeing him scrutinize his chequebook to determine whether its pattern had changed or noting that he had had the same umbrella and watch chain for nearly thirty years.[73]

Each of these details contributed to the affectionate picture of hapless innocence that she had built up of him. For his sake she put up with much that she found intolerable in less favoured friends. There was, for example, the tedium of meeting his acquaintances – Finns who spoke only a few words of English, Treasury colleagues, some unexciting Swedes, or American diplomats in evening dress. Saxon evidently viewed the Woolfs as people who could get along with anyone, a judgement almost comical in its inaccuracy. Both Virginia and Leonard were highly critical of their fellows and generally suffered fools with barely concealed impatience (on Leonard's side) or ridicule (on

Virginia's). But they made exceptions for Saxon's guests. She would be glad to meet anyone he chose, Virginia told him. They even hosted a party at Tavistock Square for several of his guests, turning down a dinner invitation from Rebecca West to do so. Saxon's old flame Barbara Bagenal later wrote of his close friendship with Virginia:

> Saxon was a very reserved man, sometimes hardly speaking at all to anyone he did not know well, but Virginia was devoted to him and managed to make him almost voluble . . . [she] was fascinated by his extraordinary mind, his accumulation of knowledge and his very odd character . . . She said to me 'There will *never* be his like again. He is unique.'[74]

Elements of Saxon's character appear in two of Woolf's novels. In *The Voyage Out* Willoughby Vinrace's friend William Pepper has Saxon's physical build and fragile constitution. A small man, bent as if by a gale, he suffers from rheumatism and is sensitive to draughts. Representing the academic world, he is learned in a range of subjects, including mathematics, history, Greek, zoology, economics, and the Icelandic Sagas, as well as Persian poetry, coins and road-making.[75] He quotes Greek to Clarissa Dalloway and has not married because he has never met a woman who has been educated, like a man, to read Greek (which Virginia could, of course). He writes monographs that are published as small yellow books and memorizes the number of any ticket given to him. Rachel Vinrace thinks of him as a fossilized fish. But if William Pepper's academic pursuits and quirks remind one of Saxon, his personality does not. He is a little fiery, like his name – even the bulky Willoughby Vinrace fears contradicting him. He lacks Saxon's humanity; he is judgemental and cold-natured, censuring a colleague for procrastination and speaking of the deaths of acquaintances without emotion.

To the Lighthouse's Augustus Carmichael, although inspired by a Professor Wolstenholme who used to stay with the Stephens at St Ives, has some of Saxon's characteristics: his feline inscrutability, his silence, his apartness. Carmichael is another academically inclined character, but his studies – in the first part of the book at least – have resulted in no substantial output. He presents a picture of what Saxon might have become if he had been more worldly and perceived his life as a failure: an opium addict with marital problems. Carmichael spends most of his time alone, lying in the Ramsays' garden, thinking about poetry; lying in wait for the right word like a cat about to pounce on a bird. He is somnolent during daylight hours and in the evenings stays up late reading Virgil. He says little, but Lily Briscoe (whose character contains aspects of Virginia) feels an empathy with him. And, significantly, it is he who is with her at the climactic moment, as together they watch the little boat sail to the lighthouse.

The strongest flavour of Saxon is captured in Virginia's unpublished memoir, 'One of Our Great Men'. The name of her subject is given as F.A.R. Rankin (nicknamed 'Fairy'), but the model for the piece is clear. Rankin reads Greek fluently but speaks rarely: 'he seemed asleep by day. In company he sat perfectly silent, like an idol, with his hands and feet drawn together.'[76] But in the early hours of the morning he pays social calls, tapping on his friends' windows, as Saxon did. His intelligence is revered and great things are expected from him. He reveals little about his background, but in the holidays a friend tracks him down to a shabby house called 'The Mimosas' (named, appropriately, after a tree whose leaves curl up on contact), reading aloud to an invalid old lady – his mother, who runs an institution for 'imbeciles'.

After Cambridge Rankin goes to work in a bank and lives in lodgings in a dingy back street. His friends still nurse their expectations about him and press him to tell them about his studies, a range of complex subjects from counterpoint to Chinese languages. Everyone waits for Rankin's great work to appear, while his reputation for brilliance turns him into a legend. People point him out as an authority on horse-racing, rabbits, crosswords. Why did he not marry? people wonder. Perhaps because of having to care for his invalid mother; perhaps because he cannot afford to keep a wife. He views a woman purely aesthetically, appreciating the beauty of her gestures rather than her person. He courts women by post, sending valentines in order to avoid speaking to them. Younger people wonder about the basis for his high reputation. But Rankin's friends still keep faith and claim he will show his genius when he retires. But when he does retire still nothing appears – Rankin continues to flit through life insubstantial as a ghost but deep in thought.

The point of these 'recollections' is pressed home in the shape of a question: Can someone be considered great on the strength of potential alone without producing a great work? Behind this question there lurk other questions of stifled genius; perhaps about Virginia's brother Thoby, who died at twenty-six without fulfilling his potential. With all his promise, why did

Saxon not become a great man? Virginia asks. Did the need to earn his living hold him back? Without inherited wealth Saxon was forced to work for money rather than for posterity, but his job at the Treasury left plenty of time to pursue his interests (one thinks of T.S. Eliot). Saxon's mind was stocked with knowledge, but somehow he could not settle to writing a book. He came to view his intelligence as something with which he amused himself and his friends; he was a champion list-maker and fact-collector who spent his time in private exercises for his brain. His meticulousness meant that even the smallest of activities resulted in hours or even days spent on decisions and arrangements.[77] In this he was the absolute opposite to Virginia, who had a single-minded drive towards her future as a writer even as a child and to whom wasted time was anathema.

Saxon had no real aspirations, no desire for fame. But despite his modesty and lack of ambition he reached a position of respect, if not power, in the Treasury and was well thought of by his colleagues. One of his tasks was to ensure that the Prime Minister was kept apprised of all the relevant news that came out of the Treasury, in order to be forearmed against awkward questions in Parliament. According to Frances Partridge, Saxon 'was reputed to be the only man beside the Chancellor who could be trusted with knowledge of the contents of the Budget'. Promotion was turned down, however, because it would mean moving to another office and losing the pleasant view from his window.[78]

For all his set ways and love of routine, Saxon could sometimes break out of character, as he did at Asheham in 1917. On his occasional weekends at Ham Spray, Lytton's country house, he would normally read or sleep under a tree, but he was also available for more offbeat entertainments. During one weekend in August 1929 he found himself surrounded by comparative youngsters (Lytton was absent), including Carrington, Rachel and Dermot MacCarthy (son and daughter of Molly and Desmond), Frances Marshall (later Partridge) and Beakus (Bernard) Penrose, who had brought a cine camera. Not content with the usual home movie, they devoted Saturday night and Sunday morning to planning a theatrical performance and organizing costumes and props. The result was a ten-minute film, 'Dr Turner's Mental Home', starring Saxon in the leading role, loosely inspired by his own father. 'Of course I forgot that Saxon's father kept a "Home",' Carrington wrote to Lytton, 'but I am sure Saxon didn't mind the coincidence.'[79] Rachel played Daisy the nurse, and the others were 'lunatics' in Dr Turner's asylum. Like a deranged Prospero, the evil doctor carried out medical experiments on the lunatics; the climax of the story was the drowning of poor 'Daisy' in the bath. Saxon, who seemed to enjoy the escapade and was applauded for his sinister grimaces, dashed off his final scenes on the Monday morning before catching the train to work.[80]

It was part of Saxon's idiosyncratic nature that, although approaching his half-century and by no means an extrovert, he more than held his own among his younger friends. In fact they often brought out his best qualities. Lytton found his old friend rather tedious company, and Saxon would often go to Tidmarsh or Ham Spray to see Carrington. Like Virginia she was charmed by Saxon's eccentricities and wrote to Barbara about how lively and amusing he was. Frances Marshall was equally appreciative of Saxon and his ways and devoted several pages of her now-famous diary to him over the years. In February 1928 she went to tea with him and marvelled at the number of esoteric but quite useless books that filled his rooms. She tried to persuade him to get rid of a few:

> 'Saxon, you must really sell some of your books,' I said.
> 'Hm – yes – hm – perhaps. I think there are one or two I could do without – possibly. There's a treatise here on ophthalmia. I *think* I can do without that.'[81]

By the mid 1940s Saxon was living in a flat at 28 Percy Street. Barbara and Nick had separated temporarily, and Barbara became very friendly with Clive Bell, now in his sixties, driving him around and accompanying him on social engagements and holidays. Saxon had retired on a small Treasury pension. Ironically, despite working for so long with government money he had not learned the value of his own and was often hard up after unsuccessful gambling on horse races and the stock market. Vanessa Bell had to lend him money to buy food on at least one occasion. Fortunately his needs were few and his surroundings less important to him than his reading material. He became something of a recluse, only partly through his own choice – Sydney Waterlow, for instance, found him a depressing companion and avoided him: 'Saxon's visits, although they are the fruit of solid affection, are devastatingly without any play of mind. They do actually devastate me.' Surprisingly, perhaps, he found Saxon 'an incredibly powerful character'.[82]

Saxon was sure to receive a warm welcome from Frances and Ralph Partridge at Ham Spray where he continued to spend his holidays.[83] If he was lucky Barbara would be staying at the same time. Frances made sure Lytton's old friend and sponsor was treated royally. Even during the war she would feed him grouse and open a bottle of vintage wine in his honour. In her diary she drew a loving character portrait of him, beginning with a typical encounter in a Ham Spray corridor:

> The first sight one catches of him in the morning is a stately figure in a once-good but now indescribably dilapidated dressing-gown over pyjamas to match, parading very slowly towards the bathroom with his false teeth in a tumbler of water held somehow rather defiantly in front of him. Unable to greet one in speech, he gives an emphatic nod. He comes down to breakfast in a prehistoric black suit (no doubt made by a first-rate tailor) and a royal blue shirt – or in summer an extremely well-cut white silk Palm Beach one frayed at the edges. Black button boots, a volume of Pindar in the original under his arm, slow but elegant movements and a face beautifully cut out of old ivory, long periods of complete silence broken by moments of sudden animation with a faint rose-petal flush appearing on his pale cheeks – all these are important elements, but nothing can add a final touch to the portrait of this lovable, exasperating, and (I'm convinced) deeply affectionate man.[84]

When he was not at Ham Spray the Partridges worried about his vulnerability to German bombs, since he lived in the centre of London. Saxon seemed unconcerned about the danger, but he was not impervious to it. While at Ham Spray in September 1940 he decided it was time to make his will; the following month bombs killed two of his Treasury friends. In July 1944 he arrived at Ham Spray grimy from a doodle-bug which had blown out the windows of his flat. On his departure Ralph thought he seemed 'the loneliest man in the world'.[85]

By 1949 Saxon's horse-racing losses had left him little money, and he had never been very good at taking care of himself. He reported to Frances Partridge that he ate bread and jam for breakfast, missed out lunch and tea and dined off bread and cheese; consequently his fragile health suffered.[86] Occasionally he would dine at his club, or the ever-sociable Clive would come to his rescue. (Naturally there were no hard feelings regarding Clive's purloining of Barbara.) A letter Saxon wrote to Clive in June 1948 gives a poignant picture of his loneliness:

As one gets older and one's friends fewer one values more meetings with old friends and kindnesses at their hands. It was therefore very pleasant to be asked out by you and to have some talk with you, especially as I had been feeling rather depressed.[87]

Clive was kind, but the Bagenals were like the family Saxon never had. Barbara took a flat over a Cypriot grocery shop on the other side of Percy Street, and Saxon grew friendly with her three children, Judith, Michael and Timothy, and their families. Michael's wife Alison accompanied Saxon to two of Wagner's operas in London in the late 1940s – she found it hard to enjoy them but was touched by his kindness. Afterwards he insisted on walking her to the door of Barbara's flat, where she was staying. 'Saxon would kindly toil up the stairs with me. Once he stopped and said that Wagner's music was his favourite of all music. Then he continued to climb upward.' She was aware that he wrote piano works himself but never heard him play, even though she and Michael shared Saxon's passion for music and owned a piano which was 'quite respectable'. When the couple later moved to Dorset he went to stay with them and was godfather to their daughter.[88] Barbara kept them in touch with Saxon's activities, which occasionally demonstrated that he was becoming even more eccentric in old age. For a long while he put up with the rather unsatisfactory services of a housekeeper-cum-cleaning-lady. Barbara, exasperated, eventually asked him why he didn't find another and received the brief and ambiguous reply, 'Because I like walking about naked.'[89] Judith's daughter Vanessa recalled Saxon as a kindly but somewhat distant figure, distributing Pierre Gourmand lollipops. His flat was crowded with furniture, pipes and chess sets, and two identical farmyard scenes adorned the walls, just as Leonard Woolf remembered.[90]

But his health was deteriorating, and in 1955, in his mid seventies, Saxon went into a house for the elderly in Hendon where he could be looked after but still retain his independence. He left his Percy Street flat to Duncan and Vanessa, who transformed his rooms into a suitable venue for Memoir Club meetings and used the flat as their London base. When in 1958 Barbara and Nick separated for good, Saxon was in no position to take advantage of the situation; besides, he still had to share her with Clive. By this time both were old men with health problems, and Saxon had been suffering from Alzheimer's disease for some time. Visiting him in hospital, Barbara's granddaughter, although only a young girl, wondered sadly what was the point of keeping alive this sick old man with his papery yellow skin who seemed unlikely to recover.[91] Frances Partridge had similar thoughts when she went with Barbara to see Saxon in hospital in October 1961. Possibly as the result of a stroke, he had a paralysed arm and was unable to speak articulately. Despite his incapacities Saxon, undemanding as ever, seemed happy enough, but to Frances (who had the year before lost Ralph to heart disease) his physical decline was a tragic sight.

> But oh, the sadness of seeing this poor old man, all his dignity gone but his delicate ivory beauty remaining, with his paralysed arm folded on his breast like the broken wing of a bird, his mumbling words, his abandoned coughs and sighs, and the look of sensitive intelligence coming from his bright eyes. Then I began to understand that he wasn't really unhappy, because for long years he has wanted but little here below and that mostly attention; and he gets that from the pretty little Malay nurses who peer into his white face with their velvet eyes.[92]

A year later, on 4 November 1962, Saxon died at the age of eighty-two, with Barbara at his side until the end. Many of his old friends were dead. Virginia and Lytton had predeceased him by two and three decades respectively, Desmond and Molly MacCarthy by one decade, Vanessa by only nineteen months. Clive and Leonard were still alive to mourn their old friend, although Clive had been far from well and was recovering from treatment for cancer.

Saxon certainly did not think of himself as a tragic figure, but many of his friends lamented his unfulfilled potential. He inspired amusement with his peculiarities, frustration with his passive nature and pity with his lack of family ties. But in a few close friends he inspired an undying affection. He achieved nothing that would have merited a *Times* obituary, but on 13 November the paper published an appreciation written by Leonard, headed 'Mr Saxon Sydney-Turner – The Bloomsbury Group'. Seeing Saxon's death ignored by the press, Leonard made this gallant attempt to bring his passing to public notice by linking his name with the more well-known ones of Lytton Strachey and Maynard Keynes. Saxon was not a major player in any particular discipline, declared Leonard, but would be remembered with 'amused affection' by friends and colleagues as 'an eccentric in the best English tradition'; 'a remarkable man and a strange character' who had 'an extraordinarily supple, subtle, and enigmatic mind'.[93] It was fitting that the last word should go to his oldest friend.

'I Was Right to Be in Love with Him':
Lytton Strachey

ETIOLATED, SPINSTERISH, HYPOCHONDRIACAL, waspish, witty, elegant, brilliant – Lytton Strachey was all of these. More than any of Virginia's suitors, save Rupert Brooke, Lytton strove to maintain a reputation built on a carefully constructed persona as well as literary output. At Cambridge he was famous for languishing in his rooms in a dressing-gown, gesticulating effeminately and talking with the high-pitched 'Strachey voice'. He made no secret of his crushes on young and handsome boys, stars of the rowing club or the rugby field. His intelligence was legendary. Virginia learned from Thoby that this strange and exotic creature was the acme of culture and wit and that the Cambridge academics flocked to hear to him talk. 'Whatever they give you, Strachey... it won't be good enough,' he was once told before an examination.[1] Lytton had a sensitivity and discrimination that matched Virginia's. Both found the other the ideal conversational partner, and they had many traits in common: the tendency to exaggerate; the sharp, critical tongue; the confidence in their own powers leavened by an occasional lack of self-esteem.

Giles Lytton Strachey was born at Stowey House in Clapham, south London, on 1 March 1880, the eighth surviving child of Sir Richard and Lady Jane Strachey. The Stracheys exceeded even the Stephen/Duckworth family in their sheer numbers: the siblings, in order of birth, were Elinor, Richard (Dick), Dorothy, Ralph, Philippa (Pippa), Oliver, Pernel, Lytton, Marjorie and James.[2] Lady Jane gave birth to her first child at nineteen and her last at forty-seven, so there was a span between eldest and youngest of nearly thirty years. Sir Richard was a generation older than his wife and the age of a grandfather to all of his children. He was forty-two when his eldest child, Elinor, was born and seventy by the time his family was completed with the birth of James. In the India of the 1870s Richard and his favourite brother John had been a formidable pair of senior administrators, nicknamed the 'Strachey Raj'.[3] Many of their ideas were as unpopular as they were innovative, but schemes that were initially rejected were often put into practice later on. On settling back in England Richard remained an indefatigable worker, remaining chair of the East India Railway almost to the end of his long life. But not for worldly rewards: a knighthood had to be bestowed without his permission after he had refused it five times.[4] Lytton knew his father chiefly as a remote but benevolent patriarch, the quiet centre of a noisy family. When he died aged ninety in 1908 Lytton was still in his twenties.

Jane Maria Grant was Richard's second wife, the first having died after only a year of marriage. She was the first cousin of John Strachey's wife and was in India with her father, the head of the Department of Public Works in which Richard was under-secretary. When they met in 1858 she was eighteen and he forty-one. They made an incongruous pair: he was small and dark, she was fair and several inches taller. Although no great beauty, her intelligence, wit and common sense gave her a more substantial appeal. Richard's choice of wisdom over a pretty face stood him in good stead: Janie proved to be a great support throughout his career, whether he needed her gift of expression for official documents or her organizational skills in raising and educating their large family.[5] Jane was a passionate reader of English and French literature, numbering among her friends Robert Browning and George Eliot (Eliot's partner G.H. Lewes was reminded of Jane by *Middlemarch*'s Dorothea), and passed her love of reading to all her children. She was also a dedicated supporter of the Suffragist cause. Her daughter Pippa later became secretary of the Fawcett Society (Millicent Fawcett had been a great friend of Lady Strachey) and helped to organize the first large-scale women's suffrage procession in February 1907.[6] Both Janie and Richard were confirmed agnostics, and the Strachey children learned to test commonly accepted ideas against their own scepticism.

In this highly cultured family Lytton was encouraged to read from a young age and was soon writing poetry – a habit that never left him – and taking lessons in French. When he was twelve years old a tutor advised his parents that Lytton was a remarkable boy with a highly original mind who should merely be guided rather than forced into a the usual mould. This perceptive man even predicted that Lytton would become a writer with an unusual style.[7] Like Virginia Lytton practised his future art in a family magazine, the *Comet*, for which he and his cousin Pat wrote stories and verses, drew illustrations and created the word puzzles that were so popular in the Strachey family. In 1893 he was sent to Abbotsholme, a precursor of Bedales, whose rigorous regime of cold baths reduced Lytton to a fever within days. He was invalided home after only a few months and moved to Leamington College, which made fewer demands on Lytton's physique. A tall, awkward and unathletic boy, Lytton still suffered from verbal and physical bullying, his skinny build earning him the nickname of 'Scraggs'.[8] But things improved: he showed an early propensity for drama; he did well in examinations (despite frequent absences owing to illness); and in 1895 he was made head of house.

Before going up to university the precocious Lytton spent two years at Liverpool University College. Here his interest in Elizabethan poetry, stirred by his mother, was fortified by the English professor Walter Raleigh, a relative by marriage.[9] This aside, Lytton considered his time at Liverpool very dull. But his mind was ever-active – observing, questioning, criticizing – and, as a diary entry of 3 March 1898 shows, was tending along the same lines as Virginia's, creating imaginary lives for people he met in the street. Shocked that morning to see a debilitating change in an old man who had seemed lively and happy the day before, Lytton invents a spiritual crisis for the stranger. Observation ceases; imagination takes over: 'Today a storm broke upon him; he was wracked by the infinite and the inevitable; his spirit heaved amidst a sea of doubts and terrors; he was overwhelmed.'[10] Lytton's taste for *Sturm und Drang* was already becoming evident.

Lytton spent the summer in France improving his French and then prepared for an Oxford scholarship examination. But he felt a closer affinity with Cambridge, following a short visit there with Walter Raleigh during which he met family friends, saw his sister Pernel, who was at Newnham College, and had dinner with the Principal of Newnham, Virginia's cousin Katharine Stephen. Fortunately, in the light of his future development, he failed the entrance examination for Oxford's Balliol College, breeder of highly competent civil servants, and went instead to study history at Cambridge's more congenial Trinity College, where he started his memorable student career on the last day of September 1899.

Most of Lytton's fellow undergraduates, startled by his elongated form, his penetrating voice and his particular way of doing quite ordinary things, did not quite know what to make of him. Nevertheless he quickly made friends who valued his eccentricity: Leonard Woolf, who would become his particular friend; Thoby Stephen, whom he idolized mainly for his physical attributes; the enigmatic Saxon Sydney-Turner; and the worldly and urbane Clive Bell. In this new environment Lytton blossomed into a more confident and contented being. History studies, however, occupied a fairly low place in his list of priorities. Like many intellectually curious undergraduates extra-curricular activities absorbed much of his time. He was a member of several literary societies including Clive Bell's Midnight Society, the weekly Sunday Essay Society and a play-reading club. He was elected to the Apostles in February 1902 and by October had brought Leonard Woolf and Saxon Sydney-Turner on board. Most of these college societies required that members prepared occasional papers to be read to the gathering; all of them required rigorous thinking and a taste for debate. In these two particulars, Lytton excelled. At last he was in company where he could parade his unorthodox opinions and his mordant (and increasingly suggestive) wit.

Lytton had known since his school days that men exerted a stronger attraction for him than women. At Cambridge this was common; there was no reason to hide his proclivities. One of his early infatuations was with the charming but unpredictable J.T. (Jack) Sheppard. For two years Jack was Strachey's intimate friend, but Lytton's attempts to shape him into a more perfect being failed, and by 1904 the glamour was wearing off. In the meantime Lytton had lost one friend and gained another – Leonard Woolf had left to be an administrator in Ceylon, but the brilliant Maynard Keynes had been elected to the Apostles. Before long Maynard had replaced both Jack and Leonard in Lytton's affections. But this new friendship was to be severely tested in the coming years.

Although Lytton expected to do well in the history tripos in June 1903, he managed only a second-class degree. Without much enthusiasm he decided that his best option was to stay on at Cambridge for another year, preparing a dissertation in the hope of winning a fellowship. His subject was Warren Hastings, the first Governor General of the East India Company, chosen because of the Strachey family connection with India. Unfortunately his subject and its handling were considered insufficiently original, and his fellowship applications were rejected two years in a row.

Lytton had been more successful in building a reputation. He was regarded as a second Oscar Wilde: decadent and effeminate, with dangerous and heretical opinions. One of Leonard's friends had deplored Lytton's atheistic influence to the extent that he had sacrificed Leonard's friendship.[11] Lytton rather enjoyed creating such a rumpus. Cambridge had given his life purpose and structure, allowing him to showcase his intellect and wit for the admiration of those he himself admired. He was loath to leave a place where so much attention was paid to him. He and Maynard were now leading lights of the Apostles. Devotees of G.E. Moore, they espoused his theory of the supreme value of human relations, ushering in to the meetings frankness about sexual desire – especially homosexual desire – while practising what they preached. Unfortunately, both sought to practise on freshman Arthur Hobhouse, the subject of their first rivalry. In this case, as in others, Lytton was the loser. They clashed again, more seriously, over Lytton's cousin, the vague but charming artist Duncan Grant. The outcome of this affair was one of the chief causes of the depression that led Lytton temporarily to reject his homosexuality and propose to Virginia.

Duncan had dominated Lytton's romantic thoughts since the summer of 1905, but he was an elusive lover and the affair was far from plain sailing. Lytton was tossed this way and that by his conflicting emotions; now bullying, now conciliatory. In late 1907, frustrated by being fobbed off with weak excuses, he wrote to Duncan of his 'hardness' and 'indifference': 'You reduce me to such despair that I can say nothing, and you exasperate me too . . . I was enraged. I don't like being treated as if I was a fool.'[12] The next day he was abject, assuring Duncan: 'You're the kindest person in the world.'[13] 'It's not you that's the cause,' he wrote a week later.

> I have a devil inside me – perhaps seven. I occasionally feel that I'm done for, & that I really should smash up, and "go under", as they say, like a decadent poet . . . I have visions of perfect love which drown me in lakes of ecstasy. Visions for evermore.[14]

On 12 February 1908 Sir Richard Strachey died. Lytton was saddened rather than distraught: his father's death at ninety cannot have been entirely unexpected, and he had always been a rather distant figure. But it was a bad beginning to a year that got steadily worse. In July Lytton found another use for his black-bordered writing paper when he found out that Duncan Grant was having an affair with Maynard Keynes. He had introduced them in late 1905, keen to have his closest friends meet and like one another. Their affair was a bitter blow that deprived Lytton of two friends at once and revived memories of the theft of Hobhouse. His feelings of betrayal were exacerbated by the recognition that Maynard had been falling in love while Lytton had been confessing his own tumultuous feelings for Duncan. To rub salt in the wound, Keynes's career had taken a turn for the better. While Lytton had twice failed to win a fellowship, Keynes not only had an academic post – he had become a don at King's College in June 1908 – but he had Lytton's lover, too.

All three tried to take a 'Bloomsbury' attitude to the situation in order to preserve their friendship, but for Lytton it was naturally more difficult, and his jealousy and resentment periodically surfaced: 'He [Maynard] will tell you, no doubt, that I am wrong, that I am foolish because I am jealous, and that I am to be pitied because I am in love,' he wrote to Duncan shortly after his unpleasant discovery.[15] He wrote to Maynard the same day, on the black-bordered mourning paper, advising him not to call round. Maynard, uncertain what tack to take until he knew the nature of Lytton's reaction, asked Lytton not to hate him.[16] Summoning up all his reserves of forgiveness and tolerance, the latter presented a front of noble suffering:

> I only know that we've been friends for too long to stop being friends now ... I
> ... don't hate you ... if you were here now I should probably kiss you, except
> that then Duncan would be jealous, which would never do![17]

He sent Maynard a present of some expensively bound books and offered to fund art tuition for Duncan, for whom he was, if not exactly content to wait until the affair spent itself, at least prepared to do so:

> [T]hough I like Maynard, I cannot think of him as you do, or else, I suppose, I
> should be in love with him too! The result is that I don't take your affair as
> seriously as you do either, and therefore imagine that you will some day or other
> return from Cythera.[18]

As 1909 dawned Lytton sought sanctuary from this atmosphere of intrigue and betrayal. He yearned for an escape from homosexual yearnings that seemed always to result in disappointment or loss. His havens during the tempests of 1908 had been Virginia and Vanessa Stephen, and he turned to them now in his distress and loneliness. Virginia's sharp wit and feeling for literature made her an especially attractive companion. She was more than a match for him intellectually and – it seemed to him – had none of the usual feminine vanities and foibles. Perhaps most importantly she did not pose a sexual threat in the way Vanessa did.

Before Virginia met Lytton she had heard tales of 'the Strache' from her brother Thoby: that he was destined to be a great poet, dashed off sonnets and imagined that he heard the music of the spheres.[19] They first met either in Cambridge, or in Lyndhurst, Hampshire, where both the Strachey and Stephen families were spending the summer of 1901. Virginia did not record her early impressions but Lytton's were of a family headed by an old man, like his own, and including two very attractive daughters.[20] In 1905 both families spent a weekend with the Douglas Freshfields at Forest Row in Sussex. Again Lytton seems to have been more impressed with Virginia than she with him; he was glad to have someone of equal sensibility to share his feeling that the opulence of the Freshfield house, stuffed with valuable antiques and carpets, was rather crushing.[21]

The following year saw the catastrophic death of Thoby Stephen, which was a great blow to all his friends as well as his family. He had been a young man of exceptional promise and his loss seemed senseless and bewildering. It was Lytton's task to convey the news to Leonard Woolf in Ceylon – to both men the death of their hero was a source of bafflement and depression. If there was a silver lining to the disaster, it was that, like Saxon, Lytton grew closer to the remaining Stephens in their collective grief. Virginia would remain a lifelong friend to those who had known and loved her brother best.

The first letter that survives from Virginia to Lytton is a short and formal invitation to 46 Gordon Square dated two days after the death of Thoby. It was during this visit, on 25 November 1906, that Lytton suggested that they use first names.[22] The friendship began in earnest, and Clive Bell's Play Reading Society did much to further the intimacy of the Bloomsbury friends, introducing a more sexually explicit atmosphere at Gordon Square. Lytton and Virginia's first substantial correspondence was during Virginia's holiday in St Ives in the spring of 1908. By now the two were great friends with much in common – both were literary reviewers with great ambitions but a self-deprecating humour, and they were aware of each other's preferences and able to respond in the same vein to each other's remarks. They were intimate enough for Lytton to confide his first impressions of Rupert Brooke (pretty in a pink-and-yellow sort of way) and for Virginia to convey her impatience with the domesticity of Bell family life. Even at this stage Lytton yearns for some private talk with Virginia, so as to explain why he thinks himself 'a wild man of the woods' (it certainly needed some explaining), and his desire to see more of her is repeatedly expressed in his letters.[23]

By the summer their friendship had brought them to the attention of others. Vanessa's radar was ever sensitive to intimations of matrimony in Virginia's life: 'Did Lytton propose to you this afternoon? . . . I would rather you married him than anyone else,' she wrote to her sister in July.[24] But she also recognized that the match was unlikely. 'I should like Lytton as a brother in law better than anyone I know, but the only way I can perceive of bringing that to pass would be if he were to fall in love with Adrian.'[25] There was no proposal yet, but Lytton had begun to think of Virginia as one of those intimates with whom he would like to flee his present circumstances. He envied what he saw as her simplicity of outlook. Life was full of difficulty and confusion to him, while he imagined Virginia's vision to be clear and untainted, with none of the complications of unrequited passion:

> There are moments – on the Heath, of course, — when I seem to myself to see life steadily and see it whole, but they're only moments; as a rule I can make nothing out. You don't find much difficulty, I think. Is it because you *are* a virgin?[26]

He felt like a caged animal in his bedsit in the family home at Belsize Park Gardens, feeling trapped in body and mind. While he was extremely fond of his family he wanted his independence; but at work as well as at home he was tied to them. (He was a reviewer for his cousin St Loe's periodical, *The Spectator*.) He railed against the restrictions that prevented him having the life he wanted – simple, unthinking, free from anxiety and disastrous love affairs – and suggested to Virginia that they should 'all' flee to the Faroe Islands and live a happy-ever-after life. But since his wallet would not stretch so far as the Faroes he contented himself with a short holiday with Virginia and Adrian at the southern-most point of England, the Lizard in Cornwall. However, Virginia's life was not as simple as Lytton pretended to think it, and he himself was partly to blame. Clive was becoming jealous at their growing closeness, and Virginia was obliged to reassure him: 'You will be glad to hear that I am not in love with [Lytton], nor is there any sign that he is in love with me.'[27] But Lytton was longing to be in love with someone who would think of him first and foremost. Ideally he wanted to be top of Duncan's list; failing that, in a category of his own – anything rather than being thought ordinary.[28] Knowing he did not come first with Duncan he cast around for another soul-mate and found one in Virginia.

For Virginia it was pleasant to have another friend with whom to discuss literary topics, but Lytton was also a potential rival. On the whole, Lytton thought more of Virginia's writing than she did of his. Lytton was not exempted from Virginia's scepticism of graduate verse, voiced privately in her review of *Euphrosyne*.[29] So when Clive rather hyperbolically claimed that Lytton's poems were second only to Catullus and a handful of others, this did not make her think any better of Clive's literary judgement.[30] To Lytton himself she cleverly avoided an actual critique of his work: 'Compliments I know mean nothing to you.' Instead she offers a pen portrait of him as 'an oriental potentate, in a flowered dressing gown'.[31] (The dressing-gown is a garment closely identified with William Rodney in *Night and Day*; see p. 133.) Sensing the appeal to Lytton of imaginative escape from his body and his circumstances, she created for him another flattering *alter ego*, with shades of the future *Orlando*: 'I think of you as a kind of Venetian prince, in sky blue tights, lying on your back in an orchard, or balancing one exquisite leg in the air . . .'[32]

Lytton had an equally colourful imagination, which concerned Virginia. Planning a novel (which never came to fruition) in 1908–9, he described his characters to her: 'My footmen are amazing, and so are my prostitutes. There's a Prime Minister who should be fine, and there's a don's wife à faire mourir de rire.'[33] Virginia made light of Lytton's fecundity but was a little alarmed at his encroachment into her territory. His lack of seriousness compared to her earnestness of purpose is hinted at in her reply. She, who wants to write of real situations and of life through a woman's eyes, has no chance against his more imaginative fictions: 'I wish you would confine your genius to one department,' she complains, although she was later to trespass into his.[34]

Both writers were able to bring into play their considerable imaginative powers for a letter-writing game that began in early 1909 and lasted for only a few exchanges. But under cover of the game Lytton (as Vane Hatherly) was able to hint at the trouble Virginia (as Eleanor Hadyng) was causing between Clive and Vanessa (James and Clarissa Philips): 'To my unaccustomed eye she [Vanessa] seemed to be watching dear James [Clive] more carefully even than usual.'[35] Virginia confirmed his suspicions, although she was careful not to admit her complicity: 'How clever you are, and how unkind! . . . I know its dangerous to imagine people in love with one . . . I am thinking of his face, as he helped me on with my cloak, and said good night.'[36]

Apart from Vanessa's hurt feelings, there was another reason for Lytton to discourage Virginia's intimacy with Clive. He was trying to matchmake between Virginia and Leonard Woolf, his closest friend, whom he believed the only man (apart from himself) to deserve her. Lytton and Leonard greatly admired the Stephen sisters – 'It was almost impossible for a man not to fall in love with them,' Leonard wrote – and both had been aghast when Clive Bell secured Vanessa in marriage.[37] Clive's place in their circle at Cambridge had been chiefly due to his friendship with Thoby Stephen, but Lytton and Leonard had grave doubts about his intellect. (See pp. 74–6 for more on attitudes towards Clive Bell and his marriage to Vanessa Stephen.)

Lytton began to encourage Leonard to marry Virginia from late 1908, hinting that if Clive could secure one of the sisters almost anything could happen. His enthusiasm was infectious. Soon Leonard, who had hardly known Virginia before his departure for Ceylon, was dreaming of making her his wife, seeing her as a saviour and his only possibility of happiness. But he did not act on his impetuous thoughts, despairing both of his life in Ceylon and any life he would have in England. Even though he had carved out a highly successful career in the East, he would be viewed as a failure at home – such was his reasoning. Virginia began to embody the spirit of hope for him. He joked to Lytton: 'Do you think Virginia would have me? Wire to me if she accepts. I'll take the next boat home.'[38] Then there was an unexpected twist. By the time Leonard's mock proposal reached England, nearly three weeks later, Lytton had proposed to Virginia himself. Evidently he had decided that the chance of Leonard returning home was slim (he surmised correctly – it was over two years before Leonard took the plunge and left Ceylon) and that Virginia was too 'astounding' to be allowed to escape. Apart from his evident intellectual attraction to Virginia and depression about his homosexuality, Lytton was also motivated by the thought that he was making a stand against Clive's annexation of both sisters.

Lytton made his proposal to Virginia at Fitzroy Square on the afternoon of Sunday, 17 February 1909 while dejected and recovering from a cold. It was an informal, low-key business, born of desperation. But whether he realized it or not, Virginia had been wondering whether she would ever find a husband, and their close friendship may have convinced her for a few brief moments that marriage was a possibility. Virginia's acceptance took Lytton by surprise, and he saw immediately that he could not renounce his homosexuality so easily.

Although intellectually she was his perfect partner, physically she was undeniably female. He feared her kisses in the same moment he was appreciating her magnificence. As they continued their conversation, both came to terms with the impracticability of the plan and agreed to back out of their hasty agreement. The episode left Lytton emotionally exhausted, but once home he wrote a short note to re-establish the *status quo*: 'whatever happens, as you said, the important thing is that we should like each other: and we can neither of us have any doubt that we do'.[39]

For a homosexual who never really doubted his homosexuality, proposing to a heterosexual (or at least virginal) woman may seem an odd decision, but during a time when homosexuality was a criminal offence, and would remain so for nearly sixty years, it was not an unusual one. Knowing that a permanent and socially acceptable relationship was unlikely to result, many gay men and women suppressed their natural instincts and married for companionship, children and – occasionally – an alibi. Even within Bloomsbury marriage was the rule rather than the exception. Maynard Keynes, James Strachey, David Garnett, Adrian Stephen and Gerald Shove all had homosexual affairs as young men and later married. Lytton and Duncan Grant maintained long-term and loving (but on the whole sex-free) liaisons with women that proved to be the most important relationships of their lives.

Virginia and Lytton were in some ways ideal companions. They were intellectually well matched, with a shared interest in literature and a desire to write. There was their lack of heterosexual desire; teamed with Lytton's need to adore and Virginia's to be adored. Although Virginia acknowledged that their marriage would have been a 'bloodless alliance', she asserted 'I was right to be in love with him 12 or 15 years ago.'[40] But there were also grave incompatibilities: Lytton was not by nature monogamous and his interest in young men was as intense as ever. Both he and Virginia were frequently ill, but neither was good with invalids. Two such hypersensitive individuals in close proximity would have caused one another serious problems. Observing Lytton's behaviour with subsequent lovers, Virginia remarked on the emotional restrictions he would have enforced on her: 'If I'd married him . . . I should have found him querulous. He would have laid too many ties on one, & repined a little if one had broken free.'[41] There was great affection but no passion between them, and in her late forties, looking back on *Orlando* and *A Room of One's Own* and in the middle of writing *The Waves*, Virginia realized that Lytton's demanding presence, like her father's, would have ended her writing career before it had properly begun: 'Had I married Lytton I should never have written anything . . . He checks & inhibits in the most curious way.'[42] (Was it partly the presence of a rival that she found inhibiting?) Fortunately both acquired devoted lovers who were prepared to nurse them through illness, admire their brilliance and take second place to their egos.

Meanwhile Lytton had some explaining to do. With linguistic acrobatics he managed the uncommon feat of commending Virginia to Leonard as a fine wife, while telling him in the same letter of his own proposal and subsequent retraction. The reason he gave Leonard was that he had come to a turning point in his life when Something Had to Be Done:

> I was brought to it by the horror of my present wobble and the imagination of the paradise of married peace. It just needed the *fact* of the prospect to show me that there simply isn't any alternative to the horror, that I must face it, and somehow get through or die.[43]

Encouraging Leonard to stick to his guns, he claimed to have asked Vanessa to relay his friend's proposal to Virginia; and, as if to prove to Leonard that he was not having second thoughts about his homosexuality, he revealed in the same letter that he had 'copulated' with Duncan that very afternoon.[44]

To his brother James he confessed his folly a few weeks later, stressing its secrecy:

> On Feb. 19th [17th] I proposed to Virginia, and was accepted. It was an awkward moment, as you may imagine, especially as I realised, the very minute it was happening, that the whole thing was repulsive to me. Her sense was amazing, and luckily it turned out that she's not in love. The result was that I was able to manage a fairly honourable retreat.[45]

After the proposal Lytton and Virginia reached a mutual understanding, and little appeared to have changed – the gossipy teas and scurrilous letters continued unabated. Lytton wrote to his sister Dorothy a week after his proposal that apart from Duncan 'the people I see and like most are two women – viz. Vanessa and Virginia, with neither of whom I'm in love (and vice versa)'.[46] He was still casting around for a way of keeping Virginia within their circle and had not given up hope of Leonard's return. He renewed his coaxing in May and again in August, representing her as a miraculous, wild and impetuous creature yearning for love and waiting to be swept away by it.[47]

But later that year a peculiar and puzzling episode occurred that threatened his plans for Virginia's future. James Strachey brought gossip of Virginia's advances towards their sister Marjorie, much elaborated but with perhaps a grain of truth. Marjorie told Duncan that Virginia had confided a secret to her which she might now regret, as they had since fallen out. Duncan speculated that Virginia's secret was that she was in love with him, and James encouraged him to propose.[48] Was this a joke on James's part? James, like Virginia, was prone to exaggeration. It was a story easily verifiable by Lytton as it involved his sister and two close friends, but he was content to take James at his word, although he was alarmed by the thought of a marriage between Virginia and Duncan. Thinking of his own aborted proposal, he warned James that anything of the kind would be a grave mistake for both parties. Duncan was unpredictable enough to propose, although Virginia would probably refuse. In his opinion, he added, the 'secret' was probably a proposal from Hilton Young, who had been courting Virginia.[49]

Lytton must have been disappointed with the inefficacy of his matchmaking, but eventually his persistence was rewarded. When Leonard came back to England on leave in June 1911 he was already seriously thinking of Virginia as a possible wife, thanks, largely, to Lytton's persistence. The story of the courtship, Leonard's proposal, Virginia's prevarication and her eventual acceptance is well known. Lytton, as his oldest and closest friend, was the first person Leonard told of their engagement. Lytton replied joyously: 'It is magnificent. I am very happy; and je t'aime beaucoup.'[50]

Finally his desire had been realized after nearly four years of persuasion. His favourite woman had married his closest male friend. Had he not encouraged the match, would Leonard have thought of it himself? Probably. He had been slightly in love with Virginia and Vanessa on first meeting them, but at the time he left for Ceylon had met Virginia only two or three times. When he returned it must have been obvious to many of their friends that they would be well matched, but it was Lytton who made Leonard believe that there was something – someone – worth coming home for.

Even when on honeymoon, Virginia kept up a lively correspondence with Lytton, describing with comic and vivid precision the filthy WC, attacks by mosquitoes, their reading matter and how she imagines Lytton to be spending his time. For his titillation she adds a striking and lyrical image of their Mediterranean paradise: 'the naked boys run like snipe along the beach, balancing their buttocks in the pellucid air'.[51] The letter-writing styles of Virginia and Lytton had much in common, including an addiction to indiscretion and exaggeration, a waspish and malicious streak, the occasional bout of ironic self-dramatization or exasperated self-deprecation, the inventive flights, the picturesque – and the grotesque – imagery and the sheer gusto. They would save up titbits of gossip and observation, confident that the other was the perfect audience. Of their correspondence those closest to them said that

> each was a little wary of the other: in writing to each other they were always on
> their best behaviour, and never felt so much at ease as they did in their dealings
> with people whom they admired and respected less.[52]

The phrase 'best behaviour' should not be confused with 'good behaviour' – Lytton and Virginia were often mischievous and rumour-mongering as well as witty and fantastic, a couple of peacocks preening their own feathers for the other's admiration.

Although the marriage of the two prima donnas would probably have proved disastrous, the friendship blossomed. Lytton continued to be frank about his feelings towards Virginia after she was married (perhaps even more so, since his motives could not now be misconstrued). After the disappointment of a meeting cut short, he wrote with simple affection and perhaps a twinge of regret: 'I saw you for such a short time the other day: it was tantalizing. I should like to see you every day for hours. I have always wanted to. Why is it impossible?'[53] Virginia was his favourite companion when he wanted conversation that was amusing, indiscreet, imaginative, fascinating and on the whole sympathetic to his point of view. Clive Bell remembered Lytton's tribute to the inspiring effect of Virginia's presence. During a rainy, murky winter afternoon he asked Clive: 'Loves apart, whom would you most like to see coming up the drive?' and after a moment answered his own question, 'Virginia of course.'[54]

Since his time at Cambridge, Lytton had been aware that he was a 'figure', and in 1905 it had struck him that more facial hair might enhance his dignity and reputation. But it was not until 1911 that he began to cultivate a beard. By 1912 the beard was already long enough to be a striking feature. The caricaturist and writer Max Beerbohm first saw Lytton at this time and described his appearance:

an emaciated face of ivory whiteness, above a long square-cut auburn beard, and below a head of very long sleek dark brown hair. The nose was nothing if not aquiline, and Nature had chiselled it with great delicacy. The eyes, behind a pair of gold-rimmed spectacles, eyes of an inquirer and a cogitator, were large and brown and luminous.[55]

Punning on his membership of the Apostles, Beerbohm said that the sceptical Lytton must be Doubting Thomas. To his disappointment he was not introduced to Lytton until 1917, when he was 'impressed by his mild dignity and benign good manners'.[56] Others, too, noticed Lytton's singular physique. His biographer Cyril Clemens, a third cousin of Mark Twain, described him thus: 'aside from his red beard with a curious rufous tinge, he was an extraordinary figure; fairly tall, his excessive thinness, almost emaciation, caused him to appear endless'.[57] Lytton's attenuated frame and high-pitched voice may be accounted for by a genetic condition called Marfan syndrome, suggests Michael Holroyd in his substantial biography.[58] This little-known condition, discovered and elucidated in 1896 by the French paediatrician Antoine Bernard-Jean Marfan (1858–1942), affects one in 5,000 of the population and is manifested in the connective tissues. It is sometimes called 'arachnodactyly', after the long fingers and toes (or 'spidery digits') common in sufferers, who tend to be lanky and long-limbed. Those with Marfan syndrome often have a narrow jaw and high palate (affecting the voice), myopia, a weak heart, a malformed spine, joints liable to injury, poor muscle development and a generally weak constitution. The condition is spread fairly evenly across populations but is more common in children of elderly fathers (Sir Richard was sixty-two when Lytton was born). Although this view detracts a little from his enigmatic standing, Lytton's much remarked-upon physique and voice may have been 'symptoms' of the syndrome.[59]

At the end of 1912 Lytton, inspired by the success of his first full-length book, *Landmarks in French Literature*, sought a country retreat where he could retire from London society and write. He toured Berkshire and Wiltshire with Hilton Young, whose cottage, The Lacket, was near Marlborough. Lytton was very friendly with Hilton during this period, finding him kind, dependable and rock-like. After failing to buy a cottage or land, he decided to take Hilton up on his offer to let The Lacket to him, despite his reservations about the colour scheme. Previously he had fantasized about redecorating in orange and magenta (this was his Augustus John period), but after months of fruitless searching the cottage looked increasingly attractive, even without the makeover.

Lytton lived at The Lacket from October 1913 to September 1915. Soon after taking up residence he wrote in hyperbolic rapture to Duncan Grant about the peacefulness and the luxury of his surroundings.[60] But peace was a temporary pleasure, and despite his pose as a solitary he feared loneliness. At weekends he would go to London or invite guests: James, Marjorie, Pippa and Pernel Strachey, Vanessa and Clive Bell, Duncan Grant, Desmond MacCarthy, Maynard Keynes, Noel and Daphne Olivier, or his great crush, Henry Lamb (who once had to nurse Lytton through influenza, to the mortification of both). Occasionally Hilton Young would come as a guest to his own cottage, and Virginia and Leonard spent a weekend there from 5 to 8 December 1914. Virginia deplored the interior decoration and the contents of the bookshelves but was very fond of the Wiltshire countryside. [61] The Lacket witnessed several notable incidents during Lytton's tenancy. At Christmas 1914 there was the first meeting of Duncan Grant and Bunny Garnett, destined to become lovers (Bunny later claimed it was Lytton's tale of youthful sexual exploration, *Ermyntrude and Esmeralda*, that inspired him to bed Duncan) and – much later – in-laws; as well as the proposal by the separated but undivorced politician Josiah Wedgwood to Lytton's besotted sister Marjorie. (Hearing of the latter brought back to Virginia memories of her own proposal from Sydney Waterlow in 1911.) But the greatest event of Lytton's time at The Lacket was the completion of the Cardinal Manning and Florence Nightingale sections of the work that would seal his reputation, *Eminent Victorians*.

Shortly after he had left The Lacket and resumed his London life Lytton met someone who would transform his life. It was the winter of 1915. This individual was not a beautiful young man, as he might have expected, but a moderately attractive young woman, with thick fair hair cut in a bob, china-blue eyes and a tomboyish way of dressing. She was Dora Carrington, a Slade painter who had been invited with her friend Barbara Hiles to Asheham by Vanessa and Clive Bell; Lytton, Duncan and Mary Hutchinson were the other guests. Carrington liked Duncan, as almost everyone who met him did, but Lytton she found rather repellent. He tried to kiss her while they walked on the downs together, and she pulled away in disgust. He seemed to her tremendously old (he was thirty-five to her twenty-two), and even when the more worldly Barbara tried to explain homosexuality to her it did not improve matters. Carrington's indignation led to an incident that has become legendary in the annals of Bloomsbury. Before dawn the next day she went into Lytton's room with a pair of scissors, intending to cut off his beloved beard; after all, it was an outward sign of the male authority by which he had pressed his unwanted attentions on her. But, blow for feminism or not, all such intentions were adandoned when he opened his eyes and – the story goes – she was transfixed with love at his gaze.[62] His awakening prevented her from the drastic act, although whether from love or embarrassment it is not possible to be sure.

In the months that followed Lytton often saw Carrington at Garsington Manor, Ottoline Morrell's house in Oxfordshire. They struck up a teacher–pupil relationship, with Lytton recommending books and advising Carrington to study French. Subterfuge soon became necessary to avoid both the prurience of Bloomsbury and the possessive jealousy of the painter Mark Gertler, who had been in love (and lust) with Carrington for several years and counted Lytton as a friend who would help secure her. Eventually Gertler's friendship was sacrificed by both of them.

Lytton was apprehensive about Bloomsbury's attitude to Carrington and rather ungenerously played down their relationship. His old friends found it difficult to adjust to a new, younger person in his life. In the past his lovers had been passing (although passionate) fancies, usually unrequited and not intended to form a part of his intimate circle. Carrington, on the other hand, appeared to be a permanent fixture and more than requited his feelings for her. Virginia was recovering from a breakdown during the first months of 1916 and did not meet Carrington until the autumn. In mid October Carrington was summoned to explain why she had broken into an empty Asheham with Barbara Hiles and Bunny Garnett (calling on the Woolfs, they had found the house unoccupied and themselves without a bed for the night). Virginia was pleased to note that a reputation for fierceness had preceded her and that Carrington's voice quavered when she spoke to her on the phone.[63] Carrington's deferential attitude was a tribute to her, and she began to warm to the new arrival. Thus the unpromising beginning turned to Carrington's advantage. But Virginia, who had been so close to Lytton, was reluctant to relinquish her hold. She asked him teasingly to tell her she was preferred to Carrington, which he did, to please her.[64] Carrington heard from Lytton only that he had successfully resisted Virginia's flirtations.[65]

Carrington remained devoted to Lytton for the rest of both their lives. Like the wife he had occasionally wished for, she took care of his domestic arrangements and entertained his friends, while both retained the independence they desired and needed. It was she who scoured the countryside for a house for them and arranged the moves to Mill House, Tidmarsh, in 1917 and to Ham Spray in 1924. She decorated the houses, planted the gardens, dealt with the servants and generally arranged everything for Lytton's convenience. Gradually his friends began to appreciate Carrington's merits – Lytton had become much more benign and contented since her arrival. But was he as good for Carrington as she was for him? For his sake she married Ralph Partridge, the well-built young officer much admired by Lytton, hoping that it would keep the household stable. Like many threesomes it was not properly balanced until it acquired a fourth leg – in this case Frances Marshall, who would later become Ralph's second wife and, after Virginia, Bloomsbury's most famous diarist.

Three years after the advent of Carrington Lytton became a celebrity. The publication of *Eminent Victorians*, with its irreverent handling of four respected figures (Cardinal Manning, Florence Nightingale, Dr Arnold and General Gordon), brought Lytton an almost overnight reputation. His radical method was to write of his subjects as people, rather than of their public roles. Unremarkable as it seems to us now, this approach was shocking, intriguing and – above all – puzzling compared to the factual and respectful Victorian biographies that appeared in Leslie Stephen's *Dictionary of National Biography*. To some Lytton was a *bête noire*, to others the champion of the new biography:

> Was this extraordinary person, at once acid and sentimental, realistic and romantic, with his eighteenth-century lucidity of style and his twentieth-century complexity of outlook, his sense of beauty, his learning, his wit, and his impertinence, a rogue or a genius, or was he both or was he neither?[66]

Before its publication, Lytton had asked Virginia to review *Eminent Victorians* for the *Times Literary Supplement*. She accepted on impulse, only to realize later how difficult it would be to review a friend's book impartially, and retracted.[67]

Virginia remained confident of the bond of friendship between them, even when they both became busy and had less time for visits and letters:

Nothing is easier or more intimate than a talk with Lytton. If he is less witty, he is more humane . . . if he were to walk in at this moment we should talk about books & feelings & life & the rest of it as freely as we ever did, & with the sense, on both sides I think, of having hoarded for this precise moment a great deal peculiarly fit for the other.[68]

But she was not blind to his faults, and only two days after she wrote this was reminded of the drawbacks and flaws of the Strachey family: 'a prosaic race, lacking magnanimity, shorn of atmosphere . . . when I think of a Strachey, I think of someone infinitely cautious, elusive & unadventurous'.[69] (Rather unfair, given the Stracheys' record in India and Pippa's suffrage activities.) Lytton is purely cerebral and lacks the creative instinct, the vitality that people such as Clive and Roger possess in spades, she continues – with Lytton she would have had endless conversation but little action. Other Bloomsberries have been innovative, creating the Omega Workshops (Roger), a publishing company (she and Leonard), an artists' retreat (Vanessa); she has forgotten Lytton's revolution in biography, *Eminent Victorians*.[70] Also forgotten or overlooked was Lytton's part in bringing sexual liberation to Cambridge and to Bloomsbury. His thoughts on the freedom of affections are expressed in an untitled paper, now known as 'The Really Interesting Question', which Lytton read to the Apostles on 20 May 1911. Here he made a plea for openness on the subject of 'all those acts, from the bright smile to the most serious copulation, which give expression to the affections that we feel'.[71] Explicit about his own desires, he complains of the English norm of repression – people closed up as though in Gothic fortresses, where an occasional wave from a parapet passes for communication. The only kind of open affection tolerated is that towards young children, he laments. Why is he not free to express his affection for adults?

In 1921 the publication of Virginia's volume of short stories and sketches *Monday or Tuesday* coincided with that of *Queen Victoria*. Lytton's book, which carried a dedication to Virginia, was almost universally praised by the critics; reviews for *Monday or Tuesday* were more mixed. During a party to celebrate his success Lytton neglected to mention her book and Virginia assumed the worst.[72] She was therefore surprised to hear through Ralph Partridge of Lytton's enthusiasm for 'The String Quartet'. Seven years later the boot was on the other foot when Lytton's *Elizabeth and Essex* and Virginia's *Orlando* were published within two months of each other. Both were experiments in biography –

a mixture of fact and fiction – but while Virginia's book benefited from the combination Lytton's book was weakened. In making biography read like fiction he had taken his method too far. Virginia, who had done the reverse, was more successful; although some literal-minded booksellers who shelved the book under Biography rather than Fiction hampered her sales.[73]

The two books had more in common than their publication date – each was a means of wooing a younger lover. By imagining the passion of the ageing Elizabeth I for Essex, Lytton explored his own feelings for Roger Senhouse and his anxieties about the liaison.[74] In *Orlando* Virginia had written a valedictory love letter to Vita Sackville-West, whose attention was straying. Although both books were lauded by reviewers (some of whom, of course, were close friends of the authors), Virginia thought that *Elizabeth and Essex* was bad. Privately she deplored Lytton's disservice to literature and was depressed to find that her personal opinion of him had been adversely affected by her dislike of his work. She never doubted that her accomplishment was greater than Lytton's and believed that for perhaps the first time he envied her gifts.[75] But he had in fact begun to envy her writing long before. On the publication of the Hogarth Press's first venture, *Two Stories*, in 1917, he had written to Leonard of his admiration for 'The Mark on the Wall': 'Virginia's [story] is, I consider, a work of genius. The liquidity of the style fills me with envy: really some of those sentences! – How on earth does she manage to make the English language float and float?'[76]

For a novelist, the opportunity to fictionalize Lytton was too good to pass up. He appears centre-stage in Virginia's first two novels: as St John Hirst in *The Voyage Out* and William Rodney in *Night and Day*. In St John Hirst Virginia conveys the intellectual and discriminating young undergraduate whom she first knew, ill-equipped for social intercourse, his shyness masking a fear of failure. His physical oddity is unflinchingly reproduced – he is 'ugly', thin and stooping, with long legs – and his incompatibility with the heroine Rachel Vinrace is highlighted. She is an untutored young woman who has experienced very little of life; he is a bookish and cultured young man who is not particularly interested in people who are not equally bookish and cultured. To young women who have not read Gibbon he has nothing much to say. When he and Rachel attempt to dance together they are out of step and each blames the other; a picture, perhaps, of Virginia and Lytton's life together had they not shied away from marriage.[77]

William Rodney is a more worldly version of Lytton, mixed with elements of Walter Headlam and George Duckworth (see p. 64). He has a high-pitched voice with a nervous stammer, appears physically peculiar and is plainly uncomfortable talking to strangers. But once one gets past his outward awkwardness his mind is intriguing – his lecture to Mary's friends on Elizabethan poetry, although badly delivered, inspires his audience. He lives in a literary universe and, seen in the intimate setting of his eighteenth-century book-filled rooms, he suddenly makes sense to Ralph Denham, who has hitherto thought him a little ridiculous. Confident and urbane when on his own ground, William dons an old crimson dressing-gown that he hopes makes him appear relaxed and at the same time scholarly – a habit he shares with Lytton.[78] He writes plays and has a passion for poetry but is fastidious and a little fussy – Katharine's description of him as 'half poet and half old maid' could clearly be applied to Lytton.[79]

There are glimpses of Lytton in other novels. The eponymous hero of *Orlando*, ostensibly based on Vita Sackville-West, embodies a desire to change sex that Lytton expressed in letters to friends.[80] Virginia's earlier image of him as a Venetian prince would have been in keeping with Orlando's Elizabethan England. Leonard detected a flavour of Lytton in Neville from *The Waves*.[81] There is a noticeable resemblance. Neville is sensitive, uncompromising and intellectual; even as a schoolboy he has a writer's talent and can imitate the style of the great poets. Too delicate to play cricket, he cares about the score only because his adored Percival does but knows that his adoration is unrequited. As an adult he seeks out a succession of lovers; his most cherished hours are spent with a book in front of the fire, in the company of someone he loves.

In later years, with Lytton tucked away in the Wiltshire countryside or at smart London parties that were not to the Woolfs' taste, Virginia noted that she seldom saw him. However, since 'seldom' to Virginia could mean eight times a year, they were not exactly estranged, and she found that they easily slipped back into their old friendship.[82] Had she known how little time was left to them she might have put up with a few more London parties for the sake of seeing him.

There were strange premonitions of Lytton's death during 1931. In March he and Carrington discussed what they would bequeath one another, and Carrington was distressed by imagining the fate of Lytton's books after his death: 'I felt suddenly serious & gloomy, & Lytton noticing the change, like a wind sweeping across the lawn through the laurels, changed the conversation.'[83] In July a mock obituary of Lytton appeared in the *Week-End Observer* signed by 'Mopsa', the winner of a two-guinea prize for a biography of the author in his own style. No one else came close to Mopsa's skill, said the judge. It was, of course, the work of Carrington, who had a flair for pastiche. She had once tricked Clive Bell into believing that he had received a letter from George Bernard Shaw, and even when Shaw denied that he had written Bell was still convinced he had.[84] This latest spoof turned out to be grimly predictive.

Lytton's frequent illnesses meant that when he began to feel unwell in November 1931 no one – including Lytton himself – realized the seriousness of his complaint. It was at first assumed to be gastric flu, but the medical diagnoses varied from paratyphoid to an ulcerated colon.[85] Virginia, knowing nothing of Lytton's illness but having by an odd coincidence dreamed of him, wrote him a letter on 10 December hoping to rekindle the friendship. Even though they saw one another infrequently, Virginia still thought of Lytton as her closest friend after Leonard. Instead of the expected jaunty reply Virginia received a letter from Ralph with the bad news. By this time Lytton was surrounded by doctors and nurses, relatives and friends, the latter journeying to Ham Spray even though there was little chance of being able to see him. Carrington was beside herself with fear and anxiety and plagued by sleepless nights. Lytton was a figure of sufficient public interest for *The Times* to carry bulletins about his health every couple of days. At Christmas, when his condition reached a crisis, Virginia recalled how much they had lived through together. She and Leonard wept to think what a crushing loss his death would be; then, hearing of a slight improvement, Virginia began making plans for visits to Ham Spray after his recovery.[86]

Several months earlier, in France, Lytton had written in his diary: 'If one's in love with life, to leave it will be as terrible as the dreadful moment when one has to leave one's beloved one – an agony, long foreseen – almost impossibly fearful – and yet it inevitably comes.'[87] But now it had come, Lytton expressed no agony – his death was nothing if not calm and civilized; as easy on his loved ones as was possible. He retained his lucidity, his capacity for rational debate and his sense of humour until the end. His doctor admired his uncomplaining swallowing of unpleasant medicines. After rallying and sinking several times, raising and then crushing the hopes of his friends, Lytton died on 21 January 1932. A post-mortem revealed an incurable stomach cancer which had perforated the colon.[88] For Virginia the loss was great – so much of her past had been tied up with Lytton. She wrote to friends who had known him and found some comfort in talking to them about her memories. Carrington, too, looked to Bloomsbury's collective past for a flavour of Lytton, reading old letters from his Cambridge friends and gaining a new understanding:

I am not surprised reading Lytton's old Cambridge letters that their friendships for each other survived all 'frenzies', even removals to other countrys [sic], & old age. When one thinks of people now who are 21, & reads Virginia's letters, & Maynard's, & Lytton's, one does not wonder Virginia is sometimes intolerant of this 'younger generation'.[89]

Now Carrington had only the past – without Lytton there was no future. The immediate fear of her friends was that she would commit suicide, which she had decided was the only rational solution. She had already made one attempt before Lytton's death but was prevented by Ralph. The next, on 11 March, did not fail – she shot herself in the side and died painfully half a day later. She was eighteen days short of her thirty-ninth birthday.

The only funeral arrangements made for Lytton were concerned with the disposal of his body. There was no service – only a cremation at Golders Green, with his brother James and Saxon Sydney-Turner as witnesses. This was in keeping with Bloomsbury's rejection of Victorian morbidity and overblown sentimentality about death, but the proceedings were a little too anonymous for some tastes – Maynard Keynes felt that he had not properly taken leave of his friend, and Virginia lamented that she did not even know where Lytton's ashes were.[90] In an odd mirroring of the situation, after Carrington's death no one could remember whether her body was cremated or buried.[91]

Lytton Strachey was mourned by admirers of his talent as well as a multitude of friends: 'When he died it seemed to those that loved his art that one of the brightest lights of the generation had suddenly gone out,' said one biographer, writing in 1935.[92] It had seemed that Lytton had much more to offer. He had planned to write a series of commentaries on the plays of Shakespeare (having begun *Othello*), saving his masterpiece for his retirement. Had he lived he might have become as renowned for literary criticism as he was for biography. *The Times* took a more traditionalist line. Carrington and Lytton's Ham Spray life were airbrushed from his obituary, which managed to combine euphemism with a veiled criticism of his work, stating that Lytton lived like a 'student' (not even a scholar) in the family home at 51 Gordon Square and was a bachelor.[93] No doubt this mixture of fact and fiction in the 'official' version of his life would have amused Lytton greatly.

6

The Baronet's Son: Hilton Young

ILTON YOUNG WAS the first serious candidate for Virginia's hand. Lytton Strachey was in certain ways ideally suited to her, but his proposal was unrealistic, and he and Virginia were not long (if at all) under the impression that the marriage would actually take place. Hilton was another kind of suitor altogether. During 1908 and the first half of 1909, when he was courting Virginia, he was a highly eligible bachelor, albeit of the Victorian school, and closely resembled the kind of man Virginia had in her youth assumed that young ladies married. He was comparatively conventional and emotionally reserved, but he was also romantic, humorous and charming. Although not unanimously esteemed in Bloomsbury circles (Vanessa, especially, had some unflattering words to say about him), he was one of the few to escape the sharper edge of Virginia's wit.

Born on 20 March 1879, Hilton came of respectable stock. His father, the third baronet, was just one in a long line of Sir George Youngs. Called to the Bar in 1864, Sir George became a Justice of the Peace and a stalwart of government committees. He stood as a Liberal candidate in Parliament four times but was never elected. He also dabbled in writing of various kinds: political articles; a translation of Sophocles; an edition of Victor Hugo's poems; and his own poems and essays. However, Sir George's talents were not limited to the intellectual. He was a keen mountaineer and a friend of Leslie Stephen, with whom in his spare time he braved icy peaks (although Leslie's agnosticism distressed him). The Youngs' London home, at 115a Sloane Street in Chelsea, was only a mile and a half from Hyde Park Gate. The Young and Stephen children sometimes played together in Kensington Gardens, although Hilton later admitted that, unknown to Virginia, a note of snobbery had entered their games:

> Among my earliest memories is bowling my hoop with the Stephen children
> in Kensington gardens, and being shocked, little snob, because I drove a

wooden hoop with a stick, they drove iron hoops with a hook, which somehow seemed plebeian.[1]

Hilton's mother, Alice Eacy Kennedy, was a striking Irish beauty who became a *grande dame* of the Victorian era. She was the daughter of Dr Evory Kennedy, an eminent Irish obstetrician from Belgard, County Dublin. Dr Kennedy, descended from a line of Northern Irish Protestants, was something of a local celebrity. A leading figure in Dublin politics in the 1860s, he entertained many distinguished guests in his home and counted Oscar and Constance Wilde among his friends. The charismatic Dr Kennedy passed on his physical and personal attractions to his daughter, a noted social hostess. Alice had married young but lost her husband after only two years. The second marriage was much longer lived: George and Alice celebrated their golden wedding anniversary in 1921, the year before Alice's death at the age of eighty-two. For all her beauty and social graces, however, Alice had a sterner side. She 'had much of the puritan in her. She used to dress her children in ugly clothes to save them from admiration, and dressed herself so too.'[2] Virginia admired Lady Young, and her esteem appears to have been returned, for in 1907 Lady Young invited her to stay at Formosa, the Youngs' family home in Cookham, Berkshire, thinking she might be lonely after Vanessa's marriage.

There were two brothers, both older than Hilton (a sister did not survive beyond childhood). The eldest son, another George, nicknamed Georis, repeated his father's pattern of public service but with an international flavour. Georis was attaché in Washington, Athens, Madrid and Constantinople, Chargé d'Affaires in Belgrade, and a newspaper correspondent in Berlin. After the First World War he turned his mind to academia. He was appointed Professor of Portuguese at the University of London, examined students on the finer points of Ottoman law and lectured American students on political science and international law, on which subject he wrote some dozen books. He married Jessie Helen Ilbert, daughter of Sir Courtenay Ilbert, Clerk of the House of Commons, and became the fourth baronet on the death of his father in 1930. Following family tradition, the eldest sons of the three subsequent generations were given the name George. The fifth Sir George Young, 6th Baronet, Conservative MP for Hampshire North West, has said rather disparagingly of his family's interest in politics: 'The Youngs are not actually serious politicians. They have dabbled in politics; they are really public servants – admirals, governor generals, diplomats, spies, civil servants.'[3] (The 'spy' was Georis's younger son, Courtenay, who worked in intelligence during the Second World War.) But politics has been an abiding interest through generations of Youngs.

Georis departed from his family's Liberal affiliations, standing as a Labour parliamentary candidate in the 1920s (with the modest slogan 'George Young is a local man'). There were even rumours of communist leanings. Georis was an authority on international politics and often consulted with Leonard Woolf, who, picking up on the contradictions in his character, referred to him as 'a nice, absurd, cantankerous man'.[4] Virginia's verdict was similar: 'a slow, stiff, kindly man, with all Hilton's romance, but less than Hilton's brain'.[5] In September 1918 Georis stayed overnight with the Woolfs at Asheham, mainly in order to have an opportunity to discuss the war with Fabian socialists Sidney and Beatrice Webb. He arrived on their doorstep, enthusiastic but soaking wet, in the middle of pouring rain. Virginia filed this in her mind as an example of the Young family's tendency to regard harsh weather conditions and cross-country walks as a welcome challenge. This propensity to rise to the challenges of nature was even stronger in Hilton's other brother, Geoffrey.

Geoffrey Winthrop Young, a mountaineer, was a colourful character. An Eton schoolmaster during the first five years of the new century, he became a good friend of sixth-former John Maynard Keynes, whom he coached for a university scholarship. He was impressed by Keynes's learning and maturity, and the admiration was mutual: Maynard called him 'the superb Geoffrey Young' and under his tutelage took up climbing in order to balance his intellectual pursuits with physical ones.[6] (Geoffrey Winthrop Young also tried – and failed – to imbue Lytton Strachey with awe for the wonders of nature. To the bookish Lytton the mountains of Skye were preposterous and the scenery merely bored him.) At times Keynes must have felt surrounded by Youngs: one of his closest friends was Gerard Mackworth Young, cousin of Hilton and Geoffrey, and Hilton himself often called at Eton at weekends, observing Keynes's mature intelligence at first hand.

During the First World War Geoffrey received a rash of bravery awards from the grateful governments of Britain, Belgium and Italy. Losing a leg did nothing to hamper his high-altitude feats, and he climbed the Matterhorn with a metal prosthetic limb. He totted up more first ascents than any other climber and was widely respected as one of the best British mountaineers of his day. He trained the younger generation of mountaineers including George Mallory, who famously climbed Everest 'because it's there'. The two were close friends: they once climbed a Cornish cliff together wearing nothing but plimsolls, and Geoffrey was best man at Mallory's wedding.[7] The energetic Geoffrey was instrumental in establishing with Kurt Hahn both Gordonstoun School and the Outward Bound Movement. A member of the Alpine Club from 1900, he was elected President for three years from 1941. Despite homosexual tendencies, he married in his early forties Eleanor ('Len') Slingsby, daughter of the famous mountaineer William Cecil Slingsby, and had two children with her.

Thus the gene pool that produced Hilton Young included a leaning towards politics, a smattering of literature and a taste for adventure, and Hilton's life and career suggest he was not neglectful of any of these. His literary heritage revealed itself when Hilton was ten or eleven years old, in a novella entitled *The Count: A Romance*, the result of a collaboration between Hilton and his two brothers. On the opening page is an early poem by Geoffrey, and the elegant illustrations of people and horses are credited to Georis. It is a charming adventure story about the abduction of the heroine, Eva Lammart, by a villain with a long mustachios, the unprincipled rascal Count De Farge (Hilton had evidently read *A Tale of Two Cities*). Eva's rescue is planned by a team of titled heroes on horseback, led by her beau, the aristocratic Sir Richard Courtenay. It opens, à la Edward Bulwer-Lytton: 'It was a cold and stormy night . . . '[8] This opening became something of a family joke and was later the preamble to stories inspired by Hilton's naval adventures. Hilton's son Wayland recalls being told numerous sea-going yarns which began: 'It was a dark and stormy night, and the bosun . . .' Typically Hilton's stories would have an unexpected twist or two in the middle.[9] *The Count* is an adventure yarn – the horseback pursuit takes centre stage and the romantic reconciliation is glossed over. Interestingly, an early story of Virginia's called 'The Midnight Ride', also featuring a flight on horseback, similarly tailed off after an exciting start.[10] Hilton's story ranks with Daisy Ashford's *The Young Visiters* and Virginia's own juvenilia, *A Cockney's Farming Experiences* and *Memoirs of a Pater-Familias*, as evidence of a precocious intelligence and youthful imagination. It is also interesting to compare the Youngs' joint endeavour for *The Count* with the young Stephens' domestic newssheet, the *Hyde Park Gate News*.

As a boy Hilton was thoughtful, questioning God, religion, sin and divine retribution, but for him 'Sex was an absolute tabu'.[11] Like many a father before and since, Sir George sounded his son out on the subject of 'how babies are born and that sort of thing' when he reached puberty.[12] To spare them both embarrassment, Hilton said he already knew, and the subject was dropped. Hilton's formal education was not entirely plain sailing: he had to be removed from Marlborough after continual bullying. There followed a spell of lessons with his father, and he ended his schooldays at Eton, where he won prizes for physics and physical geography but took away less happy memories of the troublesome Latin and Greek lessons. With these reverberating in his mind, Hilton abandoned classics on leaving Eton in 1896 and turned to science. He studied chemistry at the University of London for two terms under a respected family friend, William Ramsay, then went up to Trinity College in 1897 to read natural science. Two years later he was able to renew a childhood friendship when Thoby Stephen arrived at Trinity, along with Leonard Woolf, Lytton Strachey, Saxon Sydney-Turner and Clive Bell. It was thus that Hilton became one of the satellite members of what was later called 'Old Bloomsbury'.

Unlike Lytton, Saxon and Leonard (but in common with Thoby and Clive) Hilton did not receive the knock upon the door which was the prelude to the vetting procedure for the Apostles. Perhaps in the eyes of this elite Hilton lacked the spark of originality or was not bookish enough, his mind falling short of their exacting standards of relentless intellectual curiosity, and his manner a shade too genial and uncritical. Neither was he studying a very acceptable subject for election to the Apostles – candidates tended to be selected from among the classicists and philosophers. (John Maynard Keynes, a mathematician, was a rare exception.)[13]

While Hilton was precluded from the Apostles, he was still welcome at Thoby Stephen's Thursday evening gatherings at Gordon Square. He attended frequently, although his conversation was not always confined to the required subjects: Lytton noted disapprovingly that he had overheard Hilton discussing politics with another guest but that fortunately no one else was listening.[14] Occasionally the Stephens received return invitations to evening parties at the Youngs', but these were not regarded with unqualified joy. Hilton's family were associated with the old Hyde Park Gate years that Virginia and her siblings had rejected in their new, independent life at Gordon Square. Virginia records in her 1905 diary a minor rebellion against Hilton's 'type': 'we [Virginia and Thoby] went to the Hilton Youngs &c: evening, which was dress clothes & respectable, & I was very disreputable!'[15]

At Cambridge Hilton's political ambitions found expression, and he became President of the Union, in charge of student elections. (Maynard Keynes followed in Hilton's footsteps a few years later.) From his mother, who had formed the local branch of the Women's Liberal Association, he had inherited a loyalty to the Liberal Party. He sided with the Liberals in such debates as 'This house considers that the Unionist Government has proved itself unworthy of the confidence of the country, and would welcome a Liberal administration' and, as the *Granta* reported, 'delivered his speech in his own firm, quiet manner, sharpening his points with frequent epigrams. He was wonderfully fluent, he had a good stock of facts, and his arguments were easy to follow.' (Despite his facility as a speaker, the motion was defeated 116 to 77.)[16] As yet Hilton had manifested no desire to become a politician. His interest in science waning, he now wanted to study for the Bar but at his father's request continued with his degree and took first-class honours in the natural science tripos in 1900. In his final year he took on the editorship of the weekly university journal the *Cambridge Review*. After Cambridge he took a London house, 35 Kensington Square, with two older friends and spent the next few years in a dim Temple basement working for his legal apprenticeship.

Hilton was called to the Bar in 1904. He practised as a barrister at the King's Bench division and in Oxford on circuit but suffered a breakdown in 1907 during a trip to the University of Freiburg in Breisgau to study foreign company law. Rather quixotically he claimed that he was made ill by listening to his host, a professor of anatomy, reading *Hamlet* aloud in German – a queasy mix of business and pleasure. He took rest cures in Wales with his mother and Italy with his young friend Will Arnold-Forster – although the term 'rest' cure is not entirely appropriate for these excursions since Hilton loathed physical inactivity and spent much of his time walking long distances. In 1908 he began to look for a country cottage near Marlborough and alighted on The Lacket in Lockeridge, a cottage dating from 1701 which he purchased with a family legacy. Among his first guests was Adrian Stephen, and many of his Bloomsbury friends would later stay here. Rather half-heartedly Hilton set to work writing a book on law, but when he met Francis Hirst, the editor of *The Economist*, he jumped at the chance to change the direction of his career once again. By 1909 he was assistant editor.

In the meantime 'old' Bloomsbury had evolved to include Virginia Stephen and Vanessa Bell and was now consolidating into a close-knit group. Hilton was aware that he was largely excluded from the enchanted realm, although he gained entry at intervals to report on the lives of ordinary mortals:

> 'Bloomsbury' . . . was very exclusive: it did not suffer fools gladly. They lived in an intellectual enclosure . . . A common-place opinion astonished them all. It moved Virginia to silence, Vanessa to a sympathetic effort to give it meaning, Lytton to change the subject, and Clive to his genial but explosive laughter.

Hilton credited his own rejection of the commonplace opinion to 'those fine minds, which had so wholly freed themselves from the burden of traditions'.[17]

In the summer of 1908 Virginia was twenty-six and Hilton twenty-nine. For her own sake as well as her sister's, Vanessa was keen to help Virginia find a mate. She recognized that Virginia was drifting rather unhappily, despite her determination to manage life on her own terms. But not just any upper-middle-class bachelor would do. The choice of a husband for Virginia would be of great importance to her present and future friendships. The wrong man could, potentially, draw Virginia away from Bloomsbury and take her into quite a different world. Bloomsbury without Virginia at its centre was not an attractive prospect. Nor was Virginia herself keen to leave behind her intellectually stimulating corner of the world. So her suitor had to fit not only her own idea of a husband but also those of her sister and her friends.

Hilton had been a regular visitor to Virginia's and Adrian's Thursday evening meetings at Fitzroy Square almost from their inception. Part of his attraction to the Thursdays was to see Virginia, Vanessa supposed, picturing her sister 'in the midst of the most rarefied culture in London, with Saxon, Lytton and no doubt Hilton Young all hanging upon your words'.[18] She watched closely as Virginia's relationship with Hilton progressed through the summer of that year, in concert with a deepening friendship with Lytton and a continuing flirtation with Clive, who became very possessive in the face of the growing competition.

In August Virginia went to Wells while she worked on 'Melymbrosia', the precursor of *The Voyage Out*. Hilton's letters followed her to Somerset, and it is this period of her life that she afterwards identified with him, referring to 'that summer at Wells, when I used to get letters from Hilton'.[19] He must have made his intentions fairly clear, because the courtship progressed quickly to the point where Virginia expected a proposal at any moment. But she also knew that someone else was competing for Hilton's favours and keeping a curious eye on both of them. Olive Ilbert was Hilton's sister-in-law once removed – her sister Jessie had married Georis in 1904. Another sister, Lettice, was married to Virginia's cousin H.A.L. Fisher, so both Olive and Hilton were distant relatives, by marriage, of Virginia and Vanessa.[20] Olive and Virginia maintained a sporadic and rather uneasy friendship based on this family tie, and Virginia evidently knew of Olive's feelings for Hilton. What on earth was she to say to Olive if Hilton proposed? Virginia asked her sister, envisaging (and perhaps relishing) a dramatic scene.[21]

While she enjoyed his attentions Virginia was not convinced of Hilton's suitability as a future husband. Her delicate antennae had perceived that Hilton shared her sense of their 'incongruity' and that this was probably preventing him from hastening the courtship. She viewed a proposal from him as the climax to the courtship, about which she felt apprehensive but which her self-approbation demanded. Although still in her twenties, she felt like an old maid and considered herself entitled to a 'real' proposal. She wished her singledom to be her own decision, not simply due to the fact that nobody wanted to marry her – with her three-fold eligibility of birth, beauty and intelligence, this would be an intolerable insult.

Virginia's doubts were fuelled chiefly by Vanessa's disapproval. Hilton was handsome, amiable, charming and often impulsive but just not 'Bloomsbury' enough. Perhaps because he did not share their argumentative streak and was not so interested in breaking taboos, he was seen by some Bloomsberries as lacking in intellectual depth. Despite her eagerness to find Virginia a husband, Vanessa had no desire to see her sister take the retrograde step of marrying a 'Hyde Park Gater' and a baronet's son to boot, and she was very discouraging. She appealed to her sister's love of subtlety and originality and laid stress upon the leaden side of Hilton's nature. In one of her characteristic mixed metaphors she likens his sense of humour to 'an elephant in a china shop' – oceans apart from Virginia's own discriminating wit.[22] Vanessa's words testify as much to the sisters' closeness as to Bloomsbury's code of frankness. Her sister's opinions were very important to Virginia and must have played no small part in her own consideration of Hilton as a prospective spouse. In the minds of both sisters Hilton's Hyde Park Gate respectability scuppered his chances of a romantic conquest before he had uttered one word of love.

However, not all of the Bloomsberries had an unfavourable opinion of Hilton. Morgan Forster, his chess opponent and walking companion, found him subtle, discerning and a man of integrity. During a period of writer's block in 1920 Morgan considered Hilton's advice the most helpful he received: his sensitivity and understanding of the creative process lifted Morgan from the depression into which he had sunk. On another occasion he was so impressed with Hilton's advice that he copied it into a notebook.[23]

Virginia enjoyed Hilton's attention and did little to discourage it. Conscious that she was the object of intense speculation among her friends, she playfully sent one of Hilton's letters to Vanessa so that her sister could be a 'witness' to the courtship. Whether he intended to propose or just to talk, Virginia rationalized, she might as well provide him with an opportunity. She planned to go from Wells to Marlborough, close to The Lacket, and Hilton asked if he might call on her. But at the last minute Virginia changed her mind and decided to go to Manorbier in Wales instead, muddying the waters and no doubt confusing her suitor. He neither visited her Wells lodgings nor wrote, and Virginia began to doubt his ardour. She speculated to Vanessa on the reasons for his silence, reviewing their recent letters and meetings, wondering whether she had seemed too keen or too indifferent or whether other factors had changed Hilton's mind. She watched the possibility of a proposal fade away but was 'complacent', she told Vanessa. It seems that Hilton suffered from cold feet on this occasion – Virginia later suspected Olive Ilbert of stoking up trouble; Clive believed that Hilton had simply not received Virginia's letters. But after this hitch the courtship soon resumed and continued into the following year.

Vanessa's habitual censures against Hilton were tempered the following March when the reality of Virginia's life with Adrian was revealed. Vanessa was thrown into Adrian's company during the Stephens' holiday in Cornwall. The extent of Adrian's gloom and lethargy was remarkable – he hardly moved from his armchair for three consecutive days. Virginia told Vanessa that this was his normal condition, and Vanessa realized the strong attraction of marriage for her sister. Were she in Virginia's position, she wrote to Lytton, given a choice between life with Adrian or life with Hilton, she would almost be prepared to marry Hilton.[24] Not exactly a resounding endorsement but certainly a change from her customary attitude.

The long-awaited proposal came in the middle of May 1909, and in as romantic a setting as Virginia could have wished. Hilton asked Virginia to be his wife as they punted along Cambridge's River Cam. The backdrop implies that the proposal had been carefully prearranged, and Hilton's son Wayland Young has observed that the romantic gesture was very characteristic of his father. Virginia was pleased and flattered but refused as she had long planned to do. The odd reason she gave Hilton for her refusal was that if she were to marry she would accept only Lytton, whose proposal had taken place – and been immediately retracted – three months earlier. This effectively put her out of the reach of all and sundry. Hilton retired gracefully from the scene, not heartbroken but wondering perhaps why Virginia had led him such a dance.[25]

An echo of this incident can be found in Virginia Woolf's short story, 'Moments of Being: "Slater's Pins Have No Points"' (1928), in which Fanny Wilmot visualizes an abortive proposal made to her friend Julia Craye in a rowing boat on the Serpentine. Julia's beau, Mr Sherman, is interrupted at the crucial moment by Julia shouting an angry warning when she foresees a collision with the bridge, and each is immediately disillusioned with the other. Whether or not Virginia was recreating a real-life event, it seems likely that she cast her mind back to Hilton's water-borne proposal. (Although the near-collision is probably pure fiction, as Hilton was a very good sailor.) Typically, there is no enlightenment for us in the diary or letters from 1927, the year in which she wrote the story. Woolf was inaccurate when she said that death was the only experience she would never describe – she was also curiously silent on the subject of her proposals.[26]

Virginia soon discovered that her refusal did not end the conjecture about her liaison with Hilton. Olive continued to play sentinel, writing letters and making inquiries about Virginia's romances. Virginia found it all rather irritating but did not retaliate.[27] The following year Olive made it clear to Virginia that she interpreted her involvement with the cause of women's suffrage as a movement towards a rapprochement with the politically minded Hilton.[28] If, as Virginia suspected, there was continued speculation about Hilton and herself, it probably originated with Olive. She was an inveterate gossip (a charge from which we cannot exempt Virginia, of course) and even managed to get on the wrong side of the genial Hilton. By April 1911 he had fallen out with Olive, apparently suspecting that she had put the kibosh on his affair with Virginia. Virginia repeated to Vanessa (no doubt adding dramatic flourishes) a story told to her by Elinor Darwin. Olive, enmeshing Virginia's cousin Fredegond Maitland and poet Frances Cornford in her intrigue, had threatened to kill herself because she wanted to confess something to Hilton and he would not see her.[29] Frances intervened, telling Olive she must accept that Hilton was not interested in her. Olive soon afterwards gave up the pursuit of her handsome brother-in-law, and in June 1912 she married Michael Heseltine, son of a Norfolk clergyman. The marriage was annulled in 1921 – according to Virginia, on the grounds of his impotence. Hearing that Olive was free again and Hilton still unmarried, Virginia surmised that Olive would renew her pursuit of Hilton. If so, Olive was destined for another disappointment – Hilton had by this time met his future wife.[30]

In the aftermath of Virginia's rejection Hilton concentrated on his career. After his stint at *The Economist* he moved in 1910 to the *Morning Post* where he was financial editor until the outbreak of war. One of his initiatives here was to publish the views of his friend Maynard on the government's financial policy. Attempting to move into mainstream politics, in late November 1910 he stood as Liberal candidate for East Worcestershire against Unionist Austen Chamberlain. He had considerable personal support from his family, fellow Liberal Maynard Keynes, Sydney Waterlow (who canvassed for three days on his behalf) and Morgan Forster (who donated £5 to his campaign) but lost heavily, polling half the number of votes that Chamberlain collected. He was probably aware that he had little chance of winning. Rupert Brooke, meeting Hilton shortly before the election, thought that 'He seemed rather disillusioned & tired. He said he was a relic of Moore's generation.'[31] Brooke suggested to another friend that Hilton was in love with Alfred Brooke, his younger brother, but this was probably a typical Brookean overstatement of their close friendship.[32] They shared a house in 1912 and went travelling in the Black Forest together that summer, but no other Bloomsbury gossip links them romantically or sexually.

Although Hilton did not see Virginia for nearly a decade after his proposal, he remained in sporadic contact with Bloomsbury. He supported the Second Post-Impressionist Exhibition in 1912–13, buying several paintings by virtually unknown French artists and one of two versions of *The Dancers* by Duncan Grant. Hilton's son Wayland remembers being told a story about the exhibition that illustrates his father's eye for a good deal as well as a good painting. Hilton initially bought only one painting, but on his way out of the gallery was offered a sum ten times more than he had paid for it. He accepted the offer and went back in to the exhibition to buy more paintings with his newly acquired profit.[33] In early 1914, at the first exhibition of the Grafton Group, held at the Alpine Club in London, he bought a painting by Jean Marchand to the approval of Vanessa Bell – 'Hilton Young has bought the town by Marchand,' she wrote to Duncan.[34] His interest in art led to a sprinkling of correspondence with Vanessa and Clive Bell. He wrote to Vanessa to tell her he liked a picture of hers but had doubts about one of Duncan's recent works. Vanessa's reply was characteristically full of praise for her lover's painting.[35] In another lively letter of spring 1915 she regaled him with stories of Bloomsbury parties and offered to send him a copy of Virginia's first novel, *The Voyage Out*.[36] (Hilton's opinion of Virginia's first novel – or of any of her other works – is not recorded.) Clive found Hilton's letters extremely amiable, and Hilton found Clive a genial companion – when he and his brother Geoffrey started a Cambridge dining club Clive was an occasional visitor, along with Maynard Keynes, Roger Fry and Adrian Stephen.

Hilton sometimes found his work in the City unsatisfying, and he travelled whenever he could. But one of his friends had effected a more exotic escape from the humdrum to live a life of indulgence and adventure. In April 1914 Rupert Brooke wrote to him from Santa Fé, Arizona. In his letter Rupert gives a strong flavour, if a highly imaginative one, of his itinerant lifestyle. He appeals to Hilton, as a poor man to a rich one, to buy a yacht and come cruising to the South Seas: 'Come! It is your only chance of salvation,' he exorts.[37] He promises to teach Hilton any necessary life skills such as diving for turtles, climbing coconut trees barefoot, spearing fish, primitive dances. How tempting it must have been to leave his grey London office for the exotic and colourful world described by his friend. But Rupert was a carefree twenty-six, Hilton a responsible (and not particularly wealthy) thirty-five. He did not take Rupert up on the offer.

However, Hilton was to escape the City by a dramatically different route. On 28 June 1914 the heir to the Austro-Hungarian throne, Archduke Franz Ferdinand, was assassinated in Sarajevo by Gavrilo Princip, a Serbian nationalist. For many international observers, Leonard Woolf among them, this marked a permanent end to political stability across Europe. Clive Bell predicted an end to civilization. War broke out between Serbia and Austro-Hungary and within two months had spread to the rest of Europe. Hilton was ambivalent about the purposes of the war. Morgan Forster later recalled how they had discussed the prevention of war, and this was a topic that preoccupied Hilton until the end of his life.[38] At the beginning he shared Bloomsbury's pacifism: 'We who were unwarlike [believed that] the only way to end war was not to fight.'[39] But his urge to support the national cause proved stronger, and when he heard that volunteers were required to decode telegrams, he signed up immediately for intelligence work. He was sent to assist the Grand Fleet at Scapa Flow, off the Orkney Islands. For reasons of expediency (namely to prevent the Germans shooting him as a spy if captured), he was given a commission as lieutenant in the Royal Navy Volunteer Reserve (RNVR). He debated with himself the nature of his duty – was it to resist war or to resist the Germans? Without really having determined on an answer, he joined a fleet patrolling the North Sea on board HMS *Iron Duke*.[40] (Morgan Forster, writing to him there, considered a ship a peculiar kind of address and he wondered how the postman would know where to find it.)

Hilton was always to think of himself as a landlubber despite having a very active war. In his naval memoirs, *By Sea and Land* (Morgan Forster gave Chapter 5 an 'A' for literary merit), he says his story is about 'how a peaceable landsman fell asleep and dreamed that he was a naval officer'.[41] However, Hilton was convincing enough in the role to win himself a clutch of medals: one after a mission in Serbia, two more for overseeing the import of food and the export of refugees in the Balkans and the DSC and the Croix de Guerre for fighting at the Flemish Front.

Towards the end of the war, nine years after rejecting Hilton's proposal and having exchanged no more than half-a-dozen words with him in the interim, Virginia met him unexpectedly at the house of Katherine (Ka) Cox. Virginia felt slightly uncomfortable about seeing Hilton again, conscious that the last he had heard of her was probably through Olive Ilbert's gossip. But Hilton bore her no ill will and they 'talked hard indeed'. He appeared to Virginia 'a perfect type of naval officer, cleanshaven, shorn, red faced, all blue cloth & gold braid with a ribbon on his breast'.[42] It is difficult to imagine what Hilton and Virginia can have talked about, given the divergence in their attitudes towards the war and her dislike of any job that necessitated the wearing of a uniform, especially one with gold braid and medals. She had little interest in the war beyond the detrimental effect it had on the national consciousness, and many of her friends were conscientious objectors. Nevertheless they talked easily; Virginia, assuming they would have different views on the war, steering clear of the contentious subject. Hilton was as courteous and charming as ever: 'His dark enigmatic ways (the Sphinx without a Secret) are swept away; & yet I liked him – thought him kind & trusty & a little romantic – I'm afraid no longer romantic about me.'[43]

Virginia found herself feeling wistful on Hilton's behalf, pitying him for doing without a wife in the intervening years. He had been pursued by Olive Ilbert and Irene Noel, an early love of his friend Desmond MacCarthy before he married Molly Warre-Cornish.[44] No one had won his heart entirely, but he had developed a close friendship with Ka and they exchanged several intimate letters.[45] Virginia may have known from Ka of their friendship and imagined a romance between them. When Lytton's brother James told her of Ka's engagement that July, her immediate assumption was that Hilton had proposed. She was disappointed to find that Ka's intended was Hilton's friend, the painter and naval officer Will Arnold-Forster, who was a little too conventional for Virginia's taste.[46]

The war continued. Hilton, with no intention of marrying Ka, or she him, went back on active duty to face his greatest wartime challenge to date. On 23 April, St George's Day, he participated in a 'volunteers only' mission – the perilous Zeebrugge Raid.[47] Hilton was on deck during the raid and was wounded in the right arm. In true patriotic spirit he battled on, and it was only afterwards that he found out how serious his injury was. The nerves in his arm had been severed, the bone splintered, and he had to have the arm amputated below the shoulder. Even so he was luckier than many of his compatriots: there were around 200 killed and 400 wounded as a result of the raid. For his actions Hilton won a long-awaited promotion to lieutenant-commander and a few months' rest in England. By July he was back in the thick of war, this time in command of an alliance of Russian and foreign forces (the Whites) who were fighting against the Bolshevik revolutionaries (the Reds) in the Russian civil war. He was given charge of an armoured train. The plan was to drive the train the 350 miles from Archangel to Vologda, Russia's diplomatic capital, and consolidate the Allied position before the onset of the harsh Russian winter. The train made slow progress, with only thirty-five miles of line gained in five days – hardly the 'dash to Vologda' that had been planned but a gallant effort under the difficult circumstances. Before they could reach their target, news of the Armistice filtered through. Hilton arrived back in England with a DSO for overseas action.

Even in the exigencies of war Hilton had not relinquished his political ambitions. In 1915, after being invalided home for a period, he was elected as Liberal

Member of Parliament for Norwich. (Hilton retained his Norwich seat, with only a short break, until 1929.) After the Armistice a General Election was quickly called before the Paris Peace Conference began the following January. This was known as a 'khaki election' since it followed so quickly upon the heels of the war. The voters, faced with a mind-boggling choice between three major parties and four coalition combinations, marked their papers in favour of a Conservative/ Liberal coalition government led by Lloyd George. Their decision spelled the beginning of the end for the Liberals, who have never regained their popularity.

For his day job Hilton returned to financial journalism, becoming editor-in-chief of the *Financial News*, a free paper that was a rival to the *Financial Times*. He was appointed parliamentary secretary under the Minister for Education, Virginia's cousin H.A.L. Fisher, but his first major appointment as an MP was to a financial mission in India in 1920. The following spring he became a junior minister when Lloyd George appointed him Financial Secretary to the Treasury (a post held seventy years later by Hilton's great-nephew, the sixth Sir George Young). The 1922 election led to Hilton's appointment as Chief Whip of Lloyd George's National Liberals.

Meanwhile Hilton had met the woman he was to marry. She was the sculptor Edith Agnes Kathleen Scott, née Bruce, widow of the Antarctic explorer Captain Robert Falcon Scott (known to family and friends as Con), and she was a fascinating character – brave, strongwilled, self-contained and an inveterate traveller. The youngest of eleven children, she could trace her ancestry back to Robert the Bruce and the Graeco-Turkish rulers of the eighteenth century. A second cousin became Prime Minister of Tonga; a less exotic uncle the Archbishop of York. She was orphaned at an early age, and she and her brothers and sisters went to live with their great-uncle. A few of Kathleen's youthful experiences merit a mention, not least because they echo episodes in Virginia Woolf's life and writing. As a young child Kathleen was the victim of an attempted abduction by a drunken man while on her way home from school. She bit him on the hand and escaped but had an understandable fear of men as a teenager and a lifelong aversion to alcohol. When she was aged about twelve Kathleen's charismatic but rebellious cousin Willie came to stay. He got into the habit, after a night out on the tiles, of tapping on the window of her ground-floor bedroom as a signal for her to open the front door. He became enraged if she made the slightest sound, but, as she noted in a memoir, his gratitude (the nature of which she did not disclose) was even more alarming.[48]

Unlike Virginia, Kathleen was sent away to school – a convent – but she developed a lust for adventure. And she found it. In 1900, while Virginia was buckling down to her Greek and Latin studies, Kathleen was studying art at the Slade and three years later was learning from Rodin. In early 1904, while Virginia was looking for a house in Bloomsbury after the death of her father, Kathleen was helping refugees in Macedonia. While Virginia was sailing to Nauplia during an ill-fated trip with her siblings and Violet Dickinson, Kathleen was delivering her friend Isadora Duncan's illegitimate baby in Holland. Like Virginia Kathleen made an impression on many of the men she encountered. She was even immortalized (rather savagely) in print, in the *Confessions* of black magic practitioner Aleister Crowley.

When Kathleen met Hilton in 1919 she was immediately attracted to him. He was a war hero and, Othello-like, he wooed her with tales of daring and adventure (as did T.E. Lawrence, on whom Kathleen also had a crush). Not only was he charming and amusing – Kathleen found him 'exciting' and 'entrancing' – but he had another important weapon in his armoury: he got on wonderfully with Kathleen's adored son Peter and his menagerie of pet animals. There were two major obstacles. The first was Hilton's shyness and sexual reticence, which meant that the courtship moved very slowly – it was almost two years before he even touched her, and when he finally declared his love it was in writing rather than in person. The other problem was Kathleen's veneration of the memory of her first husband, Con, who had died returning from the South Pole in 1912. His marriage to Kathleen had been a short but intensely happy one of three and a half years. Kathleen's attraction to Hilton was countered by yearnings for her dead husband, and she even fled the country to avoid falling in love again.[49]

To understand how powerful a phantom Hilton was up against it should be noted that Scott's reputation was almost legendary, not just to his widow but to most of Britain. Reports that he and his colleagues had perished during a mission combining those heroic attributes of endurance and patriotism had sent shockwaves throughout their home country. Amundsen, the Norwegian explorer, had already returned from the South Pole with his team intact, but his successful expedition was eclipsed by the loss of the British team. Despite their failure to beat the Norwegians to the Antarctic, Scott and his cohorts became posthumous heroes.[50] It was Hilton's heroic qualities that appealed to Kathleen. He was a thoughtful, philosophical man, but he also had a drive towards physical activities such as sailing, swimming, diving and walking long distances (especially under difficult conditions). His missing right arm appeared to cause few problems – he even mastered driving in a specially adapted car. The need for constant challenge which had been so strong in Kathleen's first husband was also present in her second. As was the interest in nature that Con had exhorted Kathleen to encourage in their son. Among the things Kathleen noticed about Hilton was his knowledge of the songs of the birds; his ornithological enthusiasm was surely instrumental in Peter's later career.[51]

Eventually the reluctant lovers were won round by one another. When they married on 3 March 1922 Hilton was almost forty-three and his bride a year older. (This generation of Youngs was partial to late marriages: Geoffrey was also forty-two before he tied the knot; George was thirty-two when he wedded his first wife, but he married again at seventy-six.) The wedding was conducted by the Bishop of St Albans in the Crypt Chapel of the House of Commons amid a flurry of press attention. One of the guests was Mrs Reginald McKenna whose husband, as First Lord of the Admiralty, had received Adrian's and Duncan's apology for the Dreadnought Hoax in 1910. There were a few departures from the norm. Hilton's old rival Austen Chamberlain, a friend of the bride, gave her away in a service that lasted only ten minutes. Hilton's right sleeve was pinned to his morning coat, and for the post-ceremonial photographs Kathleen poignantly took the empty sleeve in her left arm. Kathleen's son Peter, aged twelve, got away with casual dress – an open-necked shirt and shorts. The bride and groom took a brief, rainy honeymoon at The Lacket, and Hilton was back at work three days later.

Virginia almost certainly never met Hilton's wife, but they narrowly missed meeting at Studland in the late summer of 1909, several months after Hilton's proposal to Virginia. Kathleen was at Studland in August, swimming in the sea and enjoying her first pregnancy; a month later Virginia, back from her opera trip to Bayreuth and Dresden, was staying near the Bells, swimming in the same sea in a hired 'bisexual' bathing costume.[52] One can imagine that Virginia would have derived much pleasure from hearing about the adventures of this modern-day Orlando, unrestricted by gender, and from reporting them in her diary. The diary was one of the things they had in common and meant that Kathleen's family and admirers, like Virginia's, could read about her life in satisfying detail. There were other areas of common ground; for instance, their ambivalence towards sexual matters. A robust young woman in many ways, as an art student Kathleen was physically sick the first time she was faced with a nude male model. Attractive to men, she had many male friends and lovers but, like Virginia, remained a virgin until her first marriage at the age of thirty. Both women admitted to being intellectual snobs. Both were possessive about their loved ones and cuttingly critical about those who did not come up to their high standards. Both also hated buying clothes: Virginia because she hated mirrors and being looked at by shop assistants; Kathleen because spending money on clothes seemed a frivolity.

A major point of difference was their attitude towards women: in direct contrast to Virginia, Kathleen was 'a man's woman'. That she chose to sculpt almost exclusively male figures says much about her outlook. A man with her views about gender would be labelled a confirmed misogynist. To someone who asked her opinion of women artists, she said (perhaps with a measure of exaggeration to tease her interlocutor) that women were no good for anything except childbearing. At heart she thought, like Julia Stephen, that men were worth more than women, and her determination to marry a hero was fuelled by her ambition to produce a heroic son. (Her fierce and possessive love for her son Peter resembles Vanessa's for Julian.) Neither did Kathleen approve of Bloomsbury's promiscuity: for all her gypsying she admitted to being a bit of a puritan. She might have found their dinner party talk fascinating, but she would not have condoned the sexual exploits of Vanessa, Clive, Lytton or Maynard. However, an exception in her general attitude towards Bloomsbury was made for one of its members – Duncan Grant. Duncan was almost universally liked by those who met him, and Kathleen was not immune to his charms. She found him terribly endearing, dishevelled but attractive, and couldn't help but mother him. She actively avoided meeting Bloomsbury *en masse*, but there were occasional encounters: Kathleen saw Bloomsberries at concerts, where she privately complained of their talking through the music; Morgan Forster was a friend of Hilton's as well as a Bloomsbury regular. Kathleen heard stories of Ottoline Morrell through their mutual friend H.H. Asquith; and she was also an old acquaintance of Sibyl Colefax, 'an unabashed hunter of lions' who tried to befriend Virginia.[53] On Armistice Day, in the company of Austen Chamberlain, Kathleen even met Virginia's half-brother George Duckworth, who had once been Chamberlain's private secretary.

In the year that Hilton married, Virginia published her third novel, *Jacob's Room*, feeling she had finally discovered own unique novelistic voice, and began her next novel, *Mrs Dalloway*. The characters of Clarissa and Richard Dalloway both originally featured in *The Voyage Out*; *Mrs Dalloway*'s Clarissa resembles her blueprint a little, but the two Richards are quite different. Whereas the first appears to be based on George Duckworth, the second has much more in common with Hilton Young. He shares Hilton's (and of course Leonard's) thoughtfulness, making Clarissa rest for an hour after lunch and moving her into a separate bedroom because he works so late at the House of Commons (as Hilton often did).[54] Lady Bruton observes that Richard is always very well presented, and her secretary, Milly Brush, appreciates his gentlemanly dependability.[55] Sally Seton says that Richard's second-rate intelligence will stand in the way of his ambitions to a Cabinet post (not Hilton's fate).[56] Peter Walsh acknowledges that he is a decent man but limited in imagination (the Bloomsbury view of Hilton): his views are taken verbatim from the *Morning Post* (where Hilton spent four years as financial editor) and his real metier would have been as a landowner in Norfolk.[57] Richard Dalloway is good with animals and calm in emergencies but is emotionally repressed, feeling uncomfortably like a voyeur when reading the love sonnets of Shakespeare and unable to tell Clarissa he loves her.[58] Virginia thought Hilton romantic but had perhaps sensed the emotional reserve that prevented him declaring himself.

Mrs Dalloway's Clarissa is a diluted version of Virginia. She has absorbed the ruling-class attitudes of her husband but is entirely without his interest in politics. She has not been able to develop her own opinions and has no driving force in her life to equal Virginia's drive to write. She is like a Virginia without the edge, and with vaguely formed discontents which take the form of an admiration for Septimus Warren Smith in his defiance of life. She has lost her identity, thinking of herself as 'Mrs Richard Dalloway' rather than 'Clarissa'.[59] Clarissa has twice Richard's intelligence, observes her old friend Peter Walsh, but is nevertheless subservient to his opinions.[60] Her apprehension of her physical self – narrow, with a beaky face – is an exaggeration of Virginia's physical attributes.[61] She shares Virginia's sensibilities and frailties: before the book opens Clarissa has been ill for some time.[62] Her upright posture is emphasized, reminding us of Julia Stephen's final words to her youngest daughter, 'Hold yourself straight, my little Goat.'[63] Like Virginia, Clarissa has seen death at close quarters (her sister Sylvia was killed by a falling tree). With no profession of her own, she throws parties to amuse herself and with a view to Richard's political prospects. Was Virginia imagining a parallel life in which she had married Hilton, buried her ambitions and followed in the 'angel in the house' footsteps of Julia and Stella?

Hilton's career prospered. But despite his debating success at Cambridge he confessed to his wife that he suffered from stage fright and was not a good debater. This was a view with which Kathleen concurred, and she noted his bad speeches in her diary. He told her he that did not believe he would ever be party leader.[64] Hilton's political interests were wide, and during his career he would deal with such diverse matters as manpower, iron ore, a planned East African federation, Indian currency and free school places. His main area of expertise was finance, and in the 1920s he was sent on financial missions to India, Poland and Iraq, as well as fighting to keep his seat in the political twists and turns. It was to be a rough ride – the 1920s and 1930s saw one of the most turbulent periods in British political history.

After his stint as Financial Secretary to the Treasury, effectively the second-in-command of the Chancellor of the Exchequer, Hilton resigned. Lloyd George's coalition had broken down. The Liberal Party, suffering irreconcilable internal differences, split, with Lloyd George on one side with the National Liberals and Asquith's Liberals on the other. The coalition's failure was not a great surprise to political commentators. Cartoonist Sir David Low had satirized it in the press as the 'Coalition Ass', an absurd double-headed animal, inspired perhaps by the 'pushme-pullyu' of the Dr Doolittle stories.[65] Hilton spoke to Parliament about his fears for the new government, urging it to quell the rising 'Diehardism', to govern in the interests of the 'masses' as well as the 'classes' and to adhere to the previous government's settlements – some of which he had helped negotiate – in Ireland, India and Egypt.[66] In the General Election Hilton was convincingly returned to office under a Unionist government led by the Conservative Andrew Bonar Law. Leonard Woolf, who had reluctantly been persuaded to stand as a Labour candidate for the Seven Universities' Democratic Association, lost to Virginia's Liberal cousin (and Hilton's former boss) H.A.L. Fisher and his Conservative counterpart. Leonard was not much put out, believing that little real political work was accomplished in Parliament.[67] No doubt Leonard's failure was also a relief to Virginia. She did not mind hosting meetings for the Richmond branch of the Women's Co-operative Guild or the Rodmell Labour Party, but she took little direct interest in party politics.

By now Hilton was a seasoned politician. He was selected as Britain's representative at the 1922 Hague Conference on International Finance and in December was offered the post of Chief Whip under Lloyd George. However, he was soon caught up again in the vicissitudes of political life and became a back-bencher in the Liberal/Conservative government under Stanley Baldwin, whom he came to consider his 'spiritual godfather'.[68] Rejecting the socialist tendency of the Liberals' land policy, Hilton became briefly an Independent Member of Parliament and in May 1926 wrote to Prime Minister Stanley Baldwin of his intention to join the Conservatives. He didn't burn his boats with the Liberals, though, and managed to remain on good terms with Lloyd George and Asquith as well as Baldwin. That summer there was press speculation that he would become Speaker of the House of Commons, but this came to nothing. In September he was a delegate to the Assembly of the League of Nations, the organization Sydney Waterlow and Leonard Woolf had played a role in setting up, for the first of four occasions. Only a year after he joined the Conservatives Hilton's name was submitted by Stanley Baldwin for a GBE (Knight Grand Cross; the highest Order of the British Empire), which was granted in the summer of 1927. As if in celebration of the honour the family moved from Kathleen's house in Buckingham Palace Road to Leinster Corner in Bayswater Road, the house once inhabited by Kathleen's friend J.M. Barrie.

For Virginia 1927 was the year she published *To the Lighthouse*, with another version of Hilton in the person of William Bankes. Quentin Bell believes that his aunt used Walter Headlam as a model for William Bankes (see pp. 64–5), but Hilton Young is a much better fit. He is a scientist, as Hilton was when he first met the Bloomsberries; he is calm and rational but with a romantic side. There is another clue. William Bankes's favourite painting is a rather ordinary one of blossoming cherry trees along the Kennet, an area where he spent his honeymoon (as Hilton did, short-lived though it was).[69] This is less a reflection of Hilton's literal taste in art – he had after all bought several pictures at the Second Post-Impressionist Exhibition – than of his seemingly unshakeable reputation among Virginia's circle for conventionality.

All this time Hilton and Virginia had not spoken to one another, although Hilton surely knew of Virginia's books and she of his political career, through press reports. Then in April 1931 Hilton suddenly guest-starred in Virginia's subconscious when she dreamed that Vanessa had given birth to his child.[70] She had perhaps read some of the many recent reports in *The Times* about Hilton's parliamentary speeches and public appearances or may have been reminded of him by hearing from Vita Sackville-West of her husband Harold Nicolson's plan to stand for Parliament. From time to time Virginia amused herself by indulging in 'what if I'd married so-and-so?' fantasies about the men who had proposed to her in her youth. If she had married Hilton Young, she speculates on this occasion, Vita and she might both have been parliamentary spouses.[71]

The zenith of Hilton's career was approaching. When in September 1931 he was appointed Parliamentary Secretary for Overseas Trade he was disappointed, having hoped for and expected Baldwin to select him for a Cabinet post. He only had to bear his disappointment for a matter of weeks. In early November he was offered and accepted the post of Minister of Health. Housing, including the provision of accommodation for the poor, was Hilton's chief responsibility. He took charge of local authority slum clearance in the larger towns and cities and by 1934 was able to claim great successes in this sphere: almost every town in the country had a slum clearance programme. The Archbishop of Canterbury was moved to write to *The Times* praising the housing reforms.[72] As a minister Hilton took on a working day of sixteen or seventeen hours. He was no longer a young man, and the stress began to tell on his health, causing symptoms of a condition that would have sounded very familiar to Virginia's ears: the frequently diagnosed 'neurasthenia'. This was a vague term for any upper-class pain or lethargy that was thought to have a psychosomatic basis, a broad classification that encompassed hysteria and shell-shock. Symptoms could include insomnia, headache, vertigo and depression. Its equivalent is our modern-day chronic fatigue syndrome and in Hilton's case it took the form of nervous exhaustion. Doctors, predictably enough, prescribed a rest cure, and he spent a short period at a nursing home.[73]

Hilton's sights had long been set on the post of Chancellor of the Exchequer. With his background in financial journalism and his long-standing interest in the economy, this must have seemed an attainable goal. But just as his star seemed to be rising it suddenly fell. Among the problems was Hilton's dissenting viewpoint regarding compensation for slum clearance. While seeing through amendments to housing law through Parliament, he voiced his opinion that for the government to pay slum landlords for the demolition of their property was like a public health inspector paying a butcher for confiscating his flyblown meat.[74] These remarks went against the grain of Conservative policy, which viewed private property as sacrosanct. When Stanley

Baldwin replaced Ramsay MacDonald as Prime Minister in 1935, Hilton was ousted from the Cabinet. The ostensible reason for Hilton's departure was to let in new blood such as Anthony Eden, but his successor as Minister of Health (Sir Kingsley Wood) was by no means a young man. Hilton's own version of events was given to Morgan Forster in late 1939:

> I worked as a servant of the public, without wages, for 35 years, and was prepared to go on doing so, but the public said, as it were 'Here are honours and dignities. Goodbye.' I felt that there was a misunderstanding somewhere: but that was that.[75]

As the youngest of three brothers, Hilton did not inherit his father's baronetcy, but he was otherwise well provided for in terms of honours. He had received the DSO and DSC for military service, he had been made Privy Councillor in 1922 and GBE in 1927, and in July 1935, in compensation for the loss of his Cabinet post, he was named first Baron Kennet of the Dene, a title inspired by the river Kennet near The Lacket. But Hilton's entry into the House of Lords at the age of fifty-six was, effectively, the end of his political career. The Lords was no substitute for the Commons, and he spoke there only twice. Instead he went back into business world and was co-opted on to the board of several companies including Southern Railways and Commercial Union Insurance. He acquired chairmanships left, right and centre. One of the most significant of these was the Capital Issues Committee, a collection of financial and industrial experts that advised the Treasury on monetary policy, prioritizing demands for capital. He was chair of this prestigious organization until 1959. In 1949 he declined the job of Governor of the National Bank of Iraq at a salary of £6,000, a huge sum for the time.

While pacifists considered the First World War the result of political bungling, the Second World War elicited a different response. Bloomsbury knew that there was no possibility of a diplomatic solution with the Nazis. But while Hilton was a loyal patriot Bloomsbury was more sceptical and wary of government propaganda and rose-tinted ideals. Sixty years later it is almost a public duty for the dissenters to have their say. Today we cannot imagine a war without journalists and satirists questioning the official line and presenting alternative explanations and motives. But in the 1940s such things were severely frowned upon.[76] The Nazi menace, moreover, inspired such fear that patriotism was considered compulsory.

Hilton still had intermittent points of contact with Bloomsbury. At Fritton Hithe, the Youngs' Norfolk house, there was a visit from Duncan Grant, and one of the very few trips Vanessa Bell made to war-torn London in 1944 was to see Hilton. His old friend and Treasury colleague Maynard Keynes died in 1946, Kathleen a year later, but there were a few enduring friendships. Hilton often invited Desmond MacCarthy to stay at Leinster Corner on a Friday night while he finished his review for the *Sunday Times*, having procrastinated until the last minute as usual. Morgan Forster was still a regular visitor, but between him and Hilton there was, quite naturally, some difference of feeling about the war. Morgan was a pacifist and sceptic, the author of *Two Cheers for Democracy*. Hilton was not only a decorated First World War veteran but a Conservative former Cabinet minister and a peer of the realm. What could be more establishment? Throughout the war Hilton took a patriotic line. But as the 1950s came to a close, in the face of nuclear proliferation and encouraged by his son Wayland, Hilton returned to the pacifist views of his youth: 'Better that any nation, even one's own, should be subjected to another than that humanity should be destroyed. 'So now I should be a conchy.'[77] He proposed publicly that Britain should be the first great nation to renounce the production of nuclear weapons, and in the late 1950s he became the president of the Sevenoaks branch of CND.[78] Humanism was again his religion, and his view, at least of his own life, was essentially optimistic: 'So looking backwards I see the course of life marked by the bones of dead beliefs, as the bones of camels mark the passage of a caravan; but ending in an oasis.'[79] By the end of his life he had gone full circle, back to the Mooreist beliefs he and his friends had shared at Cambridge.

Hilton died at The Lacket on 11 July 1960, aged eighty-one, from a heart attack. His life had been long, beginning in the puritanical Victorian era and ending just as the 1960s were beginning to swing. Times were a-changing in the political arena, too. Only a few weeks before Hilton's death Wayland Young had published a book on public ownership and internationalization, *The Socialist Imagination*. A new age of international politics had dawned in which America's empire was replacing Britain's. On the day Hilton died Fidel Castro's supporters were protesting about the US sanctions against Cuba, while Senator John Kennedy's popularity was increasing to legendary proportions. A few days later Jack Kerouac's beat novel *The Subterraneans* would be reviewed in *The Times* as the story of the love affair of a 'cad', nicely combining the two eras.

Virginia Stephen with her younger brother Adrian
and Duncan Grant, formally dressed for a rare studio
picture. The photograph is undated but was taken
no earlier than April 1907, when the Stephens first
met Duncan, and probably a little later.

Above left 22 Hyde Park Gate, where all the Stephen children were born and lived until their father's death in 1904. During Virginia's childhood there were eighteen adults and children living here, including the servants, but only one bathroom and three water closets.

Above 46 Gordon Square, where the four Stephen siblings lived for two happy years from late 1904. There was a library/study on the ground floor and a large drawing-room on the first floor. Virginia had her own sitting-room on the top floor. It was at this house that 'Bloomsbury' was born in March 1905.

Left Once owned by George Bernard Shaw, 29 Fitzroy Square was Virginia and Adrian's home from early 1907. Duncan Grant remarked that the Stephens were probably the only people on the square to own an entire house. Virginia's rooms were on the second floor, and Adrian's study, where visitors were entertained, was on the ground floor.

Above Virginia's first suitor, Walter Headlam, a close friend of the Stephen family. In this picture, taken in the year he went up to King's College, Cambridge, on a scholarship, he is eighteen years old. He retained his boyish looks well into his twenties.

Above right The left-hand portico in the centre of the picture is the entrance to 24 Norfolk Square, near Hyde Park, London, where Walter Headlam was born in 1866. The building is now part of the Shakespeare Hotel.

Right The Gibbs Building, King's College, Cambridge. Walter Headlam lived in rooms on the ground floor (left-hand corner) as a King's fellow from 1890 to 1894. Headlam's protégé Rupert Brooke also lived here for a few terms in 1907–8.

Above The TAF (Twice a Fortnight) Club, Cambridge. From left to right, back row: Gerald Duckworth (Virginia's half-brother), M. Sanderson, Hugh Benson, J.K. Stephen (Virginia's cousin), Walter Crum, Walter Headlam; front row: R. Can Bosanquet, Marcus Dinsdale, E.H. Douty, M.R. James, E.F. Benson, E. Sanderson.

Below Dressing-up games at Talland House, St Ives, Cornwall, *c.*1892. Virginia and Jack Hills (later Stella Duckworth's fiancé) are standing. Vanessa, apparently feigning sleep, and Walter Headlam, in don's gown (he was made a King's fellow in 1890), are both seated on the *chaise longue*.

Above Cleeve House, Seend, Wiltshire, where Clive Bell grew up. Virginia Stephen first visited here on New Year's Eve 1906 and later used the Bells' home as the basis for two of her short stories.

Below 'Bloomsbury in Sussex': Charleston Farmhouse, near Firle, Clive Bell's country home from 1916. Vanessa Bell lived here with Duncan Grant and her children, and Clive paid frequent visits from London. The house is now maintained by the Charleston Trust.

Above Clive Bell with Virginia Stephen at
Studland, Dorset, 1910 (detail). By now their
flirtation was waning, but in this picture, as in
others taken at this time, they still exude an air of
guilt and discomposure.

Right Clive Bell in a studio picture taken in
1921 (detail). Clive's fortieth year was a busy
one: he was occupied with two love affairs,
published a volume of poetry with the Hogarth
Press and was working on *Since Cézanne*
(published 1922).

Above 42 Ventnor Villas, Hove, Saxon Sydney-Turner's family home. In 1910 he took Virginia here to meet his parents, and she described the visit in great detail in a letter to Vanessa.

Below Saxon Sydney-Turner with Barbara Bagenal's daughter Judith (born November 1918) in about 1920. Barbara was the love of Saxon's life and he looked on her children as his own, despite the fact that she was married to someone else.

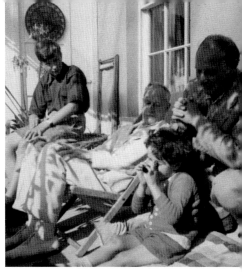

Above Saxon Sydney-Turner and Clive Bell (with unidentified children) in a picture probably taken by Barbara Bagenal, a good friend of both. Saxon is wearing the 'white silk Palm Beach' suit that Frances Partridge described him wearing at Ham Spray in 1942.

Below Saxon in old age (and in the same suit!) with Barbara Bagenal (and unidentified child) outside his Hendon lodgings in the late 1950s.

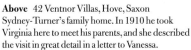

Left Sketch of Lytton Strachey by Henry
Lamb, 1910. Lytton first met Henry in 1905 and
had a crush on him for years; it was unrequited,
but Henry found Lytton a fascinating subject
and drew and painted him many times.

Below Lytton Strachey with Virginia Woolf at
Garsington, 1923, in a photograph taken by
Ottoline Morrell (detail).

Above The Mill House, Tidmarsh, near Pangbourne in Berkshire, the home of Lytton Strachey and Carrington from 1917 to 1924. Oliver Strachey, Maynard Keynes, Saxon Sydney-Turner and Harry Norton shared the rent with Lytton to enable him to leave his parents' house in Belsize Park Gardens, London.

Right 51 Gordon Square, the Strachey family's London home from 1919 to 1963 (no. 51 is the house with the plaque and plain doorway). By the 1920s 'Bloomsbury' had also colonized nos 37, 41, 42, 46 and 50.

Above Hilton Young at Cambridge in 1901, when he was President of the Union, with members of the obscurely named 'Magpie and Stump', the most long-lived of the university's debating societies. The society mascot is on the ground in front of them.

Right Hilton at the time of the East Worcestershire election in 1910, when he stood as a Liberal candidate against the Conservative Austen Chamberlain, with support from several Bloomsbury friends.

Top right The Lacket, Lockeridge, Wiltshire, purchased by Hilton Young in 1908 and still owned by the family. Lytton Strachey lived here from October 1913 to September 1915, while he was writing the first half of *Eminent Victorians*.

Above Hilton Young in naval uniform in the 1920s, after losing his right arm at Zeebrugge in April 1918. Unwilling to give up the pursuits he loved, he learned to write, drive and sail with only his left hand.

Above Walter Lamb in formal dress, probably taken when he was a Trinity fellow (1907–13). Although still young (twenty days older than Virginia), his hair has started receding, a fact that did not escape Virginia's notice.

Far Left Walter Lamb and family, *c.*1903–5. From left to right, back row: Henry, Ernest, Peggy, Walter, Helen; front row: Dorothy, Bessie (Elizabeth, their mother) and Horace (their father). Walter's sister Lettice is not in the photograph.

Left A moody nineteen-year-old Rupert Brooke in summer 1906, just before he went up to King's College, Cambridge, to study classics

Below Rupert Brooke in the garden at the Old Vicarage, Grantchester, summer 1911. Virginia stayed with him for a few days during August and met him at the Neo-Pagan camp at Clifford Bridge a fortnight later.

Left Rupert Brooke in Ottawa, July 1913, during the year he spent travelling before the First World War. This photograph, showing a neater Rupert than the Neo-Pagan of two years earlier, was given to Geoffrey Keynes by Rupert's mother in 1919.

Below This last photograph of Rupert Brooke, suffering from sunstroke on a camp bed at Port Said, Egypt, was taken on 2 April 1915. He died of septicaemia three weeks later, on St George's Day, setting in motion the myth of Brooke the patriotic hero.

Top right Sydney Waterlow in Greece where he was British Minister 1933–9. His wife Margery sits in the boat behind him. Because of his interest in the classics and in modern Greek literature Athens was Sydney's favourite posting and he was reluctant to retire.

Below right Sydney Waterlow in the garden at Parsonage House. Sydney was a keen and active gardener but later wrote to G.E. Moore that his labours there had probably contributed to his heart problems.

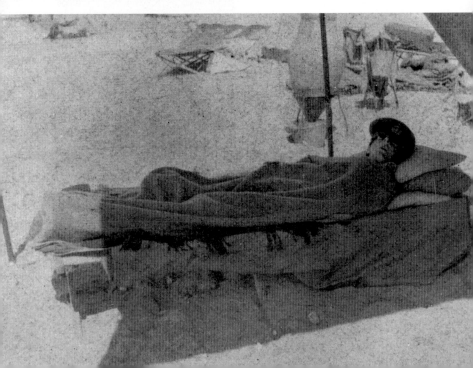

Parsonage House, Oare, Wiltshire, taken in the 1920s. This eighteenth-century house was leased by Sydney Waterlow in 1918 and remains in the Waterlow family. Virginia and Leonard Woolf first stayed here during the weekend of 15/16 June 1918.

Companion of Royals: Walter Lamb

WO YEARS PASSED between Hilton Young's proposal and Virginia's next serious suitor. Meanwhile her reviewing career was continuing apace. She had eight reviews published in the *Times Literary Supplement* between July and December 1909. Her novelist's career was as yet in embryo, but in late 1909 she submitted 'Memoirs of a Novelist' to the *Cornhill Magazine*, proposing it as the first in a series of fictional biographies. She took the editor's rejection to heart and never wrote for the *Cornhill* again. Two friendships developed. In August 1909 Virginia accompanied her brother Adrian and Saxon Sydney-Turner to Bayreuth for the opera season and found herself amused and entertained by Saxon's eccentricities. She even made some money out of the trip by writing an article for *The Times* about Bayreuth.[1] The literary hostess Ottoline Morrell, whom Virginia had met a few months previously, was becoming fond of her (as she teasingly told Violet Dickinson). Clive continued to flirt with her and sent her a poem for Christmas.

The following year began with a bang, with Virginia volunteering to address envelopes for the cause of women's suffrage in January and blacking up as a ludicrously unconvincing Abyssinian for the Dreadnought Hoax in February. (She was very much annoyed to hear that Clive disapproved of the escapade.[2]) For much of the rest of 1910, though, she was ill and undergoing rest cures with the Bells or in a nursing home. By the autumn Virginia was feeling better, and happier, attending the first Post-Impressionist exhibition at the Grafton Galleries and, as the year closed, finding her Sussex *pied-à-terre*, Little Talland House. The new year brought two new friends in the shape of Ka Cox and Jacques Raverat, and the summer yielded another – Leonard Woolf, just returned from seven years in Ceylon. This year, 1911, would be brimful of suitors. First on the scene was Walter Lamb, brother of the now more famous painter Henry but of a very different cast. A quieter, more cautious figure, he was destined for failure by Virginia's and Bloomsbury's exacting standards, but by his own and those of many others he achieved great success.

In spite of an impressive name, Walter Rangeley Maitland Lamb came from more humble beginnings than many of his Cambridge friends. Granted, his father was the celebrated mathematician and engineer Sir Horace Lamb, FRS (1849–1934), but Horace's father had been a cotton-mill foreman who died when his son was young. Horace lived with his aunt, who sent him to school at Stockport Grammar. Here he became head boy and befriended his young classics master, only three years his senior. A prodigy in both classics and mathematics, Horace was offered a classical scholarship to Queen's College, Cambridge, but instead accepted a place at Owen's College in Manchester (later part of the University of Manchester) to study mathematics. Later he took up a scholarship at Trinity College, where he continued to be an outstanding student.

Horace kept up his old school connections, and two of these proved very profitable, providing him with a wife and an income. He married Elizabeth Mary Foot, the youngest sister of the wife of his former headmaster. Elizabeth was companion to two middle-aged ladies in Manchester but came from a large Dublin family of eight daughters and seven sons. From beginnings as humble as Horace's (her great-great-grandfather, Lundy Foot, had sold snuff and tobacco in Dublin), she was, like him, rising in the social scale, thanks to her father, a solicitor and Justice of the Peace. When family misfortunes threatened to bring them down again, Elizabeth left for England to earn her living and sought out her sister in Manchester.

Unfortunately Trinity fellowships were reserved for celibate males. A timely tip from his old classics master, now in South Australia, informed Horace of a mathematics professorship at the newly formed University of Adelaide. Horace applied for the Adelaide post, was appointed and arrived in Australia in March 1876 at the age of twenty-six. He stayed at Adelaide until 1885 when, homesick during a period of leave, he accepted a professorship at his old stamping ground, Owen's College. He returned to England with his wife and children and settled in the Manchester suburb of Fallowfield.

Horace and Elizabeth were ambitious for their children. Socially self-conscious and proper, they ran their household for the most part along oppressive and restrictive lines. Alfred Ainsworth, a Cambridge friend of

Walter's and an employee at Owen's College, remembered a visit to Fallowfield during which Horace and his youngest son Henry dominated the conversation and his wife and daughters were barely permitted to speak.[3]

All but one of Horace's sons and daughters took up careers that demonstrated the legacy of their father's interest in art and literature rather than that in science. The exception was the eldest son, Ernest, who became Professor of Engineering at London's Queen Mary College. Helen became a fellow and tutor of Newnham College, Cambridge. Lettice was not at all academic and was sometimes considered silly by her siblings. Margaret (Peggy) went to be a nun in a Belgian convent. Dorothy, the youngest, went up to Newnham College where she became friendly with Ka Cox, who introduced her to Rupert Brooke. She taught at Bedales School, where the seeds of the group later nicknamed the Neo-Pagans had been sown. It was Dorothy who first introduced her brother Henry to the paintings of Augustus John, probably changing the course of his youth if not his life. In 1920 she married John Reeve Brooke, Rupert's cousin. She was an enthusiastic socialite and a friend of the publisher Victor Gollancz, the writer Rose Macaulay and Naomi Royde-Smith, the literary editor of the *Westminster Gazette*.

The maverick youngest brother, Henry, led the most eventful life of all the siblings. He left Manchester Grammar School with a talent for both mathematics and art; he was also a pianist of near-professional standard. He began to study medicine but soon switched to painting at L'Ecole de la Palette, a small academy of art in Montparnasse, Paris.[4] With his dark tousled hair and fine bones he attracted much attention. The novelist Anthony Powell described the young Henry as 'devastatingly handsome' but 'irascible'.[5] Lytton Strachey considered him beautiful but wicked.[6] Virginia thought he had evil goat's eyes and revealed to Violet Dickinson that Aunt Minna Duckworth was convinced that he was really a woman.[7]

There was a short-lived plan to share a studio with Vanessa Stephen, but this never came to fruition. Within six months Henry had impregnated and married the beautiful but vague Nina Forrest ('Euphemia'), whom he had met at medical school. Euphemia subsequently miscarried the baby, and the marriage of convenience broke down. Walter, visiting the couple in Paris in April 1908, found them broke as usual and considering divorce but amicable enough. Walter was only one year older but took a paternal interest in his reckless younger brother. However, the interest was often treated as an annoyance. Henry was strong-willed, self-centred and didn't suffer fools – among whom he included his brother – gladly.

The Byronic Henry hovered on the fringes of Bloomsbury for many years, admired and befriended by several Bloomsberries. His admirers were many and various, a testament to his wide appeal. They included flamboyant literary hostess Ottoline Morrell, intellectual and fastidious Lytton Strachey and dependable and maternal Ka Cox. Henry struck up more straightforward friendships with Carrington and with Leonard Woolf, with whom he took Russian lessons and went riding (Leonard judged him an inept horseman[8]). But there was one person he could not get along with – Virginia – and the feeling was mutual. However, it seemed that Euphemia did not share his opinion. She developed a crush on Virginia who, although fascinated by Euphemia's chaotic mind, did not return the admiration.[9]

Despite their short-lived relationship, Henry and Euphemia did not divorce until Henry's second marriage in 1928. His new wife was a well-connected aristocrat, Lady Margaret Pansy Felicia Pakenham. Twenty years Henry's junior, Pansy was the sister of Edward Pakenham, the sixth Earl of Longford, and Francis Pakenham, later the seventh Earl, the prison reform campaigner and father of the historian Antonia Fraser. When Lytton met his old flame's fiancée in 1927 he wondered if she would be able to tame the devil within him. Seeing Henry and Pansy together at a Dublin house party three years later he decided she had.[10]

Walter's and Henry's characters could not have been more different. Where Henry was creative, forceful and confident of his powers and talents, Walter was an earnest and hesitant character, prone to self-doubt and morbidly sensitive to discourtesy. Born on 5 January 1882 in Adelaide, he was educated at Manchester Grammar School and, echoing his father's early interests, went up to Trinity College in 1901 to study classics. One of his early friends was the extremely shy J.G. Frazer, later author of *The Golden Bough* which so influenced T.S. Eliot's *The Waste Land*. Here he also met for the first time Clive Bell (who became his friend), Lytton Strachey, Leonard Woolf, Thoby and Adrian Stephen and Ralph Hawtrey, who gave him his nickname 'Wat' or 'Wattie'. He joined the Shakespeare Society, the Sunday Essay Society and the X Society, and, under the influence of his new friends and having read Leslie Stephen's *An Agnostic's Apology*, he lost his Christian faith.

In Thoby's characteristic way of idealizing his friends he cast Walter in the flattering role of a Greek boy in a vineyard. (Within a few years Virginia couldn't help noticing that the Greek boy had aged and lost his hair.) Lytton was an altogether more critical friend. He thought Walter officious; bestowed on him the nickname 'the Corporal'; and, discussing his character with Henry Lamb, called him a 'eunuch' (Henry agreed). In his early letters to Lytton Walter played up his own homosexual leanings. Writing from Italy he borrowed Lytton's literary style to describe in sensuous detail Raphael's frescoes in Rome and the handsomeness of young students in Milan. For a while in late 1905 he had a crush on James Strachey (Lytton reported to Clive Bell that they adored one another[11]); then on Adrian Stephen (but Adrian was more interested in Henry and Euphemia Lamb). Like many young men of his class and time Walter was rather confused about his sexuality. Sexual experimentation, rife in boys' public schools, was sometimes carried over into the universities. Walter's uneasiness with women may also have been a factor in his dalliance with homosexuality. When his decidedly heterosexual friend Clive Bell became engaged to Vanessa Stephen, Walter admitted to him that he had been rather hard on women in the past simply because he did not know any and was unsure how to act in their company.[12] How odd this awkwardness must have seemed to the genial and lustful Clive.

Although Virginia and Vanessa had considerable respect for Thoby, his friends were not exempt from criticism. The Stephen girls' disillusionment with Thoby's 'Greek boy' began as early as May 1906. Walter complained to Clive: 'I do not know the cause of the latest gossip at Gordon Square; but for some reason or other Vanessa & Virginia were abominably rude to me at the [Friday] Club.'[13] He is still brooding on his slight ten days later:

> I am sure I should hate to think I had any quarrel with any of the Stephens: but I thought the behaviour of the ladies so strange that I saw something must have happened of which I was unaware. I suspect the mistake is theirs: I hope it may only be mine.[14]

By mid July it had blown over, with the diplomatic Walter shouldering the blame for any misunderstanding: 'I . . . confessed to my mistaken view of [Vanessa] & her sister's behaviour to me at the Club . . . [and put] everything in a satisfactory position.'[15]

The Friday Club (formed by Vanessa in 1905 and under her stewardship until 1913) was an artistic organization instrumental in promoting the work of young artists, including Henry Lamb. In its early days, Virginia noted, it had a dual identity, with half of the committee supporting the avant-garde in the shape of Whistler and the French Impressionists and the rest British traditionalists.[16] For Walter, not an accomplished painter like his brother but nevertheless with a serious appreciation of art learned during tours of Italy with his father, the Friday Club provided the opportunity to lecture alongside Clive Bell and Roger Fry to art students, painters and art critics.

By now Walter had realized that his true nature was scholarly. Two Trinity College fellowships were available in the autumn of 1906, and he made a bid for one of them, competing in an examination with thirteen other candidates. While he saw himself as the only true scholar in the group, he despaired of recognition: 'What chance is there, among a lot of electricians, plumbers, ready reckoners and chauffeurs, for a mere literary man?'[17] He awaited the fellowship selection results while preparing lectures on Tacitus 'for those good Newnhamites' but days later was able to report his failure, beaten by a chemist and a man of whom the best that could be said was that he once gave breakfast to Thoby Stephen.[18] Disenchanted with Cambridge and rather bored, he jokes about casting himself as a kind of Malvolio, donning 'a tartan pair of gaiters' to liven things up.[19] Malvolio was certainly an appropriate image for him in the eyes of friends such as Lytton, who thought him fussy and ingratiating.

He was shaken from his weary complacency by the arrival of grave news. Thoby and Vanessa Stephen had been taken seriously ill on their return from a trip to Turkey and Greece. 'I was of course very horrified by your news, & am very anxious to hear how things go on,' he wrote to Clive. 'My God, I wish I could be of some use.'[20] A week later, hearing of Thoby's misdiagnosis, he revealed his mistrust of doctors.

> I have told you how great is my horror of their vague methods and shifty behaviour, and how eager I should be to bring in a first-rate hospital surgeon to whom a mistake is really a mistake & a lie really a lie.[21]

He advised Clive to get a nurse in to control the relatives' access to the patients and asked him to confirm that Virginia and Adrian were still in good health. A fortnight later it was all over. Thoby was dead.

Walter wrote 'some sentences' about Thoby 'to show what he was like': these were published in the *Cambridge Review* a few days later.[22] Fred Maitland, Leslie Stephen's biographer and husband to Virginia's cousin Florence, asked Walter to send a copy of the article to Leslie's sister Caroline Emelia. As a result Walter was invited to her house, The Porch, where Virginia had spent part of her convalescence after her father's death. One of the subjects under discussion was, inevitably, Vanessa's recent engagement to Clive. Caroline Emelia had met Clive but evidently had her doubts about the match, quizzing Walter about Clive's prospects. Walter assured Clive that he had given him a good reference.[23]

Walter finally achieved his fellowship in 1907 and held it until 1913. For the next two years he taught a little at Cambridge, continuing to lecture in classics at Newnham, where his sister Dorothy and her friend Ka Cox were students. Needing extra income, he also took on the post of assistant master at Clifton College in Bristol, where Roger Fry and later Thoby Stephen had been pupils. Walter became depressed at the strict routines at Clifton which left him little time and inclination for reading and writing, and his mind became 'inured to vacancy'.[24] Largely out of boredom he staged a minor rebellion, challenging the headmaster on the subject of compulsory chapel attendance for the masters. On leaving he wrote with relief his final school reports, and looked forward to taking his place again among his intellectual friends. Despite his strong Cambridge connections he had viewed his situation as one of exile from both Cambridge and London.

As one of many friends of Thoby's who came under the spell of the Stephen sisters, Walter Lamb already had reason to suspect that his feelings were not reciprocated. But in his low-key fashion he continued to pursue their friendship. He visited the Stephens and the Bells in London and at their summer retreats. When Adrian and Virginia rented a house in Playden, near Rye in Sussex, in the late summer of 1907, Lamb was a guest with Saxon Sydney-Turner. It was not an ideal combination. Walter had not conquered his awkwardness with young women, and Saxon was notoriously reticent.

However, Virginia had plenty of work to keep her occupied and wrote to Violet Dickinson that she intended to ignore the guests for the most part. At the same time, seeing Vanessa (who was four months pregnant) happy and serene, she couldn't help comparing their lives. She wondered wistfully if she would ever have children herself or was destined to remain an aunt to

Vanessa's children, making up stories for them and writing egotistical letters to her friends. Despite her decision to shun the guests, she was piqued when the young men ignored her. A fortnight of Walter and Saxon left her exasperated by their lack of social skills. If her marital opportunities lay in the hands of young men like these, she wrote to Violet, she was facing a lifetime of virginity.

But while Saxon was later forgiven his reticence because of his brilliance and his eccentricities, Walter Lamb remained on the outskirts of Bloomsbury. In April 1908 he joined Clive's Play Reading Society for a reading of Swinburne's difficult 'Greek' verse drama *Atalanta in Calydon*. He was commended by Clive in the society minutes for his 'sonorous intonation'.[25] In the light of Virginia's later remarks about the monotony of Walter's voice, this may well have been a euphemistic comment or perhaps a joke at his expense. Walter was not invited to become a regular participant. Clive was annoyed by his prevarication and his last-minute decision to attend; moreover, Walter was based at Cambridge and Bristol for his two teaching jobs, and the play readings took place in London.

Walter attended only one other meeting, on 15 January 1909. This time Lytton left them in the lurch by fleeing to Cambridge on some romantic errand, and they decided to abandon their usual format and each select a passage from a book to read aloud. Clive chose Swinburne, *enfant terrible* of the previous generation; Vanessa, keeping up her racy image, read from Defoe's picaresque novel *Moll Flanders*, and Saxon chose John Payne's *The King's Sleep*. Walter read from *The Life of Sir Thomas Urquart of Cromartie*. Virginia, flirtatiously, and perhaps giving Walter false hopes, selected Edmund Spenser's *Epithalamion*, a poem written to celebrate the poet's own wedding and modelled on the classical marriage hymn, complete with the virtuous and beautiful bride ('all her body like a pallace fayre / Ascending uppe with many a stately stayre / To honors seate and chastities sweet bowre'), pagan rituals and invocations to the gods.

By the summer of 1908, Walter had decided on his opinion of Virginia: 'I have seen just enough of Virginia to wish to know her well; I fancy she has qualities of mind for which I am always looking – I mean chiefly her kind of imaginative, constructive humour.'[26] Clive passed on the flattering remarks straight to Virginia, as Walter probably intended he should. But Virginia kept Walter guessing as to what she thought of him. He observed perceptively to Clive that she seemed neither to like him nor dislike him and censured himself for his own timidity with women.[27] Seven months later Walter felt he was making headway. Like Walter Headlam before him, Walter Lamb also tried to woo Virginia with Greek – staying at Fitzroy Square as Adrian's guest, he translated Euripides for her. He had his 'first good talk with Virginia' and noted 'how friendly she made herself appear'.[28] He was still not feeling very confident, comparing his dullness with her vivacity, his hard-wrung writing with her flights of inspiration. Unfortunately he chose for a confidant his old friend Clive Bell, whom he kept apprised of the progress of his affections. Given Clive's own interest in his sister-in-law this was not the wisest course.

Walter had another opportunity to spend time with Virginia that September, when he was a guest of the Bells at Studland, near Poole Harbour in Dorset (as a substitute for Lytton who was being treated for his ongoing health problems in a Swedish clinic). But despite his strenuous efforts Walter did not inspire Virginia's affection or stimulate her intellect. In her characteristically mocking way she wrote to Lytton about the summer just past:

Now we are back again, living on culture chiefly, the Sangers, and King Lear, and the memory – alas it fades! – of conversations with Walter Lamb. I wish (as usual) that earth would open her womb and let some new creature out. They are grown very stale, and one will have to go back to nature I foresee.[29]

Perhaps Virginia did not hide her boredom: a few months later Walter, finding it difficult to envisage his place in the larger world, was experimenting with different roles. With resignation he wrote to Clive: 'I am not great myself, nor think I am or may be', and tried to recast himself as a Wildean pleasure-seeker.[30]

For Virginia, much of 1910 was swallowed up by illness. Vanessa and Clive took her to Studland and then Blean, near Canterbury, but Walter was not invited to visit, although Saxon Sydney-Turner was. Then on medical advice Virginia agreed reluctantly to enter a nursing home in Twickenham. Jean Thomas, its proprietor, was so taken with Virginia was that she took her on holiday to Cornwall to recuperate. Another stay at Studland followed. During this frustratingly prolonged period of illness, marriage and sex were much in the air: Virginia fended off Olive Ilbert's suspicions that she was making another play for Hilton Young; she fantasized about telling George Duckworth that she was to be 'confined'; she wrote to Saxon about lovers encountered on the Cornish cliffs and to Clive about the kind of man she might marry; she conversed with another *TLS* contributor on the subject of sexual relations;

gossiped that Walter Lamb had proposed to a 'Miss C' and been refused; and heard the news that Jack Hills's brother was to marry.[31]

Virginia meanwhile was feeling rather desperate about her future. On 27 May 1911 she attended the wedding of her friends Gwen Darwin and Jacques Raverat and was reminded of the emptiness in her own life. Perhaps it was to assuage this that two days later she lunched with Walter Lamb at Trinity College. If so, the relief was temporary. She wrote to Vanessa of a depression following the gloom of a summer storm: 'Did you feel horribly depressed? I did. I could not write, and all the devils came out – hairy black ones. To be 29 and unmarried – to be a failure – childless – insane too, no writer.'[32]

By this time Walter and Virginia had known each other for seven or eight years. On 3 July 1911 Walter accompanied Virginia and Duncan Grant to 46 Gordon Square where Leonard Woolf, recently returned from the colonial service in Ceylon, was the Bells' dinner guest. He had last dined there with Thoby, Virginia and Vanessa before sailing to Ceylon in 1904. Much had changed, but Leonard found that the Stephen girls' beauty had not. Virginia took to the familiar stranger straight away and invited him to Firle several days later. He could not come on this occasion, but when Virginia repeated the offer for September he accepted gratefully.

Walter continued his courtship by taking Virginia to Diaghilev's Ballets Russes (encountering Leonard, who was also in the audience, as were most of their friends) and to Hampton Court. He arranged an outing to Richmond Park for 20 July in the course of which he intended to declare himself. According to Virginia, they talked of noble souls, love and women, and she revealed that Lytton had proposed to her. Walter listed for her the reasons the obstacles that lay in his path: these included his opinions that she lived 'in a hornets' nest' and that 'marriage is so difficult'.[33] This was Walter's account of the inconclusive proposal:

> I decided that I must be in love with her, and I made my declaration. She was evidently affected, but not in the manner or degree that I hoped. I pressed my suit for some time, by interview & by letters, but did not seem to make any real headway. [A few weeks later, I] walked over the downs to Firle, where Virginia gave me lunch at her cottage, & we sat a while in Firle Park. I realised that she did not care enough for me, and I said nothing of what I chiefly felt . . . But I was getting rid of my gout, & soon began to lighten also my load of love.[34]

The full story was obviously more complicated. Walter declared his love and asked Virginia to wait for him. He even hinted that he should be one of the tenants in the house she was planning to rent with several friends (eventually 38 Brunswick Square). He was obviously fishing for a declaration from her, but Virginia claimed she talked only of the value of friendship. Walter had reservations about Virginia's critical nature, voicing his fears that she might find fault with him and flirt with other men after she was married. [35] She could not assure him otherwise.

Virginia felt sorry for Walter, whose affection and fear of rejection did at least seem to be genuine. If he had been cautious during the meeting in the park Walter made up for it in the ensuing days. He threw himself with abandon into the role of passionate lover, having obviously mistaken her lukewarm response for the beginnings of something much more promising. His usually tightly reined thoughts ran out of control, and he became uncharacteristically importunate:

I do so want to be close to you, and it is so horrible being away from you, that I must put down what I can of my thoughts and send them to you. Be your fine simple self and read them patiently and graciously. I am aching all over with the feeling that came on me when I left you on Thursday night, it makes me want to press you, body and mind and spirit, hard against me with all my strength and keep on till I have got some at least of your soul mixed in and moving with mine. Of course it is a much larger fiercer thing than that I want to do: you must understand it, for it chokes me when I try to say it. I believe I began really to feel it when I sat with you in this garden, where I am now. I am holding your arm now with one hand, just above your hand: this arm I am writing with is round your neck, and my fingers are feeling about your throat and venturing to your face, half in terror of alarming the pride of your delicate blood. Oh you must not laugh at me, or I shall kill myself: there is nothing else in the world for me but you and what we could make of the world if you could love me.

I saw you first simply as a person with an excellent mind and an imagination full of wonderful schemes. Then this year I began to feel you were a charming delicious girl, with a girl's desire of admiration and free impulse towards nice friendly people. Now what was I to do when I saw the other day that you are not arranged in separate divisions rather wickedly gaming with each other, but one whole woman whose body declares a deep wealth of feelings and passions only awaiting the decisive word from a superb intellectual taste . . . I want chiefly to do battle, passion for passion, looking to the heavenly splendour of the contest and the tremendous delight of the dance.

Dear lovely creature, it is intolerable that you should say I must not think of it. I have done something, haven't I? a very little, but something. Confess you feel a touch of me in you, tingling a little as you go about. I remember now, and go over gratefully, the delicious things you said, your tender concern, your pity, your distress. You knew I was not really ungrateful, you saw the bitterness of my despair. Every minute you seem to me more and more an angel of intelligence and love. Is it foolish to say I have made you a little in love with love, if not with me?[36]

Walter's passion was entirely unrequited, but he could not acknowledge the signs. He was also remarkably misguided on the subject of her (physically) passionate nature. Virginia, who had come to think of herself as 'a woman with very little sexual charm', must have been taken aback by Walter's advances, imaginary as they were.[37] (Or were they? Is he fantasizing, or remembering?) Did he but know it, his recurring references to her body probably did much to repel her, and this letter gave her much material justification for her scornful treatment of him in later years. The suggestion that his 'superb intellectual taste' will awaken her passions is splendidly conceived. In the same vein, he tries to flatter himself and Virginia simultaneously:

Can you see that my taste has always been a large active thing, leading me, although at rare intervals, to seize hold of the finest people? . . . It does move you, doesn't it, that a severe old priest of culture should fall down in his robes and vow with tears that you, as a human woman, are the one goddess of his adoration?[38]

Walter's impression was that, although Virginia had said quite categorically that she did not love him, she left him room for hope. He wrote to Clive: 'I am in love with Virginia, and have told her so. She does not love me. She seems touched, and treats me with perfect nobility and grace. I go on hoping.'[39] Perhaps his only percipient observation was that Virginia was in love with the romantic idea of love – that is, she was looking for a husband. Two days later he is sunk into gloom at not having heard from Virginia. His mood fluctuates from ecstasy to despair as he tries to imagine her real feelings in the matter. He imagines a walk with her during which she tells him marriage to her would only make him unhappy; he will weep and try to forgive her.[40] But his pose of melancholic lover lost him Virginia's sympathy. This fervent suitor whose ardour she could not reciprocate but who showered her with compliments soon began to exasperate her:

> I have . . . had 3 letters from W. What I say to him, I dont know. He wants to come here [29 Fitzroy Square] . . . I don't see that I can go on letting him praise me, unless I shall fall in love – and that seems as though one said unless I grow a beak.[41]

It also emerged that Clive had been making mischief in the background. Bitter at Virginia's criticisms of him, he discouraged Walter with anecdotal evidence of her shortcomings: her sharpness, her flirtatiousness, her egoism and vanity. He had given Walter an account of the Lytton episode, with what embellishments Virginia did not know, but she was angry that he had been gossiping about her. Adrian Stephen added to the anti-Virginia campaign with corroboration of her vices.[42] To complicate matters further, Sydney Waterlow passed on to Walter Clive's remarks about his own passion for Virginia, adding that Clive's attitude towards her was 'perfectly absurd'.[43] (Sydney, of course, had his own reasons for feeling proprietorial.) Walter was not entirely deterred, telling Virginia he could find no fault in her character, but his friends' reports had done their work; his elaborate caution and indecisiveness left Virginia with only an impression of his weakness. For once in the circuit of gossip Virginia was relatively blameless, and she complained to Vanessa about Clive's part in the matter.[44] Clive, annoyed that his criticism of Virginia had reached her ears, cut off his friendship with Walter, who was by now aware of Clive's jealousy: 'He seemed to regard both sisters, to one of whom only he was married, as in some sense his property or preserve.'[45]

Clive Bell was not the only obstacle to Walter Lamb's courtship of Virginia. The comparison with Leonard Woolf, recently returned from Ceylon, was not advantageous to Walter. Despite his hints to Virginia it was Leonard who was invited to Firle and to share 38 Brunswick Square, and Walter was left out in the cold. During several lengthy talks walking on the Sussex downs, Virginia had found Leonard to be an intelligent and sympathetic companion and on the same intellectual wavelength as herself. The conversation flowed smoothly. In contrast, talking to Walter was hard work. Virginia complained to Ka Cox that drawing words from him was like drawing water from a deep well.[46] Soon Woolf stepped in where Lamb had feared to tread. Leonard Woolf was a man to reckon with, vigorous and quietly self-assured. He was much closer to Virginia's idea of a husband.[47] Where Walter's caution and fear of ridicule had prevented him from risking an outright proposal, Leonard argued persuasively in favour of marriage and staked his career on Virginia's answer.

Inadvertently Walter interrupted the tête-à-tête in January 1912 during which Leonard asked Virginia to marry him. In a letter written immediately afterwards Leonard tempers his subject matter with a typically Bloomsbury joke at Lamb's expense: 'Don't you think that the entrance of Walter almost proves the existence of a deity?'[48] A few months later Virginia accepted Leonard's proposal. Walter gave in sadly but gracefully, writing to Leonard on hearing of the engagement:

> You have the love of the finest person I know of in the world, so I need hardly try and offer you anything more like a congratulation. I am sure you will do all in your power to make her happy, and that I can count on your lasting friendship as well as hers.[49]

Having lost all hope of Virginia, Walter now concentrated upon his career. In 1913 he saw the post of Secretary of the Royal Academy of Arts advertised in the *Athenaeum*. Although he had only been to the Royal Academy occasionally for the winter exhibition, he applied and was called for interview on 2 December – he bought a tail coat and silk hat for the occasion. The interview panel of seven included Sydney Waterlow's cousin Ernest Waterlow, President of the Royal Society of Painters in Water Colours. Within three days Walter heard he had been selected for the job out of 121 applicants. He was to serve at Burlington House under the President of the Royal Academy, Sir Edward Poynter.[50] His remuneration was £550 per annum, and (he told his friends proudly) he was to have his own offices with numerous staff under him. His main tasks were to prepare for councils and committees, administration work for the Summer and Winter Exhibitions and to be the spokesman on the subject of Academy selection policies and other matters. No doubt Walter expected it to be a long-term commitment on both sides, and justifiably: the previous secretary, the recently deceased Sir Frederick Eaton, had been in the position since 1873.[51] The President had to be re-elected every year, but there were no such conditions attached to the Secretary's tenure. Walter was selected for his unflappability, his talent for smoothing over difficulties, and, to some extent, his conservative attitudes in relation to art. The Academy had come to believe that a layman made a better Secretary than did an artist and strong artistic opinions would have rendered him ineligible. Walter was not a rebel or a maverick, and his chapel rebellion at Clifton was probably the nearest he got to non-conformism. While Bloomsbury sided with the modernists in art, his job required that he defended the traditionalists.

Walter's first year at the Royal Academy was particularly eventful. Early in 1914 discussions were under way for a state-funded school of art for advanced students. In May suffragettes attacked Sargent's portrait of Henry James and a portrait of the Duke of Wellington. A greater threat was posed when war broke out in August. Sir Edward Poynter patriotically offered use of the galleries to the War Office, and eight rooms were given up to the United Arts Force. It was Walter's job to prepare the rooms for military use. Like many large buildings and country houses at the time, Burlington House was transformed into a military zone: guns were stored in the galleries, and drills took place in the courtyard.[52]

There was a certain kudos for Walter in being associated with the Royal Academy, and its conformist line and conservative outlook suited him. One example serves to demonstrate the conservatism of the Academy at this period and its complete identification with government aims and policies. In autumn 1914 Poynter, concerned about the destruction of art and architecture by German troops in continental Europe, wrote to the US Ambassador in London asking him to use his influence with the hitherto neutral US government to protest against it. A few weeks later Walter received a letter from A.R. Powys, Secretary of the Society for the Protection of Ancient Buildings. Powys proposed a letter asking Lord Kitchener, Secretary of State for War, whether British and Allied troops had been instructed to treat with respect the art and buildings of Germany. Knowing that his reply would commit the Royal Academy to a political position on the war, Walter passed Powys's letter to Poynter, who wrote an outraged reply, retorting that he deemed it an insult to consider the British capable of such acts of destruction as were being committed by the Germans. He declined absolutely to associate the Academy with Powys's letter.[53]

The self-righteous Poynter was only one of seven Presidents under whom Walter served during his thirty-eight-year tenure. They were a mixed bag. When Poynter retired his place was taken by Aston Webb, the architect of Admiralty Arch, who was followed by the Pre-Raphaelite-style painter Frank Dicksee. His successor, William Llewellyn, broke Academy rules by retiring at eighty instead of seventy-five, having subtracted five years from his real age.[54] Edwin Lutyens, the prolific architect and designer of the Cenotaph at Whitehall, was elected in 1938 and teased Walter by calling him his 'pet lamb'. Despite his reputation for fine architecture, the softly spoken Lutyens was not ideally suited to a position that demanded frequent public speaking. A colleague complained that Lutyens was almost inaudible at meetings, and as a result Lamb was often his mouthpiece. Lutyens found his assistant invaluable; one of his favourite sayings was 'The Lamb is my shepherd, I shall not want'. During meetings he would look for approval from Lamb to see if he was doing the right thing.[55]

After Lutyens's death in 1944 the painter A.J. Munnings was elected.[56] Gerald Kelly, elected in 1949, was the last President under whom Walter served, and he did much to popularize fine art. (For more on Kelly, see pp. 69-70 and p. 253.) To have a brother who was Secretary of the Royal Academy should have been good news for Henry Lamb, an ambitious painter who had begun to cast off his reckless youth. But Henry only became a full member of the Academy in 1949, during Gerald Kelly's presidency, having rejected Walter's offers of help. In December 1954, on Kelly's retirement and three years after Walter had left the Royal Academy, Henry put himself forward for the presidency and received two of the forty-six votes cast. He stood again in 1956 but received only one vote.[57]

Despite the status of his job – and often because of it – Walter Lamb became a target of mockery for Virginia and Leonard. But they did not dislike him enough to avoid his company. When they moved to 17 The Green in Richmond in October 1914, and thereafter to Hogarth House, Lamb was a neighbour in nearby Kew, and they saw him relatively frequently. He prided himself on his taste, collecting rare books (Leonard couldn't see the point of such a practice) and with an interest in eighteenth-century architecture. He told Virginia that he would answer 'To Let' advertisements for local Georgian houses in order to view the interior.[58] His own house was tastefully decorated and immaculately neat; but after a visit there Virginia pronounced him 'a sham man of the world . . . Art interests him less and less.'[59] There may have been a grain of truth in this. Walter's post at the Royal Academy of Arts required him to smother his artistic opinions and develop his skills as an administrator. But to Virginia establishment art was sterile, and she satirized it in the character of Sir Harry in *Mrs Dalloway*. Sir Harry represents for Virginia all that is bad about the Royal Academy: he paints nothing but 'refined' pictures of cattle or stags standing in sunsets, having to suppress the sybaritic side of his character that is fond of music halls and brandy and wants to ask Clarissa to sit on his knee.[60]

For Virginia, one of the advantages of maintaining a friendship with Walter was to hear his gossip. His position at the Royal Academy brought him into contact with the royal family. Twice a year, the King received the Academy's President and Secretary in order to sign the diplomas of new Academicians. To amuse Virginia Walter began to relate indiscreet anecdotes about King George V. One of these, which reminded a gleeful Virginia of George III in the journals of Fanny Burney, concerned a royal visit to the Royal Academy, when the King, turning away from the paintings, asked his sister Princess Victoria where she got her false teeth from – his were always falling out.[61] This may have been the origin of the 'dentist' conversation in *Between the Acts* which mixes royalty with false teeth. Isa Oliver repeats to Lucy Swithin her dentist Mr Bates's remark that false teeth were invented in ancient Egypt and recalls that his partner Mr Batty talks only of royalty: when Isa was a child, one of his patients was a princess.[62] Virginia was fascinated by royal gossip and encouraged Walter whenever the chance arose. She became convinced that Walter came to call on them every time he had seen the King, expressly to tell his stories. She observed that Walter was not relating these incidents solely for the amusement of his audience and suspected him of an ulterior motive: 'each story throw[s] a gleam of light upon his own success, or tact, or prosperity'.[63] In 1920 Walter's royal connections reached an apogee: he was charged with writing a speech to be delivered by Prince Albert (the future King George VI) at a Royal Academy dinner.[64]

But whatever his storytelling merits, listening to Walter Lamb was wearing to Virginia because of his monotonous tone of voice: flat and grey, in her opinion, without passion or poetry. Even when his gossip is above par, 'the wildest romance would be flattened ... by that voice'.[65] In private Virginia and Leonard performed impersonations of him, and Virginia, spotting him at an afternoon concert, recorded his bald head shining like an alabaster monument.[66] She often remarks on his lack of hair as if it is a symbol of his officious nature; in Kew Gardens in 1916 he is 'as spruce as a Bank Clerk, and as bald as an egg'.[67] Alternatively he is depersonalized, talked of as a wax figure with an abnormally smooth head like an egg or a billiard ball.[68]

There is something faintly ridiculous about one's friends growing up before one's eyes, dressing up in formal clothing, becoming an authority on something or other and consorting with the great and the good. To Virginia it was often risible: to her the least accomplished of her acquaintance had become the most outwardly successful. When she meets Walter in the street she at first sees him as a stranger might: 'A gentleman in frock coat, top hat, slip, umbrella &c. accosted me.' A second later she recognizes 'old Wat'.[69] Virginia held in contempt the 'uniforms' and insignia donned by men to signify their importance. One item of clothing anathema to her was the 'slip', a kind of under-waistcoat which provided a white border for the waistcoat proper and which for her personified all that was fussy and vain in 'gentlemanly' dress. George Duckworth wore one, as did (in Virginia's imagination) Philip Morrell's *alter ego* Sir Julius in the letter-writing game of 1909.[70] Two years later Virginia encounters Walter at a Kew pillar box and has a shock of recognition: 'a smooth, sleek provincial looking man' turns out to be 'our Walter'.[71] He is enslaved by his profession, has given up writing, reading, culture; in short, he has become that most disgraceful of all objects in Virginia's eyes, a respectable philistine. In Virginia's fiction Clarissa Dalloway is less critical of her old friend Hugh Whitbread, who mirrors Walter Lamb's dress code and manners. When they meet in St James's Park the 'almost too well dressed' and 'perfectly upholstered' Hugh makes Clarissa feel 'skimpy' and self-conscious about her own outfit – she wonders fleetingly if her hat is acceptable for morning wear.[72] Like Walter, Hugh is fond of royal gossip, much to the distaste of Peter Walsh, who pronounces him 'a first-rate valet'.[73] Peter's assessment of Hugh echoes Leonard's opinion that King George V treated Walter as 'a superior footman'.[74]

Accompanying Leonard in 1921 to Manchester, where Walter was brought up (and where his father had been Professor of Mathematics at the university), Virginia claimed she had tracked down his spiritual family as well as his real one. The academics, never her favourite people, are all peculiarly similar to Walter: 'provincial, smug, destitute of any character, hopelessly suburban'.[75] Actually Walter agreed with her in this prejudiced judgement of the people of his home town, whom he likened to gnomes. Leonard, in retrospect, described Manchester in terms of the London of Eliot's *Waste Land*: grimy, grey, noisy, foggy, melancholy, the citizens moving like ants through the cityscape.[76]

Virginia was not enamoured of Manchester (or indeed of any British city except London) and had already used it as a metaphor for tediousness in *Night and Day* (1919).[77] The Hilberys discuss a relative who has married and gone to live in Manchester, which Katharine and Mrs Hilbery consider a social cul-de-sac.[78] In *Mrs Dalloway* Peter Walsh thinks with amazement of the change in Sally Seton, who used to ride her bicycle on parapets and smoke cigars, now Lady Rosseter, married to a rich cotton-mill owner and living in Manchester.[79]

Manchester is a metaphor for stinginess and provincialism in *Jacob's Room*. Mrs Plumer, wife of a Cambridge don, gives Sunday lunch to Jacob and three other undergraduates. She is worried that the rate at which Jacob consumes the mutton (a thrifty choice of meat) means that there will be nothing left for the next day's lunch. Her upbringing in a Manchester suburb has taught her to be careful with money but ambitious for her husband and daughters (plain, of course). George Plumer, the author suggests rather satirically, is a future Professor of Physics – Horace Lamb was Professor of Mathematics at Manchester but taught and researched in mathematical physics.[80]

Occasionally Virginia was brought up short by someone else's good opinion of Walter. After a dinner at Hogarth House she revealed in mock astonishment to Vanessa that T.S. Eliot and his wife Vivien were very taken with him. Did this justify a reassessment of her old lover? The other guest, Marjorie Strachey, was in scatological mood and talked of enemas and lavatorial matters. Meanwhile Walter told stories of the royals: it was perhaps the contrast of sensibilities that made the Eliots think him attractive, charming and witty.[81] But, Virginia conceded, 'He has a nimble mind, & makes himself much at home in his corner of the world.'[82] She liked being brought into imaginative contact with a number of other people about whom she was curious; for instance, the poet A.E. Housman, Professor of Latin at Cambridge and a great friend of Walter's, and Celia Noble (née Celia Brunel James), a wealthy social hostess who was the granddaughter of the celebrated engineer Isambard Kingdom Brunel and the wife of arms manufacturer Saxton Noble. There were also interesting invitations extended to her, such as dinner in June 1920 at the house of Celia Noble's daughter Marjorie Madan, which had once been inhabited by an eccentric sister of the writer and social reformer Mrs Humphry Ward.[83] Marjorie's daughter Nicola, Lady Campbell of Croy, says that Virginia 'formed a poor impression of my mother, pregnant and limp, and the house untidy and the garden overgrown'. Of Walter's friendship with her mother, she says:

My mother, Marjorie Madan, was Walter's great love, I'm sure. He first met her when she was young, in about 1912, I should think, when he was tutoring her elder brother, Humphrey Noble, before the '14 war. I remember Walter Lamb when I was a child, playing under the tea table at home when he came to consult my mother about marrying ... My mother encouraged him warmly to marry, which he did ... He continued to give my mother special treatment and tickets for the Royal Academy ... I know he remained devoted to my mother and gave her books, inscribed lovingly *'For those days'*.[84]

After the Woolfs gave up Richmond to live in Tavistock Square in 1924 they did not make very much effort to keep in touch with Walter. So infrequent was their contact that Virginia did not even mention in her 1927 diary the fact that, having reached his mid forties, Walter married Rose Brooks.

A statuesque and free-spirited American born in Chicago in 1900, Rose was eighteen years younger than Walter. He met her in early September 1926 during a trip to France; his first impression was of a 'dark girl wearing tortoiseshell glasses over fine eyes ... I thought her very charming in her self-reliant yet greatly enquiring manner.'[85] An artist and designer by trade, she had won a scholarship to the Chicago Institute of Art and worked as a fashion illustrator in New York. Having saved her money carefully, she had embarked on a three-year tour of Europe. She and Walter shared an interest in art but were absolute opposites in character. While Walter was fascinated by 'this pretty, smart, and vivacious American lady' who had Russian and Polish ancestry, she was equally intrigued by his erudition and sheer Englishness.[86] Within a week, Walter wrote, 'I realised that I was strongly attracted to her', and after another week he proposed:

I had grown so fond of my charming clever friend that I tried to persuade her to come & live with me as my wife, although neither of us had any money besides what we could earn, and she was 26 while I was 44.[87]

Walter's uncharacteristic haste may have been motivated by the fear of another man stealing his treasure. Despite her youth, Rose had been married and divorced and had recently been engaged to a wealthy American. She and Walter both agreed to go home and think about their future. Rose returned to Paris and Walter to Richmond. On 30 September he received a letter from

Rose that prompted him to repeat his proposal, and on 4 October he arrived home to find a telegram announcing Rose's imminent arrival at Victoria. He was perturbed by the suddenness of her decision and began to have his first doubts – how would she get on with his friends and his colleagues? Rose was introduced to his sister Dorothy and Walter's sister-in-law Euphemia. Both women liked her immediately.[88] She returned to Paris, but by now the plans were definite, and Walter told his friends A.E. Housman, Lawrence Haward, Arthur Hobhouse and the Nobles about his impending marriage. There was an awkward moment when Cynthia Noble, Marjorie's younger sister, asked Walter if he preferred Rose to her. Walter told Cynthia she would always be his dear friend, but it suddenly struck him that she might have expected him to propose to her. He visited his sister Helen and his parents in Cambridge to tell them of his plans and discussed his engagement with Henry. For once the boot was on the other foot, with Henry advising caution.[89] He thought it very amusing to begin with that his austere brother should lose his head over a bright and breezy American. But his attitude towards Rose softened enough to paint her portrait as a wedding present, and he became very fond of her.

On 15 January 1927 Rose and Walter were married in Richmond Registry Office, with a small family party in attendance. The marriage was not without its problems. Walter had decided he was too old to start a family, and Rose, only in her twenties, had to agree to a life of childlessness. There were, under-standably enough, some cultural misunderstandings, as well as a few small calamities. Rose once arrived at a royal garden-party fashionably but colourfully dressed to find that the other guests were wearing tweeds and sombre colours. On another occasion she missed an opportunity to meet the Prince of Wales when, stepping behind Walter to check her dress, she fell backwards into a hedge as the Prince was passing. Then there was an invitation to a palace ball. Since they were travelling by train from Kew in the rain, she wore waterproof boots with her ball-gown but on arriving at the palace realized she had forgotten to bring her shoes and had to go home to fetch them. When she finally arrived back at the palace Walter remarked wryly that she was just in time for dessert.[90] Virginia, who liked telling stories of her own *faux pas*, would have enjoyed these anecdotes enormously, but unfortunately probably never heard them.

Walter had grown apart from his old Cambridge friends, but he retained an interest in their lives. He wrote to Lytton in 1928 that he had followed his literary career and was proud to have known him. Walter does not seem to have received similar approbation for his own success, as his institutional career was not the kind that Bloomsbury valued. The psychological distance Walter had travelled from his Bloomsbury roots was demonstrated in a chapter he wrote for a book, *Art in England*, published in 1938. His contribution bore the unequivocal title 'What the Royal Academy Stands For'. In this book he found himself in an artistic debate with his old friend Clive Bell, who wrote the preceding chapter on 'Victorian Taste', which expresses profoundly different sentiments. Clive deplores the Victorian fashion for 'collectibles', worthless in artistic terms, and for the imitative practices of the nineteenth century. He levels a few insults at Queen Victoria and Prince Albert: she is a barbarian and he a philistine, and between them they tried to ensure that the art of their day was uncomplicated, unchallenging and immediately comprehensible. (Lytton Strachey, of course, had laid the foundations for this kind of royal-bashing two decades previously with *Eminent Victorians*.) The difficulty of judging what is good and bad in contemporary art is that it takes sensibility, Clive states, hinting that this is what the traditionalists lack, and so fall back on accepted tastes.

Walter's opinion, or that of the Royal Academy, is that people must be familiar with the traditional before they can accept and appreciate modern and experimental art. He points out (perhaps thinking of his brother) that if good artists are missing from the list of Academicians this may be due to a refusal on their part and not neglect of their talent by the Royal Academy. The purpose of the Academy exhibitions is to show the main route of progress in art rather than all the short-lived offshoots of fashion – he concedes that its function is to educate, not to innovate. There is a hint of criticism of avant-garde movements such as those promoted by Clive Bell and Roger Fry. Some artistic endeavours, he says, ignore the past and are designed simply to shock, the artist seeing himself as a crusading reformer. In fact, what is valuable is that core of art which generations of critics have decided is significant and worth while; thus, posterity will be the ultimate judge.

Walter Lamb stayed with the Royal Academy for rest of his working life. He had been in retirement for a decade when he died in Northwood, Middlesex, on 27 March 1961, almost twenty years to the day after Virginia's death. (Henry Lamb, born a year after his brother, died a year before him.) He had become a figure prominent enough to merit a notice in *The Times*. The obituarist wrote of a man who had become a functionary of arts administration, so identified with the Royal Academy that he seemed to have no outside life; so absorbed was he by his role as guard dog that he was unconscious of it. He had always been quick to defend the Academy against criticism, firing off occasional letters to *The Times* when it was necessary to clarify policy on membership and the selection of pictures. The accompanying photograph shows Walter Lamb in old age, his hair having receded into a fringe at the back but retaining the bright, watchful eyes of his youth, resembling a young man made up to look old. [91]

At his memorial service the former President of the Royal Academy, Sir Albert Richardson, gave the address. Richardson praised Walter's 'unswerving loyalty', his classical scholarship, his detachment from artistic bickering and his reticence at disclosing his own opinions on art. He had possessed 'the intuitional skill of a diplomat' and with his 'silent influence' was able to 'mould opinion . . . with greater success than is commonly supposed'. Most importantly of all,

> he never submitted to the influence of groups or actions. For Walter Lamb understood his place and his duties to perfection. Although walking in the full blaze of the art world he maintained the dignity his post demanded. For he was endowed with that most hallowed of gifts, self criticism. He held most steadfastly to his purpose of maintaining equilibrium in all his doings. He realised by reason of his historical knowledge that all can contribute something vital to the benefit of posterity and that although the arts are subject to fashion and change, in general purpose they remain constant.[92]

These tributes give a picture of a rather strait-laced, humourless man who has subsumed his character in an institution, of whom the best that can be said is that he knows just the right thing to do and doesn't indulge in any jumped-up ideas – in fact, the perfect public servant. This concept, perhaps admirable in an earlier era, has lost currency in the twenty-first century – most of us would be appalled to think that adherence to the status quo was our most prominent virtue. Walter's main personal failing as far as Bloomsbury was concerned was a lack of the creativity that its members rated so highly. He was analytical rather than theoretical or innovative and pondered at length rather than giving free rein to his imagination. This would certainly have made him an unattractive suitor in the eyes of Virginia, whose flights of fancy were her life-blood. Walter recognized that he was dull where Virginia was vivacious and that this would limit his horizons, both in terms of his Bloomsbury friendships and his career. His Royal Academy post demanded the development of those qualities that Bloomsbury deplored and the suppression of those they most valued. Therefore his entry into its hallowed portals effectively drew a line under his intimacy with his Bloomsbury friends. But he was comfortable with his sacrifice, having found a place in the world – where the qualities that they had perceived as shortcomings were viewed as virtues.

Dark Angel: Rupert Brooke

IRGINIA WOOLF SAID that all good-looking men who die young leave a legend behind them.[1] She was writing of her mother's first husband, Herbert Duckworth; the same is certainly true of her brother Thoby and of Rupert Brooke. To his friend and fellow poet Frances Cornford Rupert was a 'young Apollo'; to D.H. Lawrence he was a pretender to the sun-god's throne; to Winston Churchill he was a glorious symbol of self-sacrifice. Subsequent generations would learn to recognize him in two or three iconographic images – tumbling hair, floppy tie, androgynous good looks – without knowing anything of his poetry or his person, except perhaps that he was an English patriot who liked honey for tea and died during the First World War. Many of his friends and acquaintances remembered his charisma, his enthusiasm and vitality, his self-deprecating irony, the light he shed on less illuminated lives. He had a sunny and magnetic charm and golden-boy good looks but remained for the whole of his short life essentially adolescent – Peter Pan was an acknowledged role model. The darker side of his character made him moody, with a streak of malice, narcissistic, quick to take offence and prone to bouts of suspicion and self-dramatization, as those who were close to him found out. Virginia Stephen was one of the lucky ones. She was drawn within the compass of his flame briefly but did not stay long enough to get burned.

The son of a Rugby schoolmaster, Rupert Chawner Brooke was born on 3 August 1887. Although she idolized her son after his death, Rupert's mother was initially disappointed. She already had a boy, Richard, and had hoped for a girl, to replace a daughter who had died in infancy. Some comfort, perhaps, was the undeniable fact of Rupert's beauty, inherited from his mother and the subject of many compliments from his early youth.[2] But this superficial sublimity was to haunt Rupert and perhaps hinder his emotional development, in the years to come.

The Brooke family claimed ancestry from Matthew Parker (1504–75), Anne Boleyn's chaplain and Archbishop of Canterbury under Elizabeth I. Rupert's grandfather, Richard England Brooke, Rector of Bath Abbey, was a graduate of Gonville and Caius College, Cambridge, and the Cambridge connection was continued by his offspring. Of the rector's six children, one of the four sons (Alan England) became Dean of King's College. Another son, William Parker (Rupert's father, generally known by his middle name), initially found great academic success, becoming head boy at Haileybury and winning numerous prizes in classics. He secured a place at Trinity College but transferred to King's College on a fellowship. Because of the historic link between Eton and King's (both were founded by Henry VI), this was the first King's fellowship to be awarded to anyone who had not been to Eton. It was a small step towards democracy, but the move was not universally popular among the senior academics. This achievement apart, Parker was not particularly remarkable, being rather shy, diminutive, conventional in outlook and sadly unequal to the task of husband to his eventual bride.[3]

Rupert's mother, Mary Ruth Cotterill, came from a family of Anglican priests. Her uncle was a bishop, and her brother was housemaster at Fettes public school in Edinburgh, where Parker Brooke was his colleague. Mary was house matron and assisted her brother. Tall, dominating, wilful and with a sense of humour deficit, she set her sights on the diffident Parker and they were married on 18 December 1879.[4] Parker's next position was as housemaster of School Field House, Rugby, where his mild disposition and absent-mindedness met with henpecking from his domineering wife and ridicule from his pupils. Rupert's friend Geoffrey Keynes (younger brother of Maynard) was a friend of Rupert's at Rugby and knew his schoolmaster father. In Geoffrey's opinion Parker had no understanding of his pupils.[5] Rupert, too, thought his father lacking in personality and drive and realized early on that Mary, a woman of decided views, held sway in the family. Her single-mindedness is evident from a family autograph album of around 1900 in which she reveals in a questionnaire that the qualities she most values in a person are steadfastness (for a man) and moral courage (for a woman); Rupert chose faithfulness for a man – ironic in the light of his many affairs – and wit for a woman. Significantly Mary omits all the questions about literature, art, theatre and music, while other members of the family, including Rupert, name Kipling as a favourite author.[6] Rupert's relationship with his mother was ambiguous. Her love for him was possessive and stern; he admired her more than any other woman but was frustrated by her dominance. He employed charm and cunning, rather than more straightforward means, to win her approval. It was in his interests to keep her sweet: she held the purse-strings and if he wanted anything he generally had to apply to her.

Rupert was in his element at Rugby and, unusually for a schoolboy, was conscious that it was likely to be the happiest time of his life. Capable rather than talented in the classroom and on the sports field, he did enough to get by but not so much as to be regarded as a swot. After his death schoolfriends chiefly remembered his sense of fun, his love of books and his lack of pretension.[7] But he was not entirely without affectation: one of his friends admitted that Rupert would sometimes allow himself to be found enraptured by romantic poetry. There were few who could withstand his charm, and he was selected as head of house in his final school year. From the reminiscences of his Rugby friends, the picture that emerges is the kind of idealized schoolboy (athletic but sensitive) found in the boarding-school fiction of a century ago.[8]

The Brookes lived on school premises. With so little separation between school and home, life cannot have been easy for the young Rupert. It seems likely that during the Rugby years he learned the duplicitous tricks on which he would often call in adult life. In his ambiguous position as son of the house-master, double-dealing was perhaps the only way he could secure the regard of both pupils and parents. He quickly learned how to 'spin' a story in mutually exclusive ways for different audiences. His Janus-like tendency prompted a fear of his mother meeting his friends and lovers for what they would reveal about him. He was especially keen to keep his female friends under wraps, as Mrs Brooke was sure to take a dim view of them. On one occasion Rupert was so alarmed by Noel Olivier's plan to visit him at his mother's house that he sent a telegram to stop her. Geoffrey Keynes was exhorted to tell Mrs Brooke absolutely nothing about their friends. When a group of Fabians came to lunch they were enjoined to keep their socialism – and his own – under their hats. Rupert's fear of his mother's disapproval almost amounted to an obsession.

The same fertile imagination that was used to safeguard his privacy appeared in his letters, where he practised literary effects. He displayed the kind of wit and penchant for fantasy that is often found in Virginia Woolf's correspondence. In one letter, wallowing in the grotesque, Rupert claims he has embarked upon a novel in which the main protagonist is a 'dropsical leper' who resembles a giant slug and sings indecent ditties.[9] Then he laments that the gods misheard him when he prayed in Greek for the poetic-sounding 'rose-rash' and have given him 'pink-eye' (the decidedly unpoetic ophthalmia) instead.[10] As with Virginia, a robust and vivid wit belied his precarious health, closely monitored by his mother, with spells in bed giving him more time to hone his poetic skills. Fantasy and real life are often deliberately confused in his remarks, so that it proves difficult to separate fact from fiction. So far this will sound familiar to readers of Virginia's letters. But where her purple prose is spontaneous and brief, and often ends in bathos, Rupert's is more studied and sustained.

In the autumn of 1906 Rupert went up to read classics at King's College, where his uncle Alan England Brooke was dean. But, like many successful schoolboys away from their home turf, he found he had to build his reputation all over again. He began to take himself more seriously and dropped the ironical pose and the Wildean parodies he had been so fond of at school. He did not spend a lot of money on clothes but paid great attention to his 'image' and was very particular about his trademark floppy-collared shirts. He was indignant when, during a trip to Florence, the limp collar was starched by the hotel laundry.[11] It was not long before Rupert's 'artistic' look and handsome face attracted the attention of his peers, and he was cast as the Herald in a university production of Aeschylus's *Eumenides*. Rupert's non-speaking role required him to wear a costume with a short skirt and to mime blowing a trumpet while the sound effects were created offstage. The scantiness of his costume led to great excitement among certain members of the audience. One of these was Eddie Marsh, who would take a demi-mentor role in Brooke's life and have a profound influence on his posthumous standing.[12] Meanwhile Rupert's status at Cambridge was being enhanced by his old schoolfriend James Strachey, Lytton's younger brother, who was in his second year at Trinity and made no secret of his high regard – or for that matter his ardour – for Rupert.[13]

But amid the pleasures and friendships of Cambridge there was a family loss: on 13 January 1907 Rupert's older brother Dick died from pneumonia aggravated by heavy drinking. He was twenty-six. It was a great shock for the whole family but especially for Parker, who was at his son's bedside when he died. Coincidentally, Dick was just about to be promoted by his employers, a firm of engineers.[14] Rupert went back to Cambridge at his parents' request, where they thought he might better cope with the loss. He agreed but could not prevent himself breaking down in tears during a tutorial.[15] Several weeks later he channelled his emotions into verse, producing 'The Call' for the *Cambridge Review*. While the poem features a glorification of youthful death, it seems to express his own longing for immortality as much as a desire to immortalize his brother:

> Your mouth shall mock the old and wise,
> Your laugh shall fill the world with flame
> I'll write upon the shrinking skies
> The scarlet splendour of your name.[16]

While Rupert had no fear of death he dreaded getting old, associating middle age with mediocrity, conventionality, apathy and loss of beauty, as his poems 'Jealousy' ('Senility's queasy furtive love-making') and 'Menelaus and Helen' ('her golden voice/Got shrill as he grew deafer. And both were old') make clear.[17] Was it possible that one day he would embody these things? While his brother had not exactly gone out in the blaze of glory suggested by 'The Call', Rupert almost envied him dying in his prime – he himself liked to pose as the young poet destined to a tragically early grave. Tragically, all three of the Brooke brothers would die before they reached thirty, leaving their widowed mother to a childless old age.

One valuable although short-lived Cambridge friendship was with Walter Headlam, Rupert's lecturer in Greek, another victim of premature death. Walter extended the hand of friendship to his pupil at around the time his own flirtation with Virginia was reaching its peak. It was through Walter that Rupert's interest in Webster and the Elizabethan dramatists, as well as in the classics, grew and deepened. In October 1907, perhaps as a mark of respect, Rupert moved into Walter's old rooms in the Gibbs Building in the grounds of King's College. With his mentor's support Rupert stage-managed in 1908 an ambitious production of Milton's *Comus* for the New Theatre in Cambridge, celebrating Milton's centenary. This attracted a star-studded audience including Thomas Hardy, the future poet laureate Robert Bridges and Edmund Gosse. Brooke was working on the production when news of Walter's sudden death reached him. He wrote to his mother of his admiration and affection for him and his devastation at the loss of his role model.[18] Without Walter's encouragement Rupert found it increasingly difficult to maintain his interest in classics and was advised by his tutors to drop the subject in favour of English literature for his fourth year – realistically, they said, he would never be a classics fellow. (In the event, he scraped a low second in the classical tripos.) By now literature had assumed the foremost place in his intellectual pursuits.

Politics was added to his list of enthusiasms, and he started attending Fabian Society meetings. Both his parents held Liberal beliefs, and he concurred with them until he began to feel that a more radical philosophy might suit him better. He threw himself into his new interest with great energy, amassing newspaper cuttings from *The Labour Leader*, reading William Morris and studying Fabian tracts. He was elected to the committee of the university Fabian Society, discussed the 'new society' with H.G. Wells and campaigned for Poor Law reform. He was even a signatory to the Fabian manifesto which advocated financial democracy and sexual equality (even though he believed men superior). Fabian socialism was a cause that attracted a great many young people, and Rupert was perhaps not alone in being drawn as much by them as by their principles. During a holiday in the Swiss Alps with a group of Cambridge and Fabian friends, he met Ka Cox and Brynhild Olivier, one of the four beautiful daughters of the distinguished Fabian Sir Sydney Olivier and cousins of the actor Laurence.[19] Later Rupert met Bryn's sisters, Noel, Margery and Daphne, one of whom would play a crucial part in his life.

Rupert became part of another 'family' through Cambridge. To his great gratification he was elected to the Apostles in early 1908. Nominated by James Strachey for reasons less closely connected with intellect than with lust, Rupert found himself in a circle dominated by homosexuals. His first Apostles meeting was a reading party in April 1908, in the company of Lytton Strachey, Maynard Keynes, Desmond MacCarthy, E.M. Forster and G.E. Moore. Lytton, rather bored, wrote to Virginia that Rupert's yellow hair and pink cheeks provided a spark of interest, even when the intellectual pursuits on offer were not all he had hoped for.[20] He was only mildly interested in Rupert, however, too aware of his 'pose' and too surfeited with hearing of his brother James's adoration to fall in love himself. It may have been Lytton's reservations about Rupert's intellectual powers that prevented him from introducing him into the Bloomsbury circle. Rupert also had doubts about mixing the Apostolic and the Neo-Pagan parts of his life. But his links with Bloomsbury, and with Virginia, were mounting up.

Virginia and Rupert first met as children at St Ives. Virginia remembered playing cricket with Rupert and his brother when he was five or six and she ten (probably eleven).[21] The childhood connection had faded with the years, and in the interim Virginia had seen Rupert perhaps only once, with the Fabians at Newnham.[22] Then there were two encounters in quick succession. She and Adrian met Rupert for tea on 28 February 1909 and reminisced briefly about their childhood holidays in St Ives.[23] There was another meeting the following day, in the company of James Strachey and Harry Norton in Strachey's Cambridge lodgings. This was less to Virginia's taste, with much of the flavour of Thoby Stephen's Thursday evenings – the young men were reduced to silence under the pressure of discussing only what was important and 'true'. She and Norton tried to keep the conversation flowing but received no support from Brooke or Strachey.[24] Perhaps this experience deterred her; in any case it would be another two years before their friendship progressed. Virginia was not attracted to Rupert's Mooreist or socialist incarnations, but his next metamorphosis would interest her.

Rupert's English tutor, George Macaulay, an old friend of the family, became concerned that he was spending more time on social activities than on his work – a dissertation on John Webster. He advised his charge to seek out-of-town lodgings. During the summer of 1909 Rupert moved to the Orchard and later to the Old Vicarage in Grantchester, where he was only two miles from his tutor's family home in Great Shelford. Macaulay's daughter Rose, later a well-known novelist, was an occasional visitor.[25] He was immediately taken with his rural surroundings and wrote rapturously to Noel Olivier of his new Arcadia.[26] In Grantchester Rupert was transformed from a Cambridge sophisticate into a child of nature, reinventing himself as a Pan figure, leading a group of happy, laughing acolytes. His 'decadent' pose was replaced by its exact opposite: the outdoor life, with simple (usually meatless) food, casual dress, cross-country treks, swimming in rivers and plenty of mixed company. (By the end of 1909 Rupert's diet had reached wider attention, and he was asked by Earl Lytton to promote the National Food Reform Association.[27])

Drawn by his enthusiasm, a number of his friends gathered in his wake, anticipating a return to a natural and uncomplicated way of life, and soon the Neo-Pagans included Ka Cox, the Frenchman and ex-Bedalian Jacques Raverat, Gwen Darwin (who married Jacques in May 1911), Frances and Francis Cornford, the Olivier sisters, Geoffrey Keynes, Justin Brooke (no relation to Rupert), economics students Dudley Ward and Gerald Shove, and Noel Olivier's childhood playmate, David Garnett.[28] Their picnics evolved into fully fledged camping trips with tents and campfires. Augustus John had been gypsying around with wagons, mistresses and children for some years, but for the 'Neo-Pagans', as Virginia nicknamed them (the name was soon taken up by others), it never became a way of life. All would return to comfortable homes after a couple of weeks. And whereas John earned a living by his art, the wealthy families of the young 'pagans' provided them with financial backing.

Brooke's new principles had their origin in the pioneering Bedales School at which several of Rupert's friends had spent their formative years. Bedales, progressive and experimental, provided a milieu which was very different from the traditionalism of Rugby, advocating vegetarianism and mixed nude (but chaste) bathing.[29] To all intents and purposes Rupert was reborn as an old Bedalian. The attraction of the outdoor life was enhanced by hopes that it might improve his general state of health. His letters reported proudly his new regime of cold baths, cross-country walks and frequent exercise with a chest expander. Dudley Ward was informed that he intended to take up six sports, including fencing, boxing and ju-jitsu.[30] For perhaps the first time he felt manly and robust. The bonus of female company convinced him of the suitability of this new way of life. He was attracted by several of the young women around him, including all four of the Olivier girls. But Noel, the youngest, was the main focus of his attentions.

When Rupert first met Noel, at a Fabian social gathering in May 1908, she was a fifteen-year-old schoolgirl and he was twenty. He was immediately attracted by her beauty and aloofness and contrived to encounter her wherever possible. But his devotion was not monogamous, and it did not prevent him from making overtures to her sister Bryn. Noel reciprocated Rupert's ardour to an extent, but even as a youngster she was a cool and detached judge of his character. She was one of the few prepared to castigate Rupert if he grew over-amorous or melodramatic, and indeed that was probably part of her attraction for him. Despite his tirades against her lack of passion, it is clear that she was one of the few women he respected. They had much in common. Noel had inherited from her father, and Rupert from his mother, a streak of hardness: neither was given to displays of sympathy. Unfortunately Rupert had also inherited from his mother a puritanical tendency, which did not sit well with his desire for sexual conquest. Desire proved the stronger, and he bombarded Noel with Marvell-like persuasions to elope with him.

Eventually Noel must have been convinced of his sincerity – at least temporarily. While on a camping trip at Bucklers Hard, Hampshire, in 1910 their affair reached a peak and they became secretly engaged. Perhaps for Noel it was just a schoolgirl lark: she was still only seventeen. In the event, neither of them stuck to their agreement and Noel remained as cool as ever in her affections. By the spring of 1911, while in Munich to learn German, Rupert acquired another love interest in the shape of Elisabeth van Rysselberghe, a Flemish sculptor whose father was a painter and whose mother was a friend of André Gide.[31] Things moved quickly and Rupert decided that the time might be right for ridding himself of his troublesome virginity (although, strictly speaking, Rupert had already lost his virginity with the brother of a school friend in 1909[32]). He wrote to James for contraceptive advice and was rewarded with explanations and diagrams obtained from Oliver Strachey (who rather naïvely thought James was asking for his own purposes). Extra advice was provided by Henry Lamb, who preferred the risky withdrawal method.[33] Elisabeth changed her mind when faced with the complicated and messy procedures, and she afterwards claimed they never had sexual intercourse.[34]

It was during this year that Virginia and Rupert properly resumed the friendship begun eighteen years before. Rupert's memory of this time was stirred on finding two old photographs showing a gauche and chubby Virginia dating from around 1893.[35] When Virginia told Lytton Strachey in 1908 that she had seen Rupert in the company of the Fabians, she wrote as if this was her first glimpse of him.[36] It was perhaps the first time she had seen the adult Rupert Brooke. They finally became reacquainted through their mutual friend Ka Cox.

Rupert had turned to Ka in his frustration at Noel's lack of passion and the loss of his friends Jacques Raverat and Gwen Darwin to marriage. Much as Rupert hated his friends to marry, Ka was the more closely affected, since Jacques had been in love with her, too, and she was beginning to regret having spurned him.[37] Ka was the antithesis of the cool but girlishly beautiful Noel, being plain, maternal and earthy. Virginia nicknamed her 'Bruin' for her solid physique and character. Unlike most women of her age she was financially independent. Her mother had died while she was a child, and her father, a stockbroker, followed in 1905, leaving

Ka well provided for. She was a kind and loyal friend, warm, sympathetic and open-handed with her inherited wealth. For the wavering and uncertain Rupert Ka seemed to provide a haven of reliability. An additional appeal to his vanity and his purse was that she was a skilled needlewoman and hand-made Rupert's limp-collared shirts just the way he liked them.[38]

By the spring plans were being made to bring Bloomsbury and the Neo-Pagans closer together by means of a camping trip. The groups were already intertwining. James Strachey was a solid link because of his adoration of Rupert, but he never entered wholeheartedly into the Neo-Pagan spirit, agreeing with Lytton that the outdoor life was much too uncomfortable. Virginia was friendly with several Neo-Pagans and was fascinated by the Ka–Jacques–Gwen triangle, having rather hoped it would end with a marriage between Ka and Jacques.

It was time for the generals from each camp to rendezvous. James Strachey prepared the ground, bringing Rupert flattering reports of Virginia's opinion of him: 'The poor Goat last night fairly "went it" over you – thought your poems must be so good, as you had such a wonderful Grasp of Things.'[39] (Strachey's phrasing suggests that Virginia had not actually read Brooke's poems but was expecting them to be good.) Rupert confessed to Ka a slight nervousness before Virginia's stay at the Old Vicarage, set for 14–19 August. It was the meeting of two serious-minded but largely unknown writers from very different circles, and curiosity would have been natural on both sides. Among their friends, who expected great things from them, both were considered to have great promise. Virginia was the progeny of a respected literary figure and had published articles for newspapers and journals such as the *Times Literary Supplement* and the *Cornhill Magazine*. She had been working on her first novel 'Melymbrosia' (the forerunner of *The Voyage Out*, published in 1915) for four years and had obtained encouraging and constructive criticism from her astute brother-in-law Clive Bell. The manuscript now accompanied her to Grantchester for further revision. The charismatic Rupert had no literary forebears to boast of but had made a widely favourable impression on a number of his masters and peers at Cambridge (including most of Virginia's friends), as well as on his Neo-Pagan companions, and had a few published poems under his belt.

That August Rupert was working on the dissertation about John Webster which would, in 1913, win him a King's fellowship.[40] He was also writing last-minute verses for his first collection of poems. Having been rejected by

Dent, he had been in negotiation with the recently founded publisher Sidgwick and Jackson and a major step towards his career as a poet was about to take place. The resulting book would be the only volume of Brooke's poems published during his lifetime. During Virginia's stay he produced the contract and asked her to act as witness to his signature.

Rupert was on excellent form that week. He recited some of his poetry on the lawn – Virginia thought it overworked, but she looked back on her visit with fondness years afterwards: 'He was all that could be kind and interesting and substantial and goodhearted.'[41] There is only one letter that survives of Virginia's week at Grantchester, sent to Ottoline Morrell with whom she had spent the previous weekend.[42] One of the reasons for her unusual lack of correspondence may have been, as she tells Ottoline, that Rupert kept no pens or writing paper in the house, pencilling his verses on the backs of old envelopes. (If true, this would correspond with his reputed unwillingness to spend money.) Or less prosaically it may have been, as Virginia also says, that they talked without pause day and night and there was little time for letters.[43] Most of the undergraduates had left Cambridge for the summer, but Rupert summoned a few people for her amusement: the Cornfords and Sydney Waterlow, recently separated from his wife and already involved in a new love affair. Love was certainly in the air that season: barefoot pagans Olwen Ward and A.Y. Campbell dropped in casually to announce their engagement.[44]

One evening Rupert, treating Virginia as a fully fledged Neo-Pagan, suggested that they strip off for a moonlight bathe. She was by no means the first or last to receive this invitation: Rupert was famous for it. Perhaps prepared for such an eventuality Virginia rose to the challenge. She told Vanessa of her small adventure, and immediately the story spread through the Bloomsbury grapevine. Vanessa wrote in suggestive rhyming couplets to Saxon Sydney-Turner: 'I heard from Virginia. She bathed with her Brook. / And now they're at Firle. For what next must we look?'[45] Virginia was proud of her daring escapade, seeing it as an act of sexual liberation – normally Vanessa's strong suit rather than her own. Virginia was not by nature a bohemian but was keen to divest herself of her virginal image. She had started the summer feeling decidedly old-maidish but had within a few weeks received a proposal from Walter Lamb and expressions of romantic interest from Leonard Woolf. It was the combination of these things, perhaps, that gave her the confidence to experiment with the Neo-Pagan lifestyle.

Rupert accompanied Virginia back to Firle on 19 August. There was a national railway strike, which gave Rupert an opportunity to wax lyrical about his socialist beliefs. But his semi-vegetarianism appears to have been based on thrift rather than principle; Virginia revealed to Vanessa that he ate meat during his stay at Firle.[46] A few days afterwards, persuaded by Rupert at the instigation of Bryn Olivier, Virginia opted for the full Neo-Pagan experience: camping at Clifford Bridge in Devon.

The other campers had been specially selected to appeal to Virginia. Among them were Rupert, James Strachey, Geoffrey and Maynard Keynes, Noel, Bryn and Daphne Olivier, Justin Brooke, old Bedalian Paulie Montague and Maitland Radford (a cousin of Hugh Popham, the man who would eventually marry Bryn). Gerald Shove visited from a cottage in nearby Becky Falls, where Lytton Strachey was staying with Leonard Woolf and G.E. Moore. In spite of the trouble taken to ensure Virginia's participation her welcome was not as warm as she might have liked. When she and Ka Cox arrived at the camp on the evening of 30 August the others had decided to walk to nearby Crediton. The unfortunate newcomers, who had hiked eight miles from the station, had to make do with stale leftovers for supper, while the earlier party were treated to afternoon tea by Paulie's mother and went on to Crediton Fair. However unpleasant for Virginia and Ka back at the deserted camp, the day was very productive for Rupert – he was inspired to finish his poem 'Dining-Room Tea', a celebration of friendship which featured in his début collection ('When you were there, and you, and you, / Happiness crowned the night').[47] Still, Virginia was able to report with pride that she had slept on the ground and swum in rivers, like a true pagan.[48]

Adrian Stephen took to referring to Virginia's 'Rupert romance', teasing her as much for her sudden interest in the outdoor life as for her renewed friendship with the handsome poet.[49] When her own Bloomsbury circle was more established, she would see a threat in rival circles such as the Hampstead set (including Katherine Mansfield, John Middleton Murry, S.S. Koteliansky, Dorothy Brett and Sydney Waterlow). But during this earlier period Virginia was more open to the existence of other groups and, being single, found it easy to dip her toe in their waters. Besides, the Neo-Pagans were not on the whole writers, and those that were wrote poetry, which was no threat to her novels. She was interested in knowing more about their self-styled leader, this golden boy whose reputation preceded him. Virginia's friendship with Rupert was an adventure for her, a rebellion against type. He was not one of Thoby's circle like her other male friends; he and his 'set' professed to believe in fresh air and sunshine rather than indoor intellectualism. But it was not much of a rebellion; and he was not very far from type. Although Brooke's boyish twenty-four compared to her spinsterly twenty-nine must have represented a considerable age gap, his background was in reality very similar to those of her other friends.

No real courtship was involved in the 'Rupert romance'. Rupert was busy with his other romances (Noel, Ka, Elisabeth) and with building his reputation as a poet. He was more straightforward with Virginia than he ever was with his lovers, telling her that he was not yet ready for marriage but that sex was definitely on his agenda.[50] If he had harboured any romantic notions about her, they did not last. She was too much a part of sceptical Bloomsbury. Any propositions he had made would soon have been fodder for the Bloomsbury gossip-shop. On Virginia's side, the attraction to Rupert was intellectual rather than romantic; more curiosity than hero-worship. No doubt his good looks, charm and popularity reminded her a little of Thoby. But the Neo-Pagan period was, ultimately, merely a series of minor adventures for Virginia, allowing her to cast off her virginal reputation for a while. (The effect may have lasted some time. James Strachey told Rupert Brooke in April 1912 that Virginia had succumbed to the Neo-Pagan lifestyle.[51])

The friendship of these two complex people was largely a simple one. Instead of the disastrous collision of two powerfully self-absorbed minds, as might have been expected, it was as if all the neuroses and sharp edges on both sides had cancelled each other out. Evidently the two liked each other enough to explore the friendship further. After Clifford Bridge Rupert paid several visits to Virginia at Little Talland in Firle, and they met occasionally in London. It was during one sojourn at Firle that Virginia played muse to Rupert in the composition of his poem 'Town and Country'. In a review of his *Collected Poems,* Virginia described Rupert's peculiar method of composition: creating the skeleton and then fleshing it out later. Searching for an image, Rupert asked Virginia what was the brightest natural thing she could think of. Never at a loss for images, Virginia suggested a leaf illuminated by sunshine.[52] Sure enough, her idea was transmuted into 'Cloud-like we lean and stare as bright leaves stare'.[53]

Rupert was a denizen of Bloomsbury for a few weeks, geographically speaking, but did not feel at ease there. In October 1911, shortly before Virginia moved to set up her experiment in communal living at 38 Brunswick

Square, Rupert decided he need to be nearer the British Museum while researching for his Webster dissertation. He took Maynard Keynes's and Duncan Grant's rooms on the second floor of 21 Fitzroy Square (they were away) but complained to Noel Olivier that his accommodation was filthy and uncomfortable.[54] He was already beginning to consider Bloomsbury alien territory, and he felt uncomfortable about inhabiting rooms normally shared by a homosexual couple. Within weeks he had moved to other rooms at Charlotte Street, found for him by the trusted Ka. But Rupert's antagonism towards Bloomsbury was as yet nascent. His friendship with Virginia would be threatened and eventually destroyed by his delusion of a Bloomsbury conspiracy to separate him from Ka.

The crisis was triggered at an Apostles-type reading party in Lulworth in Dorset at the tail-end of 1911. A group of the Neo-Pagans, including Rupert, Ka and Justin Brooke, gathered together with Bloomsberries Lytton, James and Marjorie Strachey, Maynard Keynes and Duncan Grant. Other guests were the painter Henry Lamb and Ferenc Békássy, a young ex-Bedalian originally from Hungary who was being pursued by Maynard Keynes but was in love with Noel Olivier. Virginia had been invited to Lulworth but did not go, perhaps feeling that her new Brunswick Square house-mate, Leonard Woolf, would provide better entertainment. The trip had been intended to cement the friendship of Bloomsbury and the Neo-Pagans, and no doubt Rupert had cast himself as the leader, or at least the main focus of attention, of this hybrid group. There was a rude awakening in store for him.

Having his own agenda in relation to Ka, Rupert had arranged that the Olivier sisters would not be invited to Lulworth, in order to reassure her (and presumably to keep Noel out of Békássy's reach). But Ka had complicated matters by persuading Lytton to invite Henry Lamb, with whom she was beginning to fall in love. Lytton, nursing a passion for Henry, was happy to oblige. A rival for Ka's affections was one thing that Rupert had not counted on. And, as a rival, Henry Lamb was Rupert's worst nightmare. Handsome, strong and virile, with a heterosexuality that was never in question, Henry was a potent threat to Rupert's more sensitive and androgynous sexuality. Never sure what to be – passionate or cynical, romantic or realist, charmer or predator – Rupert was faced with an adversary who was unambivalent about his role in life.

Ka disappeared with Henry on a long walk soon after his arrival at Lulworth. She compounded the insult to Rupert's vanity by telling him she thought she was in love with Henry. Rupert's jealousy was aroused, and he convinced himself that he had been deeply in love with Ka, while Henry was a heartless philanderer who had come between them. He suspected a plot, and, perhaps knowing that it was useless to fire darts at Henry's armour, Rupert turned his ire and his latent homophobia on Lytton. In Rupert's mind Lytton was the means by which the three others had been duped into playing the parts designed for them. Meanwhile, the supposedly machiavellian Lytton was writing to Henry to advise him that Ka was not the right person for him either as wife or mistress and asking him to back off, leaving the field open for Rupert.[55] These Bloomsbury dramas, he told Ottoline Morrell, put Dostoyevsky in the shade.[56]

Rupert's fit of sexual jealousy led to a mental breakdown during which he returned to his mother's care. He was still in the grip of a kind of madness when he made a serious misjudgement, for which the unfortunate Ka would suffer as much as he would. In early 1912 he set about trying to convince Ka that his jealousy signified that he was in love with her. He bombarded her with passionate love letters in which he related every movement of his rollercoaster emotions and the dark thoughts that circled his disturbed mind. At first she was understandably confused at his sudden ardour. In the same letter he would flatter and curse her with equal vehemence. Ka finally agreed to meet him so that they could resolve the situation. But she had been waiting for the right moment to make a confession. She was still in love with Henry Lamb whom she had been meeting at Bloomsbury gatherings. Rupert, confident that Ka had come to him out of love and loyalty, was shattered to hear she had come out of pity. He insisted that they prove their love through sex, and Ka consented. But this served only as a palliative, and Rupert's feeling of betrayal returned.

Then Ka announced her fear that she was pregnant – a false alarm, as it turned out. But when Rupert felt he might be trapped into marriage he recoiled in horror. His deep-seated disgust about sex clouded his judgement further. He began to feel that Ka had contaminated him, and his letters from this period are full of images of dirt and filth. Like Lady Macbeth, he wanted to rid himself of past events that he had instigated, to wash his hands of the whole affair. Sexual fulfilment had not met with his romantic expectations. He was still unsatisfied, yearning for Noel. He had been driven more by jealousy than love, and now his suppressed puritanism broke out. With misogynistic logic he blamed Ka for giving in to him. He cast her off, clumsily, disgusted and exhausted with the whole affair. Although it precedes the Ka episode, Rupert's poem 'Lust' could have been written in its aftermath:

> Love wakens love! I felt your hot wrist shiver,
> And suddenly the mad victory I planned
> Flashed real, in your burning bending head . . .
> My conqueror's blood was cool as a deep river
> In shadow; and my heart beneath your hand
> Quieter than a dead man on a bed.[57]

The extent of Rupert's antipathy towards Bloomsbury did not surface for several months. He continued to correspond with his enemy's brother, James Strachey, regretting the passionate scenes at Lulworth.[58] In March he wrote to Virginia on hearing of her mental collapse, grateful to communicate with a fellow sufferer. Sensing a commonality, he aligns himself with her, being literary and of a sensitive physical and mental condition, professing to 'hate' James and Ka for their robustness. He entreats her not to have a nervous breakdown, as he has just done. Whatever sympathy he may have felt, the focus of his letter soon moves from her mental health to his. The tone is flippant, which could be read as light-headed relief for his emergence from the blackness, or, alternatively as a pose of suffering, an addition to the Rupert myth. Given the seriousness of Virginia's illness, his remarks, clearly intended to bear the stamp of authority from his recent sufferings, sound insensitive and suggest a scant knowledge of her mental history. There is particular lack of feeling in his gratuitous tale of two choirboys raping a ten-year-old boy during a church service, an indication that the 'filthiness' of sex was preying on his mind.[59] The following month Rupert took Bryn Olivier to tea with Virginia at Asheham, and she summed them up for Ka: Bryn's eye was cold and glassy; Rupert was a cut-price Byron.[60]

Rupert was now uneasy about Bloomsbury's influence on his other friends, especially Noel. He patronizingly asked Jacques Raverat to keep an eye on Noel when she spent a weekend with Virginia in May 1912, anxious about 'the subtle degradation of the collective atmosphere' and a weakening of his own influence.[61] Noel sensibly told her possessive lover that while she might avoid James and Adrian for her own reasons (they were both in love with her), she looked forward to seeing Virginia and would by no means avoid a meeting.[62] Ignoring the youthful Noel's unusual toughness, Rupert repeatedly warned her against being tainted by Bloomsbury.[63]

Although Brooke feared the influence of those he and Jacques Raverat called 'the Jews', the only Jew among them was a man he hardly knew and didn't particularly dislike. When Leonard Woolf met Rupert Brooke his first impression was of a young Adonis.[64] That Rupert thought little of him is evident from his words to James Strachey: 'Was Woolf, who seems very nice, ever more than minor?'[65] As he usually did when his female friends were annexed by another man, Rupert became proprietorial on finding out Virginia was engaged to Leonard in the summer of 1912. 'His attitude to all other males within a short radius of any attractive female was ridiculously jealous – the attitude of the farmyard cock among the hens,' remembered Leonard.[66] Because he connected Bloomsbury with pestilential taint Rupert rarely visited Virginia in Fitzroy or Brunswick Squares. Physical distance from WC1 reduced his anxiety. When Virginia moved with Leonard to Clifford's Inn at the end of October he had fewer qualms about visiting her. He noted that she was 'calmer' after her marriage but that a psychological distance had crept between them.[67] The lack of rapport was understandable. Rupert looked upon her marriage – as he looked upon all his friends' marriages – as a fall from grace, an abandonment of the golden circle that he had created. The situation could hardly have been improved by the fact that he had declared war on Lytton, one of her closest friends.

The wound began to fester. Rupert's preoccupation with insects (surely a disadvantage to one who regularly camps out of doors) developed into an obsession, and he ranted to James about woodlice invading his room at night as though they were Bloomsbury-induced nightmares, like D.H. Lawrence's black beetles.[68] There was a final showdown with James in which Rupert, levelling wild accusations even at Virginia and Duncan whom he liked, effectively ended the friendship.[69] James, as Lytton's brother, and Virginia, as Lytton's friend, were debarred from Rupert's society. Although in theory he was able to cope with Lytton or Virginia as individuals, Rupert's suspicion of 'Bloomsbury' en masse never died. (Ironically, Lytton had also been distancing himself from Bloomsbury during 1912.) Rupert fumed to Noel Olivier that he would no longer tolerate carriers of disease such as the Stracheys. In the same letter he threatens suicide, laments Noel's stupidity for not seeing he will be the greatest poet in England and insists that they must marry.[70] Little wonder that his friends believed that he had lost all sense of proportion and become mentally unstable.

The tragedy of Rupert's situation was that he never recognized his distorted view for what it was – mental illness, a kind of temporary insanity, that needed medical attention. This was very different to Virginia's attitude to her bouts of 'madness'. From childhood she had been under strict medical supervision, although her doctors' knowledge of the dysfunctional mind was limited. Her submission to rest cures was extremely reluctant, but she became accustomed to putting her life on hold for months at a time. She chafed at the bit her doctors imposed on her but never completely rejected their advice, even when their 'treatment' seemed to do little good.

Rupert consulted one of Virginia's doctors, Dr Maurice Craig of Harley Street. Craig prescribed, as he did for Virginia, the standard regime of complete rest, plenty of food ('stuffing') and abstinence from physical exercise and intellectual stimulation. Naturally there was little for Rupert to do but brood on the wrongs he had suffered. Cognitive therapy was then a long way off. But Virginia recognized the difference between illness and wellness. Like Rupert she railed when ill at her nearest and dearest, suspecting Leonard and Vanessa of conspiring to keep her in nursing homes, and she wrote some very unsettling letters to friends. But when she was better she realized that her mental instability had affected her outlook. When Rupert was well he continued to nurse his enmities and accuse his friends, without recognizing that he had subjected them and himself to a frenzy of jealousy for a woman he did not even love.

During the two years before the outbreak of the First World War Rupert drew away from his Cambridge and Bloomsbury friends and began to cultivate his friendship with Eddie Marsh, now Winston Churchill's private secretary. The wealthy and open-handed Marsh, fifteen years older than Rupert, had followed with interest Rupert's burgeoning poetic career. He now acted as his devoted publicist and sponsor – as he did for several others, including the painter Mark Gertler. He and Rupert came up with the idea of an anthology of contemporary poetry that led to the five-volume series, *Georgian Poetry*. Through Marsh Rupert became acquainted with other poets and writers, including Katherine Mansfield, John Middleton Murry, Lascelles Abercrombie, Walter de la Mare, Harold Munro, John Drinkwater and Wilfrid Wilson Gibson. He courted the modernizers, purchasing a sculpture by Eric Gill and receiving an invitation to dine with W.B. Yeats and Ezra Pound. He was rehabilitated to the extent that even Geoffrey Keynes's admission that he was courting Ka Cox was greeted calmly.[71] But he was still unequal to the task of regarding the happiness of his married friends with equanimity: their loving glances and caresses continued to touch a raw nerve.

In 1913–14 Rupert spent a year out of England, travelling in Canada, America and the South Seas. He took on a commission from the *Westminster Gazette*, for which he had written many poems, to write a series of articles about his American experiences.[72] While he did not entirely shake off his past, he managed to put some space between his new travel-writer self and the old bitter persona of 1911–12. He certainly had plenty to keep him occupied, moving on to a new town or a new country every few weeks and meeting dozens of adoring strangers. With oceans between them it was easier to distance himself mentally from the women he had left behind, and before long he met another, the Marchesa Capponi, the American widow of an Italian aristocrat. She, too, was kept at arm's length, and he kept travelling. In a South Seas paradise he had a sensual and for once trouble-free affair with a Tahitian girl, Taatamata, who spoke very little English, precluding the usual complications.[73] It was probably one of the happiest and most fulfilling years of his life. But it had to come to an end, and Brooke was not entirely sorry. On 5 June 1914 he arrived back in England.

He barely had time to slip back into his 'new' old life before the blow came that was to put on hold the lives of millions across Europe. War was declared on 4 August, the day after Rupert's twenty-seventh birthday. He would not live to see another. He was not, like many of the Bloomsbury Group, a conscientious objector during the First World War. Part of his anti-outsider pose was to disdain Germans, an attitude that seems to have been shared by his family – aged nineteen Rupert had written to his father from Florence that attempts to attract German tourists to the city were fortunately failing.[74] But this had not deterred him from travelling to Munich and Berlin subsequently. One of his most famous poems, 'The Old Vicarage, Grantchester', was written when he was feeling homesick in Berlin. Like many patriots he appreciated his home best when he was away from it.

Rupert yearned to make his mark somehow, and war gave him the opportunity. Even before the call for volunteers went out he turned his attentions to his own part in the approaching struggle. The war for him was a superior, and – importantly – external 'cause' that could help to free him, once and for all, from his inner turmoil. Instead of fighting his own demons he had foreign ones to battle with. He considered a posting as an interpreter, a labourer on a French farm and a war correspondent, but got nowhere. Characteristically, he balked against becoming an ordinary soldier, just one more cog in the military machine. But other avenues having failed, at the end of September he applied to join up.

First Lord of the Admiralty Winston Churchill was assembling a new type of unit – the Royal Naval Division, designed to be seagoing but to fight on land. Rupert's devoted friend Eddie Marsh ensured there was no delay in securing him an RND commission to the post of sub-lieutenant. But if Rupert had hoped to distinguish himself at the Front, he was doomed to disappointment. The nearest he came was the retreat from Antwerp in the autumn of 1914.[75] Then, the following February, his division started out for the Dardanelles and Gallipolli.

In his absence Rupert was becoming a highly successful poet. The *Times Literary Supplement* reviewed the fourth issue of *New Numbers*, devoted to the verse of Rupert Brooke, John Drinkwater, Lascelles Abercrombie and Wilfrid Wilson Gibson. The reviewer's praise was unalloyed: Rupert's poetry was full of promise and his sonnets were comparable with Philip Sidney's.[76] On 4 April 1915, Easter Sunday, Dean Inge read 'The Soldier' in St Paul's Cathedral as a tribute to the war dead. Brooke's sonnet struck the right note with a public desperate to hear that their dead sons, husbands, brothers and fathers had not been lost in vain. He had unquestionably reached the establishment, but fame had arrived too late.

Despite his gung-ho enthusiasm to be in the middle of the action Rupert's lifelong physical frailty meant he was not able to withstand the demands of navy life. He began the trip with seasickness, and by the end of March he had developed sunstroke. Probably the last photograph ever taken of him (2 April 1915) shows him lying asleep in his officer's cap and sunglasses on a simple wooden-framed bed in a patch of shade, covered by a blanket even in the heat of Port Said. Weakened by agonizing headaches, diarrhoea and vomiting, he developed a sore on his upper lip – probably an infected mosquito bite – that led to septicaemia. His decline was swift. He slipped into semi-consciousness on 22 April and died on the afternoon of the following day –St George's Day – on a French hospital ship anchored off the island of Skyros in Trebuki Bay. He was buried in an olive grove on Skyros, where he had spent 20 April on manoeuvres with his fellow soldiers (several of whom were personal friends), and admired its beauty. In spite of its remoteness, his grave, with a tomb commissioned by his mother replacing the original stone cairn and wooden cross, has become a place of pilgrimage for his admirers. In 1931 a statue on a pedestal was erected in Brooke Square, Skyros town, as a tribute to him. Another whisper added to the rumour mill was that the model was a Belgian male prostitute. Mrs Brooke, having died the previous year, was spared this last indignity.[77]

Rupert's posthumous reputation was helped along by friends in high places. For the Prime Minister, Herbert Asquith, whose son Arthur was Rupert's fellow officer, his loss was the greatest of the war so far.[78] His daughter Violet, with whom Rupert had carried on a flirtation (as well as having an affair with her friend Eileen Wellesley), was distraught. Staying in Dublin with friends, she was comforted by Kathleen Scott, the widow of Captain R.F. Scott and future wife of Hilton Young.[79] Winston Churchill, who had secured Rupert's naval commission and unwittingly set him on the road to dissolution, contributed a memoir for his obituary. But it was more a call to arms than a commemoration of a life lost. The stirring rhetoric mythologized Rupert as a young god, symbol of all that was best and noblest in English manhood, conveniently neglecting to mention all his more human aspects.[80] But then Churchill had hardly known him: a few conversations across dining tables was all their acquaintance had amounted to.[81] D.H. Lawrence, perhaps partly drawn to Rupert through their mutual loathing of Bloomsbury, was devastated by the news of his death. Believing initial reports that he had died from sunstroke, he muttered about the hubris of the faux sun-god being slain by the true sun-god. Significantly, he does not ignore the artificiality of Rupert's concocted image, referring to his self-deifying 'pose'.[82]

Rupert's mother received dozens of letters and elegies dedicated to the fallen hero, and dozens more were sent to the press. One of these, from his friend and admirer Maurice Browne, was a sentimental poem with almost religious overtones, written in 1916 and published in the March 1918 issue of *The Dial*. Evidently he concurred with Lytton Strachey's first impression ('Rupert Brooke – isn't it a romantic name?') since he writes: And a myriad lovers shout your name, / *Rupert! Rupert!*, across the earth.'[83] He seems to have been besotted with Rupert, asserting in his *Recollections of Rupert Brooke* 'the man *was* the myth' and

The beauty of the outer man was as the beauty of a young god; the beauty of the inner man outshone the beauty of the outer by so much as the glory of the sun is outshone by the glory of the human heart.[84]

Henry James, equally smitten, wrote the preface to Rupert's posthumously published *Letters from America* in 1916. He sketched him rather misleadingly as one who 'young, happy, radiant, extraordinarily endowed and irresistibly attaching, virtually met a soldier's death . . . if one liked him . . . one liked absolutely everything about him, without the smallest exception'.[85] Virginia Woolf, and most of Rupert's former Bloomsbury friends, profoundly disagreed.

Many years after his death, Rupert's friend Hilton Young, with whom he had often stayed when in London, wrote of him:

> Rupert looked like an archangel . . . there was no trace of effeminacy in Rupert's golden glory. Pheidias might have chiselled his face and form for a Pheobus, and Midas touched the waves of his hair to gold. The Muse . . . gave him the gift of song.[86]

Hilton had perceived the steel beneath the golden surface. Valhalla, not Olympus, would be Rupert's natural resting place, he said. 'There is something stark and tough about his poems, and there was something stark and tough about his ways and talk. He was for beef and beer, not nectar and ambrosia.'[87] Rupert's appeal was just as wide among those who had not known him personally. Such was his posthumous celebrity that J.M. Barrie found that he only had to mention his name during a lecture to elicit a round of applause.[88]

There were a few dissenting voices amid the general chorus of praise. Poet Charles Sorley, like Rupert, had very little time to assimilate his wartime experiences before his death. And, like Rupert, his chosen poetic form was the sonnet. But he took a very different approach, claiming that it was not the purpose of war poetry to soothe the reader. He was dismissive of Rupert's playing to the gallery with his 'sentimental' attitudes.[89] But it appears that the public wanted soothing. Certainly Sidgwick and Jackson had no cause to regret taking a risk on this relatively unknown poet, but their initial print run of five hundred copies for *Poems* (1911) was a little on the conservative side. Between the wars Rupert Brooke's poetry sold in six-figure quantities – *'1914' and Other Poems* alone sold 147,219 copies by 1930 (it was first published in May 1915), and even his Webster dissertation sold in the thousands.[90]

Successful though his poetry was, Virginia's opinion was that Rupert would eventually have found other outlets for his energies. He was better than his verse, she thought, and the critical consensus today is that his output is patchy and derivative. Writing verse was a common accomplishment among Cambridge graduates. It was only after his death that Rupert Brooke was characterized as a poet – more specifically, a war poet, although the war sonnets were only a small part of his output. Rupert's personal qualities – his ambition, his gift of charming people, his force of character – as well as his involvement with the Fabians suggested to Virginia that, had he lived, he might have stood for Parliament, even become Prime Minister.[91] His connections with the Asquiths and Churchill certainly would not have hindered his political ambitions.

Virginia knew that Rupert had not been simply a patriotic hero. James Strachey, despite his ardour for Rupert during his lifetime, admitted that he had been ill-balanced. Virginia agreed but knew that it was impossible and useless for his friends to attempt to reveal his real character in all its bewildering complexity, however they might resent his translation from a human being into a public icon.[92] Virginia lamented his canonization in her 1917 review of *Prose Papers* by John Drinkwater entitled 'The New Crusade':

> If the legend of Rupert Brooke is not to pass altogether beyond recognition, we must hope that some of those who knew him when scholarship or public life seemed even more his bent than poetry will put their view on record and relieve his ghost of an unmerited and undesired burden of adulation.[93]

It was Eddie Marsh's memoir, a lengthy introduction to the 1918 edition of Rupert's *Collected Poems*, that most irritated Rupert's friends, many of whom, including Virginia, thought the article gave an unrepresentative picture that served only to feed the public appetite for First World War heroes. Virginia's review of the book, entitled simply 'Rupert Brooke', criticized Marsh for his undue reverence of his subject; Rupert's very English handsomeness was almost a cliché, she suggested, and his Neo-Pagan lifestyle as much a pose as his earlier incarnations. He had been self-conscious, sensitive, sceptical and unsentimental (his lovers might have added jealous, manipulative, misogynistic and egotistical), and his poetry was born of meticulous construction and a workmanlike attitude, not a fey romanticism.[94]

Despite half-a-dozen biographies Rupert still remains a mystery. Even Virginia found it difficult to adapt his character for fiction; there are no visible models of him until her last, posthumously published novel *Between the Acts*, and even this does not seek to duplicate his personality. Only the name is borrowed for Rupert Haines, the gentleman farmer who is the object of Isa's romantic fantasies. That the physical description of Isa resembles Ka Cox is probably no coincidence.[95] The shadowiness of Haines's character – Isa's only contact with him has been when he handed her a teacup at a village fête and a racquet at a tennis party – indicates that he is a symbol of romance rather than a portrayal of the reality of love.[96] Isa knows him as slightly as did some of the people who were charmed by Rupert. Haines has a 'ravaged face', suggesting that he is a veteran of the First World War – or that Rupert's inner flaws have become flesh. These endear him to Isa, who feels 'mystery' in his injuries and 'passion' in his silences.[97] Her husband Giles embodies the other side of Rupert – passionate, possessive, vengeful, homophobic – but even with all his faults Isa feels herself bound to him and lets slip her romantic vision.[98]

Between the two extremes Virginia knew there was a complex human being who had not been fully revealed. After the death of Rupert's mother in 1930 she was keen for the Hogarth Press to publish Rupert's letters, in order to balance what had been written about him with some of his own prose.[99] The plan came to nothing, and the letters remained unpublished until 1959. For Virginia the private Rupert was never completely swamped by the public image. A decade after his death she reflected on his relationship with Bloomsbury, and her own personal memories of him, in a letter written to Gwen Raverat:

> Rupert was a little mythical to me when he died. He was very rude to Nessa once, and Leonard, I think, rather disliked him; in fact Bloomsbury was against him, and he against them. Meanwhile, I had a private version of him which I stuck to when they all cried him down, and shall preserve somewhere infinitely far away.[100]

⚮ 9 ⚮
Pomp of Circumstance:
Sydney Waterlow

V IRGINIA'S PENULTIMATE SUITOR, rejoicing in the name of Sydney
Philip Perigal Waterlow, was the last man to propose to Virginia
before her marriage. Sydney's brief courtship of her in late 1911
coincided with Leonard's and came close on the heels of Virginia's rejection
of Walter Lamb. Quentin Bell's impression was that Virginia 'found [Sydney] amiable but not exciting'.[1] To G.E. Moore's biographer Paul Levy, on
the other hand, he seemed 'an interesting and colourful man'.[2] In Virginia's
diaries and letters a two-dimensional and rather comic figure emerges. She
talks disparagingly about Sydney's physique and his mind and mentions
only in passing his wide-ranging interests, his work at the 1919 Paris Peace
Conference and his role in founding the League of Nations. He was a career
diplomat who was decorated with the Legion of Honour, represented Britain
as British Minister in Siam, Abyssinia, Bulgaria and Greece and was
knighted in 1935. But his professional success alone was not enough to
satisfy his personal longings. Sydney was a lifelong seeker for spiritual truths
and a romantic who was happiest when he had made a new beginning –
whether he had discovered a philosophy of life, started a new job in an
unfamiliar country or had fallen in love.

Through his mother, Charlotte Beauchamp, Sydney had a family whose
branches extended as far as New Zealand and Australia. His great-grandparents
lived in Hampstead (to which London suburb their great-grandson would
eventually return), but their seven surviving sons, including Sydney's grandfather Henry Heron Beauchamp, emigrated to Australia. Two of them went from
there to New Zealand, where in the 1860s they claimed a piece of land belonging
to an aunt. Henry ran a successful business in Sydney and married an Australian
heiress, Louise Lassetter. (In a neat parallel his brother Horatio married Louise's

sister.) After having made his fortune in the New World, Henry returned to the Old World and settled in suburban Bexley, in Kent.[3]

According to Henry's nephew Harold, the Beauchamps could trace their lineage back to a Richard Beauchamp who came to England with William the Conqueror in 1066. A Beauchamp ancestor who was a gold- and silversmith sold a gilt tankard to Samuel Pepys in 1660. Four generations later John Beauchamp (born 1781) was running the same business.[4] There were literary connections too. Sydney's aunt, Mary Annette, was better known under her pen-name Elizabeth von Arnim. Her first book was *Elizabeth and Her German Garden*, based on her experience of resurrecting a derelict garden on her husband's estate at Nassenheide. Published in 1898, the book provoked much interest in Britain. The budding writer Virginia Stephen was one of Elizabeth's early admirers, and the admiration was returned when their mutual friend Kitty Maxse relayed Elizabeth's praise for one of Virginia's articles, 'Street Music'.[5] Another writer in the family was destined to become Virginia Woolf's nearest rival. This was Harold's third daughter, born Kathleen Mansfield Beauchamp, later known as Katherine Mansfield.

Other Beauchamp relatives, far removed from the aristocratic or the literary world, were concealed so effectively by the previous generation that they were not discovered for nearly a century. Organizers of a large Beauchamp family reunion in New Zealand in 1974 estimated that the seven brothers who decamped to Australia bred 400 descendants, 150 of whom were present at the gathering. The reunion brought to light a number of Maori relatives about whom Sydney and Katherine almost certainly knew nothing. It emerged that Elizabeth and Charlotte's wayward cousin Fred had had five sons in New Zealand by a Maori woman and bestowed on them the quintessentially English names of his father and four uncles – George, Sam, John, Henry and Arthur.[6] Katherine and Sydney were second cousins to these five as well as to each other.

Sydney's father, George Sidney Waterlow, had a less remarkable range of relatives than his wife. However, George's father was Sir Sydney Hedley Waterlow (1822–1906), the Lord Mayor of London from 1872 to 1873. Sir Sydney was one of the great Victorian philanthropists and is today chiefly remembered as the man who gave London's Waterlow Park and Lauderdale House, now an arts and education centre, to the public. A statue of him stands in the park in memory of the bequest. He also founded a social housing company, the Improved Industrial Dwellings Company, which at his death was running 6,000 tenements capable of housing 30,000 people. Sir Sydney was a doughty businessman, establishing the family printing company that would become world famous and survive for 150 years. He was a tireless chairman, director and president, sitting on almost every board and committee in London. A wealthy man at his death, he left a fortune of almost £90,000 – all of it to his second wife, deeming that he had made ample provision for the rest of his family during his lifetime.[7]

George Sidney Waterlow was by no means as successful as his remarkable father. He was a City merchant, but he lacked his father's business brain and was often in financial difficulty. (In the summer of 1904 Sydney had to take a year's leave from the Diplomatic Service to help sort out his father's money problems.[8]) The details of George's life and his personality are shadowy. His four sons and daughter became estranged from their father when their parents' marriage failed, and George departed, leaving his family financially provided for – Sydney, a young man by that time, helped negotiate the terms of the settlement – but without a husband and father.[9] Sydney spent much of his adult life seeking a role model, a spiritual adviser or mentor – a surrogate father. He told his own children little about their grandfather, but his son John remembers accompanying him, as a boy of nine, to George's funeral in 1925.[10]

Sydney was the eldest son, born 22 October 1878. From the start he was marked out for a glowing academic career. At Eton he was considered a prodigy. He excelled in examinations and was the youngest boy ever to win Eton's most prestigious prize, a Newcastle scholarship. He went up to Trinity College, Cambridge, in 1896, where he lived up to his Eton reputation. He was a brilliant student and went down in 1900 with a double first in classics. He relished the competitive nature of examinations and prizes, as his friend Desmond MacCarthy observed. 'Just before he entered the Foreign Office I remember asking him if he would not be glad when the examination was over. "Glad!" he replied, "I shall be extremely sorry; I love examinations."'[11]

Like his first mentor G.E. Moore Sydney Waterlow began his Cambridge career studying classics but developed a passion for philosophy. He first got to know Moore in the summer of 1898, and for the next two years they saw one another frequently. When Sydney left Cambridge they corresponded on questions of philosophy and aesthetics, examining minutely the works of other philosophers and exchanging theories of their own, with Sydney always deferring to his mentor's views. Many Cambridge men of Sydney's age were influenced by Moore, whose meticulous pursuit of the meaning of words reverberated through the university – and Bloomsbury – for years afterwards. Thoby Stephen, who knew Sydney through their mutual friends Clive Bell and Jack Pollock, gives an interesting glimpse of his cogitatory Mooreish style of thinking in a letter to Leonard Woolf:

> Waterlow is a serious cove and devilish Cambridge. 'What is poetry? Well, there you ask me a difficult question – I am not sure that it *is* anything – It depends on what you mean by being' and so on the old round . . . His wife lags behind him but struggles gallantly 'Sidney, Sidney, what do you mean by Mon-og-amy?' However he has a bottom of good sense and is not a bad fellow.[12]

Such was his admiration for Moore that, with historian G.M. (George) Trevelyan, Sydney concocted an ambitious plan for a collection of papers dedicated to Moore and his influence: other contributors included the philosopher Bertrand Russell and the economist Ralph Hawtrey. The kind of tribute that is normally used to sum up an senior academic's lifetime achievement, it was intended in this case to celebrate the thinking of a thirty-one-year-old ex-Trinity fellow of no fixed employment. Meetings were held to discuss 'Waterlow's project', as it became known, but problems soon began to arise. Moore was a modest man, but he was exceedingly precise. After a year of deliberation over the book, the plan ran aground in late 1905 over Moore's anxieties about the founding principle of the book – the unity of thought among the contributors.[13] Sydney later lost faith in Moore's theory of good and did not flinch from telling him so, but their friendship survived, and among Sydney's last correspondence was a ten-page letter to him, written nineteen days before his death.

Because of his outstanding academic record Sydney was able to step straight into a good position at the Foreign Office on leaving Cambridge. His fortunes rose swiftly. In 1901 he was appointed attaché in Washington and was soon promoted to third secretary. He was known for writing insightful and well-expressed dispatches, and many of his juniors were grateful for their training under his auspices. However, he was not merely a yes-man, a puppet of the government. Rather the reverse – Desmond MacCarthy believed that Sydney's official reports:

may have been sometimes over-emphatic; for I recall his saying about a memorandum he had sent up as head of an FO department to Sir Austen Chamberlain, 'I couldn't help putting the case strongly because I knew he wanted me to say the exact opposite.' I was not very surprised when shortly afterwards he was recommended for foreign service.[14]

In 1902 he married Alice Isabella Pollock, the sister of John (Jack) Pollock, his friend and Cambridge contemporary, and daughter of Sir Frederick Pollock, 3rd Baronet, Corpus Professor of Jurisprudence at Oxford.[15] They may have met at the Trinity College Ball in 1900, Sydney's last ball before leaving Cambridge, since Virginia remembered seeing Alice Pollock there. (This may also have been where he first met Virginia.) The Pollocks were friends of the Stephen family, but their Surrey house, Hindhead Copse in Haslemere, would have held sad memories for Virginia. It was while she and Leslie were staying there in April 1902 (the month in which Sydney and Alice were engaged[16]) that he was taken ill and subsequently diagnosed with intestinal cancer.[17]

Virginia almost certainly met Sydney through her brother Thoby, but they only became properly acquainted in 1910, as a result of two dinner parties. The first was on 29 September at Studland, when Sydney dined with Virginia who was recuperating from illness.[18] The second was at Gordon Square on 8 December. Sydney, making a foursome at dinner with the Bells and Virginia, felt that their intimacy was growing.

> Dined with the Clive Bells: what a relief & change! No one else but Virginia S. We had talk that begins to be really intimate. Vanessa very amusing on paederasty among their circle. I realized for the first time the difference between her & Virginia: Vanessa icy, cynical, artistic; Virginia much more emotional, & interested in life rather than beauty.[19]

His friend Henry James had expressed great disapproval of the rather shabby *modus vivendi* and equally shabby friends of the daughters of the venerable Sir Leslie Stephen, but this did not deter Sydney from seeking their company.[20] He began to frequent Gordon Square and recorded in his diary the following January a fact that would have shocked Henry James profoundly: '[Vanessa] wants to form a circle on the principle of complete sexual freedom.'[21] Sydney's thoughts tended along the same lines. That spring

Vanessa and Clive stayed at Hillyfields, the Waterlows' house in Rye. In the absence of his wife Sydney talked frankly about his weakness for beautiful, openly sensual women. More daringly still, he claimed that the two barriers to his having affairs were time and money.[22]

Talk about it though he might, sexual freedom was not something Sydney was able to practise. He had been incapable of consummating his marriage and was forced to presume himself impotent. Within a few years he and Alice began to drift apart, and they increasingly spent time away from each other. While he saw old Cambridge companions with whom Alice had little in common, she was more interested in her brother Jack's theatrical friends. The gap between the couple widened: she sought happiness through diversion and entertainment; he through spiritual truths and philosophy.

Sydney and Alice separated in June 1911 after a fierce quarrel. Both knew the marriage was over. Presented with his freedom, Sydney felt elation mixed with a self-reproaching depression: 'I've never brought anything but misery to others & am likely to be more & more of a curse to myself.'[23] Unknown to him, he had already met his second wife, although he would endure several misadventures before they were united. Meanwhile Alice was being courted by Orlando (Orlo) Williams, Clerk to the House of Commons and later a literary critic, although Sydney suspected nothing for several months.[24]

A legal separation was quickly put in train. Divorce – which had a highly unsavoury reputation – would have been a last resort. The divorce law was archaic, almost unchanged since 1857. In 1911 only the husband was permitted to sue for divorce on the grounds of adultery alone. Until the Matrimonial Causes Act of 1923 women seeking to divorce faithless husbands had to produce a second reason such as desertion, extreme cruelty, rape, sodomy, bigamy, incest or bestiality. (Remarkably, it was not until 1937 that desertion, cruelty and insanity joined adultery as the sole basis for a divorce case.) Annulment was therefore the lesser of two evils, despite the embarrassment it caused for Sydney, and meant that the separation could be accomplished amicably. Sir Frederick acted as their legal adviser and no doubt favoured annulment as the less painful option for his daughter.

Leonard Woolf observed that 'Sydney's life was in some ways stranger than fiction', referring to confidences he had received from Sydney about his private affairs.[25] What Leonard may have considered a twist worthy of a potboiler was that, even as the annulment of his own marriage was progressing on the grounds of impotence, Sydney was being cited as co-respondent in someone else's divorce case.

Two days after Alice left him Sydney met a woman called Norah, wife of the art historian Alexander Finberg, in a London park.[26] Highly susceptible to attractive women, he was immediately – although temporarily – smitten. That evening he took Norah to dinner, and they walked through London hand in hand like young lovers. They began a whirlwind romance that changed the course of Sydney's life – the psychological barrier that had caused the conjugal problems with Alice was suddenly lifted. To his great relief, he discovered he was not impotent after all: 'I am renewed in body & soul: the cloud of horror is gone from my life,' he rejoiced.[27] The affair, which satisfied Sydney physically but not intellectually, petered out within a few months. But not before Norah's husband discovered the truth and ejected her from their house. Gratitude to the woman who had given him back his sexuality long outlasted Sydney's passion. He considered marrying Norah, and for a while he contemplated setting her up in the dressmaking trade, but his friend H.O. Meredith (Hom to his friends) pointed out that she might not know how to run a business. Norah had meanwhile fallen ill with typhoid, and Sydney decided the best thing he could do was to take charge of arrangements for her divorce and provide her with funds until she was on her feet again.[28]

The tangle of Sydney's love life became even more knotted in the latter half of 1911. While still seeing Norah and waiting anxiously to see if he would be named in her divorce, he struck up a friendship with a Cambridge graduate, Eva Ward, and began to spend a good deal of time with her. On 15 August, following lunch with Eva, he had tea with Rupert Brooke and Virginia Stephen at the Old Vicarage in Grantchester, and they dined with him the following evening. Virginia noted that he was revelling in his freedom, seeing everything as if for the first time.[29] On 5 November there was more juggling of his social engagements – Virginia, staying with the Cornfords, and Ka Cox were slotted in for tea; lunch, supper and the following morning's breakfast were reserved for Eva.[30] But what had been intended by Sydney as a light-hearted flirtation developed on Eva's side into a full-blown passion. She declared her feelings – Sydney pondered his choice of words for four days, then wrote to say that, although he had greatly enjoyed her company, he did not feel as she did.[31]

Virginia's life was equally full of possibilities. She had just cast off a cautious but persistent suitor, Walter Lamb (who confided to Sydney that he had proposed[32]), and enjoyed a friendly fling with Rupert Brooke. She was now planning a household run along cooperative lines at 38 Brunswick Square, with her brother Adrian, Maynard Keynes, Duncan Grant and Leonard Woolf – who, unknown to Sydney, was his rival for Virginia's affections. With her thoughts full of this new adventure and her growing friendship with Leonard, Virginia had little attention to spare for Sydney, and hitherto he had given her no reason to expect romantic advances from him.

But Sydney's delight at gaining his liberty was subsiding and he began to feel he would like to settle down again. After turning it over in his mind and eliciting advice from friends, he decided that Norah and he were not compatible.[33] Whether Virginia knew about the Norah affair is debatable. It was certainly common knowledge by 1918, Virginia and Leonard discussed it with Sydney's second wife.[34] But as Sydney had unwisely chosen to confide in Clive Bell in July 1911 it seems likely that Clive passed this tasty piece of gossip on almost immediately.[35]

By November 1911 Sydney had been separated from Alice for several months. Knowing Virginia only from their occasional meetings, he suddenly alighted on the idea that she was the remedy for his loneliness. She was of his own class and intellectual level; she was familiar but still slightly mysterious; she was beautiful, cultivated, discerning and witty. Moreover, she was single and appeared inclined towards marriage. On the strength of these reasons Sydney decided to propose, knowing that Walter Lamb had recently been rejected. He confided his intentions to Hom before speaking to Virginia. Hom, although married, was susceptible Virginia's appeal himself: 'I shall certainly be jealous of you if you succeed for my thoughts turn towards her pretty often. She would certainly be a divine mistress, but I incline to think she would be a good wife.'[36] Sydney was invited with Vanessa and Roger Fry to stay with Virginia in Firle the weekend of 25–7 November. The decree nisi for his separation from Alice was granted on the last day of his visit.[37] He must have found the timing propitious: two days later he went to see Virginia in London 'in a state of electrical agitation' to propose marriage.[38] The entries he made in his diary at the time, although brief, speak volumes: 'W. 29. Spoke to Virginia. Th. 30. Back to Cambridge in despair.'[39]

Virginia, as Vanessa had done on her first proposal from Clive, had reacted with well-bred surprise and let Sydney down as gently as she could. But he was distraught at her refusal. He was overcome with self-loathing and felt foolish for having proposed to a woman with whom, he realized later, he was not even intimate. An exaggerated self-consciousness told him he had insulted both Virginia and himself, and he must now be a gentleman and disappear abroad for a few months.

Hom took a more robust line:

Forgive me if I am brutal – but why all this pother & self abusement? Assuming that she was not in love with you & we had no reason for any other assumption what could she do but fall back on the traditional 'oh sir, this is so sudden' tricked out of course in the manner & phrase which are the right of her birth & education? The *reasons* you give for feeling self disgusted are absurd – as she herself insisted. Of course you 'dont know her'; but what has that to do with it? Do people ever know one another when they fall in love? The proof of the pudding is in the eating.[40]

He advised Sydney to be pragmatic and persuaded him it would be better to let the dust settle, take stock of his life and his affairs and approach Virginia again in six months if he still wanted to marry her. It was this calmer tone that Sydney adopted in a letter to Virginia, to which she replied a week or so later. In a short and businesslike reply she agreed that he had no reason to reproach himself but confessed frankly that she could not consider him as a husband. His desire to marry her was merely temporary; she urged him not to waste his time and energies dwelling on her as a suitable wife, when all she could offer was friendship.[41]

Unlike Virginia's prevaricating response to Walter's proposal, this one has an air of finality about it. She did not keep Sydney dangling as she had Walter Lamb (perhaps having learned the disadvantages of this) but disposed of the proposal cleanly and unambiguously. Presumably Virginia already had an inkling of what she should feel for the man she would marry and could be certain that she did not feel it for Sydney. Over the last few months she had spent a lot of time with Leonard. Although they had been little acquainted before his departure for Ceylon in 1904, they had been making up for lost time since his return. By late November she knew that he would be a natural fit for the Brunswick Square arrangement and that they had much in common; this was not true of Sydney, as Virginia was forced to tell him. Unfortunately for Sydney, his anguish was highlighted by its contrast with the seasonal celebrations. He spent the last days of 1911 in the darkest misery, avoiding Christmas and New Year parties and wandering the streets of London searching for a friendly female face.[42]

Gradually he recovered his equanimity, and with it came the realization that marriage to Virginia would not satisfy his yearnings. But he continued to value Virginia's friendship and rated her intellect highly, even when he had grown away from his Bloomsbury friends. His younger daughter Judith remembered him remarking to Nancy Catty, a family friend: 'My dear Nancy, you must know perfectly well that the only woman worth talking to is Virginia Woolf.'[43] He still saw the Bells regularly and on 26 January attended an all-male dinner at Gordon Square with Clive Bell, Roger Fry, Leonard Woolf and Saxon Sydney-Turner.[44] Leonard had proposed to Virginia two weeks earlier, but the fact was not widely known and was almost certainly not under discussion that evening.

Sydney remained on good terms with other Bloomsberries, too. In March H.G. Wells held a fancy-dress ball where Sydney, dressed as an Indian rajah, encountered Duncan Grant, James Strachey and Adrian Stephen and admired their exotic costumes. He teased James about his androgynous appearance (he wore a low-necked dress, bangles and pantaloons) and thought Duncan Grant looked beautiful in a purple turban and a Turkish robe borrowed from Virginia (who was absent, recovering from a period of illness).[45] He was also interested in the art they produced: he went to Roger Fry's one-man show at the Alpine Club, and seeing the Borough Polytechnic mural painted by Duncan he declared: 'Duncan Grant's Swimmers [are] magnificent.'[46] After enjoying the first Post-Impressionist exhibition (the brain-child of Roger Fry) he agreed to take Leonard Woolf's place as Secretary when the second exhibition was extended into January 1913. This was a brave decision, as the first exhibition had been greeted with derision and even laughter, even though there were hundreds of visitors a day. The second caused a similar uproar but had even more visitors and, importantly, more buyers.[47]

Marriage plans were put on hold for a year or two but not abandoned – Sydney was thirty-four and yearned for a wife and family. The 'right' woman was closer at hand than he had imagined. For several years he had been friendly with a Manchester family called Eckhard, who were at the hub of the city's cultural community. When Sydney took charge of the extra-mural programme at the University of Manchester in 1905 his path was bound to cross theirs. The Eckhards belonged, according to Leonard, to 'the well-to-do Manchester bourgeoisie'.[48] The nominal head of the family was Gustav Eckhard, an émigré from Frankfurt who worked for Reiss Brothers, a cotton trader. Leonard stayed with the Eckhards during his lecture tour in the north of England in 1917 and described his host to Virginia: 'He is the queerest little gray German you can imagine, with a little wrinkled twitching face.'[49] There was one son, Oscar, and five Misses Eckhard, one of whom was distinguished with the name of 'Beetle' (the nickname of Beatrice), another of whom, Margery, went to Somerville College, Oxford, and a third, Edith, to Newnham College, Cambridge. Their mother, Marie, was a Jewish matriarch of a type with which Leonard was familiar and towards whom he was not entirely unsympathetic – although he was rather exasperated on one occasion when Mrs Eckhard insisted he help her cut down a large tree in her garden on a sudden whim. 'Mrs E is really rather nice, very impulsive & downright & at first sight objectionable,' he wrote to Virginia.[50] Marie was considered by Sydney as a personal friend and confidante, and he thought highly enough of her to introduce her to his distinguished friend Henry James. Sydney was friendly with the whole Eckhard family, as an entry from his 1910 diary shows:

> To Manchester, to stay with Mrs. Eckhard. To a meeting on Sat. night in Ancoats to hear Sir George Kemp. Wonderful sensations walking back from Ancoats to Oxford Road, & thence out to Palatine Road on top of a tram, as of old. Walk on Sunday with Gustav & Margery through fog & slush ... Talks with Marie about Oscar's troubles.[51]

Of the younger Eckhards Sydney spent most time with Margery, and soon he began to approach her with matrimonial intent. They were oddly matched in physical terms – he was six feet two and stoutly built; she was only five feet tall. Curiously, Virginia never explicitly mentioned the Waterlows' contrasting physiques, although individually she was insulting about them. She observed that when Sydney bathed in the River Ouse he made the river look much smaller and that his mind and his body were one: 'His fat pink body always seems to me boneless and hairless like that of a gigantic child; & his mind is the same.' More charitably, she added: 'But there is a charm about him.'[52] Plunging into caricature, she described Margery variously as 'gnome like', 'squat & vivacious' and 'a squawking dab chick'.[53]

Virginia's unkindness about Margery may have been defensive, prompted by her own sense of 'womanly' inadequacy. Margery was a capable woman in possession of all the domestic virtues: an eye for hygiene, a keen gardener, good with servants and a consummate manager of children. On top of this she was university-educated and had an adventurous streak. She rode horses and motor cycles and in 1912 went up in an aeroplane, at a time when air travel was in its infancy – 'She had great physical courage,' remembers her son John.[54] She would need courage of a different kind to take on a man with Sydney's chequered past, and she must have known about his extra-marital affairs, if not from Sydney then from her mother.[55] Margery took the risk, and they married in the summer of 1913; and for a time they were extremely happy.

Delighted to be enjoying the physical relationship that had been lacking in his first marriage, Sydney regained his natural ebullience and confidence. He continued to cultivate his Bloomsbury friends, and in October 1914 the Waterlows rented Asheham from the Woolfs. But there was soon a clash of ideologies. The fastidious Margery did not share the *laissez-faire* Bloomsbury attitude to hygiene and complained that the house was dirty and the chimney needed sweeping.[56] Sydney was keen to explain his objections to Virginia, anxious lest this should cause a rift between them.[57] Despite the inauspicious start to their sojourn the Waterlows found Asheham charming.[58] They decided to extend their lease to the following July, and their first child, Charlotte, was born there at the end of May. But they had evidently outstayed their welcome. Virginia wrote damningly to Lytton that Sydney was 'a bore' and 'palpably second rate', and she was repulsed by the thought of him having sex in her house. Ignoring Margery's enthusiasm for cleanliness, she fancifully imagined she could detect olfactory evidence of the Waterlows' sexual exploits for months afterwards.[59]

Insults about Margery may be explained by Virginia's defensiveness and an element of anti-Semitism, but why was she so malevolent about Sydney? A clue lies in the identity of her correspondent – she wrote some of her most cutting and amusing letters to Lytton Strachey, who replied in a similar style. In her correspondence with him can be found unkind comments about many of her friends – she even ventures to criticize her adored Vanessa. Virginia and Lytton were both quick to appreciate beauty but found lapses from physical perfection distasteful. This attitude serves, of course, to create a sense of superiority and to deflect attention from one's own imperfections. Both were unsatisfied with their physique. Lytton believed that although he possessed some grace the numerous handsome young men he admired would seldom harbour lustful thoughts about his elongated and spindly form. Virginia, in spite of her beauty, had a complex and ambivalent attitude towards her body. When ill, she shunned food; yet she believed that a good diet helped keep her sane. On one occasion, speculating that Sydney's semen was little more than 'mutton fat', Virginia disclosed frankly to Lytton that she weighed twelve stone instead of her usual nine as a result of the 'stuffing' regime prescribed by her doctors to restore her mental balance.[60] But her own plumpness was 'evidently good for the health'.[61] She used body weight as a means of criticizing Sydney but congratulating herself (although her frequent antipathy to food betokens some kind of eating disorder). Seemingly insignificant incidents such as this were exploited in order to build up her picture of him as a comic character, while other 'evidence' that showed him in a different light was ignored. Thus the Sydney Waterlow that emerges from Virginia's writings is more a caricature than a real person. Virginia became accustomed to writing and talking of him in a particular way and found it difficult to appreciate the qualities that did not fit the picture she had carefully honed.

From her own vantage point as happily married wife, Virginia looked critically at the Waterlows' *ménage*. She observed Sydney's attitude towards his wife and saw that Margery was often left at home to look after the children while Sydney traversed London and the home counties calling on friends. Virginia was not particularly friendly with Margery but at times sympathized with her for being trapped in a marriage to a professionally successful man while having no intellectual outlets of her own.

There is another reason, political rather than personal, for Virginia's attitude towards Sydney Waterlow, connected with the sentiments expressed in her 'feminist' books, *A Room of One's Own* and *Three Guineas*. For this reason, too, it was necessary to cast Sydney as a two-dimensional character, a human representation of something she disliked. It was irksome to Virginia to see her male peers achieve public success when she considered their intellect below par. Sydney, like Walter Lamb, had reached a position of public prominence for which his gender qualified him. Virginia, on the other hand, would have been ineligible. She was not in the least attracted by the idea of working for the government or any other organization; nevertheless a principle was at work for which she had a profound aversion. That she, an intellectual on a level with the best of men, should be disqualified merely because she was female was unacceptable. It was not personal dislike that drove her malice – she was railing against a principle.[62]

Virginia's perception of Sydney's professional life fed into the creation of Hugh Whitbread in *Mrs Dalloway*. The oleaginous Hugh revels in his position, 'a little job at Court', which requires him to carry a dispatch box emblazoned with the royal coat of arms.[63] He dresses impeccably, if fussily (there is a touch of Walter Lamb in the characterization). Hugh's letter to *The Times* on behalf of Lady Bruton is pompous but expresses crowd-pleasing sentiments; it is sure to be published because of his contacts. Clarissa feels affection for her old friend, but Peter Walsh thinks him 'a positive imbecile' and Richard Dalloway 'was nearly driven mad by him'.[64] Sally Seton considers him 'a perfect specimen of the public school type ... No country but England could have produced him.'[65] But Hugh is Sydney without the colour, without the unconventionalities; with only his professional pride.

Virginia never acknowledged the fact, but intellectual interests she shared with Sydney played a part in her literary development. In 1912 Sydney wrote an article on the philosophy of Henri Bergson for the *Quarterly Review*.[66] Bergson's theory of *la durée* ('real time' or 'internal time'), which expands and contracts, is related to her work; either by coincidence or indirect influence. For Virginia, time is an elastic concept and most especially in *Orlando*, the events of which stretch over three centuries, bringing the eponymous hero/heroine into the present day having aged by only twenty years.[67] Leonard would state at this point that Virginia very seldom read philosophy of any kind. But it is clear that either Virginia or Leonard (and probably both) certainly knew of Bergson's theories of *unanimisme* – 'unanimity' or shared consciousness of a group of individuals – because one of them reviewed the work of Jules Romains, which draws on the same concept. Indeed, Bergson was a celebrity in England as well as in France, and it would have been difficult for anyone with a claim to being an intellectual to ignore his ideas.

In 1911 Romains published a novel, *Mort de Quelqu'un*, which stirred much interest in Bloomsbury. It is the deceptively simple tale of the effects of a man's death on others. The nature of immortality is pondered: do the dead become 'non-existent' when there is no one who remembers them? Is existence not merely a corporeal state but also spiritual, surviving in the minds of others? What is the meaning of 'I', and does it disappear after death? On 7 August 1913 a review of Romains' second novel, *Les Copains*, appeared in the

Times Literary Supplement, written by either Virginia or Leonard Woolf.[68] The article discusses *Mort de Quelqu'un* and *unanimisme* as well as *Les Copains*, suggesting a familiarity with the earlier work.[69] It was not until 1914 that Sydney Waterlow and Desmond McCarthy published their English translation, *The Death of a Nobody*; therefore it appears that the Woolfs read the novel first in French.

Ideas similar to *unanimisme* reverberate throughout Virginia's novels. Jinny Carslake in *Jacob's Room* acquires spirituality through Indian philosophy and gazes at her collection of pebbles picked off the street to prove to herself how 'multiplicity becomes unity'.[70] Like Jacques in *The Death of a Nobody*, Mrs Flanders's dead husband becomes one with the landscape:

> Had he, then, been nothing? An unanswerable question, since even if it weren't the habit of the undertaker to close the eyes, the light so soon goes out of them. At first, part of herself; now one of a company, he had merged in the grass, the sloping hillside, the thousand white stones . . . Seabrook was now all that.[71]

Mrs Dalloway's Clarissa and Septimus can easily be imagined as two aspects of the same consciousness. Although they never meet, Clarissa feels instinctively that she understands what precipitated Septimus's suicide: 'Death was an attempt to communicate . . . There was an embrace in death.'[72] The early title of *The Waves* – 'The Life of Anybody' – echoes Romains's title and suggests that that the six main characters represent a single self.[73]

Desmond MacCarthy, in his dedication to the translation, predicted that Romains' writing style and ideas would influence the influential. Sure enough, his discussion about Romains' literary style could easily apply to Virginia's later work:

> [It is] a style which passes easily from fixing, with odd intensity, details so ordinary that other novelists omit them as things taken for granted, to describing emotions so elusive, so large and so obscure that they too have been ignored.[74]

By the end of 1917 Sydney's diplomatic career was blossoming. He was involved in negotiating the Paris Peace Treaty (the Treaty of Versailles) in 1919; although Virginia pretended amazement that he could be such a great influence in international politics. But slowly she mellowed towards him, writing to Saxon: 'His absurdity is really delightful and even lovable.'[75] During a visit to the Woolfs just before Christmas Sydney told them rather shyly about his professional activities and his family: 'He . . . rolled out the word "I" with a sort of tremor of pride . . . Being self conscious & diffident his triumphs give him enormous pleasure.'[76] Sydney was in general very concerned with the opinions of his friends. 'He desperately wanted to be liked and admired; he was somewhat vain in a naïve way,' his daughter Charlotte has written of him.[77] But in 1919 Virginia detected his growing independence from the opinions of Bloomsbury. He had grand ambitions. His career plans, she claimed, were a wholesale reform of the Foreign Office or else to earn £10,000 a year in the City and co-write books with Desmond MacCarthy. Why not write his own books? Virginia wondered; but he enjoyed intellectual teamwork and the company of his friends.[78]

For several years the Waterlows and the MacCarthys lived in close proximity. The Waterlows took a twenty-eight-year lease of Parsonage House, in Oare, Wiltshire, in the summer of 1918. Built in the early eighteenth century, the accommodation was basic – thatched roof (not so desirable then as now), no electricity and no indoor lavatory. Light came from oil lamps and candles and water from a well.[79] Characteristically, Virginia criticized their decision and their taste, thinking the house dull and lacking a decent view; a bad choice among a wealth of choices. Others admired the Waterlows' Wiltshire home: John Middleton Murry found it very cosy and solid and wrote to Katherine Mansfield commending it; she expressed envy of their luck in getting such a house.[80] Virginia's negative attitude was symptomatic of her fear of a rival coterie which would supplant Bloomsbury-in-Sussex. In 1919 Desmond and Molly MacCarthy moved into Home Farm across the road from the Waterlows. Hilton Young's cottage, The Lacket, stood a few miles away in Lockeridge. Bryn (née Olivier) and Hugh Popham lived in an ancient farmhouse about a mile west of Oare. Maynard Keynes and Lydia Lopokova joined the Wiltshire clan briefly when they borrowed Oare House from a colleague of Maynard's in 1922. But the colony that Virginia feared did not materialize, although Sydney and Desmond were great friends and occasionally worked on literary projects together.

Desmond was not Sydney's only collaborator. Leonard, who had fingers in a number of political pies, was occasionally associated with him in a professional capacity. In 1918 Sydney used verbatim much of Leonard's book *International Government* (1916) for a Foreign Office report entitled 'International Government under the League of Nations'. There was no point in doing the research and analysis over again, he said, since Leonard had done it very competently the first time.[81] This report was sent to Woodrow Wilson and eventually became the basis of the League of Nations, leading to the modern United Nations.

Leonard and Sydney may have seen eye to eye on politics, but Virginia was very dubious of Sydney's opinions on literature. One point distinctly not in his favour was his friendship with John (Jack) Middleton Murry, a literary critic and editor and husband of Sydney's second cousin Katherine Mansfield. Virginia's attitude towards Murry was ambivalent from the beginning: she was interested in the way his mind worked, but she believed him fundamentally dishonest and thought little of his writing.[82]

Sydney's admiration of Murry threw into doubt not only his literary but his professional capacities as far as she was concerned. Virginia's antagonism towards Murry was fanned by Sydney, who unwisely repeated Murry's negative opinions of her writing.[83] For a few months Sydney lodged with Murry in Hampstead, while Katherine recuperated from tuberculosis in the south of France. Sydney and Katherine, although related, had never known each other very well, but during the summer of 1920, which Katherine spent in England, their friendship blossomed. When Katherine had to return into exile in France she found Sydney's letters a great consolation. After one of her own letters went astray in the postal system, she was anxious that he should not feel himself neglected.

> Friendly letters, letters such as you write me, dear Sydney, are so rare – so awfully rare in my life – it grieves me to think I should have appeared unappreciative ... I want to tell you I've always felt such real affection for you; it has always been so very pleasant to hear your 'well, Katherine', & I have regretted we have seen so little of each other.[84]

In her lonely convalescence his letters were an extremely welcome diversion. Although Sydney wrote that he was afraid of boring her, she loved hearing even the minor details about his life.[85] She had imagined him reading her new story, 'The Daughters of the Late Colonel', while she was writing it at Villa Isola Bella in Menton and found it very easy to discuss 'serious' topics with him.[86] She encouraged her cousin to write a play and offered her own insights into his psychology. 'You have been a hidden, secret spectator when *les autres* did not even know that you were by. You have lived by apprehensions far far more than most people, I imagine.'[87] The two shared a feeling of isolation – Katherine's because of her illness, Sydney because of his frequent depressions – and a need for a deep mutual understanding with their friends.

Despite his growing friendship with Murry and Katherine, Sydney's gloom crept back. An inner demon periodically reminded him he had not been an Apostle at Cambridge, setting off anxieties about his psychological inferiority and about his reputation among his Bloomsbury friends. He was often self-conscious and sensitive, in constant need of reassurance. While at times proud of his achievements, at others he doubted his powers and questioned the way of life he had chosen, contemplating a drastic action – such as absconding abroad. He wrote a heartfelt letter to Hom, who admitted: 'It brought me back with a shock to the fact that you have a problem.'[88] Hom sympathized but dissuaded Sydney from a 'bunk' to the South Seas, wondering prophetically if he would benefit from a posting abroad: 'I wonder sometimes if you and Mar. would get more out of life if you took up a foreign appointment.'[89] Sensitive to slights, Sydney wrote to Virginia Woolf to correct her impression that his unhappiness was simply a pose:

> Your attitude to me seems to have been that I am a rather absurd creature, but not unloveable by those who have worked through what is distasteful in me, & that, while I imagined myself to be unhappy, I am really quite satisfied by my ridiculous activities. This is a misconception that I feel almost as an insult.[90]

His periods of happiness are rare, he confesses, and arise from a period of romantic idealism when he is freed from the constraints of his own self-consciousness:

> I know what real happiness is, so that, if you do, you will understand me. I've hardly ever experienced it: only at the times when I thought I was in love, & when A. [Alice] left me. There were then some weeks, even months, when the bliss of feeling free to start life again was incredible.[91]

Most of the time his spirits are prevented from soaring: 'My life is like climbing a mountain with lead tied to one's feet: one has got to go on, and the strain is almost unbearable.'[92] He feels that people do not feel attracted to him as they do to others who have

> some sort of solid core, either some inner circle of intimacy or some absorbing interest, from which they draw strength & wh. makes the outer circle of people instinctively curious about them, interested in them & pleased by their society . . . I've no spontaneity, I'm inhibited all the time; so the result is that no one wants to see me or takes pleasure in my society.[93]

For once Virginia put aside her mockery, concerned at his evident distress – the sensation of being without a core was very familiar to her. But she reminded him that his perceptions were skewed; that when one is depressed 'all one's external relations become febrile and unreal'.[94] She assured him that her own ridicule was only a 'method' and promised to help him regain his equanimity. His self-doubt was surprising, she suggested, because his merits were so clear to her. His letter revealed a quality that she appreciated and found interesting in him: 'this sensibility – this introspection – this sense of the importance of things'.[95] It is a kind and perceptive letter and one that demonstrates affection and empathy. Virginia could be a sympathetic friend when appealed to sincerely, and disclosures of depression or illness often brought out the best in her.

Sydney's depressions, like Virginia's, were probably hereditary. Members of preceding and succeeding generations of his family committed suicide. His great-uncle Walter Blanford Waterlow, the former Mayor of Reigate, killed himself in his seventies. His estranged father shot himself in the head at Plymouth's Grand Hotel in 1925, also in his seventies. His younger brother Cecil threw himself from a railway bridge. After Sydney's death the pattern continued when his daughter Judith, a successful psychoanalyst, killed herself in her mid forties. Sydney was not driven to suicide, but he confided to Virginia in early 1921 that he had contemplated it, as he had nine years ago; that is, during the depression following her refusal of his proposal of marriage.[96]

One of the remedies he frequently called upon to assuage his depression was change: a new way of life or a new way of thinking. His daughter Charlotte describes her father as:

the eternal seeker for the truth which lies beyond reason and emotion; he was always *pondering* . . . There was no point at which he said: 'Here I will stop, and rest my oars on what I think I know or believe' – people who rest their oars are always threatened by what lies upstream.[97]

Desmond MacCarthy believed that Sydney was 'perpetually searching after spiritual truths, he was what the Germans call a "God-struggler"'.[98] Another friend, S.S. Koteliansky ('Kot'), the translator of Tolstoy for the Hogarth Press, mentioned in a letter to Sydney 'the awareness of a need for harmony . . . with which you have been struggling for so long'.[99] Like a true evangelist Sydney tried to interest his Bloomsbury friends in the ideals revealed to him by Augustine's *Confessions* or the Ramayana but received replies such as this one from Morgan Forster: 'You have undergone conversion, I not, and consequently I cannot guess what you are, and you cannot remember what I am.'[100] On the other hand, Forster found that Sydney's 'mysticism' made him easier to confide in:

> Since you took up with 'that mystic stuff' I have found it possible to talk to you and, in particular, to consult you on my own difficulties, in a way that I have not found possible during the previous years I've known you. [Therefore] one up to the mystic stuff from my own point of view.[101]

Even though Virginia had been kind, Sydney was convinced he would never be part of Bloomsbury's 'inner circle'. He found it hard to let go but gradually acquired a new set of friends, including S.S. Koteliansky and the artists Dorothy Brett and Mark Gertler.[102] The group began to meet on Thursday evenings at Brett's house in Hampstead. Other regulars to the Thursday evenings were John Middleton Murry, Herbert J. Milne and J.W.N. Sullivan.[103] Sullivan was one of a series of men whom Sydney regarded as 'the authentic voice of god'.[104] Virginia met Sullivan and was not impressed – 'too black and hairy and singular for my taste' – but for Sydney's sake curbed her mockery.[105]

The existence of the 'Thursdayers', a potential rival to Bloomsbury, rang alarm bells for Virginia. But there was much in-fighting among them, she noted with satisfaction and perhaps some relief. (On one occasion Gertler took offence when Sydney asked, rather Lytton-like, if he conducted sexual relationships with his models.[106]) Virginia was disparaging about them: 'if

[they] with one voice denounced me, I should sleep the sounder. It is a group without teeth or claws.'[107] She measured the Hampstead set against her own and claimed to find it wanting, boasting ebulliently to Sydney that Lytton alone was worth more than the whole pack of them. Provocatively she invited Sydney to come and hear more of her opinions, promising to bulldoze his.[108]

Much of her hostility was due to the fact that the Hampstead group was a male coterie, with women only allowed by unanimous vote. Brett was admitted because the meetings were held at her home; D.H. Lawrence's wife Frieda was allowed to come with her husband, as was Katherine Mansfield; and occasionally an exception was made for Iris Tree, the bohemian daughter of theatre impresario Herbert Beerbohm Tree. Of the regulars, only Sydney and Murry were married.[109] Kot and Murry believed that women could not possibly appreciate the genius of D.H. Lawrence. Virginia concluded that they were misogynists.[110] Both the Woolfs were 'elected' to attend the Thursday meetings in December 1922 but declined, Virginia noting with *schadenfreude* that Margery Waterlow had been blackballed.[111] Despite their occasional spats, the Thursdayers became for Sydney the group of friends he had feared he would never have, who would take pleasure in his company and respect his ideas. He now felt liberated from Bloomsbury, and by 1923 the friendship between Virginia and Sydney was cooling. Leonard sometimes saw Sydney to discuss politics, but he largely disappeared from Virginia's life, although at intervals she added a note to her 'collection of Sydneyana'.[112] After seeing Sydney in June 1923 Virginia realized how fond she was of him, warts and all: 'I cant help liking Sydney – fundamentally honest; fundamentally weak; gullible; & now settling down to "repose", which is very delightful. And he's a vegetarian ... Vegetarianism is part of a whole revolution.'[113] Once more, he had found short-term salvation through new spiritual beliefs.

But his 'repose' was interrupted. In 1926 a new phase of his life began when he was appointed to the first of a series of foreign diplomatic posts. As Hom had predicted, his diplomatic postings were very good for him. Sydney's son and daughter remember their father's elated letters during the first few weeks or months of a new posting in Bangkok, Sofia or Athens, then his returning gloom as the excitement of being in fresh surroundings died down. Information that he had become British Minister to Bangkok was relayed to Virginia through the grapevine, and she joked in a letter to Vita Sackville-West: 'Had I married Sydney

Waterlow I should have gone to Bangkok.'[114] Naturally when he was abroad for much of the year Sydney became estranged from many of his former friends. But his bond with Kot had been strengthened when in 1924 Sydney took his part against Murry, who had quarrelled with Kot over editorial control of the *Adelphi*. They now began a regular correspondence. Kot appreciated Sydney's openness to new experiences, writing in response to his impressions of Bangkok: 'I liked the way you can still feel freshly and unsophisticatedly, and give yourself wholly to an experience.'[115] He was openly fond of Sydney and prompted none of the doubts Sydney had about his Bloomsbury friends: 'I wish you were here, for we really miss you,' Kot wrote to him in 1927.[116]

When he was satisfied with his lot Sydney's demeanour could convey an impression of smugness. In 1920, T.S. Eliot remarked to his mother that as a result of making himself indispensable to Lord Robert Cecil at the Foreign Office Sydney had become pompous and had taken up smoking cigars.[117] When she felt fond of him Virginia interpreted his self-satisfaction as a shy pride in his successes.[118] When she was out of sympathy with him her interpretation was different. In 1933 she wrote to Dorothy Brett (who had fallen out with some of the Thursdayers before emigrating to New Mexico in 1924) of 'Sydney Waterlow . . . whose pomp of circumstance surpasses belief'.[119] But Desmond MacCarthy believed that these impressions of his complacency were misleading:

> one of his endearing characteristics was the amusing contrast between the self-assured pomposity of his utterances & the honest diffidence and sensitive naivety which it concealed. No one at bottom could be less a man of the world; no one temperamentally less of a diplomat.[120]

Desmond thought Sydney's sincerity was 'a fundamental trait in him'.[121] Occasionally, though, it led him to voice an unpopular opinion. When British Minister in Athens in 1936, Sydney received a visit from King Edward VIII and Wallis Simpson. Sydney was in the minority who thought marriage to Mrs Simpson might do the unfocused Edward – and directionless Britain – a power of good, and he was not afraid to say so. To Lord Hardinge, the King's Private Secretary, he wrote that the union between Edward and Mrs Simpson was a harbinger of the burgeoning relationship between Britain and the United States, and that, since British civilization was disintegrating, they had better embrace their American future.[122] (From today's standpoint, this sounds almost prophetic.)

In Athens Sydney cut a great figure. His statuesque physique and authoritative demeanour impressed his colleagues, who held him in awe but recognized his eccentric side. One of his attachés remembered:

> By his whims – and these were frequently incalculable – our life in the Legation was circumscribed. Tall, with a flowing upturned moustache meeting his side-whiskers ('the built-up areas' someone once called them) and a man of great intellectual achievement . . . There was nothing colourless about him. His eccentricities were both exasperating and endearing. He was a personality to be reckoned with. Everyone in Athens knew H.M. Minister . . . [123]

Rebecca West, in Athens in 1936 for a British Council lecture tour, formed a very vivid opinion of Sydney's virtues and vices:

> He represents the type of eccentric English gentleman at its very best . . . The Greeks adore his superb floridity, his kingly bearing, his arrogance and courtliness . . . He is kindly, generous, full of enthusiasm for what pleases his scholarly and aesthetic sense, and is obviously shrewd enough when it is borne on him that he has to be. But he has the defects of his qualities. He is a character whom only those with a certain amount of talent and breeding can appreciate . . . He is also impulsive, spoiled and given to breaches of good manners whenever he feels like it.[124]

Virginia Woolf briefly acknowledged Sydney's role in Greece in *The Years* (1937) where she has Sir William Whatney and Morris Pargiter discuss whether Athens has an embassy or a legation. Sir William himself bears some similarities to the older Sydney, being stout and walrus-like with white hair and whiskers. Significantly Virginia places this incident in the '1911' section of the book: this was the year when Sydney proposed to her.[125] But it was twenty-two years later that he became British Minister there.

The Athens posting fitted Sydney like a glove. It was three decades since his Cambridge days, but his interest in Greek and the Greeks remained. He schooled himself in the modern language and literature, published several translations of ancient Greek texts and became friendly with a circle of Greek writers. No doubt he made the acquaintance of Hilton Young's cousin and Maynard Keynes's friend, Gerard Mackworth Young, who was Director of the British School at Athens from 1936 to 1946. He was interested in the local excavations and joined the Greek Archaeological Society. His superiors in the British government wondered if he had 'gone native'.[126] But they acknowledged his skill in keeping the dictator Metaxas on their side, to prevent him joining forces with his Italian neighbour, Mussolini.

When Sydney reached retirement age (he turned sixty in October 1938) a year's extension of his tenure was proposed. But he then took a step that proved very unpopular with his superiors. Predicting that the severity of Metaxas' regime would bring about revolution, Sydney advised the Greek king to distance himself from it to avoid his own downfall. The king believed that his adviser was exaggerating and did not act. The Foreign Office considered Metaxas the best of a bad bunch and were alarmed both at Sydney's intervention and the king's evident loss of trust in his opinions. Meanwhile word that the British Minister had spoken against him reached a furious Metaxas. By spring 1939 Sydney's relations with both Metaxas and the king had deteriorated to such a degree that the extension of his contract was curtailed by several months. Officially he was told that the extension had caused unrest among ambitious junior diplomats who were keen to succeed to senior posts such as his, but the real reason was clear.[127]

Although he would have been happy to continue in Athens, Sydney was forced to retire in early June 1939. He never quite got used to not being in the thick of international politics, although he tried to direct his energies to tending his garden at Oare, reading and playing chess. One of his companions in his retirement was another career diplomat, Sir Eric Phipps, formerly ambassador to Berlin and Paris, who lived in nearby West Stowell with his family.[128] (In another of those ubiquitous Bloomsbury links, Sir Eric Phipps's son later married Henrietta, the niece of Walter Lamb.) Only three months after Sydney returned from Athens for the last time war was declared. His last few years were not happy ones: he felt useless without employment, feared invasion and coped badly with the privations of the war.[129]

Sydney did not live to see peace established. He died from heart failure on 4 December 1944, after several years of heart problems. He was sixty-six. He retained his enquiring mind until the end, writing shortly before his death a lengthy letter to G.E. Moore containing various interesting facts about heart disease (Moore also had a heart problem) and urging his friend to refrain from exertions such as gardening – as he had not. He had been reading a little philosophy and told Moore that if he had not been forbidden over-stimulation he could have constructed a few theories of his own.[130] A few days after his letter to Moore he wrote a pragmatic letter to *The Times*, rejecting an argument that a civil servant who disagrees with government policy should resign on principle.[131] After his death *The Times* printed his obituary but, adhering to the principles of the age, omitted all the most interesting parts.

Epilogue

EONARD WOOLF'S COURTSHIP of Virginia Stephen was brief and concentrated, although apparently discreet on both sides – neither Walter Lamb nor Sydney Waterlow seem to have noticed during their pursuit of Virginia that they had a rival. Leonard proposed in January 1912 and, after much prevarication, was finally accepted in May. In Leonard Virginia had found a man who interested her intellectually, to whom she could talk for hours but who was at the same time a man of action. In describing Leonard to Madge Vaughan and to Lady Robert (Nelly) Cecil, Virginia mentioned the fact that he had shot tigers. To Nelly Cecil she over-extended his talents and claimed that he had ruled India.[1] He had in fact been an administrator, although a very good administrator, in Ceylon. In Virginia's eyes, it seems, Leonard possessed some of her dead brother's physical and personal qualities.[2] Years later she was even more certain she had made the right decision, telling Jacques Raverat that she could not have married anyone else.[3]

On her honeymoon she continued to write to her closest friends. She hinted to Lytton at her lost virginity, telling him that she and Leonard had been interrupted in bed by mosquitoes.[4] But she gave out that she was not impressed by the nuptials – she felt no different as Mrs Woolf than she had done as Miss Stephen.[5] She remained unimpressed, and the Woolf marriage was practically a celibate one. Virginia had warned Leonard of her physical coldness, and to his credit he seems to have been content with his lot.[6] He came to think of Virginia as a genius – indeed the only genius with whom he had been on close terms.[7] He supported her desire to write, encouraged her and nursed her through numerous periods of mental disturbance, several of which occurred in the three years following their wedding. His self-discipline and rigour provided a stability that Virginia's life had hitherto lacked. It cannot be entirely coincidental that it was only after her marriage that she started to publish books and to keep a regular diary. Leonard also provided Virginia with a respite from the stresses of writing when he set up the Hogarth Press in 1917. An additional advantage (perhaps foreseen by Leonard) was that the Press brought her into touch with a new generation of writers. Most importantly it meant that she could publish her own books and attain complete authorial freedom.[8]

Virginia's idea of the kind of man she wanted to marry had been refined by the approaches of other men. She was in no hurry to lose her virginity; she was financially independent; therefore her choice could be made on the basis of love, intellectual compatibility and, to a lesser but still important extent, her suitor's relationship with her friends. The only other man she could even contemplate marrying was Lytton, thoroughly acceptable to Bloomsbury because he was one of its central 'members'. An important factor in Virginia's acceptance of Leonard was Vanessa's wholehearted endorsement of him. Vanessa wrote letters to Leonard and her sister after his first proposal, telling them both she could imagine no one else married to Virginia (although within months she was to be exasperated by Leonard's obduracy). But she had to admit that her faith in his rightness was based on instinct rather than a thorough knowledge of his character.[9] She desired her sister's happiness but also her own. She needed a little distance. It was in her interests to separate Virginia from Clive once and for all and to ensure that her sister did not interfere in her affair with Roger Fry.

How much of Virginia's choice was determined by the person her parents brought her up to be, and how much by her subsequent character development or her peers? This is perhaps the same as asking: Did she marry the person she was expected by her family or her friends to marry? When announcing her engagement Virginia assumed that Leonard would be an unexpected choice in the eyes of her family and her older friends, a fact of which she was fully aware when she boasted with glee that her fiancé was a Jew with no inherited money.[10] Her choice was evidently meant to reflect the bohemian and exotic aspects of her character, but Leonard was in reality neither of these, if by bohemian we mean *laissez-faire* and sexually free and by exotic we mean outlandish and glamorous. On the contrary, he had the reassuring and rock-like qualities – which became increasingly essential to Virginia – of decisiveness, stability and complete reliability.

Virginia was devastated when her mother died and when, less than a decade later, her father succumbed to cancer. In her middle age she admitted that, acutely as she missed him for years afterwards, had he lived she would have had no career: his life would have absorbed hers and left no time or energy for novels.[11] Virginia was very much aware of those women whose lives had been ruined by having to look after an elderly parent, a responsibility that always fell to the unmarried daughter. Had Julia lived, her ideas of female duty and submission would have had the same stunting effect on Virginia's writing – could Virginia have ignored or suppressed the angel in the house while living with the angel? And what effect would her parents' longevity have had on her choice of a husband? As he did for Stella Duckworth, Leslie would probably have left Virginia to make her own decision, while hoping (and frequently hinting his hope) that she would remain a spinster at 22 Hyde Park Gate and would spend her afternoons talking to him about books.

But what of Julia, the confirmed matchmaker? It doesn't seem possible that she would have sat back without trying to influence her younger daughter's opinions, encouraging in some quarters and discouraging in others. She would quietly have quashed the Walter Headlam affair. Whatever his virtues, it was clear that there was a family prejudice against him, whether based on fact or rumour. The flirtation with Clive, had Julia allowed Vanessa to marry him (and it is possible Vanessa would have married him anyway; being always more rebellious than her sister), would not have taken place under the altered circumstances. Saxon would have been indulged and pitied but not taken seriously as a possible husband. Lytton would have provided much entertainment for the older Stephens, as he did for the younger ones and their friends (although of a less racy character), but would certainly not have proposed and retracted so lightly had he had Julia to contend with. Walter Lamb might perhaps have been under consideration, but his Byronic brother would have been a black mark. Sydney Waterlow, with a wife already under his belt, would definitely not have been a candidate. Hilton Young would certainly have been Julia's favourite: handsome, romantic, charming, wealthy, a baronet's son and with a career in serious journalism and politics: what Victorian mother could have resisted him for their daughter's hand? Virginia was almost tempted herself.

Would Leslie and Julia have looked approvingly on Leonard? Well, perhaps. He was intelligent and serious-minded enough to have made a favourable impression on Leslie (certainly Leslie did on Leonard, when he saw him from a distance in 1901[12]) but was perhaps not a sufficiently romantic figure for Julia's taste, in spite of his career in Ceylon. Perhaps, torn between her yearning for companionship, the call of the 'nunnery' and love and respect for her mother, Virginia would not have married at all, not published a single book and become one of those daughters-at-home whose fate she deplored.

How close did Virginia come to making a different decision? Not very close, I think. With the scholarly Walter Headlam she enjoyed a mild flirtation which fed her vanity and made her feel less lonely, less spinsterish. The intimacy with Clive – which Virginia later referred to as her 'affair' with Vanessa *and* Clive – was undertaken in a bid to be close to them both and as such was not likely to result in anything that excluded Vanessa.[13] Her friendship with the gentle Saxon was never more than that, although she always had a soft spot for him and – like many other women – thought him charming. In Lytton she found an intellectual soulmate but one who was highly strung and emotionally demanding of those he loved. Her acceptance of his hasty proposal shows that she considered him, at least briefly, the kind of man she could marry. And he was the only man apart from Leonard with whom she admitted to being in love.[14] But years later she declared that she would not have published anything if she had married him, such was his strangely inhibiting presence.[15]

Hilton might have had a better chance had he been less interested in politics and more in literature; or if he had found his way to Bloomsbury's heart. Virginia found him kind and romantic, and his pursuit (although this is too strong a word for it) was the nearest to a conventional courtship that Virginia experienced before Leonard. But without Vanessa's approbation Hilton's prospects were limited. Walter Lamb was rather strung along by Virginia after a fallow period of suitors; cautious and hesitant by nature, his almost-proposal did not merit an outright refusal but surely would have received one. A marriage between Virginia Stephen and Rupert Brooke was never a possibility – Brooke had too many other women on his mind, and Virginia recognized the unacknowledged mental instability under the smooth, golden exterior. Sydney Waterlow, like Lytton, saw in Virginia a saviour from the rough and tumble of life. It took him a little longer than Lytton, but after a few months he saw that the match was not the answer to all his problems. For Virginia Sydney was a friend who alternately charmed and wearied her. His chief disadvantage is that he stood in comparison to Leonard, who was in the process of making an extremely favourable impression while Sydney contemplated marriage to Virginia.

Remaining single was not a permanent option for Virginia, who longed to regain an intimacy she had first enjoyed with Vanessa. She liked being on her own for short spells occasionally but was not psychologically equipped to live a solitary life. However she might complain about a constant stream of visitors, the visitors were obviously made to feel welcome or else they would have stopped coming. Contact with people was her life-blood. She had many reservations about marriage (would her husband expect passion? how would they live? would she still be able to write?) but even more about staying single. She wanted and needed emotional stability and companionship, and if her flirtations with her suitors tell us nothing else, they tell us that she loved being loved.

There is some dissent among Woolf's biographers as to whether Virginia Stephen married the right man. While Spater and Parsons conclude that the marriage was overall a happy one for both, Poole and Trombley view Leonard as domineering and restrictive.[16] Certainly there were rocky patches during their early years together; and it is possible that the stresses which led to her mental instability in 1912–15 were increased by the marriage – as they might have been whomsoever she had married. If we believe she might have been better off with someone else, we must consider how her life would have been improved. Perhaps her periods of mental instability would have been treated more sympathetically; perhaps she would have had children? But although Leonard had some influence in these matters they were chiefly the result of medical advice. Despite his flaws Leonard was perhaps the only man of Virginia's acquaintance who could have so assiduously attended to her needs – physical, emotional and intellectual – and helped to make her the writer she became.

Ultimately we must judge Virginia's attitude to her marriage by her own words, those she wrote in her letters and diaries. Of Leonard she had, except on rare occasions, only good words to say. Her periods of illness aside, there seem to have been no major disturbances in the marriage, the diaries recording only minor disagreements that were soon smoothed over. For two people with such different characters – one imaginative and sensitive to a high degree, the other priding himself on rationalism and self-discipline – this is quite a feat. No doubt Virginia's gratitude for Leonard's loyalty and care played its part in mitigating any criticisms she might have made about his character or behaviour; and for Leonard Virginia's genius diminished her transgressions. To Virginia, clearly, Leonard was the most suitable of suitors; the best of husbands; she could not imagine that any couple could have been happier.

Family Trees

Note: Family trees have been compiled for the lesser-known suitors discussed in this book: Walter Headlam, Hilton Young, Walter Lamb and Sydney Waterlow; Clive Bell is also included because, well known as he is in Bloomsbury circles, no biography or family tree has yet been published. Much though I would have liked to include details and dates of Saxon Sydney-Turner's forebears, he remains as elusive in death as he was in life, and I was not able to unearth enough genealogical information to make a family tree worth while. The little information I did find appears in Chapter 4.

The family trees in this book were compiled using information from *Who's Who* and *Who Was Who*, *Debrett's Handbook*, *Burke's Peerage and Baronetage*, the *Dictionary of National Biography*, the *Annual Register*, personal interviews and correspondence and the Registers of Births, Deaths and Marriages at the Family Records Centre in London. Other sources are listed in the notes.

Virginia Woolf's family tree can be found in Volume 1 of Quentin Bell's *Virginia Woolf*, Volumes 1 and 2 of Woolf's *Letters*, Volume 1 of *The Diary of Virginia Woolf* and Hermione Lee's *Virginia Woolf*. A fairly shallow tree showing three generations of Leonard Woolf's family is in Leonard Woolf's *Letters*, ed. Frederic Spotts, and a slightly more detailed one in the third volume of Virginia Woolf's *Letters*, p. 522.

Lytton Strachey's family tree and much information about his ancestors are in Barbara Strachey, *The Strachey Line*.

Rupert Brooke's antecedents are covered in Nigel Jones's biography, *Rupert Brooke: Life, Death and Myth*, pp. 1–4.

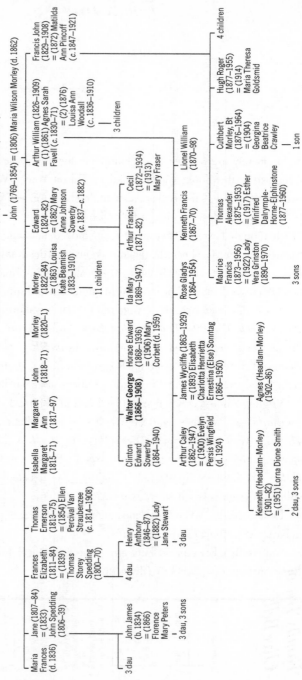

Family Tree of Walter Headlam[1]

Family Tree of Clive Bell [2]

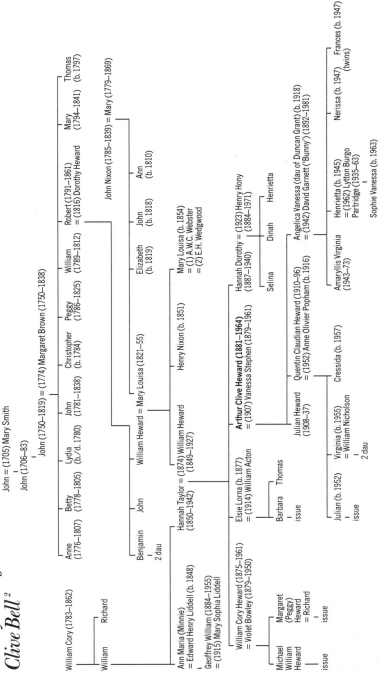

Family Tree of Hilton Young[3]

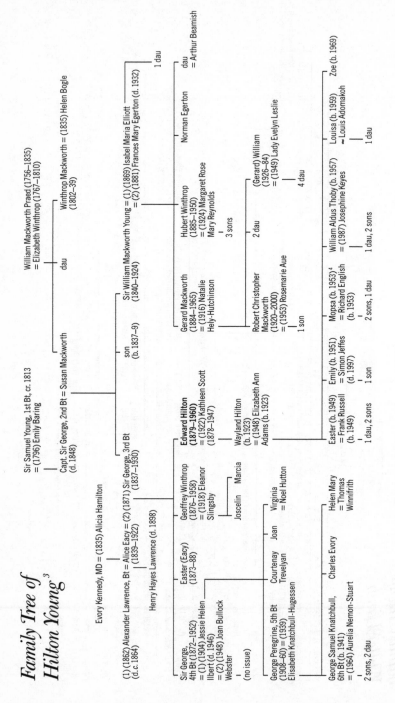

Family Tree of Walter Lamb [5]

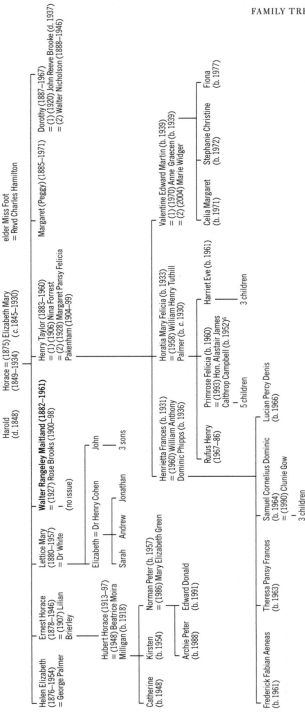

Reuben Rangeley

William Lamb

Mrs Holland

dau (b. 1817) = John Lamb of Stockport (1816/17–51)

Simon Foot of Dublin

Harold (d. 1848)

Horace = (1875) Elizabeth Mary
1849–1934   (c. 1845–1930)

elder Miss Foot
= Revd Charles Hamilton

Henry Taylor (1883–1960)
= (1) (1906) Nina Forrest
= (2) (1928) Margaret Pansy Felicia Pakenham (1904–99)

Margaret (Peggy) (1885–1971)

Dorothy (1887–1967)
= (1) (1920) John Reeve Brooke (d. 1937)
= (2) Walter Nicholson (1888–1946)

Helen Elizabeth (1876–1954)
= George Palmer

Ernest Horace (1878–1946)
= (1907) Lilian Brierley

Lettice Mary (1880–1957)
= Dr White

Walter Rangeley Maitland (1882–1961)
= (1927) Rose Brooks (1900–98)
(no issue)

Hubert Horace (1913–97)
= (1948) Beatrice Moira Milligan (b. 1918)

Elizabeth = Dr Henry Cohen

John

Sarah   Andrew   Jonathan

3 sons

Catherine (b. 1948)

Kirsten (b. 1954)

Norman Peter (b. 1957)
= (1986) Mary Elizabeth Green

Archie Peter (b. 1988)

Edward Donald (b. 1991)

Henrietta Frances (b. 1931)
= (1960) William Anthony Dominic Phipps (b. 1936)

Horatia Mary Felicia (b. 1933)
= (1958) William Henry Tuthill Palmer (b. c. 1930)

Harriet Eve (b. 1961)

Valentine Edward Martin (b. 1939)
= (1) (1970) Anne Graecen (b. 1939)
= (2) (2004) Marie Widger

Celia Margaret (b. 1971)

Stephanie Christine (b. 1972)

Fiona (b. 1977)

Rufus Henry (1967–86)

Primrose Felicia (b. 1960)
= (1993) Hon. Alastair James Calthrop Campbell (b. 1952)[6]

5 children

Lucian Percy Denis (b. 1966)

3 children

Frederick Fabian Aeneas (b. 1961)

Theresa Pansy Frances (b. 1963)

Samuel Cornelius Dominic (b. 1964)
= (1990) Clunie Gow

3 children

Family Tree of Sydney Waterlow[7]

Walleran Waterlo of Lille (fl. 1628)
|
Walran Waterlo of Lille (d. 1684)
|
Walran Waterlo of Canterbury (1634–1712)
|
Samuel Waterlo of Canterbury (b. 1663)
|
Samuel Waterlo of London (bap. 1701)
|
Josiah Waterlow (fl. 1740s–1760s)
|
Josiah Waterlow of London (c. 1762–1817)
|
James Waterlow (1790–1876) = (1812) Mary Crakell (1792–1872)

Mary Valentina (1814–95) = (1848) William Stones (1820–66)
3 dau

Alfred James (1815–86) = (1838) Isabella Jameson (b. 1815)
6 dau, 5 sons

Charles William (1817–97) = (1842) Louisa Masters (b. 1815)

Walter Blanford (1819–91) = (1) (1842) Rebecca Stones (1822–69) = (2) (1874) Maria Waterlow (née Corss)

Ellen Celia (b. 1821) = (1842) George Hickson (1819–89)
5 sons, 4 dau

Sydney Hedley, 1st Bt, cr. 1873 (1822–1906) = (1) (1845) Anna Maria Hickson (1824–80) = (2) (1882) Margaret Hamilton (b. 1850)

Albert Crakell (1824–56) = (1846) Maria Corss (1823–1918)

Emily Kate (b. 1829) = (1854) Philip Stephen King (b. 1819)
3 dau, 5 sons

Josiah (1830–1)

Philip Hickson, 2nd Bt[8] (1847–1929) = (1) (1869) Amy Grace Lutwyche (1848–97) = (2) (1898) Laura Marie Jones (b. 1858)
2 sons, 4 dau

Ruth (b. 1850) = (1873) Francis Wilkes Homan (d. 1880)
2 dau, 2 sons

George Sidney (1852–1925) = (1876) Charlotte Elizabeth Beauchamp (1859–1944)

Charles Hickson (b. 1854) = (1881) Frances Anne Latimer (b. 1856)
4 dau, 2 sons

David Sydney (1857–1924) = (1883) Edith Emma Maitland (1864–1932)
6 sons

Hilda Maria (b. 1861) = (1886) Alfred Ford (b. 1860)

Paul Langbourne (b. 1863) = (1892) Kathleen Holmes (b. 1871)

Celia Agnes (b. 1865)

Ernest Albert (1850–1919) = (1876) Marie Hofman (1856–99)
2 dau, 2 sons

4 dau

Zoe Beauchamp (b./d. 1877)
(no issue)

Sydney Philip Perigal (1878–1944) = (1) (1902) Alice Isabella Pollock (1876–1953) (no issue) = (2) (1913) Helen Margery Eckhard (1884–1973)

John Beauchamp (1880–1916)

Margery (b. 1881) = (1909) John Herbert Norton (d. 1963)

Guy Walron (b. 1884)

Cecil Beauchamp (b. 1887)

Charlotte Mary (b. 1915)
(no issue)

John Conrad (b. 1916) = (1939) Angela Gray
1 dau, 2 sons

Judith Matilda (1921–66)
(no issue)

Janet = Harry Eeles
3 children

Peter John (b. 1913) = (1944) Olive Mary Deacon
1 dau, 1 son

Richard Christopher (b. 1919) = (1945) Margaret Thomas
3 sons, 1 dau

Notes

A page reference to a footnote or an end note is given in the style p. 163 n. 10, or p. 163n if the note is unnumbered. I have assumed some familiarity with the names of Virginia Woolf's family and friends, and therefore their names, along with the titles of archives and institutions, have generally been abbreviated. Virginia Woolf is AVS before her marriage (10 August 1912) and VW afterwards. Vanessa Bell is VB or VS before her marriage (7 February 1907). Other abbreviations in the notes are:

ATL/NLNZ	Alexander Turnbull Library/National Library of New Zealand
BB	Barbara Bagenal (Barbara Hiles before 1 February 1918)
Berg	Berg Collection of English and American Literature, New York Public Library, Astor, Lenox and Tilden Foundations
BH	Barbara Hiles (Barbara Bagenal from 1 February 1918)
BL	British Library
CB	Clive Bell
CP	Charleston Papers
CUL	Cambridge University Library
DC	(Dora) Carrington
Dept MSS	Department of Manuscripts
DG	Duncan Grant
DM	Desmond MacCarthy
EMF	(Edward) Morgan Forster
FP	Frances Partridge (née Marshall)
GLS	(Giles) Lytton Strachey
HY	Hilton Young
JMM	John Middleton Murry
JS	James Strachey
KAF	Ka (Katherine) Arnold-Forster (Ka Cox before 9 September 1918)

KC	Ka Cox (Ka Arnold-Forster from 9 September 1918)
King's	King's College Modern Archive, Cambridge
KM	Katherine Mansfield
KP	Kennet Papers, Cambridge University Library
LW	Leonard Woolf
LWP	Leonard Woolf Papers, University of Sussex Library
MHP	Monks House Papers, University of Sussex Library
MM	Molly MacCarthy
QB	Quentin Bell
RB	Rupert Brooke
RCBP	Rupert Chawner Brooke Papers, King's College Modern Archive
SP	Strachey Papers, British Library
SST	Saxon Sydney-Turner
Sussex	Special Collections, University of Sussex Library
SW	Sydney Waterlow
SWP	Sir Sydney Waterlow Papers, Alexander Turnbull Library
Trinity	Trinity College Library, Cambridge
VD	Violet Dickinson
WH	Walter Headlam
WL	Walter Lamb

INTRODUCTION

1. AVS to VD, 31 December 1906, in VW, *Letters* 1, p. 274.

2. AVS to VD, 3 January 1907, in ibid., p. 276.

3. AVS to Lady Robert Cecil, May(?) 1907, in ibid., p. 296.

4. AVS to VD, March 1907, in ibid., p. 289.

5. J.R. Noble (ed.), *Recollections of Virginia Woolf*, p. 11.

6. For reasons of space I have limited myself to Woolf's early admirers, that is, those from before her marriage. There were of course others who admired or courted her after her marriage; for instance, Hugh Walpole, Philip Morrell and, most famously, Vita Sackville-West.

7. Hermione Lee says five, possibly six, but does not name them. See H. Lee, *Virginia Woolf*, p. 214.

8. Some biographers, such as George Spater and Ian Parsons, number H.T.J. (Harry) Norton among Virginia's admirers, but although he was a great fan of Vanessa's and accompanied her, Clive and Roger Fry to Turkey in 1911 I have found no evidence of a close friendship with Virginia.

9. VW, *Diary* 4, 30 July 1933, p. 170. Owing to the remarkable recent discoveries of unpublished writings by Virginia Woolf, I must add to the list of possibilities that the memoir may be lying dusty and undiscovered in a drawer somewhere.

10. C. Headlam, *Walter Headlam: His Letters and Poems*, Part I, pp. 103–4, 106.

CHAPTER 1: THE HIGHLY ELIGIBLE MISS STEPHEN

1. VW, '22 Hyde Park Gate', in *Moments of Being*, pp. 31–2; 'Old Bloomsbury', in ibid., pp. 44–6.

2. For more about Virginia Woolf's childhood home, see VW, 'A Sketch of the Past' and '22 Hyde Park Gate', in *Moments of Being*; J.M. Wilson, *Virginia Woolf: Life and London*; and S.M. Hall, ' "House of All the Deaths": 22 Hyde Park Gate', in *Virginia Woolf Bulletin* (the journal of the Virginia Woolf Society of Great Britain), Issue 2, July 1999.

3. Although they never lived at 22 Hyde Park Gate again, the house was let until May 1928, when it was sold for £4,925. VW to VB, 26 May 1927, in VW, *Letters 3*, p. 385 and n. 1.

4. VW, 'A Sketch of the Past', in *Moments of Being*, p. 131.

5. Ibid., p. 105.

6. H. Lee, *Virginia Woolf*, pp. 116–17.

7. QB, *Virginia Woolf*, Vol. 1, pp. 89–90.

8. LW to GLS, 12 December 1906, in LW, *Letters*, p. 122.

9. VW, 'Old Bloomsbury', in *Moments of Being*, p. 52.

10. Ibid.

11. VS to Madge Vaughan, 25 March 1905, in F. Spalding, *Vanessa Bell*, p. 54.

12. VW, 'Old Bloomsbury', in *Moments of Being*, p. 53.

13. Violet Dickinson, older than the Stephens, was originally a friend of Stella Duckworth. Organized and responsible, she became a mother-figure to all the young Stephens, as well as Virginia's literary confidante.

14. VW, 'A Dialogue upon Mount Pentelicus', in *Complete Shorter Fiction*, pp. 63–8.

15. VW, *Jacob's Room*, p. 133.

16. The Noels' estate, Achmetaga, had been given to an ancestor in 1832 for fighting alongside Byron for Greek independence.

17. VW, *A Passionate Apprentice*, p. 340.

18. VW, 'Greece 1906', in *A Passionate Apprentice*, pp. 317–47.

19. VW, 'A Dialogue upon Mount Pentelicus', in *Complete Shorter Fiction*, pp. 63–8.

20. VW, *Jacob's Room*, pp. 24, 27, 38–40.

21. Ibid., pp. 41–2, 51, 64.

22. Ibid., pp. 65, 66, 69, 70.

23. Ibid., pp. 70, 71, 112.

24. Ibid., pp. 121, 125.

25. Ibid., pp. 133–5.

26. Ibid., pp. 139, 147, 149, 166.

27. Ibid., pp. 167, 170, 173.

28. VW, 'A Sketch of the Past', in *Moments of Being*, p. 143.

29. VS to CB, 7 November 1906, in VB, *Selected Letters*, pp. 43–4.

30. AVS to VD, 18 June 1905, in VW, *Letters* 1, p. 192.

31. J.R. Noble (ed.), *Recollections of Virginia Woolf*, p. 18.

32. Ibid., pp. 21–2.

33. See, for instance, AVS to VD, December(?) 1903, in VW, *Letters* 1, p. 112; AVS to VD, 22 December 1906, in ibid., p. 269.

34. QB, *Virginia Woolf*, Vol. 1, p. 117.

35. AVS to VD, February 1907, in VW, *Letters* 1, p. 279.

36. QB, *Virginia Woolf*, Vol. 1, p. 115n.

37. Noel Olivier to RB, 3 January 1914, in RB/N. Olivier, *Song of Love*, p. 261.

38. Quoted in J. MacGibbon, *There's the Lighthouse*, p. 106.

39. GLS to AVS, 23 April 1908, in VW/GLS, *Letters*, p. 12; also in GLS, *Letters*, p. 141.

40. J. MacGibbon, *There's the Lighthouse*, p. 2.

41. QB, *Virginia Woolf*, Vol. 1, p. 118.

42. VW, 'A Sketch of the Past', in *Moments of Being*, p. 113.

CHAPTER 2: A FINE ROMANCE: WALTER HEADLAM

1. An interesting exploration of the cause(s) of Stella's death is to be found in V. Curtis, *Stella and Virginia: An Unfinished Sisterhood*.

2. VW, 'Outlines: Dr Bentley', in *The Common Reader* (First Series), pp. 190–5.

3. C. Headlam, in *Walter Headlam: His Letters and Poems*, Part I, pp. 14ff.

4. It is interesting, if not entirely germane, to note that in 1866 a man stood before Morley Headlam on a charge of 'unlawfully attempting to carnally know a certain greyhound at Barnard Castle'. Durham Quarter Sessions Calendar of Prisoners, Durham Record Office, quoted on the 'Rogues' Gallery of Wanlesses', http://www.riverduck.com/wanlessweb/UK/rogues.html.

5. For details of Walter Headlam's family and ancestors I am indebted to Stephen Headlam, whose website provided much valuable information. Readers interested in Walter's genealogy are directed to http://www.dheadlam.freeserve.co.uk, where many branches of the family are noted.

6. C. Headlam, *Walter Headlam: His Letters and Poems*, Part I, p. 2.

7. VW, *Jacob's Room*, pp. 34, 103.

8. E.F. Benson, *As We Were*, pp. 135–8.

9. L. Stephen, *Sir Leslie Stephen's Mausoleum Book*, p. 78.

10. WH to Julia Stephen, 1893. Quoted in C. Headlam, *Walter Headlam: His Letters and Poems*, Part I, p. 84.

11. VW, 'A Sketch of the Past', in *Moments of Being*, p. 113.

12. Ibid., p. 108.

13. C. Headlam, in *Walter Headlam: His Letters and Poems*, Part I, p. 31.

14. Quentin Bell suggests that Jem Stephen's injury was caused by a blow from a moving train. See QB, *Virginia Woolf*, Vol. 1, p. 35n.

15. T. Caramagno, *The Flight of the Mind*, pp. 100–3.

16. VW, 'A Sketch of the Past', in *Moments of Being*, p. 108.

17. T. Caramagno, *The Flight of the Mind*, pp. 101–3. It was at St Andrew's that Lucia, the mentally ill daughter of James Joyce, was confined and died in 1982.

18. 'In Memoriam J.K.S.', in C. Headlam, *Walter Headlam: His Letters and Poems*, Part II, p. 20.

19. QB, *Virginia Woolf*, Vol. 1, p. 118.

20. VW, 'A Sketch of the Past', in *Moments of Being*, p. 131.

21. AVS to Emma Vaughan, 17(?) June 1900, in VW, *Letters* 1, p. 35.

22. See, for example, Virginia's letter to Thoby dated July 1901, in VW, *Letters* 1, p. 42.

23. WL, 'Notes of My Life, 1882–1922', Trinity.

24. AVS to VD, 10 December 1906, in VW, *Letters* 1, p. 259.

25. C. Headlam, *Walter Headlam: His Letters and Poems*, Part I, p. 94.

26. AVS to VD, 6 December 1904, in VW, *Letters* 1, p. 163.

27. Ibid.

28. VS to AVS, 7 December 1904, in VB, *Selected Letters*, pp. 27–8.

29. 'Hunting-crop', in C. Headlam, *Walter Headlam: His Letters and Poems*, Part I, pp. 27–9.

30. Or was it? Apparently Walter 'loved to *represent* himself as naïvely simple' (my italics), and this may have meant he got away with a certain suggestive humour. Ibid., p. 30.

31. WH to Mrs George Wherry, 29 August 1906. Quoted in ibid., p. 100.

32. E.F. Benson, *As We Were*, p. 138.

33. C. Headlam, *Walter Headlam: His Letters and Poems*, Part I, p. 131–5.

34. AVS to VD, 10 December 1906, in VW, *Letters* 1, p. 259.

35. Ibid., 28(?) December 1906, p. 272.

36. VW, *A Passionate Apprentice*, p. 232.

37. AVS to VD, March 1907, in VW, *Letters* 1, p. 289.

38. AVS to CB, 22 March 1907, in ibid., p. 289.

39. AVS to VD, 12 April 1907, in ibid., pp. 291-2.

40. Ibid., 23(?) April 1907, p. 293.

41. Those who are interested in reading the letter from Walter to Virginia are referred to QB, *Virginia Woolf*, Vol. 1, p. 119.

42. Margaret Lushington's diary for 21 September 1893. Quoted in A. Curtis (ed.), *Before Bloomsbury*, p. 34. Many thanks to Stephen Barkway for bringing Margaret Lushington's diary to my attention.

43. Stella Duckworth's diary for 22 September 1893. Quoted in QB, *Virginia Woolf*, Vol. 1, p. 119n.

44. A. Curtis (ed.), *Before Bloomsbury*, p. 35.

45. QB, *Virginia Woolf*, Vol. 1, p. 118.

46. C. Headlam, *Walter Headlam: His Letters and Poems*, Part I, p. 88.

47. WH to Mrs Lancelot Sanderson, 1897. Quoted in ibid., p. 84.

48. 'Seven Years Old', in ibid., Part II, pp. 40-1.

49. Michael Harrison, in his book *Clarence: The Life of HRH the Duke of Clarence and Avondale (1864-1892)*, London: W.H. Allen, 1972, has suggested that stylistic similarities between J.K. Stephen's poetry and notes purportedly written by Jack the Ripper are evidence that J.K. Stephen himself was the Whitechapel murderer of 1888.

50. AVS to VD, May 1907, in VW, *Letters* 1, p. 294.

51. Ibid., p. 295.

52. 'Seville', in C. Headlam, *Walter Headlam: His Letters and Poems*, Part II, p. 59.

53. Ibid., Part I, pp. 155-60.

54. AVS to Madge Vaughan, 28 June 1908, in VW, *Letters* 1, pp. 335-6.

55. Ibid., p. 336.

56. G. Murray, quoted in C. Headlam, *Walter Headlam: His Letters and Poems*, Part I, p. 7.

57. RB to M.R. Brooke, 28 June 1908, in RB, *Letters*, pp. 132-3.

58. C. Headlam, *Walter Headlam: His Letters and Poems*, Part I, pp. 51-2.

59. Ibid., Part II, p. 111.

60. AVS to GLS, 4 January 1909, in VW, *Letters* 1, p. 378.

61. AVS to DG, 29 November 1918, in VW, *Letters* 6, p. 495. (This letter appears in Vol. 6 of the *Letters* because it was discovered too late for inclusion in Vol. 2.)

62. VW to J.T. Sheppard, 5 January 1920, in VW, *Letters* 2, p. 414.

63. QB, *Virginia Woolf*, Vol. 1, p. 118n.

64. VW, *To the Lighthouse*, pp. 26-7.

65. VW to VB, 23 March 1919, in VW, *Letters* 2, p. 342.

66. VW, 'A Sketch of the Past' in *Moments of Being*, p. 145.

67. VW, *Diary 3*, 23 November 1926, p. 117.

CHAPTER 3: TURNING THE KNIFE: CLIVE BELL

1. QB, *Elders and Betters*, p. 23. Cleeve House now has a much more peaceable purpose. Since the 1970s it has been owned by a charitable organization, the Family Federation for World Peace and Unification, which unites families from across the world in the study of 'ethical and spiritual principles'. See www.cleevehouse.org.uk.

2. Ibid., pp. 25-7.

3. AVS to Madge Vaughan, 17 December 1906, in VW, *Letters* 1, p. 265; VW, *A Passionate Apprentice*, p. 383. According to Leonard Woolf, Clive's interest in art, which became so large a part of his life, began not at Cambridge but later, when he lived in Paris. See LW, *Sowing*, p. 128 n. 2.

4. VW, 'Old Bloomsbury' in *Moments of Being*, p. 49.

5. LW, *Sowing*, p. 128.

6. VS to Margery Snowden, 2 May 1904, in VB, *Selected Letters*, p. 17.

7. AVS to VD, 6(?) May 1904, in VW, *Letters* 1, p. 140.

8. Outside the limits of this book, strictly speaking, but interesting nevertheless, is the curious story of Gerald Kelly's friendship with Aleister Crowley, whom he met at Cambridge in 1898. Crowley married Kelly's sister Rose in 1903 to save her from being forced to marry someone else. He had lived with Kelly in Paris in the early 1900s, so the Stephens narrowly missed meeting him.

9. In fact Clive did not give up hunting after he married Vanessa. In August 1908 Virginia mentioned in a letter to Saxon Sydney-Turner that Vanessa was upset by Clive's shooting rabbits. See AVS to SST, 28 August 1908, in VW, *Letters* 1, p. 362.

10. VS to Margery Snowden, 13 August 1905, in VB, *Selected Letters*, p. 34.

11. Thoby Stephen to CB, August 1905. Clive Bell I, Box 5/11 (38), Trinity.

12. Ibid., October 1905 (40); WL, 'Notes of My Life, 1882–1922', Trinity.

13. See Appendix C in QB, *Virginia Woolf*, Vol. 1.

14. LW to GLS, 3 September 1905, in LW, *Letters*, pp. 100–1.

15. AVS to VD, 16 November 1906, in VW, *Letters* 1, p. 246.

16. Ibid., 19 November 1906, p. 247.

17. Ibid., 29 November 1906, p. 253.

18. AVS to Lady Robert Cecil, 2(?) December 1906, in ibid., p. 256.

19. AVS to VD, 14(?) December 1906, in ibid., p. 262.

20. Ibid., 2 January 1907, p. 274.

21. VB to AVS, 11 April 1908, in VB, *Selected Letters*, p. 60.

22. Through his mother Clive was related to Alice Liddell, the inspiration behind Lewis Carroll's 'Alice' stories: Hannah Taylor Bell's sister married Alice's brother.

23. QB, *Elders and Betters*, p. 25.

24. Stella Duckworth was the daughter of Leslie Stephen's second wife Julia. In 1897 Stella married John (Jack) Waller Hills after a protracted courtship. Leslie, by then a widower, did not dislike Jack but resented the loss of his capable and sympathetic housekeeper.

25. AVS to Madge Vaughan, 17 December 1906, in VW, *Letters* 1, p. 265.

26. AVS to CB, 20 December 1906, in ibid., p. 268.

27. AVS to VD, 28(?) December 1906, in ibid., p. 272.

28. Ibid.

29. Ibid., 30(?) December 1906, p. 273.

30. GLS to LW, 4 July 1905, in GLS, *Letters*, p. 73.

31. LW to GLS, 30 July 1905, in LW, *Letters*, p. 98.

32. Ibid., 17 December 1906, p. 123.

33. GLS to LW, October 1908. Quoted in ibid., p. 139 n. 1.

34. Henry James to Lucy Clifford, 17 February 1907, in H. James, *Letters*, Volume 4, p. 437.

35. RB to JS, 5/6 July 1910, in RB/JS, *Friends and Apostles*, p. 124. After being publicly and heavy-handedly teased by Clive about that 'secret' society, the Apostles (of which James and Rupert were members and Clive was not), Rupert was embarrassed and exasperated enough to exclaim to James 'What a weasel!' Ibid., p. 125.

36. VW, 'A Sketch of the Past' in *Moments of Being*, p. 146.

37. Ibid., p. 90.

38. AVS to VD, 12 April 1907, in VW, *Letters* 1, p. 291.

39. The society was re-formed with different players between October 1914 and February 1915.

40. VW, 'Old Bloomsbury' in *Moments of Being*, p. 56.

41. Play Reading Society Minutes for 16 December 1908. CP, CHA 5/1, King's.

42. Ibid., 7 April 1908.

43. Ibid., 15 January 1909.

44. CB to AVS, 3 May 1908. Letters III, MHP, Sussex.

45. Ibid., 7 May 1908.

46. AVS to CB, 6 May 1908, in VW, *Letters* 1, p. 330.

47. AVS to VB, 11 August 1908, in ibid., p. 350.

48. *Melymbrosia* has now been published in its own right, edited by Louise DeSalvo (see Bibliography).

49. CB to AVS, October 1908. Quoted in QB, *Virginia Woolf*, Vol. 1, p. 207.

50. Ibid., p. 208.

51. Ibid., p. 207.

52. CB, *Old Friends*, p. 95.

53. Clive was not so keen on Woolf's feminist writings. He thought *A Room of One's Own* 'amusing' but 'bitter' and *Three Guineas* her 'least admirable production' (see CB, *Old Friends*, pp. 101, 102).

54. AVS to GLS, 1 February 1909, in VW, *Letters* 1, p. 382.

55. VW to Gwen Raverat, 22 March 1925, in VW, *Letters* 3, p. 172.

56. CB to AVS, 12 August 1908, Letters III, MHP, Sussex.

57. Ibid.

58. Ibid., 23 August 1908.

59. Ibid., September 1910.

60. Ibid., spring 1911.

61. AVS to VB, 6 April 1911, in VW, *Letters* 1, pp. 456–7. Rachel (Ray) Costelloe was the sister of Karin, who married Adrian Stephen on 31 October 1914.

62. AVS to Ottoline Morrell, 1 January 1911, in ibid., p. 449. A draft letter from CB to GLS concerning a quarrel is reproduced in GLS, *Letters*, pp. 203–5. It is provisionally dated autumn 1911, but the content seems appropriate for the 1910 quarrel, even containting the ban from Gordon Square.

63. AVS to CB, 4 September 1910, in ibid., p. 434.

64. Ibid., 14(?) November 1910, p. 439. Mary Sheepshanks was until 1913 head of Morley College in London's Waterloo Road. It was through her that Virginia became involved in teaching working men and women in 1905–7.

65. CB to AVS, summer 1912. Letters III, MHP, Sussex.

66. VW, *Diary 3*, 23 July 1927, p. 149.

67. VB to AVS, 19 April 1908, in VB, *Selected Letters*, p. 61.

68. VW, *Diary 2*, 5 February 1921, p. 89.

69. For more on Clive Bell and Molly MacCarthy, see H. and M. Cecil, *Clever Hearts*, pp. 132–9.

70. Mary Hutchinson also had 'celebrity' connections through her offspring: her son Jeremy married actress Peggy Ashcroft and her daughter Barbara married first Lord Rothschild and then the poet Rex Warner.

71. VB to GLS, 27 April 1916, in VB, *Selected Letters*, p. 195.

72. DC to Gerald Brenan, 12 January 1920, in DC, *Letters*, p. 152.

73. Reproductions of the portrait and a photograph of Mary Hutchinson can be found in F. Spalding, *Vanessa Bell*, opposite p. 208.

74. VW to SW, 3 May 1921, in VW, *Letters* 2, p. 467.

75. VW, *Diary* 2, 22 January 1921, p. 157.

76. Juana de Gandarillas to CB, 6 March 1921, 25 May 1921, 14 August 1921 and two undated letters, probably also from 1921. CP, CHA/1/225, King's.

77. VW to QB, 11 May 1929, in VW, *Letters* 4, pp. 55–6.

78. VW to VB, 30 June 1929, in ibid., p. 70.

79. For more on Benita Jaeger, see F. Spalding, *Vanessa Bell*, pp. 242–4.

80. AVS to GLS, 21 May 1912, in VW, *Letters* 1, p. 498. Beatrice Meinertzhagen married Robert (Robin) Mayor, King's fellow and later Secretary to the Board of Education, in 1912. The couple occupied Little Talland House after Virginia left.

81. 'Manet and the Post-Impressionists' was held at the Grafton Galleries from 8 November 1910 to 15 January 1911 and featured the paintings of Manet, Cézanne, Van Gogh, Gauguin, Picasso and Matisse, among others. The second Post-Impressionist exhibition ran from 5 October 1912 to 31 January 1913. Alongside the French and Russian paintings was displayed the work of lesser-known British artists, including Vanessa Bell, Duncan Grant, Frederick Etchells, Stanley Spencer, Eric Gill and Wyndham Lewis. See F. Spalding, *Roger Fry*, pp. 126–33, 148–54.

82. F. Spalding, *Roger Fry*, p. 155.

83. QB, *Elders and Betters*, p. 41.

84. VB to Angelica Garnett, 16 October 1957 and 13 March 1960. Quoted in F. Spalding, *Vanessa Bell*, pp. 356, 359.

85. H. and M. Cecil, *Clever Hearts*, p. 165.

86. Garsington Manor was the Oxfordshire country house of Ottoline Morrell (1873–1938) and her husband Philip. Most of Bloomsbury was invited here regularly and also D.H. Lawrence, Bertrand Russell, Dorothy Brett, Mark Gertler, Aldous Huxley (whose novel *Crome Yellow* was based on Garsington and its guests), Katherine Mansfield, John Middleton Murry, Henry Lamb and Siegfried Sassoon.

87. VW, *Between the Acts*, p. 52. There is also a hint of Clive's first lover, Annie Raven-Hill, in the depiction. Virginia had heard about her from Vanessa and in Clive's 1921 paper for the Memoir Club (see pp. 82–3 above).

88. *The Times*, 19 September 1964, 10d.

CHAPTER 4: THE STRANGEST MIND: SAXON SYDNEY-TURNER

1. Alison Bagenal, letter to the author, 11 June 2004.

2. *Dictionary of National Biography*, Vol. XIX, 1973; *Annual Register*, 1847.

3. FP, *Memories*, p. 144.

4. VW to SST, 31 December 1916, in VW, *Letters* 2, p. 134.

5. VW to KAF, 5 February 1919, in ibid., p. 326.

6. Worth £41,459.17 in 2002. John J. McCusker, 'Comparing the Purchasing Power of Money in Great Britain from 1264 to 2002', Economic History Services, 2003. URL: http://www.eh.net/hmit/ppowerbp.

7. AVS to VB, 27 December 1910, in VW, *Letters* 1, p. 444.

8. M. Holroyd, *Lytton Strachey*, p. 61.

9. McTaggart may have spotted a twin spirit in Saxon. According to Leonard Woolf, McTaggart was equally silent but more intimidatingly so than Saxon and was known as an eccentric. See LW, *Sowing*, pp. 132-3.

10. See P. Levy, *Moore*, pp. 71-3.

11. LW, *Sowing*, p. 103.

12. Ibid., pp. 105-8.

13. Ibid., pp. 115-16.

14. The other members were Lytton Strachey, Leonard Woolf and A.J. Robertson. Thoby Stephen was later invited to join. The unfortunate Robertson was dropped by the others when they discovered that his father was a clergyman.

15. VW, 'Old Bloomsbury', in *Moments of Being*, p. 50.

16. AVS to VD, 1 October 1905, in VW, *Letters* 1, p. 208.

17. Ibid., 26(?) November 1906, p. 252. In this letter to Violet Dickinson Virginia was pretending that Thoby was still alive in order not to endanger her friend's chance of recovering from typhoid, but there is no reason to believe that the accompanying news is fictional.

18. VW to SST, 24 November 1916, in VW, *Letters* 2, p. 126.

19. AVS to VD, 22 September 1907, in VW, *Letters* 1, p. 311.

20. These appeared in *Euphrosyne*, a volume of graduate verse compiled by Clive Bell. See p. 71-2 above. Although he later squirmed when he read the poems, Leonard Woolf thought Saxon's contribution was not bad but as insubstantial as Saxon himself.

21. The manuscript of Saxon's play is in the Trinity College Library (Wren Library) in Cambridge, Bell II, D2. Saxon evidently thought the play good enough to make this fair copy - there are almost no errors, additions or deletions in the manuscript.

22. Play Reading Society Minutes for 10 January 1908. CP, CHA 5/1, King's.

23. Ibid., 14 February 1908.

24. Ibid., 14 February 1908.

25. Ibid., 12 March 1908.

26. Ibid. In the new-look society of 1914 *Aureng-Zebe* was reread by Saxon, Clive and Vanessa,

together with Roger Fry, Duncan Grant, Molly MacCarthy and Marjorie Strachey. Demonstrating that he, if no one else, had been reading the earlier minutes, Clive remarked: 'Saxon, I suspect, would have liked more rant'. Ibid., 4 November 1914.

27. Ibid., 12 March 1908.

28. AVS to SST, 10 August 1908, in VW, *Letters* 1, p. 347.

29. LW, *Beginning Again*, p. 29.

30. AVS to SST, 14 August 1908, in VW, *Letters* 1, pp. 352-3.

31. AVS to VB, 7, 8 and 10 August 1909, in ibid., pp. 403-5.

32. Ibid., 10 August 1909, p. 405.

33. Ibid., 16 August 1909, p. 408.

34. Ibid., 19 August 1909, p. 409.

35. Now classified as an 'autism spectrum disorder', Asperger's syndrome was first identified as a separate condition in 1944 by the Austrian paediatrician Hans Asperger (1906-80).

36. SST to BB, 3 February 1918. Bagenal family papers.

37. AVS to VB, 24 August 1909, in VW, *Letters* 1, p. 410.

38. VW to SST, VW to BH, both 16 January 1917, in VW, *Letters* 2, p. 136.

39. AVS to VB, 19 August 1909, in VW, *Letters* 1, p. 409; GLS to LW, 19 February 1909, in GLS, *Letters*, p. 174.

40. GLS to LW, 21 August 1909, in GLS, *Letters*, p. 187.

41. AVS to VB, 10 August 1908, in VW, *Letters* 1, p. 349.

42. Ibid., 24 June 1910, p. 429. This comic scenario was close to a prediction. During Virginia's engagement, George Duckworth, to whom money mattered greatly, wrote to Leonard asking him to settle a sum on Virginia. At the time Virginia was at least fifteen times wealthier than her fiancé through family legacies. George Duckworth to LW, 8 August 1912. Letters II, MHP, Sussex. See also LW, *Beginning Again*, pp. 54-5 and 89-90.

43. AVS to SST, 13 June 1910, in VW, *Letters* 1, p. 427.

44. Ibid., June 1910, p. 427. On another occasion Virginia compared Saxon to a Siamese cat. See VW to Nicholas Bagenal, 15 April 1918, in VW, *Letters* 2, p. 230.

45. AVS to SST, August 1910, in VW, *Letters* 1, p. 432. One interpretation of her comments is the denial of passion in her own nature.

46. An (absent) brother, Cuthbert, seemed from his mother's account to be the antithesis of Saxon – indeed, unlike the rest of the family. He was 6 foot 1 inch tall, handsome and had shot three elephants. See AVS to VB, 27 December 1910, in ibid., p. 444.

47. Ibid.

48. VW to LW, 31 October 1917, in VW, *Letters* 1, p. 194.

49. Ibid., 29 and 30 October 1917, pp. 191-3.

50. Carrington and Brett were known to friends by their last names. Carrington became Lytton Strachey's companion until his death in 1932 (see Chapter 5 above). Brett grew away from Bloomsbury and by the early 1920s her closest friends included D.H. Lawrence, Mark Gertler, S.S. Koteliansky, Katherine Mansfield and John Middleton Murry. She began an affair with Murry after Katherine's death but emigrated to New Mexico with the Lawrences in 1924. Faith, the sister of Nicholas Bagenal, married Hubert Henderson in 1915. Alix Sargant-Florence married James Strachey, Lytton's younger brother, in 1920. They studied psychoanalysis under Sigmund Freud; their translations of his works were published by the Hogarth Press.

51. VW to VB, 27 February 1919, in VW, *Letters* 2, p. 337.

52. SST to BB, 5 February 1918. Bagenal family papers.

53. VW to SST, 24 November 1916, in VW, *Letters* 2, p. 126.

54. DC to GLS, 29 Jan 1917, in DC, *Letters*, p. 54.

55. Ibid., p. 55; 4 February 1917, p. 57.

56. VW to LW, 30 October 1917, in VW, *Letters* 2, p. 192.

57. Ibid., 31 October 1917, p. 194.

58. SST to BB, 31 December 1918. Bagenal family papers.

59. VB to VW, 13 February 1918, in VB, *Selected Letters*, p. 212.

60. VW to VB, 29 Jan 1918, in VW, *Letters* 2, p. 214.

61. SST to BB, 5 February 1918. Bagenal family papers.

62. VW to VB, 23 February 1918, in VW, *Letters* 1, p. 218.

63. Ibid., 19 October 1918, p. 284.

64. VW to VB, 26 November 1918, in VW, *Letters* 2, p. 299.

65. Ibid., 9 December 1918, p. 302.

66. SST to BB, 31 December 1918. Bagenal family papers.

67. Ibid., 11-12 January 1919. Bagenal family papers.

68. VW, *Diary* 2, 8 May 1920, p. 35.

69. VW to VB, 20 February 1922, in VW, *Letters* 2, p. 506.

70. VW to CB, 25 February(?) 1922, in VW, *Letters* 2, p. 508.

71. VW, *Diary* 2, 3 November 1923, pp. 272-3.

72. VW to BB, 25 July 1924, in VW, *Letters* 3, p. 122.

73. VW to VB, 17 September 1925, in VW, *Letters* 3, p. 210; VW, *Diary* 3, 13 May 1929, p. 225.

74. J.R. Noble (ed.), *Recollections of Virginia Woolf*, p. 146.

75. VW, *The Voyage Out*, p. 12.

76. VW, 'One of Our Great Men'. MHP, MH/A 13c, Sussex.

77. A tendency to focus on small details together with a failure to see the bigger picture is another characteristic of those with Asperger's syndrome.

78. FP, *Everything to Lose*, p. 46.

79. DC to GLS, 19 August 1929, in DC, *Letters*, p. 414.

80. 'Dr Turner's Mental Home' (1929) is now housed at the British Film Institute National Film and Television Archive in London.

81. FP, *Memories*, p. 144.

82. SW to LW, 18 January 1942. LWP, Part III, Sussex.

83. The Partridges had taken Ham Spray after the deaths of Lytton Strachey and Carrington in 1932.

84. FP, *A Pacifist's War*, p. 146.

85. Ibid., p. 172.

86. FP, *Everything to Lose*, p. 97.

87. SST to CB, 13 June 1948. CP, CHA/1/616, King's.

88. Alison Bagenal, letters to the author, 4 April and 11 June 2004.

89. Alison Bagenal, conversation with the author, 6 May 2004.

90. Vanessa Pawsey, conversation with the author, 14 April 2004.

91. Ibid.

92. FP, *Hanging On*, p. 79.

93. LW, *The Times*, 13 November 1962, 14e.

CHAPTER 5: 'I WAS RIGHT TO BE IN LOVE WITH HIM': LYTTON STRACHEY

1. VW, 'Old Bloomsbury', in *Moments of Being*, p. 49. In the end it wasn't – Lytton left Cambridge with a double second.

2. Three more infants – Caroline, Olivia and Roger – did not reach maturity. See B. Strachey, *The Strachey Line*, p. 173.

3. Ibid., p. 155. One of John Strachey's granddaughters was Mary Hutchinson, sometime lover of Clive Bell (see pp. 80–1 above).

4. Ibid., pp. 168–9.

5. Ibid., pp. 148, 156.

6. It was Pippa Strachey's invitation to Virginia Woolf to speak to the London and National Society for Women's Service (an organization seeking to place more women in the professions) in 1931 that inspired Woolf to write *Three Guineas*.

7. M. Holroyd, *Lytton Strachey*, pp. 23.

8. Ibid., pp. 33, 35.

9. John Strachey's son Charles (Lytton's cousin) married Ada, sister of Walter Raleigh.

10. GLS, 'Diary 1898', in *Lytton Strachey by Himself*, p. 94.

11. LW, *Sowing*, p. 158.

12. GLS to DG, 16 November 1907. Add. MS 57932, LSDG 72 (146), Dept MSS, BL.

13. Ibid., 17 November 1907. LSDG 73 (148).

14. Ibid., 23 November 1907. LSDG 76 (151).

15. Ibid., 16 July 1908. LSDG 78 (175-6). Quoted in M. Holroyd, *Lytton Strachey*, p. 183.

16. JMK to GLS, 20 July 1908. PP/45/316/4, King's.

17. GLS to JMK, 21 July 1908, in GLS, *Letters*, p. 145.

18. GLS to DG, 31 July 1908. Add. MS 57932, LSDG 80 (178-9), Dept MSS, BL. Quoted in M. Holroyd, *Lytton Strachey*, p. 184. Cythera is the southernmost of the Ionian islands. In ancient times it was the site of a temple of love dedicated to Aphrodite – according to legend the goddess was carried here by the waves after her birth from the sea foam.

19. VW, 'Old Bloomsbury', in *Moments of Being*, p. 49.

20. GLS to LW, 10 September 1901, in GLS, *Letters*, p. 6.

21. GLS to B. Swithinbank, 1 July 1905, in ibid., p. 70.

22. Preface to VW/GLS, *Letters*, p. 7.

23. GLS to AVS, 23 April 1908, in GLS, *Letters*, p. 141.

24. VB to AVS, 30 July 1908, in VB, *Selected Letters*, p. 66.

25. Ibid., 11 August 1908, p. 67.

26. GLS to AVS, 27 September 1908, in GLS, *Letters*, pp. 162-3.

27. AVS to CB, 25 December 1908, in VW, *Letters* 1, p. 377.

28. GLS to DG, 26 December 1908. Add. MS 57932, LSDG 85 (187), Dept MSS, BL.

29. See Appendix C in QB, *Virginia Woolf*, Vol. 1. See also pp. 71-2 above.

30. AVS to VB, 30 August 1908, in VW, *Letters* 1, p. 366.

31. AVS to GLS, 30 August 1908, in ibid., p. 365.

32. Ibid., 20 November 1908, p. 374.

33. GLS to AVS, 27 January 1909, in GLS, *Letters*, p. 168.

34. AVS to GLS, 28 January 1909, in VW, *Letters* 1, p. 381.

35. GLS to AVS, 31 January 1909, in VW/GLS, *Letters*, p. 30. (GLS, *Letters*, p. 169 omits 'even'.)

36. AVS to GLS, 1 February 1909, in VW, *Letters* 1, p. 382. Virginia's *nom de plume* might have been derived from Eleanor Hayden, the author of a book she reviewed in July 1905.

37. LW, *Sowing*, p. 186.

38. LW to GLS, 1 February 1909, in LW, *Letters*, p. 145.

39. GLS to AVS, 17 February 1909, in GLS, *Letters*, p. 172.

40. AVS to MM, March 1912, in VW, *Letters* 1, p. 492; VW, *Diary* 2, 17 October 1924, p. 317.

41. VW, *Diary* 1, 15 November 1919, p. 311.

42. VW, *Diary* 3, 14 December 1929, p. 273.

43. GLS to LW, 19 February 1909, in GLS, *Letters*, p. 174.

44. Ibid.

45. GLS to JS, 9 March 1909, in VW/GLS, *Letters*, p. 32. (GLS, *Letters*, p.175 has 'February'.)

46. GLS to Dorothy Bussy, 25 February 1909. Quoted in M. Holroyd, *Lytton Strachey*, p. 200.

47. GLS to LW, 21 August 1909, in GLS, *Letters*, p. 185.

48. JS to GLS, 6 December 1909. Add. MS 60708 (70-1), in SP, Vol. LIV, Dept MSS, BL. (Donald T. Blume reported on this exchange in the *Virginia Woolf Miscellany*, Spring 2004, p. 11.)

49. GLS to JS, 7 December 1909 (72), in ibid.

50. GLS to LW, 6 June 1912. Letters II, MHP, Sussex. Quoted in M. Holroyd, *Lytton Strachey*, p. 257.

51. AVS to GLS, 1 September 1912, in VW, *Letters* 2, p. 5.

52. Preface to VW/GLS, *Letters*, p. 8.

53. GLS to VW, 8 November 1912, in GLS, *Letters*, p. 210.

54. CB, *Old Friends*, p. 118.

55. M. Beerbohm, *Lytton Strachey*, p. 5.

56. Ibid., p. 6.

57. C. Clemens, *Lytton Strachey*, p. 29.

58. See M. Holroyd, *Lytton Strachey*, p. 49n.

59. For further information about Marfan syndrome, see the website of the National Marfan Foundation at http://www.marfan.org and the AccessMed Health Information Library's Marfan syndrome page at http://www.ehendrick.org/healthy/000875.htm.

60. GLS to DG, 28 October 1913. Add. MS 57932, LSDG 120 (236), Dept MSS, BL.

61. VW to GLS, 8 December 1914, in VW, *Letters* 2, pp. 52-3.

62. M. Holroyd, *Lytton Strachey*, p. 353.

63. VW to David Garnett, 21 October 1916, in VW, *Letters* 2, p. 124. Carrington went with Lytton to brave the Woolfs' den on 25 October, but it is possible that Virginia had already met Carrington before this occasion. See VW, *Letters* 2, p. 122 n. 2.

64. VW, *Diary* 1, 9 December 1917, p. 89.

65. GLS to DC, 11 December 1917. Add. MS 62888, Dept MSS, BL.

66. G. Boas, *Lytton Strachey*, p. 3.

67. VW, *Diary* 1, 18 April 1918, p. 142.

68. Ibid., 22 January 1919, p. 235.

69. Ibid., 24 January 1919, pp. 235 -6.

70. Ibid.

71. GLS, *The Really Interesting Question and Other Papers*, p. 124.

72. VW, *Diary* 2, 8 April 1921, p. 106.

73. VW, *Diary* 3, 22 September 1928, p. 198. This was not the first time Virginia had attempted a fictional biography. In 1909 her story 'Memoirs of a Novelist' had been rejected by the *Cornhill Magazine*.

74. Lytton first met Roger Senhouse, twenty-odd years his junior, at Garsington and by 1926 they had become lovers. Roger was considered handsome and charming by most of Lytton's friends, but Virginia thought him not intellectually up to scratch. He was a graduate of Magdalen College, Oxford, and later became a partner in the publisher Secker and Warburg.

75. VW, *Diary* 2, 28 November 1928, pp. 208-9; 15 June 1929, p. 234.

76. GLS to LW, 17 July 1917, in GLS, *Letters,* p. 358.

77. VW, *The Voyage Out*, pp. 139-40.

78. VW, *Night and Day*, pp. 65, 126.

79. Ibid., p. 60.

80. For example, GLS to DG, 17 January 1907. Add. MS 57932, LSDG 69 (85), Dept MSS, BL; GLS to VB, 21 October 1909, in GLS, *Letters*, p. 188.

81. LW, *Sowing*, p. 123.

82. VW, *Diary* 3, 2 September 1930, p. 316.

83. DC, 'D.C. Partride [*sic*] Her Book', 20 March 1931, p. 35. Add. MS 65159, Dept MSS, BL. Quoted in M. Holroyd, *Lytton Strachey*, p. 657.

84. DC to CB, February 1922, in DC, *Letters*, p. 202; VW to GLS, 23 February 1922, in VW, *Letters* 2, pp. 507-8.

85. M. Holroyd, *Lytton Strachey*, pp. 670, 672; VW, *Diary* 4, 29 December 1931, p. 57.

86. VW, *Diary* 4, 27 December 1931, p. 56.

87. GLS, 'A Fortnight in France' (6 September 1931), in *Lytton Strachey by Himself*, p. 169.

88. M. Holroyd, *Lytton Strachey*, p. 683.

89. DC, 'D.C. Partride [*sic*] Her Book', 6 March 1932, p. 36 verso. Add. MS 65159, Dept MSS, BL.

90. VW, *Diary* 4, 4 February 1932, p. 72.

91. M. Holroyd, *Lytton Strachey*, p. 694n.

92. G. Boas, *Lytton Strachey*, p. 21.

93. *The Times*, 22 January 1932, p. 12a.

CHAPTER 6: THE BARONET'S SON: HILTON YOUNG

1. HY, 'In and Out', unpublished autobiography, p. 22. KP, Dept MSS, CUL.
2. Ibid., p. 4.
3. See Sir George Young's personal website at: http://www.sir-george-young.org.uk/articles/newsitem.cfm?newsid=720.
4. LW, *Beginning Again*, p. 116.
5. VW, *Diary* 1, 18 September 1918, p. 194.
6. R.F. Harrod, *The Life of John Maynard Keynes*, p. 105.
7. Mallory's strong-boned features and classical good looks were much admired by Lytton Strachey and Duncan Grant, who in 1912 painted a portrait of him, stripped to the waist, in pointillist style. (Duncan jokingly offered his services as the official Everest expedition artist.) Tragically Mallory died during an expedition climbing the notorious peak in 1924, aged thirty-seven. So difficult were the conditions on the mountain that his body was not found until 1 May 1999. It was buried on the mountain.
8. E.H. Young (=HY), *The Count*, p. 5.
9. Wayland Young, conversation with the author, 6 February 2004.
10. See QB, *Virginia Woolf*, Vol. 1, p. 29.
11. HY, 'In and Out', p. 193. KP, Dept MSS, CUL.
12. Ibid, pp. 8, 9.
13. See Appendix in P. Levy, *Moore*, for a list of Apostles to 1914.
14. GLS to CB, 17 January 1906, in GLS, *Letters*, p. 90.
15. VW, *A Passionate Apprentice*, 20 March 1905, p. 254.
16. *Granta*, 29 November 1902. Thanks to Stephen Barkway for bringing this article to my attention.
17. HY, 'In and Out', pp. 22–3. KP, Dept MSS, CUL.
18. VB to AVS, 30 July 1908, in VB, *Selected Letters*, pp. 64–5.
19. AVS to VB, 8 April 1911, in VW, *Letters* 1, p. 458.
20. A diagram makes the Young–Ilbert–Fisher–Stephen interrelationships easier to follow

Hilton Young's family tree can be found on p. 244 above.
21. AVS to VB, 4 August 1908, in VW, *Letters* 1, p. 341.
22. VB to AVS, 11 August 1908, in VB, *Selected Letters*, p. 67.
23. EMF to HY, 16 August 1922. KP, Part I, 28/10, Dept MSS, CUL.
24. VB to GLS, 8 March 1909, in VB, *Selected Letters*, pp. 79–80.

25. The evidence that a proposal took place comes from Quentin Bell in his biography of Woolf, suggesting that the story circulated among the family. Most other Woolf biographers take his lead. Hilton's son and daughter-in-law believe that they heard of it from Hilton himself in the 1950s (Wayland Young, conversation with the author, 6 February 2004). Virginia refers only to an 'interview' with Hilton (VW, *Diary* 1, 18 March 1918, p. 130), but this is a word she reserves for intimate discourse, usually involving a proposal. Many thanks to Geoff Burrows for reminding me that the evidence is persuasive rather than infallible.

26. VW, *Diary* 3, 23 November 1926, p. 117.

27. AVS to VB, 19 August 1909, in VW, *Letters* 1, p. 409.

28. Ibid., 1(?) May 1910, p. 424.

29. Ibid., 20 April 1911, p. 464. Elinor, née Monsell, was married to a grandson of Charles Darwin. Fredegond Virginia's cousin, was the daughter of Florence (née Fisher) and F.W. Maitland, Leslie Stephen's biographer. In 1915 she married the economist Gerald Shove. Frances, née Darwin, was another grandchild of Charles Darwin. She and her husband, Francis Cornford, both poets, were friends of Rupert Brooke.

30. Olive Heseltine (née Ilbert), under the pseudonym Jane Dashwood, later became the author of a novel of London society life, *Three Daughters* (1930). She also wrote non-fiction books under her own name, including *Conversation*, a history of talk through the ages, and *Essays and Sketches*.

31. RB to GLS, 11 September 1910, in RB/JS, *Friends and Apostles*, p. 133.

32. Ibid., n. 6.

33. Wayland Young, conversation with the author, 6 February 2004.

34. VB to DG, 14 January 1914, in VB, *Selected Letters*, p. 153. Jean Marchand (1883–1941) is the subject of an article in Roger Fry's *Vision and Design*. He became a good friend to Gwen and Jacques Raverat in the early 1920s. After Jacques's death on 7 March 1925, he and Gwen fell in love, but he eventually married someone else.

35. VB to HY, 13 January(?) 1914. KP, Part I, 5/4, Dept MSS, CUL.

36. VB to HY, 15 April 1915, in VB, *Selected Letters*, pp. 175–6.

37. RB to HY, April 1914, in RB, *Letters*, p. 575.

38. EMF to HY, 13 August 1920. KP, Part I, 28/9, Dept MSS, CUL.

39. HY, 'In and Out', p. 30. KP, Dept MSS, CUL

40. Virginia Woolf has the fictional character of Lieutenant John Craig, in the 1935 version of *Freshwater*, attached to a ship called *Iron Duke*.

41. HY, *By Sea and Land*, p. 10.

42. VW, *Diary* 1, 18 March 1918, p. 130. Ka Cox's dinner party was actually on the 19th, but Virginia describes it under her 18 March diary entry.

43. Ibid.

44. Irene Noel and her family were friends of the Stephen family, and the four siblings stayed with the Noels when they went to Greece in 1906 (see pp. 39 and 249 n. 16 above). Thoby Stephen admired her, and Sandra Wentworth-Williams in *Jacob's Room* is probably based on the self-willed, independent and accomplished Irene.

45. Thanks to Geoff Burrows for bringing their correspondence to my attention.

46. Will Arnold-Forster had been a friend of Hilton's since their youth, despite the six-year gap in their ages. As well as accompanying Hilton on a horse-drawn omnibus trip in about 1903, they went to Sicily together after Hilton's breakdown in 1907. Hilton thought Will a gifted painter and hung some of his pictures at The Lacket, but the subtle watercolours were too insipid for Bloomsbury tastes.

47. It was three years to the day since the death of Hilton's friend Rupert Brooke.

48. L. Young, *A Great Task of Happiness*, p. 12.

49. Ibid., pp. 198–200.

50. It is now known that the tragedy was due chiefly to continual blizzards and a sudden and prolonged drop in the temperature. This meant that other problems, such as leaking fuel tins (meaning fewer fires), no animals to pull the sledges (the ponies had died or been shot for food; the dogs had been sent back when their rations ran out) and delays through injury took on a much greater importance.

51. Peter Scott became a renowned ornithologist, founding the Severn Wildfowl Trust, which evolved into the Wildfowl and Wetlands Trust, and co-founding the World Wide Fund for Nature. A popular broadcaster, the David Attenborough of his day, he hosted *Look*, a BBC natural history programme, for seventeen years. He also participated in a radio programme, *Nature Parliament*, for twenty-one years. He was the illustrator of Hilton's ornithology book, *A Bird in the Bush* (1936).

52. Studland, a few miles south of Poole in Dorset, was a favourite Bloomsbury seaside resort and was the subject of a painting by Vanessa Bell (*Studland Beach*, 1912–13). The beach is now under the administration of the National Trust and is known for its nudists.

53. LW, *Downhill All the Way*, p. 101

54. VW, *Mrs Dalloway*, pp. 134, 33.

55. Ibid., pp. 121, 119.

56. Ibid., p. 135.

57. Ibid., p. 85. Coincidentally, Hilton later lived in Norfolk, but this was not until 1936.

58. Ibid., pp. 83, 132. James King, a Woolf biographer, also descries Hilton Young in the character of William Rodney in *Night and Day* (1919), but I do not see any resemblance. See his *Virginia Woolf*, London: Hamish Hamilton, 1994, p. 251.

59. Ibid., p. 9.

60. Ibid., p. 85.

61. Ibid., p. 9.

62. Ibid., p. 2.

63. Ibid., p. 2; VW, 'A Sketch of the Past', in *Moments of Being*, p. 95.

64. Lady Kennet [Kathleen Young], *Self-Portrait of an Artist*, 31 July 1921 and 24 March 1922, pp. 194, 204. The fact that Hilton thought this needed saying, though, was an indication that he was considered, and considered himself, a senior politician

65. The pushme-pullyu was a double-headed llama created by Hugh Lofting in *The Story of Dr Doolittle* (1920).

66. *The Times*, 21 October 1922, 12d (late edition).

67. LW, *Downhill All the Way*, pp. 33–40, 46.

68. Note by HY. KP, Part I, 4/1, Dept MSS, CUL.

69. VW, *To the Lighthouse*, p. 60.

70. VW to VB, 24 April 1931, in VW, *Letters* 4, p. 319.

71. VW to VSW, 28 April 1931, in VW, *Letters* 4, p. 323.

72. Another part of Hilton Young's remit as Minister of Health included the welfare of the mentally handicapped, or 'idiots', as Virginia would have termed them. The issues under discussion had still not been resolved decades later: the possibility of 'boarding-out' patients to free up hospital beds; whether the condition was hereditary; and the contentious matter of sterilization. But at least the terminology was changing: in 1930 the Lunacy Act of 1890 was supplemented by the more humane-sounding Mental Treatment Act.

73. L. Young, *A Great Task of Happiness*, p. 223.

74. Wayland Young, conversation with the author, 6 February 2004.

75. HY to EMF, undated reply to EMF's letter of 17 November 1939. Quoted in EMF, *Selected Letters* 2, p. 174.

76. It is interesting to ponder just how recently dissent has become widely acceptable. During the Falklands War in 1982 Margaret Thatcher protested publicly when the press presented the Argentinian point of view on an equal footing with that of the British.

77. HY, 'In and Out', p. 85. KP, Dept MSS, CUL.

78. *The Times*, 25 July 1960, 17e.

79. HY, 'In and Out', p. 205. KP, Dept MSS, CUL.

CHAPTER 7: COMPANION OF ROYALS: WALTER LAMB

1. Published in *The Times*, 21 August 1909, and as 'Impressions at Bayreuth' in VW, *Essays*, Vol. 1, pp. 288–93.

2. GLS to JS 8/9 February 1910. SP, Vol. LIV, Add. MS 60708 (84), Dept MSS, BL.

3. Alfred Ainsworth was also a friend of Lytton Strachey and Morgan Forster. The latter modelled Ansell in *The Longest Journey* on Ainsworth. The restrictive environment apparently extended to Owen's College which Ainsworth claimed did not encourage original thought.

4. Duncan Grant, also studying here, was disconcerted by the promiscuity of Henry Lamb and his circle.

5. A. Powell, introduction to *Henry Lamb*, Manchester City Art Galleries, 1984. Powell, a generation younger than Henry Lamb, became his brother-in-law in 1934 when he married Violet Pakenham, the sister of Henry's wife, Pansy.

6. GLS to LW, 23 October 1905, in GLS, *Letters*, p. 84.

7. AVS to GLS, 4 January 1909, in VW, *Letters* 1, p. 378; AVS to VD, April 1906, in ibid., p. 219. Sarah Duckworth, called 'Minna' by the family, was the sister of Julia Stephen's first husband Herbert Duckworth.

8. LW, *Beginning Again*, p. 55.

9. AVS to VD, 3(?) January 1906, in VW, *Letters* 1, p. 215.

10. GLS to Mary Hutchinson, 27 July 1927, in GLS, *Letters*, p. 569; GLS to DC, 9 August 1930, in ibid., p. 627.

11. GLS to CB, 17 January 1906, in GLS, *Letters*, p. 90.

12. WL to CB, 27 November 1906. CP, CHA 1/352/1, WLCB 16, King's. He seems to have forgotten his four sisters.

13. Ibid., 14 May 1906. WLCB 1(2).

14. Ibid., 24 May 1906. WLCB 2(3).

15. Ibid., 13 July 1906. WLCB 8(2).

16. AVS to VD, July 1905, in VW, *Letters* 1, p. 201.

17. WL to CB, 9 October 1906. CP, CHA 1/352/1, WLCB 9, King's.

18. Ibid.; 16 October 1906. WLCB 11.

19. Ibid.

20. Ibid., 6 November 1906. WLCB 13(2).

21. Ibid., 13 November 1906. WLCB 14(2).

22. Ibid., 27 November 1906. WLCB 16(2).

23. Ibid., 4 December 1906. WLCB 17.

24. WL to VB, 24 August 1908. CP, CHA 1/352/2, WLVB 2, Sussex.

25. Play Reading Society Minutes for 7 April 1908. CP, CHA 5/1, King's.

26. WL to CB, 16 August 1908. CP, CHA 1/352/1, WLCB 46, King's.

27. Ibid.

28. Ibid., 21 March 1909. WLCB 51.

29. AVS to GLS, 6 October 1909, in VW, *Letters* 1, p. 413.

30. WL to CB, 7 March 1910. CP, CHA 1/352/1, WLCB 63, King's.

31. AVS to VB, 1(?) May 1910, in VW, *Letters* 1, p. 424; ibid., 24 June 1910, p. 429; AVS to SST, August 1910, in ibid., p. 432; AVS to CB, 4 September 1910, in ibid., p. 434; ibid., 8 September 1910, p. 435; ibid.; AVS to Jack Hills, 5 October 1910, in ibid., p. 435.

32. AVS to VB, 8(?) June 1911, in VW, *Letters* 1, p. 466.

33. Ibid., 21 July 1911, p. 469.

34. WL, 'Notes of My Life, 1882-1922'. Trinity.

35. AVS to VB, 21 July 1911, in VW, *Letters* 1, pp. 469-71.

36. WL to AVS, 23 July 1911. Letters III, MHP, Sussex. I am greatly indebted to the Lamb family for permission to reproduce this letter and others written by Walter Lamb.

37. AVS to VD, 15(?) April 1909, in VW, *Letters* 1, p. 392.

38. WL to AVS, 23 July 1911. Letters III, MHP, Sussex.

39. WL to CB, 23 July 1911. CP, CHA 1/352/1, WLCB 71, King's.

40. WL to AVS, 25 July 1911. Letters III, MHP, Sussex.

41. AVS to VB, 25(?) July 1911, in VW, *Letters* 1, p. 472.

42. Ibid., p. 471.

43. WL to AVS, late July(?) 1911, Letters III, MHP, Sussex.

44. AVS to VB, 25(?) July 1911, in VW, *Letters* 1, p. 471.

45. WL, 'Notes of My Life, 1882-1922'. Trinity.

46. AVS to KC, April 1912, in VW, *Letters* 1, p. 495.

47. Leonard's and Virginia's exchange of letters – his urgings, her resistance – have much in common with those that passed between Leslie and Julia (which Virginia had read in 1904 for F.W. Maitland's biography of her father).

48. LW to AVS, 11 January 1912, in LW, *Letters*, p. 169.

49. WL to LW, 4 June 1912. LWP, Part II C, Sussex.

50. Sir Edward Poynter had been elected in 1896. One of his rivals for the presidency had been Julia Stephen's cousin, Valentine Prinsep, RA Professor of Painting, 1900-3, who managed to collect only one vote.

51. Royal Academy, *Annual Report . . . 1913*.

52. Royal Academy, *Annual Report . . . 1914*.

53. Ibid.

54. S.C. Hutchison, *The History of the Royal Academy*.

55. J. Ridley, *Edwin Lutyens*, pp. 405-6, 411.

56. Among Munnings' rivals for the post were Henry Lamb's old friend Augustus John, Clive Bell's friend Gerald Kelly and Laura Knight. Neither John nor Knight was ever

elected (to this day, no woman has ever been President).

57. S.C. Hutchison, *The History of the Royal Academy*.

58. VW, *Diary* 1, 10 January 1915, p. 14.

59. VW to VB, 14 May 1916, in VW, *Letters* 2, p. 96.

60. VW, *Mrs Dalloway*, pp. 197–8.

61. VW, *Diary* 1, 10 January 1915, p. 14.

62. VW, *Between the Acts*, pp. 38–9.

63. VW, *Diary* 1, 20 October 1917, p. 64.

64. VW, *Diary* 2, 17 April 1920, p. 31.

65. VW, *Diary* 1, 13 April 1918, p. 138.

66. Ibid., 13 February 1915, p. 34.

67. VW to VB, 14 May 1916, in VW, *Letters* 2, p. 96.

68. VW, *Diary* 1, 20 October 1917, p. 64; *Diary* 2, 17 April 1920, p. 31.

69. VW, *Diary* 1, 15 February 1915, p. 35.

70. AVS to VD, 14 November 1910, in VW, *Letters* 1, p. 438; AVS to GLS, 28 January 1909, in ibid., p. 381.

71. VW, *Diary* 1, 20 October 1917, p. 64.

72. VW, *Mrs Dalloway*, p. 4.

73. Ibid., p. 81.

74. VW, *Diary* 1, 10 January 1915, p. 14.

75. VW to VB, 17 March 1921, in VW, *Letters* 2, p. 458.

76. LW, *Downhill All the Way*, p. 41.

77. The dislike of Manchester was common in Bloomsbury. Saxon Sydney-Turner, telling Virginia in 1917 about Sydney Waterlow's recent leave, said 'he spent [it] in Manchester which I should imagine would be depressing'. SST to AVS 19 July 1917. Letters III, MHP, Sussex.

78. VW, *Night and Day*, pp. 8–10.

79. VW, *Mrs Dalloway*, p. 211.

80. VW, *Jacob's Room*, pp. 27–9.

81. VW to VB, 9 April 1919, in VW, *Letters* 2, p. 347.

82. VW, *Diary* 2, 17 April 1920, p. 31.

83. Ibid., 5 June 1920, pp. 46–7.

84. Letter from Lady Campbell of Croy to the author, 8 February 2004. The Madan–Lamb connection was cemented in 1993 when Marjorie Madan's grandson, the Hon. Alastair Campbell, later married Primrose Palmer, one of Henry Lamb's granddaughters. (See Walter Lamb's family tree on p. 245.)

85. WL, 4 September 1926, in 1923-6 diary, p. 138. Trinity.

86. Beatrice Newton, 'Lady Rose Lamb, 1900-1998', unpublished memoir.

87. WL, 18 September 1926, in 1923-6 diary, p. 145. Trinity.

88. Ibid., 30 September, 4-7 October 1926, pp. 147, 150-3.

89. Ibid., 11 October -5 November 1926, pp. 155-67.

90. I am indebted to Beatrice Newton for these anecdotes, recounted in her unpublished memoir, 'Lady Rose Lamb, 1900-1998'.

91. *The Times*, 28 March 1961, 14a.

92. Sir Albert Richardson, KCVO, PPRA, Memorial Service Address, dated 4 April 1961, Royal Academy of Arts Library. The memorial service was held at St James's Church, Piccadilly, on 21 April.

CHAPTER 8: DARK ANGEL: RUPERT BROOKE

1. VW, 'A Sketch of the Past', in *Moments of Being*, p. 100.

2. Rupert's mother, however, was highly suspicious of those who dwelled too insistently upon her son's beauty. He was often teased at school for his girlish looks, not just by fellow pupils but by masters as well.

3. N. Jones, *Rupert Brooke*, pp. 1-3.

4. Ibid., pp. 3-4, 7.

5. G. Keynes, *The Gates of Memory*, p. 36.

6. 'Answers & Autographs'. RCBP, M2, King's.

7. E. Marsh, 'Memoir', in RB, *Collected Poems* , pp. 25-9.

8. Ibid., pp. 27-9.

9. Quoted in E. Marsh, 'Memoir', in RB, *Collected Poems*, p. 32.

10. Ibid., p. 33.

11. RB to W.P. Brooke, April 1907. RCBP, L/8/6, King's.

12. E. Marsh, 'Memoir', in RB, *Collected Poems*, p. 38.

13. JS to RB, 30 November 1906, in RB/JS, *Friends and Apostles*, p. 26.

14. RB to St John Lucas, 22 January 1907, in RB, *Letters*, pp. 76-7.

15. C. Hassall, *Rupert Brooke*, pp. 114-15.

16. RB, *Collected Poems*, pp. 193-4.

17. Ibid., pp. 237-8, 234-5.

18. RB to M.R. Brooke, 28 June 1908, in RB, *Letters*, pp. 132-3.

19. Bryn Olivier was the mother of Anne Olivier Bell, editor of Virginia Woolf's diaries and wife of Quentin Bell.

20. GLS to AVS, 23 April 1908, in GLS, *Letters*, p. 141.

21. VW to KC, 13 August 1918, in VW, *Letters* 2, p. 268.

22. AVS to GLS, 28 April 1908, in VW, *Letters* 1, p. 328.

23. RB to M.R. Brooke, 2 March 1909, in RB, *Letters*, p. 157.

24. The full account of Virginia's visit was first published in *Carlyle's House and Other Sketches* in 2003, but she quotes from her diary entry in 'Old Bloomsbury', *Moments of Being*.

25. Formerly the Brookes and the Macaulays had lived a few doors apart in Hillmorton Road, Rugby. Rose's mother had nursed hopes of a match between her eldest daughter Margaret and Rupert's brother Dick. See S. LeFanu, *Rose Macaulay*, pp. 60, 80.

26. RB to Noel Oliver, 25 July 1909 (postmark), in RB/N. Olivier, *Song of Love*, pp. 12-15.

27. 3rd Earl Lytton (Neville Stephen Lytton) to RB, 6 December 1909. RCBP, L/1/36, King's.

28. In 1915 Gerald Shove married Virginia's cousin, Fredegond Maitland (see p. 265 n. 29). David Garnett, in middle age and after several homosexual affairs (one notably with Duncan Grant; see p. 128), would marry Angelica, Vanessa Bell's daughter by Duncan.

29. It was Noel Olivier who was responsible for the rescinding of nude bathing at Bedales, after she practised it in public view.

30. RB to Dudley Ward, 8-21 September 1909, in RB, *Letters*, p. 184.

31. RB to Jacques Raverat, March 1911, in RB, *Letters*, pp. 288-9.

32. RB to JS, 10 July 1912, in RB/JS, *Friends and Apostles*, pp. 249-52.

33. JS to RB, 10 April 1911, in ibid., pp. 170-2.

34. Years later, Elisabeth van Rysselberghe became André Gide's lover. She bore him a daughter, Catherine, on 18 April 1923.

35. RB to JS, 21 March 1910, in RB/JS, *Friends and Apostles*, p. 112.

36. AVS to GLS, 28 April 1908, in VW, *Letters* 1, p. 328.

37. Ka Cox disappointed Virginia in 1918 by marrying Hilton Young's friend, painter-cum-naval-officer Will Arnold-Forster, instead of someone Virginia considered more worthy, such as Rupert Brooke, Jacques Raverat or Hilton Young himself. See p. 150 above.

38. Ka's shirts were much admired by W.B. Yeats, who saw Rupert wearing one and asked where it came from. Rupert said he would find out where the material was bought but boasted that no shirt-maker could match Ka's handiwork. C. Hassall, *Rupert Brooke*, p. 374.

39. JS to RB, 27 July 1911, in RB/JS, *Friends and Apostles*, p. 192.

40. The dissertation was published under the title *John Webster and the Elizabethan Drama* by Sidgwick and Jackson, 1916.

41. VW to Gwen Raverat, 8 April 1925, in VW, *Letters* 3, p. 178.

42. There was almost certainly a letter to Vanessa that has not survived. On 20 August Vanessa wrote to Saxon Sydney-Turner from Cleeve House that she had heard from Virginia. See VB to SST, 20 August 1911, in VB, *Selected Letters*, p. 106.

43. AVS to Ottoline Morrell, 16 August 1911, in VW, *Letters* 1, pp. 474–5.

44. VW to Janet Case, 12 April 1924, in VW, *Letters* 3, p. 97; VW to Gwen Raverat, 8 April 1925, in ibid., p. 178. Olwen Ward became a literary critic; Archibald Young Cambell became a poet and Professor of Greek at the University of Liverpool.

45. VB to SST, 20 August 1911, in VB, *Selected Letters*, p. 106.

46. AVS to VB, 22(?) August 1911, in VW, *Letters* 1, pp. 475–6.

47. RB, *Collected Poems*, pp. 247–9. Paul Delany has interestingly compared Brooke's poetic valediction with Mrs Ramsay's dinner party in *To the Lighthouse*. See his *The Neo-Pagans*, p. 136.

48. AVS to DM, 4 September 1911, in VW, *Letters* 1, p. 477. Virginia's forays into the simple life were not entirely uncharacteristic, as her later lifestyle shows. Although she was fond of rugs and furniture, both she and Leonard were fairly ascetic and did not require luxurious surroundings. For example, there was no flushing lavatory at Monk's House until 1926, when Virginia purchased two from the proceeds of *Mrs Dalloway* and *The Common Reader*.

49. Adrian Stephen to CB, 25(?) August 1911. CP, CHA/1/598, King's.

50. Ibid.

51. RB to KC, 12 April 1912, in RB, *Letters*, p. 296.

52. Virginia describes this episode in 'Rupert Brooke' (*Essays* 2, pp. 277–84; first published in the *Times Literary Supplement*, 8 August 1918, 371a–b) but does not identify herself as the supplier of the image, as does Leonard Woolf in *Beginning Again*, p. 19.

53. RB, *Collected Poems*, pp. 231–2.

54. RB to Noel Olivier, 19 October 1911, in RB/N. Olivier, *Song of Love*, p. 122.

55. GLS to Henry Lamb, 4 and 6 October 1911. Quoted in M. Holroyd, *Lytton Strachey*, pp. 242–3.

56. GLS to Ottoline Morrell, 14 August 1912. Quoted in ibid., pp. 260–1.

57. RB, *Collected Poems*, p. 236. The poem was probably written during Brooke's affair with Elisabeth van Rysselberghe. The title was altered to 'Libido' – a word deemed less offensive by the publisher – for *Poems* (1911).

58. RB to JS, 27 January 1912, in RB/JS, *Friends and Apostles*, p. 218.

59. RB to AVS, 9 March 1912, RB, *Letters*, pp. 364–5.

60. AVS to KC, April 1912, in VW, *Letters* 1, p. 495.

61. RB to Jacques Raverat, 24 May 1912, in RB *Letters*, p. 380.

62. Noel Olivier to RB, 31 August 1912, in RB/N. Olivier, *Song of Love*, p. 216.

63. RB to Noel Olivier, 30 May and 5 September 1912, in RB/N. Olivier, *Song of Love*, pp. 176–7, 219.

64. LW, *Beginning Again*, pp. 18–19.

65. RB to JS, 19 June 1911, in RB/JS, *Friends and Apostles*, p. 183.

66. LW, *Beginning Again*, p. 19.

67. RB to Noel Oliver, 12 November 1912, in RB/N. Olivier, *Song of Love*, p. 224 and n. 1.

68. RB to JS, 16 July 1912, in RB/JS, *Friends and Apostles*, pp. 254-5 (see also p. 186 n. 4); D.H. Lawrence, *Collected Letters*, 1, pp. 332-3 (see also QB, *Bloomsbury*, p. 72).

69. Although he included Duncan Grant in his tirades on this occasion, Rupert's attitude towards him was generally friendly. After Brooke's death Duncan dedicated an abstract painting to him, *In Memoriam: Rupert Brooke* (1915).

70. RB to Noel Olivier, 28 August 1912, in RB/N. Olivier, *Song of Love*, pp. 212-14.

71. C. Hassall, *Rupert Brooke*, p. 364. This was in 1912, but the following March Rupert proved his animosity towards WC1 was alive and kicking, when he asked Geoffrey Keynes to spit at Bloomsbury on his behalf (Keynes was living at Brunswick Square at the time). RB to Geoffrey Keynes, 25 March 1913, in RB, *Letters*, p. 440. Six months later Keynes saved Virginia's life after she took an overdose of a sleeping drug.

72. These were later collected as *Letters from America*, with a preface by Henry James.

73. The affair may have resulted in a child. A letter from Taatamata to Brooke, lost *en route* but finally delivered in January 1915, told him in broken English that she was getting fat. The letter is quoted in its entirety in N. Jones, *Rupert Brooke*, pp. 398-9; see also p. 438.

74. RB to W.P. Brooke, April 1907. RCBP, L/8/6, King's.

75. Despite his enduring reputation as a war poet, Rupert Brooke was never involved in actual combat.

76. *Times Literary Supplement*, 11 March 1915, p. 85.

77. Rupert's younger brother Alfred was killed in action in May 1915. Mary Brooke outlived her husband and all three of her sons, surviving Rupert and Alfred by fifteen years. There were no grandchildren, apart from the child Taatamata may have had by Rupert (see note 73).

78. H.H. Asquith to Venetia Stanley, 23 April 1915, in H.H. Asquith, *Letters to Venetia Stanley*, p. 569.

79. Ibid., 25 April 1915, p. 571 n.2.

80. *The Times*, 26 April 1915, 5e.

81. While the language has a Churchillian ring, there is a possibility that the tribute was written on Churchill's behalf by Eddie Marsh, in which case the idolization takes on another dimension.

82. D.H. Lawrence to Ottoline Morrell, 30 April 1915, in D.H. Lawrence, *Collected Letters* 1, p. 337.

83. GLS to AVS, 23 April 1908, in GLS, *Letters*, p. 141; M. Browne, *Recollections of Rupert Brooke*, p. 9.

84. M. Browne, ibid., p. 58.

85. H. James, preface to RB, *Letters from America*, pp. xii, xvii.

86. HY, 'In and Out', unpublished autobiography, p. 24.

87. Ibid.

88. J.M. Barrie to M.R. Brooke, 14 May 1922. RCBP, Xf/3, King's.

89. Quoted in introduction to RB, *Collected Poems*, p. 21.

90. Sidgwick and Jackson sales chart. RCBP, Xf/11, King's.

91. VW to Gwen Raverat, 8 April 1925, in VW, *Letters 3*, p. 178. Curiously enough, James Strachey speculated jokingly in an early letter to Rupert about his (and James's own) ambitions to be Prime Minister. See JS to RB, 12 July 1905, in RB/JS, *Friends and Apostles*, p. 19.

92. VW, *Diary 1*, 27 July 1918, p. 172.

93. VW, 'The New Crusade', in *Essays 2*, pp. 201-3. First published in the *Times Literary Supplement*, 27 December 1917, 647c-d.

94. VW, 'Rupert Brooke', in *Essays 2*, pp. 277-84. First published in the *Times Literary Supplement*, 8 August 1918, 371a-b.

95. VW, *Between the Acts*, pp. 19, 22.

96. Ibid., pp. 9, 20.

97. Ibid., p. 9.

98. Ibid., pp. 255-6.

99. VW to Gwen Raverat, 3 February 1931, in VW, *Letters 4*, pp. 287-8; VW to KAF, 1 May 1936, in VW, *Letters 6*, pp. 31-2.

100. VW to Gwen Raverat, 8 April 1925, in VW, *Letters 3*, p. 178.

CHAPTER 9: POMP OF CIRCUMSTANCE: SYDNEY WATERLOW

1. QB, *Virginia Woolf*, Vol. 1, p. 166.

2. P. Levy, *Moore*, p. 251.

3. H. Beauchamp, *Reminiscences and Recollections*, p. 43.

4. Hugh Norwood Papers, MS-Papers-6498, ATL/NLNZ.

5. AVS to VD, May 1905, in VW, *Letters 1*, p. 190. The article Elizabeth liked was 'Street Music' was published in the *National Review* in March 1905 and reprinted in *Essays 1*, pp. 27-32.

6. R. Beauchamp, 'A Family Affair or What Became of Fred?' Hugh Norwood Papers, MS-Papers-1458, ATL/NLNZ.

7. *Dictionary of National Biography Supplement 1901-1911*, 1912.

8. SW to G.E. Moore, 22 July 1904. Waterlow family papers.

9. John Waterlow, conversation with the author, 8 July 2003.

10. Ibid.

11. DM, unpublished memoir, written 1944/5. Desmond MacCarthy Literary Estate.

12. Thoby Stephen to LW, 15 January 1905. Quoted in LW, *Sowing*, p. 126.

13. P. Levy, *Moore*, pp. 251–9 (note that Alice Pollock was the *daughter* of Sir Frederick Pollock and not his sister, as stated on p. 252).

14. DM, unpublished memoir, written 1944/5. Desmond MacCarthy Literary Estate.

15. Sir Frederick Pollock co-founded the *Law Quarterly Review* in 1885. He was an old friend of the Stephen family. A keen walker, he belonged to Leslie's walking club, the Sunday Tramps (N. Annan, *Leslie Stephen*, p. 97). He and Leslie had mutual friends in the American jurist Oliver Wendell Holmes, with whom Frederick kept up a sixty-year correspondence, and in Henry James, who later became a great friend of Sydney Waterlow's.

16. SW to G.E. Moore, 29 April 1902. Waterlow family papers.

17. AVS to VD, April 1902, in VW, *Letters* 1, p. 50 and n. 1.

18. SW, Diary, 28 September 1910. Berg.

19. Ibid., 8 December 1910.

20. Henry James to Lucy Clifford, 17 February 1907, in H. James, *Henry James Letters, Volume IV*, p. 437; LW, *Sowing*, pp. 107–8.

21. SW, Diary, 3 January 1911. Berg.

22. CB to AVS, February/March 1911. Letters III, MHP, Sussex.

23. SW, Diary, 13 June 1911. Berg.

24. In October 1911 Sydney accidentally opened a packet of Alice's photographs forwarded in the post from Rye. One showed Orlo Williams's arm round Alice's waist. Sydney concluded that they were engaged; they were in fact married on 15 June 1912. SW, Diary, 5 October 1911. Berg. Williams wrote an (anonymous) obituary of Virginia Woolf for the *Times Literary Supplement*, 12 April 1943.

25. LW, *Sowing*, p. 107n.

26. The editors of Virginia Woolf's letters identified Norah's husband as Alexander Finberg (See VW, *Letters* 2, p. 252 n. 1). Alexander Joseph Finberg (1866–1939) studied art in London and Paris and was employed as an illustrator and an art critic by several newspapers. He founded the Walpole Society in 1911 and wrote, lectured and advised widely on art. An authority on J.M.W. Turner, he was highly critical of Roger Fry's Second Post-Impressionist Exhibition. He married again in 1914 and had two sons.

27. SW, Diary, 19 June 1911. Berg.

28. The payments to Norah continued until well into Sydney's second marriage and were made

with the full knowledge and consent of his second wife, Margery. Their daughter Judith Waterlow told Leonard Woolf that one of the few things her parents agreed on was that the money should continue to be paid. Judith Waterlow to LW, 27 September 1960. LWP, Part III, Sussex.

29. AVS to Ottoline Morrell, 16 August 1911, in VW, *Letters* 1, pp. 474-5.

30. SW, Diary, 5 and 6 November 1911. Berg.

31. Ibid., 19 and 23 November 1911.

32. Ibid., 24 July 1911.

33. H.O. Meredith to SW, 26 November 1911. Waterlow family papers.

34. VW to VB, 18 June 1918, in VW, *Letters* 2, p. 252. See also VW to QB, 11 May 1929, in VW, *Letters* 4, p. 56.

35. SW, Diary, 8 July 1911. Berg.

36. H.O. Meredith to SW, 30 November 1911. Waterlow family papers. The letter arrived too late to have any influence on Sydney's decision.

37. SW, Diary, 25 to 27 November 1911. Berg.

38. Ibid., 29 January 1912. (In this diary entry Sydney describes the events of 29 November 1911.)

39. Ibid., 29 and 30 November 1911.

40. H.O. Meredith to SW, 1 December 1911. Waterlow family papers.

41. AVS to SW, 9 December 1911, in VW, *Letters* 1, p. 485.

42. SW, Diary, 'Christmas', 28 and 31 December 1911. Berg.

43. Judith Waterlow to LW, 27 September 1960. LWP, Part III, Sussex.

44. SW, Diary, 26 January 1912. Berg.

45. Ibid., 8 March 1912.

46. Ibid., 28 March 1912.

47. F. Spalding, *Roger Fry*, p. 152.

48. LW, *Beginning Again*, p. 112.

49. LW to VW, 1 November 1917, in LW, *Letters*, p. 219.

50. Ibid., 31 October 1917, p. 217.

51. SW, Diary, 26 November 1910. Berg. Oscar Eckhard's 'troubles' may have been his pursuit by Goldsworthy Lowes Dickinson, which had begun in March, the story soon spreading through the King's College grapevine. When Oscar consulted his mother she broad-mindedly advised him to avoid hurting Dickinson's feelings. He and Dickinson later had a long-term affair. See G.L. Dickinson's *Autobiography*.

52. VW, *Diary* 1, 8 January 1915, p. 12.

53. VW, ibid., 17 June 1918, p. 155; ibid., 19 October 1919, p. 306; VW, *Diary* 2, 13 November 1920, p. 74.

54. John Waterlow, letter to the author, 26 December 2003.

55. As mentioned on p. 216, in 1918 Margery discussed the Norah affair with Virginia and Leonard Woolf while they were staying for the weekend. See VW to VB, 18 June 1918, in VW, *Letters* 2, p. 252.

56. VW, *Diary* 1, 1, 4 and 5 January 1915, pp. 3, 6, 7.

57. Ibid., 8 January 1915, p. 12.

58. Ibid., 6 January 1915, p. 8.

59. VW to GLS, 22 October 1915, in VW, *Letters* 2, p. 67.

60. Sydney had undergone a similar regime a few years previously: during a rest cure in 1907, his weight had risen from 11 stone 2 pounds in August to 15 stone 3 pounds in November. SW, Diary, 14 August to 9 October 1907. Berg.

61. VW to GLS, 22 October 1915, in VW, *Letters* 2, p. 67.

62. It is interesting to note that, although Sydney was not a feminist, he accompanied friends who were taking part in the 1908 Women's Suffrage procession and carried a banner from the Embankment to Hyde Park Corner. SW, Diary, 13 June 1908. Berg.

63. VW, *Mrs Dalloway*, p. 4.

64. Ibid., p. 5.

65. Ibid., p. 81.

66. 'The Philosophy of Henri Bergson', in *Quarterly Review* 430 (1912).

67. Woolf was one of many writers of her time whose work bore the hallmarks of Bergson's thought. T. S. Eliot, who attended Bergson's lectures in Paris in early 1911, was struck by his theory of *la durée* and referred to 'The Love Song of J. Alfred Prufrock' (published June 1915) as his Bergsonian poem.

68. The review is included in the second volume of Virginia's collected essays, but the fourth edition of B. J. Kirkpatrick's bibliography notes that the *Times Literary Supplement* archive records it as Leonard's work.

69. Romains was impressed with the 'excellent article' and wrote to the editor of the *Times Literary Supplement* 'J'ai trouvé son étude aussi judicieuse que sympathique' ('I found the study as judicious as it was sympathetic'), asking for the name of its author and for his thanks to be passed on.

70. VW, *Jacob's Room*, p. 126.

71. Ibid., p. 10.

72. VW, *Mrs Dalloway*, p. 208.

73. See M. Whitworth, 'Virginia Woolf and Modernism', in S. Roe and S. Sellers (ed.), *The Cambridge Companion to Virginia Woolf*, pp. 159-60.

74. DM, Dedication, in J. Romains, *The Death of a Nobody*, pp. iii–iv.

75. VW to SST, 18 September 1917, in VW, *Letters* 2, p. 181.

76. VW, *Diary* 1, 14 December 1917, p. 92.

77. 'Father' by Charlotte Waterlow, unpublished memoir.

78. VW, *Diary* 1, 19 October 1919, p. 306.

79. John Waterlow, conversation with the author, 27 February 2004.

80. VW, *Diary* 1, 17 June 1918, p. 155; KM to JMM, 21 November 1919, in KM, *Letters*, p. 400.

81. SW, 'International Government under the League of Nations', Foreign Office, 3 January 1919.

82. VW, *Diary* 1, 18 March 1918, p. 129; VW to Roger Fry, 29 August 1921, in VW, *Letters* 2, p. 478; VW to Janet Case, 20 March 1922, in ibid., p. 515.

83. VW, *Diary* 2, 22 August 1922, p. 190.

84. KM to SW, 27 January 1921. SWP, MS-Papers-1157, ATL/NLNZ.

85. Ibid., 16 March 1921.

86. Ibid., 9 February 1921.

87. Ibid., 16 March 1921.

88. H.O. Meredith to SW, 22 January 1921. Waterlow family papers.

89. Ibid.

90. SW to VW, 16 January 1921. Waterlow family papers.

91. Ibid.

92. Ibid.

93. Ibid.

94. VW to SW, 19 January 1921, in VW, *Letters* 2, p. 455.

95. Ibid., pp. 455-6.

96. SW to VW, 16 January 1921. Waterlow family papers.

97. 'Father' by Charlotte Waterlow, unpublished memoir.

98. DM, unpublished memoir, written 1944/5. Desmond MacCarthy Literary Estate.

99. S.S. Koteliansky to SW, 21 June 1927. SWP. MS-Papers-1157, ATL/NLNZ.

100. EMF to SW, 1 January 1923. Waterlow family papers.

101. Ibid., 6 November 1923.

102. Gertler painted a portrait of Sydney which hung over the fireplace in the dining-room at Oare, but its placing proved inauspicious – it was later destroyed in a fire. John Waterlow, conversation with the author, 8 July 2003.

103. Milne was an assistant keeper of manuscripts in the British Museum. Sullivan was an Irish scientist and journalist with a 'mop of black hair à la Beethoven' whose conversation, said Sydney, 'at its best could hold us spellbound'. SW, 'Recollections of J.W.N. Sullivan', unpublished memoir. Waterlow family papers.

104. VW to EMF, 21 January 1922, in VW, *Letters* 2, p. 499.

105. Ibid.

106. VW, *Diary* 2, 18 December 1921, p. 150

107. Ibid., pp. 149–50.

108. VW to SW, 24 August 1922, in VW, *Letters* 2, pp. 522–3.

109. Sullivan was not married but set up house with a woman called Sylvia, who, Sydney later remembered, had to be headed off by Sullivan and Aldous Huxley on her way to Sicily to join Aleister Crowley's harem. SW, 'Recollections of J.W.N. Sullivan', unpublished memoir. Waterlow family papers.

110. VW, *Diary* 2, 11 December 1921, p. 149.

111. VW to VB, 22 December 1922, in VW, *Letters* 2, p. 595.

112. VW, *Diary* 2, 16 November 1921, p. 143.

113. Ibid., 4 June 1923, p. 245.

114. VW to Vita Sackville-West, 29 March 1926, in VW, *Letters* 3, p. 251.

115. S.S. Koteliansky to SW, 20 July 1926. SWP, MS-Papers-1157, ATL/NLNZ.

116. Ibid., 30 August 1927.

117. T.S. Eliot to his mother (Charlotte Eliot), 22 February 1920, in T.S. Eliot, *Letters* 1, p. 368.

118. VW, *Diary* 1, 14 December 1917, p. 92.

119. VW to Dorothy Brett, 8 July 1933, in VW, *Letters* 5, p. 202.

120. DM, unpublished memoir, written 1944/5. Desmond MacCarthy Literary Estate.

121. Ibid.

122. SW to Lord Hardinge, 1 September 1936. Quoted in Appendix to Charlotte Waterlow, 'From Bloomsbury to Balham and Beyond', unpublished memoirs. I am indebted to John and Charlotte Waterlow for allowing me to see this letter.

123. C. Mott-Radclyffe, *Foreign Body in the Eye*, p. 2.

124. R. West, *Selected Letters*, p. 163 n. 10.

125. VW, *The Years*, pp. 160–3.

126. John Waterlow, conversation with the author, 8 July 2003; J.S. Koliopoulos, *Greece and the British Connection*, p. 101.

127. Ibid., pp. 102–8.

128. John Waterlow, conversation with the author, 8 July 2003.

129. Ibid.

130. SW to G.E. Moore, 15 November 1944. Waterlow family papers.

131. *The Times*, 21 November 1944, 5e.

EPILOGUE

1. AVS to Madge Vaughan, June 1912, in VW, *Letters* 1, p. 503; AVS to Lady Robert Cecil, June 1912, in ibid., p. 504.

2. AVS to VD, 24 June 1912, in ibid., p. 505.

3. VW to JR, 25 August 1922, in VW, *Letters* 2, p. 554.

4. VW to GLS, 1 September 1912, in ibid., p. 5.

5. VW to KC, 4 September 1912, in ibid., p. 6-7.

6. AVS to LW, 1 May 1912, in VW, *Letters* 1, pp. 496-7.

7. LW, *Beginning Again*, p. 28.

8. *Night and Day* (1919), like *The Voyage Out* (1915), was published by Virginia's brother-in-law Gerald Duckworth. Thereafter her major works were published under the Hogarth Press imprint, although the Woolfs did not print the books themselves.

9. VB to LW, 14 January 1912, in VB, *Selected Letters*, p. 113.

10. AVS to VD, 4 June 1912, in VW, *Letters* 1, p. 500; AVS to Janet Case, June 1912, in ibid., p. 501.

11. VW, *Diary 3*, 28 November 1928, p. 208.

12. LW, *Sowing*, pp. 180-2.

13. VW to Gwen Raverat, 22 March 1925, in VW, *Letters 3*, p. 172.

14. VW, *Diary 2*, 17 October 1924, p. 317.

15. VW, *Diary 3*, 14 December 1929, p. 273.

16. G. Spater and I. Parsons, *A Marriage of True Minds*; R. Poole, *The Unknown Virginia Woolf*; S. Trombley, *'All That Summer She Was Mad'*. Thanks to Hilary Newman for reminding me of this point.

FAMILY TREES

1. The Headlam family is partly based on information from Stephen Headlam's website at http://www.dheadlam.freeserve.co.uk.

2. Clive Bell's family tree is based on information gathered from the Bell Family History papers in Clive Bell II, E1, Trinity; Q. Bell, *Elders and Betters*; and the website of the Cory Family Society, http://www.coryfamsoc.com.

3. Further information for Hilton Young's family tree came from KP 83/26/b, Trinity, and from a diagram supplied by Wayland and Elizabeth Young.

4. Hilton's granddaughter was named after a shepherdess in *The Winter's Tale*. Coincidentally 'Mopsa' was also Carrington's nickname for herself when writing to Lytton Strachey.

5. Many thanks to Henrietta Phipps for supplying details of the Lamb family tree, and for

directing me to Hubert Lamb's autobiography, *Through All the Changing Scenes of Life*.

6. The Hon. Alastair James Calthrop Campbell is the son of Baron Campbell of Croy and Nicola Madan.

7. Information about Sydney Waterlow's family was derived from *Memoranda as to the Waterlow Family*, privately printed *c*. 1900 and annotated by hand by members of the Waterlow family.

8. In this generation there was also a son who died in his youth, Frank William, 1846–71, and three sons who died during the year of their birth: Walter in 1849, Sydney Albert in 1856 and Albert Hedley in 1859.

Bibliography

Annan, Noel, *Leslie Stephen: The Godless Victorian*, London: Weidenfeld and Nicolson, 1984

Annual Register (1847 volume), London: F. and J. Rivington, 1848

Asquith, H.H., *Letters to Venetia Stanley*, ed. Michael and Eleanor Brock, Oxford: Oxford University Press, 1982

Beauchamp, Harold, *Reminiscences and Recollections*, New Plymouth: Thomas Avery, 1937

Beerbohm, Max, *Lytton Strachey* (1943 Rede Lecture), Cambridge: Cambridge University Press, 1943

Bell, Clive, *Old Friends*, London: Cassell, 1988 (first published London: Chatto and Windus/Hogarth Press, 1956)

Bell, Clive, 'The Tragedy of Gainsborough' and 'Victorian Taste', in *Art in England*, ed. R.S. Lambert, Harmondsworth: Penguin, 1938

Bell, Quentin, *Bloomsbury*, London: Weidenfeld and Nicolson, 1986

Bell, Quentin, *Elders and Betters*, London: John Murray, 1995

Bell, Quentin, *Virginia Woolf: A Biography*, two volumes, London: Hogarth Press, 1972

Bell, Vanessa, *Selected Letters of Vanessa Bell*, ed. Regina Marler, London: Bloomsbury, 1994

Benson, E.F., *As We Were: A Victorian Peep-show*, London: Hogarth Press, 1985

Boas, Guy, *Lytton Strachey*, English Association Pamphlet No. 93, November 1935

Brooke, Rupert, *Letters from America*, with preface by Henry James, London: Sidgwick and Jackson, 1916

Brooke, Rupert, *The Letters of Rupert Brooke*, ed. Geoffrey Keynes, London: Faber and Faber, 1968

Brooke, Rupert, *Rupert Brooke: The Collected Poems*, ed. Edward Marsh, London: Sidgwick and Jackson, 1989 (first published 1918)

Brooke, Rupert, and Noel Olivier, *Song of Love: The Letters of Rupert Brooke and Noel Oliver*, ed. Pippa Harris, London: Bloomsbury, 1991

Brooke, Rupert, and James Strachey, *Friends and Apostles: The Correspondence of Rupert Brooke and James Strachey, 1905-1914*, ed. Keith Hale, New Haven, Connecticut, and London: Yale University Press, 1998

Browne, Maurice, *Recollections of Rupert Brooke*, Chicago: Alexander Greene, 1927

Burke's Peerage and Baronetage (106th edition), ed. Charles Mosley, London: Fitzroy Dearborn, 1999

Caramagno, Thomas C., *The Flight of the Mind: Virginia Woolf's Art and Manic-Depressive Illness*, Berkeley and Los Angeles: University of California Press, 1992

Carrington (Dora), *Carrington: Letters and Extracts from Her Diaries*, ed. David Garnett, New York/Chicago/San Francisco: Holt, Rinehart and Winston, 1971

Cecil, Hugh and Mirabel, *Clever Hearts*, London: Victor Gollancz, 1990

Clemens, Cyril, *Lytton Strachey* ('An extract from the *Dalhousie Review*'), n.p., 1940 (also published Webster Groves: International Mark Twain Society, 1942)

Clements, Keith, *Henry Lamb: The Artist and His Friends*, London: Redcliffe, 1985

Curtis, Anthony, ed., *Before Bloomsbury: The 1890s Diaries of Three Kensington Ladies: Margaret Lushington, Stella Duckworth and Mildred Massingberd*, London: The Eighteen Nineties Society, 2002

Curtis, Vanessa, *Stella and Virginia: An Unfinished Sisterhood*, London: Cecil Woolf, 2001

Curtis, Vanessa, *Virginia Woolf's Women*, London: Robert Hale, 2002

Debrett's Handbook 1982, London: Debrett's Peerage, 1981

Delany, Paul, *The Neo-Pagans: Friendship and Love in the Rupert Brooke Circle*, London: Hamish Hamilton, 1988

Dickinson, Goldsworthy Lowes, *Autobiography*, ed. Dennis Proctor, London: Duckworth, 1973

Dictionary of National Biography, ed. Sir Leslie Stephen and Sir Sidney Lee, Oxford: Oxford University Press, 1973; 1993 (first published London: Smith, Elder and Co., 1885-1900). *Supplement 1901-1911*, 1920 (first published London: Smith, Elder and Co., 1912)

Dunn, Jane, *A Very Close Conspiracy: Vanessa Bell and Virginia Woolf*, London: Jonathan Cape, 1990

Edel, Leon, *Bloomsbury: A House of Lions*, Harmondsworth: Penguin, 1981 (first published London: Hogarth Press, 1979)

Eliot, T.S., *The Letters of T.S. Eliot*, ed. Valerie Eliot, Vol. 1, *1898-1922*, London: Faber and Faber, 1988

Forster, Edward Morgan, *Selected Letters of E.M. Forster*, ed. Mary Lago and P.N. Furbank, two volumes, London: Collins, 1983-5

Furbank, P.N., *E.M. Forster: A Life*, two volumes, London: Secker and Warburg, 1977-8

Harrod, R.F., *The Life of John Maynard Keynes*, London: Macmillan, 1951

Hassall, Christopher, *Rupert Brooke: A Biography*, London: Faber and Faber, 1996 (first published 1964)

Headlam, Cecil, *Walter Headlam: His Letters and Poems, with a Memoir by Cecil Headlam and a Bibliography by L. Haward*, London: Duckworth, 1910

Henry Lamb, introduced by Anthony Powell, Manchester: Manchester City Art Galleries, 1984

Holroyd, Michael, *Lytton Strachey: The New Biography*, London: Chatto and Windus, 1994 (first published London: Heinemann as two volumes, 1967–8)

Howard, Elizabeth Jane, *Slipstream: A Memoir*, London: Macmillan, 2002

Hutchison, Sidney C., *The History of the Royal Academy 1768–1986*, London: Robert Royce, 1986

James, Henry, *Henry James Letters, Volume IV, 1895–1916*, ed. Leon Edel, London and Cambridge, Massachusetts: Belknap Press, 1984

Johnstone, J.K., *The Bloomsbury Group*, London: Secker and Warburg, 1954

Jones, Nigel, *Rupert Brooke: Life, Death and Myth*, London: Richard Cohen Books, 1999

Kennedy, G.L., ed., *Henry Lamb*, Contemporary British Artists series, general editor Albert Rutherston, London: Ernest Benn, 1924

Kennet, Lady [Kathleen Young], *Self-Portrait of an Artist*, London: John Murray, 1949

Keynes, Geoffrey, *The Gates of Memory*, Oxford: Oxford University Press, 1981

Knatchbull-Hugessen, Sir Hughe, *Kentish Family*, London: Methuen, 1960

Knight, Charles, ed., *The English Cyclopaedia*, Vol. V, London: Bradbury and Evans, 1857

Koliopoulos, John S., *Greece and the British Connection, 1935–1941*, Oxford: Clarendon Press, 1977

Lamb, Hubert, *Through All the Changing Scenes of Life: A Meteorologist's Tale*, East Harling, Norfolk: Taverner Publications, 1997

Lamb, Walter, 'What the Royal Academy Stands For', in *Art in England*, ed. R.S. Lambert, Harmondsworth: Penguin, 1938

Lamb, Sir Walter R.M., *The Royal Academy: A Short History of Its Foundation and Development*, London: G. Bell and Sons, 1935, revised edition, 1951

Lambert, R.S, ed., *Art in England*, Harmondsworth: Penguin, 1938

Lawrence, D.H., *The Collected Letters of D.H. Lawrence*, ed. Harry T. Moore, two volumes, London: Heinemann, 1962

Lee, Hermione, *Virginia Woolf*, London: Chatto and Windus, 1996

Lees-Milne, James, *Diaries 1942–1945: Ancestral Voices and Prophesying Peace*, London: John Murray, 1995 (first published London: Chatto and Windus as two volumes, 1975–7)

LeFanu, Sarah, *Rose Macaulay*, London: Virago, 2003

Lehmann, John, *Rupert Brooke: His Life and Legend*, London: Quartet, 1981 (first published London: Weidenfeld and Nicolson, 1980)

Levy, Paul, *Moore: G.E. Moore and the Cambridge Apostles*, Oxford: Oxford University Press, 1981

MacGibbon, Jean, *There's the Lighthouse: A Biography of Adrian Stephen*, London: James and James, 1997

Mansfield, Katherine, *Katherine Mansfield's Letters to John Middleton Murry, 1913–1922*, ed. John Middleton Murry, London: Constable, 1951

Mott-Radclyffe, Charles, *Foreign Body in the Eye*, London: Leo Cooper, 1975

Murry, John Middleton, *The Letters of John Middleton Murry to Katherine Mansfield*, sel. and ed. C.A. Hankin, London: Constable, 1983

Noble, Joan Russell, ed., *Recollections of Virginia Woolf*, London: Peter Owen, 1972

Oldfield, Sybil (ed.), *Afterwords: Letters on the Death of Virginia Woolf*, Edinburgh: Edinburgh University Press, 2005

Partridge, Frances, *Everything to Lose: Diaries 1945–1960*, London: Victor Gollancz, 1985

Partridge, Frances, *Hanging On: Diaries 1960–1963*, London: HarperCollins, 1990

Partridge, Frances, *Memories*, London: Victor Gollancz, 1981

Partridge, Frances, *A Pacifist's War*, London: Hogarth Press, 1978

Poole, Roger, *The Unknown Virginia Woolf*, Cambridge: Cambridge University Press, 1978

Read, Mike, *Forever England: The Life of Rupert Brooke*, Edinburgh: Mainstream, 1997

Ridley, Jane, *Edwin Lutyens: His Life, His Wife, His Work*, London: Pimlico, 2003 (first published 2002)

Roe, Sue, and Susan Sellers, ed., *The Cambridge Companion to Virginia Woolf*, Cambridge: Cambridge University Press, 2000

Romains, Jules, *The Death of a Nobody*, trans. by Desmond MacCarthy and Sydney Waterlow, London: Howard Latimer, 1914

Royal Academy, *Annual Report from the Council of the Royal Academy to the General Assembly of Academicians . . .* , London: William Clowes and Sons, various editions

Sanders, Charles Richard, *Lytton Strachey: His Mind and Art*, New Haven, Connecticut: Yale University Press, 1957

Spalding, Frances, *Duncan Grant: A Biography*, London: Pimlico, 1998 (first published London: Chatto and Windus, 1997)

Spalding, Frances, *Roger Fry: Art and Life*, Norwich: Black Dog Books, 1999 (first published London: Granada, 1980)

Spalding, Frances, *Vanessa Bell*, London: Papermac, 1984 (first published London: Weidenfeld and Nicolson, 1983)

Spater, George, and Ian Parsons, *A Marriage of True Minds: An Intimate Portrait of Leonard and Virginia Woolf*, London: Jonathan Cape/Hogarth Press, 1977

Stephen, Leslie, *Sir Leslie Stephen's Mausoleum Book*, London: Clarendon Press, 1977

Strachey, Barbara, *The Strachey Line*, London: Victor Gollancz, 1985

Strachey, Lytton, *The Letters of Lytton Strachey*, ed. Paul Levy, London: Viking, 2005

Strachey, Lytton, *Lytton Strachey by Himself: A Self-Portrait*, ed. Michael Holroyd, London: Vintage, 1994 (first published London: Heinemann, 1971)

Strachey, Lytton, *The Really Interesting Question and Other Papers*, ed. Paul Levy, London: Weidenfeld and Nicolson, 1972

Tomalin, Claire, *Katherine Mansfield, A Secret Life*, Harmondsworth: Penguin, 1987

Trombley, Stephen, *'All That Summer She Was Mad': Virginia Woolf and Her Doctors*, London: Junction Books, 1981

Waterlow, Sydney, 'International Government under the League of Nations', Foreign Office report, 3 January 1919

West, Rebecca, *Selected Letters of Rebecca West*, ed. Bonnie Kime Scott, New Haven, Connecticut: Yale University Press, 2000

Who's Who and *Who Was Who*, London: A. and C. Black, various editions

Wilson, Jean Moorcroft, *Virginia Woolf: Life and London: A Biography of Place*, London: Cecil Woolf, 1987

Woolf, Leonard, *Beginning Again*, New York and London: Harcourt Brace Jovanovich, 1972 (first published London: Hogarth Press, 1964)

Woolf. Leonard, *Downhill All the Way*, New York and London: Harcourt Brace Jovanovich, 1975 (first published London: Hogarth Press, 1967)

Woolf, Leonard, *Letters*, ed. Frederic Spotts, San Diego, New York and London: Harcourt Brace Jovanovich, 1989

Woolf, Leonard, *Sowing*, New York and London: Harcourt Brace Jovanovich, 1975 (first published London: Hogarth Press, 1960)

Woolf, Virginia, *Between the Acts*, London: Hogarth Press, 1981 (first published 1941)

Woolf, Virginia, *Carlyle's House and Other Sketches*, ed. David Bradshaw, London: Hesperus Press, 2003

Woolf, Virginia, *The Common Reader* (First Series), ed. Andrew McNeillie, London: Hogarth Press, 1984 (first published 1925)

Woolf, Virginia, *The Common Reader* (Second Series), ed. Andrew McNeillie, London: Hogarth Press, 1986 (first published 1932)

Woolf, Virginia, *The Complete Shorter Fiction of Virginia Woolf*, ed. Susan Dick, revised edition, London: Hogarth Press, 1989

Woolf, Virginia, *The Diary of Virginia Woolf*, ed. Anne Olivier Bell, five volumes, Harmondsworth: Penguin, 1979–85 (first published London: Hogarth Press, 1977–84)

Woolf, Virginia, *The Essays of Virginia Woolf*, four volumes, London: Hogarth Press, 1986–94 (a total of six volumes is planned)

Woolf, Virginia, *Jacob's Room*, London: Hogarth Press, 1992 (first published 1922)

Woolf, Virginia, *The Letters of Virginia Woolf*, ed. Nigel Nicolson and Joanne Trautmann, six volumes, London: Chatto and Windus, 1980-3 (first published 1975-80)

Woolf, Virginia, *Melymbrosia*, ed. Louise DeSalvo, San Francisco: Cleis Press, 2002

Woolf, Virginia, *Moments of Being*, ed. Jeanne Schulkind, London: Pimlico, 2002 (first published London: Chatto and Windus, 1976)

Woolf, Virginia, *Mrs Dalloway*, Everyman edition, London: David Campbell, 1993 (first published London: Hogarth Press, 1925)

Woolf, Virginia, *Night and Day*, Harmondsworth: Penguin, 1969 (first published London: Duckworth and Co., 1919)

Woolf, Virginia, *A Passionate Apprentice: The Early Journals*, ed. Mitchell A. Leaska, London: Hogarth Press, 1990

Woolf, Virginia, *To the Lighthouse*, Everyman edition, London: David Campbell, 1991 (first published London: Hogarth Press, 1927)

Woolf, Virginia, *Travels with Virginia Woolf*, ed. Jan Morris, London: Hogarth Press, 1993

Woolf, Virginia, *The Voyage Out*, ed. Jane Wheare, Harmondsworth: Penguin, 1992 (first published London: Duckworth and Co., 1915)

Woolf, Virginia, *The Waves*, ed. Gillian Beer, Oxford: Oxford University Press, 1992 (first published London: Hogarth Press, 1931)

\Woolf, Virginia, and Strachey, Lytton, *Virginia Woolf and Lytton Strachey: Letters*, ed. Leonard Woolf and James Strachey, London: Hogarth Press/Chatto and Windus, 1956

Young, E.H., *The Count: A Romance*, n.p., 1890

Young, E. Hilton, *By Sea and Land: Some Naval Doings*, London: T.C. and E.C. Jack, 1920

Young, E. Hilton, *A Muse at Sea*, London: Sidgwick and Jackson, 1919

Young, Louisa, *A Great Task of Happiness*, London: Macmillan, 1995

There are several organizations that may be of interest to Woolfians. The Virginia Woolf Society of Great Britain (www.virginiawoolfsociety.co.uk) offers a variety of events to members and publishes the *Virginia Woolf Bulletin* three times a year (free to members). The International Virginia Woolf Society (www.utoronto.ca/IVWS) is based in the USA; membership includes the biannual *Virginia Woolf Miscellany* (a separate subscription is available for non-members). There are also Virginia Woolf societies in Japan (wwwsoc.nii.ac.jp/vwsj, or wwwsoc.nii.ac.jp/vwsj/index-e.html for the English-language version), France (Société d'Etudes Woolfiennes; www.utoronto.ca/IVWS/SEW.htm) and Korea.

Text Permissions

EXTRACTS FROM VIRGINIA Woolf's novels and essays are used with the permission of the Society of Authors as the literary representative of the estate of Virginia Woolf. Extracts from the following works of Virginia Woolf, published by the Hogarth Press, are reproduced with the permission of the Random House Group Ltd and Harcourt Brace: *The Letters of Virginia Woolf*, edited by Nigel Nicolson and Joanne Trautmann; *Moments of Being*, edited by Jeanne Schulkind; *A Passionate Apprentice*, edited by Mitchell A. Leaska; *The Diary of Virginia Woolf*, edited by Anne Olivier Bell. Extracts from Leonard Woolf's published letters and from the Preface to the *Letters* of Virginia Woolf and Lytton Strachey (Hogarth Press, 1956) are used with the permission of the University of Sussex and the Society of Authors as their representative. Extracts from *Sowing, Beginning Again* and *Downhill All the Way*, by Leonard Woolf, are reproduced with the permission of the Random House Group Ltd. and Harcourt Brace. Extracts from the *Selected Letters of Vanessa Bell*, edited by Regina Marler, are used with the permission of Bloomsbury Publishing. Extracts from Clive Bell's Play Reading Society minutes, his unpublished letters and *Old Friends* are reproduced with permission of the Society of Authors as the literary representative of the estate of Clive Bell. Extracts from Quentin Bell's *Virginia Woolf* are used with the permission of the Random House Group Ltd. Extracts from Quentin Bell's *Elders and Betters* are used with the permission of John Murray. Extracts from the published and unpublished works of Lytton Strachey are reproduced with the permission of the Society of Authors as agents of the Strachey Trust. Extracts from Frances Partridge, *Memories*, London: Victor Gollancz, 1981; Frances Partridge, *A Pacifist's War*, London: Hogarth Press, 1978; Frances Partridge, *Everything to Lose*, London: Victor Gollancz, 1985; and Frances Partridge, *Hanging On*, London: HarperCollins, 1990, are reproduced by permission of the author, c/o Rogers, Coleridge and White, 20 Powis Mews, London W11 1JN. Copyright © the Estate of Frances Partridge 1981/1978/1985/1990.

Extracts from Dora Carrington, *Carrington: Letters and Extracts from Her Diaries*, edited by David Garnett, New York/Chicago/San Francisco: Holt, Rinehart and Winston, 1971, and Dora Carrington's unpublished diary are used with the permission of Rogers, Coleridge and White on behalf of the estate of Dora Carrington. Extracts from unpublished letters of E.M. Forster are used with the permission of the Society of Authors as agent for the Provost and Scholars of King's College Cambridge. Extracts from *The Letters of Rupert Brooke*, edited by Geoffrey Keynes, are used with the permission of Faber and Faber. Extracts from Sydney Waterlow's diary are published with the permission of John and Charlotte Waterlow and of the Berg Collection of English and American Literature, New York Public Library, Astor, Lenox and Tilden Foundations. Quotations from the letters of Katherine Mansfield are made with the permission of the Alexander Turnbull Library, New Zealand, and the Society of Authors as the literary representative of the estate of Katherine Mansfield. Quotations from the letters of S.S. Koteliansky are made with the permission of the Alexander Turnbull Library.

Index

Note: Titles of works can be found under the name of the author.